# ANTIQUE
# SILVER SERVERS
# FOR THE
# DINING TABLE

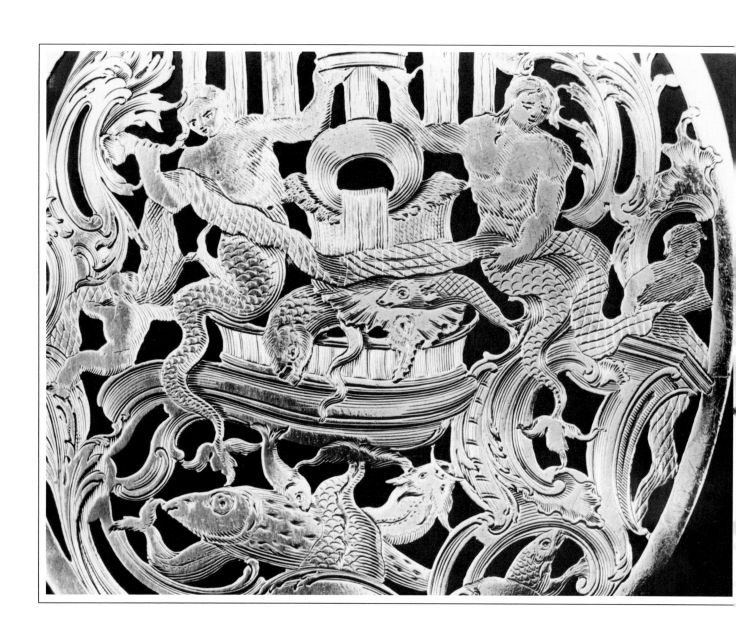

DETAIL OF THE BLADE OF THE MOUNTRATH SLICE BY
PAUL DE LAMERIE. SEE FIG. III 1b.
FROM THE DAWSON-DAMER COLLECTION.

# ANTIQUE SILVER SERVERS FOR THE DINING TABLE

## *Style, Function, Foods and Social History*

**Benton Seymour Rabinovitch**

**Major Photography Paul M. Macapia**

**Joslin Hall Publishing**
Concord, Massachusetts

Library of Congress Catalog Card Number: 90-85233
ISBN 0-9628570-0-9

Printed in the United States of America

JOSLIN HALL PUBLISHING
P.O. Box 516
Concord, Massachusetts 01742

*to Marilyn and Flora*

# TABLE OF CONTENTS

ACKNOWLEDGMENTS

The author has drawn on many sources for helpful figures and illustrations. He is very appreciative of the cooperation and help that he has received from museums, publishers and dealers. Where acknowledgment is absent, the object depicted is from the author's own collection. An effort has been made to acknowledge previous authority for information derived or quoted. In some instances, the learning process has represented a type of osmosis wherein knowledge was gained and accreted during many unascribable conversations over a number of years with silver devotees and dealers. Assignment of specific credit in such cases is impossible, and the author acknowledges his debt to these experts. In the assignment of British maker's marks, recourse has been had to the well-known work of C.J. Jackson and of A.G. Grimwade in the great majority of cases.

The following individuals have been particularly helpful: Dr. R.J. Baarsen, Ms. Anneke Bambery, Mr. David Beasley, Mr. S.A.C. Begeer, Mr. Gudmund Boesen, Dr. C. Boschma, Mr. Karel A. Citroen, Dr. Helen Clifford, Mrs. Teje Colling, Mr. Geoffrey Corbett, Mr. C.B.R. Deacon, Dr. Gerhard Dietrich, Dr. Alain Gruber, Miss Susan Hare, Mr. Christopher Hartop, Dr. Carl Hernmarck, Mr. J.W. James, Dr. A.M. Koldeweij, Mr. J. van Loo, M. Jean-Daniel Ludmann, Ms. Molly Pearce, Dr. Ulrich Pietsch, Dr. Kenneth Quickenden, Dr. Wolfgang Scheffler, Mr. C.J. Shrubsole, Mr. Eric Smith, Dr. Albert Steen, Mr. Gerald Taylor, Miss Dagmar Thormann, and Dr. M.L. Wurfbain. In some instances, such helpfulness has been all the more valuable because of geographic remoteness that has tended to restrain as free access to original sites and sources as the author would have desired.

Special thanks go to Mrs. Philippa Glanville who read the manuscript and made several helpful suggestions and gave support. The author is indebted to the late Mr. Henry W. Smart for the privilege of his friendship, for the pleasure of many discussions of fish slices, and for the opportunity to read unpublished writing and to view his collection. He also wishes to thank his friend Dr. Dale Bennett for the opportunity to view his collection.

He thanks Mr. Bernard Nist for several photographs (Figs. I 7-14, V 105, 106, VII 1, 6-8, 10, 11, 37, 38). His warm appreciation goes to Mr. Paul Macapia of the Seattle Art Museum, who did most of the photography of the author's collection, both for his skill and judgement and for the pleasure of the collaboration.

The writer is grateful to his secretaries, Mrs. Barbara Jaeger and Miss Ruth Buehrer, for their dedication and patience in the several retypings of this manuscript, and to the latter for proofreading the manuscript. He thanks copy editor Ms. Suzanne Copenhagen and, particularly, book designer Ms. Roselyn C. Pape for her many useful suggestions.

And, finally, he acknowledges his debt to his department, to the College of Arts and Sciences, and to the Graduate School Research Fund for grants-in-aid of publication.

B. Seymour Rabinovitch
Department of Chemistry
University of Washington
Seattle, WA 98195, U.S.A.

Chapter I

# BACKGROUND

*The collecting of antique silver is in part a science*
*and in part an art, governed…by the reason and the passions.*
*— Jonathan Stone, English Silver of the Eighteenth Century (1965).*

## *Prefatory Remarks*

SPECIALIST MONOGRAPHS in the field of antique silver cover a diverse range of wares, geographic regions, periods, and decoration. In this volume, the author indulges his interest in British broad-bladed and other silver servers. At the same time, some companion description of other regional developments, primarily Western European and American, has proven desirable. The author's original vehicle into this subject was an interest in silver fish servers. They represented a lacuna of knowledge — specialized articles that were out of the mainstream of stylistic development. When first approached as an area for study and collection, the subject seemed sufficiently narrow to be amenable to a modest expenditure of time, while the objects themselves seemed well adapted to a collector's purse. Unlike baskets, tankards, and tureens, they are sufficiently minor in nature so as to be light in weight and not too costly on that account. But they are not so small, like vinaigrettes, snuff boxes, wine labels, and caddy spoons, as to be eminently collectible and competitively expensive for that reason. Moreover, they are sufficiently large and variable in shape and character so as to give considerable scope for the display of the silversmith's craftsmanship. But above all, their blades provide inviting surfaces for the piercing, engraving, and chasing thereof, resulting in objects whose beauty and variety are a joy and inspiration.

One aspect of the author's original, untutored appraisal of their character, however, has proven inadequate. The subject is not as narrow as he had first thought. On the one hand, this has been a bonus, for, as the proverb states, "all is fish that cometh to net." On the other hand, one of the difficulties attending the treatment of this subject has been the sometimes ill-defined distinction between fish servers and a number of others. Thus, fish servers are related to cake, pastry, pie and pudding servers in shape and function, and these are interrelated themselves. Moreover, there is further overlap between these categories and a variety of others such as ice cream and aspic. Single-bladed asparagus servers resemble their fish counterparts in some respects. Miniature trowels also relate to butter spades; small scimitars appear as letter openers, fruit and butter knives, and fish eaters — a graceless name, as G.B. Hughes (1)* has remarked. Double bladed servers have also been termed chop servers, salad or, especially, asparagus servers. Trowels are strainers of a sort; they have been compared to strainer spoons. Pairs of fish servers — a fish slice and fork — that emerged in the second quarter of the nineteenth century connect with serving sets of all kinds. An attempt has been made here to examine this congruity of nomenclature, classification and function.

Some unusual Regency toothed shapes occur whose nature and function, whether for the service of fish, or melon, or fruit, or otherwise, are presently still speculative. These objects interrelate to a host of later toothed servers of the latter part of the nineteenth century. American manufacture of the latter period presents a bewildering and inconsistent array of implements of proliferated *ad hoc* uses and designs (2). Their number and frequently discordant designations suggest great inventiveness and business acumen, although perhaps less discretion on the part of customers. For example, one company's tomato server design was another's cheese server, while one's orange knife was yet another's cheese knife; and, as has been noted also by others (2,3), one company's pastry server might be quite dissimilar to that of another manufacturer. Any self-respecting hostess could scarcely do without a tomato-, or waffle-, or croquette-, or pasta-, or cracker-, or lemon-, or cucumber-, or oyster-, or entree-, or asparagus-, or cake-, or fish-, or ice cream-server, *inter alia*, in her silver service. The pressure on the *nouveau riche* must have been irresistible. At this point, the author's net developed large holes!

Some conservatism and discretion has proven necessary in limiting the scope of this undertaking. Thus, an attempt has been made to reveal some of the historical, constructional, functional, and stylistic relationships involving various types of broad-bladed and other servers, particularly since no accurate account appears to exist. The evolution of form, function and decoration has taken place over a period of two centuries (the eighteenth and nineteenth), and the culinary and social context is also described. But a comprehensive review of all possible implements could not be attempted, for reasons of space amongst others. Fortunately, several broad surveys of silver articles by authors of great scholarship have appeared; Clayton's Dictionary (4a) is one such example. Insofar as possible, the author has refrained from detailed exposition and expansion on subject matter that has been described by authorities whose works are well known. Thus,

*Note. Citations of references and figures within a given chapter are made without chapter designation. Citations of references or figures that are in another chapter include the chapter designation.

ordinary cutlery items, i.e., knives, forks and spoons, which have been treated in references such as (2), (III 25), and (III 33b), are largely excluded, as well, for example, as some servers such as ladles and stuffing spoons.

The arrangement of the text is as follows. Chapter I provides some background and a general introduction. In Chapter II a presentation of culinary practises and social customs of the times is made. Chapters III, IV and V give an account of the history, construction, decoration and function of the principal fish, cake, pastry and pudding server shapes — trowels, long-ovals and scimitars in the period 1700-1900. Chapter VI takes up some transient shapes that appeared over the sixty-year period, 1780-1840. A variety of other servers are described in Chapter VII. Throughout the presentation, the textual material is illustrated by a coherent chronological presentation of some four hundred articles. When date of manufacture is specified, only the first of a split pair of years is cited. British servers are of sterling composition (92.5% silver); those of other countries vary between 75%-95% and are not further specified.

The term *never* when used in the text is to be understood as synonomous with *rarely*, in the sense that an example of the feature or article in question has not yet been seen. Similarly, when a time period is specified it should be understood that if past experience has any lessons of value, earlier, or later, examples will probably be found even if none has yet surfaced. From time to time, the author has been led to express various deductions or hypotheses. These are intrinsically not rigorously provable, but it is hoped that they are at least stimulating, plausible, and, possibly, even correct.

Emphasis has been placed on the illustration of actual utensils. Two alternative arrangements of the figures seemed plausible. The first was the presentation of the illustration of an implement when it was first cited in the text, for whatever immediate purpose. The second was the presentation of the utensils in chronological order whenever the organization of the material of the text did not forbid. This arrangement, somewhat less convenient for immediate reference, has the advantage that the historical development and evolution of the shape, style and decoration of the serving pieces becomes immediately evident by inspection. This option was adopted. One caveat must be sounded, however. To depict all of the wondrous detail of blade shape (especially American) and ingenuity of decoration could have required a much larger collection of illustrations. Indeed, new piercing patterns and blade designs still come constantly to notice. Nonetheless, since the examples number in the hundreds, it seems fair to assert that the presentation is representative. As feasible, an effort has been made to depict relative sizes qualitatively.

It is hoped that readers may be stimulated to undertake further study of these implements — both to further knowledge and to have as much pleasure in their collection as has been the author's good fortune. The activity of collection is an illuminating pursuit. It may take the collector into areas of art and art history, craft technique, and design and design evolution, all of which relate to social, economic, and technologic influences, and the reactions to these. It is a broadening and civilizing experience. It can lead further into a better understanding of the art and craft of silversmithing and, for some, even into the rewarding, if amateurish, practise of this craft.

## *Early Origins*

The very earliest serving instruments were undoubtedly human fingers, wooden scoops of various sorts, shells, and carved horns and animal bones. The bone marrow scoop has survived in the earliest middens of society. All of these have continued in common use in some societies up to the present. To move forward quickly from the beginnings (see Ref. (4b) for a history), one of the earliest servers of high society in early renaissance and late medieval times was the broad knife used by the Carver to offer the product of his skill (5). As illustrated in Plate 4 of Ref. (6), a complete carving set might include a handled skewer and a primitive fork, one or two sharp knives for cutting, and a long broad-bladed knife for serving; the blade might be six to ten inches long, and one-and-a-half to two-and-a-half inches wide — a spatulate shape. The handles might be of ivory or ebony, or of marble or jasper, or of iron or bronze, or of other metal or material.

In the kitchens of large homes, and in humbler abodes, something resembling a more familiar, short broad-blade such as an iron or wooden spatula or shovel, perforated or otherwise, was in use. It is these which are the predecessors of the earliest eighteenth-century broad-bladed silver server. Reference to the dictionary (7) is useful at this point to make more precise the meanings of the nomenclature used. The word *spoon* is derived from the Anglo-Saxon word for wooden chip or the Middle German term for spatula. A spatula or spatulate form refers technically to a flat implement of elongated form that (frequently) has a wide rounded end. By contrast, the term slice seems to be a broader designation with historical precedent extending back at least to the fifteenth century. This term encompasses a wide variety of shapes and refers to any of various broad flattish utensils employed in cookery and the kitchen, including the spatula and shovel or spade. The word has also been specialized to specific uses, as for example, an egg- or fish-slice. In modern practise, the term spatula has been given very wide application, also, and is favored in American usage (8). The word *slice* should not be confused with *knife*. Although certain silver slices were used to cut and serve foods, they were not intended to play the role of an iron or steel knife, notwithstanding evidence of abuse to the contrary.

The use of wooden or metal (iron, pewter, copper, brass) food servers in the kitchen and dining hall is well known and well documented from the sixteenth to the twentieth centuries (9-12). Figures 1-6 show some earlier examples of such articles. There is considerable variety in shape and construction, particularly as

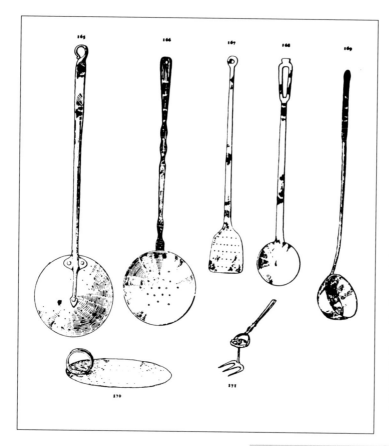

1.    Some common kitchen implements typical of the seventeenth through nineteenth centuries: 165. SKIMMER, cast brass, length 60 cm; 166. SKIMMER, brass and iron, length 57 cm; 167. FISH SLICE, cast brass, length 46 cm; 168. LADLE, cast brass, length 47 cm; 169. LADLE, brass/copper and iron, length 51 cm; 170. CREAM SKIMMER, brass. These objects are representative of these types of utensils, which may include copper variants in the sheet components or be made all of iron as in the articles of Fig. 2.
Courtesy of Academy Editions, London, from J.S. Lindsay, *Iron and Brass Implements of the English House*, Copyright 1970, Academy Editions.

2.    Some early iron kitchen implements typical of the seventeenth through nineteenth centuries: 3,8 SPATULAS; 6. PEEL. A spatula similar in shape to 3, and having a raised back edge, is called a fish slice by J.D. Eversleigh, *Old Cooking Utensils*, Shire, Princes Risborough, 1986; compare also item 167 in Fig. 1. It is evident that the distinction between some pierced spatulas and fish slices is a semantic matter.
Courtesy of the Wiltshire Folk Life Society from Ref. 10.

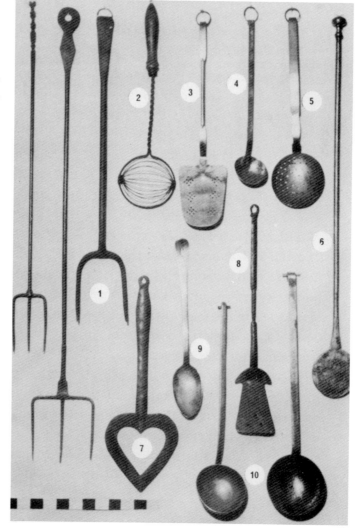

3.    An early eighteenth century Swedish CAKE SLICE ("tårtspade"); length 35 cm. The blade is of highly pierced sheet brass and has a short raised back edge (apron). The handle is attached to the underside of the blade and was forged from solid rod; the hook identifies its "kitchen" character, although the total artistic expression is superior to the items of Figs. 1 and 2. The style is characteristic of a type in use also in the seventeenth century, and is universal in its nature and shape. Note that despite the extensive piercing it is titled by present local authority as a "cake slice, probably."
By kind cooperation and courtesy of the Nordiska Museet, Stockholm.

4.    An early eighteenth century Swedish FISH SLICE ("fiskspade"); length 28 cm. The blade is pierced sheet brass in a simple scrolling vine and leaf design. The cannon-end handle of rolled sheet has an underblade attachment and carries a ring for hanging. The article would be used in the kitchen and, doubtless, would not have to move far in a modest home to be useful also at the dinner table. This style of handle appears frequently in Swedish silver servers of the first half of the eighteenth century (Chapter III). Again, the form of the article is universal in nature and was in use, also, in the previous century. This article is designated as a "fiskspade, probably," by local authority, but comparison with Fig. 3 makes the distinction somewhat invidious; either that or both articles, because of their piercing, are preferably to be called fish servers. The matter of function and nomenclature is discussed in more detail in Chapter III.
By kind cooperation and courtesy of the Nordiska Museet, Stockholm.

5.    An English KITCHEN SPATULA of pierced sheet brass and iron, probably late eighteenth century; length 37.5 cm. The handle attachment is under-blade with copper rivets and carries a hook for hanging. Another universal form. Modern steel articles of this shape, having wooden handles carved with the word "fish," are presently still made.

6.    An English cast brass shovel FISH SLICE; length 40 cm. It is allegedly eighteenth century but more probably is nineteenth century. The blade is pierced and has slightly raised sides and back. The handle terminal carries a hole for hanging. The implement resembles the fish slices of Figs. 1 and 2 and the silver server shown in Fig. III 27.

between pierced and unpierced blades. Undoubtedly, the former acted as strainers or skimmers as well as lifters, turners and servers, whereas the solid blades presumably performed only the latter functions. The specialized designation *fish slice* has been applied by some authorities (9) to the pierced shovel spatula of the type illustrated in Fig. 6. As a practical matter, however, unless the blade is dished, i.e., is curved, or has raised sides as for some spades, shovels, or spittles, it makes little practical difference whether it is pierced or not — a flat surface retains little liquid in any case. Indeed, in the circumstance in which fish was presented on a mazarine strainer, the need for a pierced server, ostensibly to act also as a strainer, becomes questionable. In fact, inexpensive late-nineteenth century fish slices were frequently not pierced.

    The name, fish slice, for fish servers has persisted from the eighteenth through the nineteenth and twentieth centuries. But slices or spatulas have also been termed by a variety of other special designations, including pudding and pastry slices, strainers (not to be confused with the larger skimmers), tart shovels, cake turners, paddles, lifters, and so on. In general, pre-eighteenth-century and

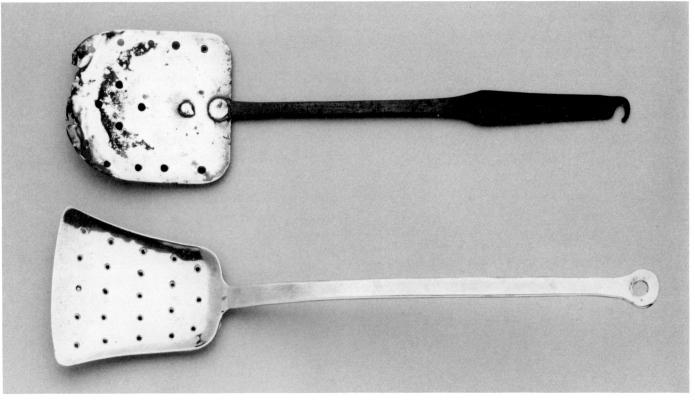

later base-metal kitchen slices were very frequently of (modified) rectangular or (near-) circular conformation; oval and especially triangular shapes were of less frequent occurrence. Contradictorily, the broad rectangular or oblong shape found expression less often in eighteenth-century silver slices. Likewise, although circular strainers, skimmers, salamanders, and such, were of common form in kitchen ware, the shape never was used in eighteenth- century silver servers. For the first three-quarters of the eighteenth century, most British silver servers were of triangular or oval shape. A circular, long-handled silver strainer with pierced holes was occasionally made in the nineteenth century (Fig. VI 22), and more frequently in the present century as plated wares, with ladle-like cutlery handles; they are usually called rice servers.

The iron and brass servers of the eighteenth and nineteenth centuries are occasionally seen in elongated oval form in the abstract shape of a fish. It is possible that some were made in this latter shape even earlier, although they have not come to present attention. The general use of base metal blades in earlier times raises a question. It is commonly stated that silver servers for fish and fruit were introduced in order to avoid an unpleasant sharp taste otherwise generated by contact of copper or iron or steel with these foods and their juices. The implication is that before service came to the table in the eighteenth century with consequent refinement and expansion of dining room and table accoutrements, even the nobility and gentry must have suffered from this degradation of flavour customarily experienced by the less affluent.

In the period covered by this account, three principal shapes of British silver server blades have occurred. They are the trowel or triangular shape, c. 1740-1780, including the oval shape discussed later; the long-oval or near-elliptical shape, from 1775 to the present; the scimitar shape, from 1790 to the present. Variations on these as well as other variant forms have appeared, governed in many instances by the artistic expression of their makers. In the sequel, we shall discuss dates, shapes and construction in more detail. It is sufficient here to notice that the handle is joined to the server blade *via* a stem or shank, and thence to a boss, or bolster, or junction, which is attached at the rear of the blade. If the handle proper is not made of silver, but of some other material such as wood or ivory, then a conical socket to receive it may be interposed between the stem and the handle; alternatively, a protruding tang from the stem may extend into the body of the handle. Reference to the figures of Chapters III, IV and V and the discussion thereof should make the arrangement quite clear.

## Other Materials

Fish, pudding and cake slices have been made in a wide variety of materials. Examples of trowels, long-oval and scimitar-shaped servers in Old Sheffield (fused silver on copper) (13-15) are considered in later chapters along with silver implements. It may be mentioned here, however, that examples of these types in fine condition are scarce. The heavy work of cutting, especially, has taken a heavy toll. In the early decades of the nineteenth century, many scimitar shapes were made in the more rugged close plate (silver on iron or steel) (13). They resemble their silver and Old Sheffield counterparts. Apart from certain examples and minor allusions, the discussion of electroplated articles is outside the scope of this volume. Although resembling their silver complements, they proliferated enormously in the last half of the nineteenth century and must be left to other accounts (2).

Pewter examples are very rare. Apart from health considerations, they were either not made in large number or have not survived — on both counts because of the comparative softness and malleability of the tin-lead alloys, which rendered them unsuitable for stressful use. The writer has not experimented with their effect on fish flavour; this exercise has been left to someone having a more adventurous palate. A fine nineteenth-century example of a pewter scimitar slice is shown in Fig. 7. It is decorated with zigzag work, thread, flower and scrolling foliage. Most unusually, it is also decorated on the underside with a floral zigzag pattern at the rear of the blade, a feature almost totally absent from British scimitar shapes. The elemental composition of nineteenth-century pewter objects is both variable and not well characterized (14,15).

Although brass and white metal (especially non-silver alloys such as German silver, Britannia metal) scimitar-shaped servers are not uncommon, in almost every instance their pseudomarks reveal their origin as stripped, electroplated servers. Early Paktong servers are of extremely rare occurrence. An occasional brass one, however, was specifically made. An example is shown in Fig. 8; the blade carries a rear apron and is in the style of the Continental, especially Dutch, scimitars of the nineteenth century. Its folkcraft nature is revealed by the simple tubular handle, the naive technique in the pierced-hole fish pattern on the blade, as well as in the employment of soft (tin-lead) solder to attach the handle. However, this otherwise unnoteworthy article is remarkable in the fact that it is an extremely rare example of a left-handed fish slice. Of thousands of scimitar shapes that have been viewed, this is the sole example noted of a left-handed server. Figure 9 shows a brass scimitar slice of English type. The style of engraved decoration, however, and detail of the fish eye suggest an Indian or Eastern origin. Moreover, it is of such thin construction as to belie ascription as the carcass of a silver-plated article — notwithstanding the presence of a row of crude pseudo marks on the underside of the handle that were probably applied to mimic British custom.

7.      A very rare pewter scimitar FISH SLICE by John Yates, Birmingham, c. 1840; length 30 cm. It is almost impossible to find examples of these; the author has never seen a trowel or long-oval pewter server. This one is in remarkably pristine condition. The zigzag scrolling blade decoration which embraces the V-junction of the handle is very fresh. The heel of the underside of the blade also is decorated — an unusual feature. The piercing pattern of stars and fish-backbone is characteristic of silver slices of fifteen, or twenty, or more years earlier [see Figs. V 23, V 43, V 65 for example]. The handle is standard English fiddle.

8.      A brass scimitar FISH SLICE, first half of the nineteenth century, Continental style [see Fig. V 138 for comparison]; length 34 cm. The naively pierced fish is a welcome verification of its intended function although the flat blade, more common for Continental than British slices, also makes it quite suitable as a cake server. The server has a small apron and that feature, as well as the under-apron attachment of the cannon-end handle, is also a common Continental characteristic. The handle end carries a swing-loop (just visible) for hanging the implement. The unusual left-handed character of this article may be telling us something about its folkcraft maker.

9.      A brass scimitar FISH SLICE, probably middle or late nineteenth century; length 30 cm. The horseshoe style of simple comma piercing is typical of the first quarter of the century in English provincial and American manufacture [see Figs. V 73, V 108]. The extended lines of the fish eye is typical of Indian decoration. These two features, together with the very light weight of the article, atypical of brass silverplated English wares, as well as its pseudo-marks, support its British Empire Eastern origin.

10.     A pierced triangular enamelled iron KITCHEN SERVER, c. 1900; length 46 cm. It bears a close resemblance in shape to item 3 of Fig. 2. The handle has a hook terminal for easy hanging. These utilitarian articles were widely manufactured in the nineteenth and early twentieth centuries in various styles, as revealed by the two succeeding figures. White and blue enamelling predominated; the enamelling prevented degradation of flavour quite effectively. They were ultimately displaced by stainless steel and plastic implements.

11.     A pierced enamelled iron TROWEL SERVER; this one is all white; length 36 cm. The handle has a pierced hole for hanging. The blade shape resembles that of early Georgian silver oval trowels [see, for example, Figs. III 31, III 46]. The history and character is similar to that of Fig. 10.

Two common types of kitchen implements in use in the late nineteenth and early twentieth centuries are shown in Figs. 10-12. These (frequently blue and white) enamelled iron slices — either trowel-, or spatula-, or scimitar-shaped — were of wide occurrence. Their shapes may assume all the variations described in Chapters III and V. The enamelling was functional and prevented contact of the metal with the food. The right side of the scimitar blade is sometimes raised, as in this example, which is provided with a simple tubular handle. These examples are furnished with provisions for hanging. No doubt they served all of the functions mentioned in the previous section. They are quite evidently a product of mass manufacture. Examples may be seen in the Castle Museum, York, and are sometimes encountered at fairs and flea markets.

A variation on the iron server is the homely tin-plated one shown in Fig. 13.

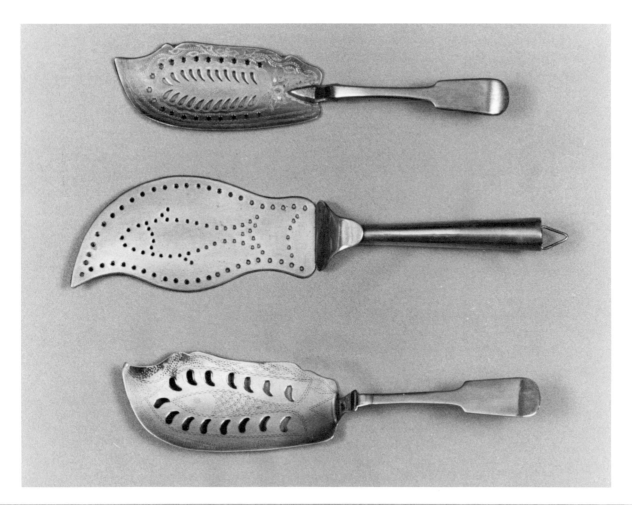

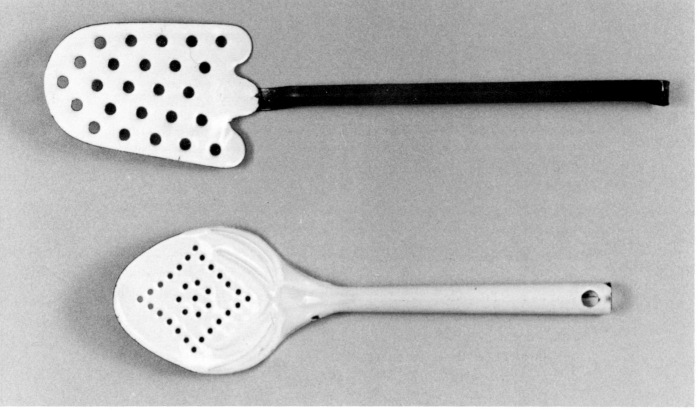

12.     A pierced enamelled iron scimitar FISH SLICE, with kitchen hanging hook; length 30 cm. The handle, which is a rolled sheet conical cannon end type, is seamed. It is continuous with the blade that it joins *via* a short tapering raised apron, which is convex shaped for strength. The blade has a stamped up-rolled right edge that also acts as a strengthening feature. The history and character of the article resembles that of the two preceding items.

13.     A pierced tinned iron FISH SLICE of Continental proportions, nineteenth century; length 32 cm. Although collected in the Northwest of the United States, it was either imported from Europe or made in the U.S.A. by an immigrant European craftsman. The handle is wooden, painted black, and has an underside junction beneath the apron and blade; the conical iron tube that receives the handle extends as an underside hollow box rat-tail (whose partial outline is visible topside as a recess at the rear of the blade) to the start of the diamond-shaped hole piercing. The generous use of soft (lead-tin) solder to attach the blade and the homely character of the implement indicates its non-commercial nature.

14.     A sheet aluminium kitchen FISH SLICE, early twentieth century; length 31 cm. The style is similar to that of the slice of Fig. 12, including the ribbed apron and up-rolled right side for strength. Such slices were made in cast aluminium in several industrialized countries. The handle is a rolled-sheet, seamed cannon end tube continuous with the blade, analogous to Fig. 12.

15.     A flat creamware FISH TROWEL by Wedgwood, c. 1785; length approximately 28 cm, of which the blade is exactly half. These articles are so-named in contemporary manufacturer's catalogues (Ref. 16). The blade is heavy, being approximately 2mm thick, and is pierced in geometric petal and other patterns. This one has no colour decoration, unlike many other contemporary articles of this kind. The handle has an Onslow (ribbed volute) finial from which a molded acanthus leaf pattern leads down the stem. The edge of the blade is rounded and this implement can in no way function as a cutter or parter of flesh. It can serve only as a lifter, whether of a small fish, or white bait, or other food stuff.
By cooperation and courtesy of Libra Antiques, London. Photograph by J.C. Holdaway.

16.     A pearlware FISH TROWEL by Wedgewood which carries the British Patent Office design registration mark for 1846, and whose date of manufacture is estimated as c. 1865; length 30 cm. The flat blade is 2.5mm thick and is pierced with a pattern whose layout is somewhat similar to that of Fig. 16; the blade edges are rounded. The article is decorated with a branch-leaf-and-flower, aubergine-coloured, transfer-printed, central pattern called Bouquet by the maker. The blade perimeter is circumscribed by a C-scroll-circle-and-diamond pattern. The handle, which is also completely transfer-printed, has an Onslow terminal that carries down the handle in broad ribbing, accentuated by gold striping; it goes over into a molded acanthus leaf, which is almost camouflaged by the transfer printing.

It is allegedly American and of nineteenth-century vintage. If American, the particular scimitar shape evinces the Continental influence on U.S.A. metal design, as does the under-blade attachment of the handle (Chapter V); it is more plausibly Dutch or French. An example of a twentieth-century aluminium scimitar slice is given in Fig. 14.

Rather large earthenware trowels were made in the late eighteenth century and nineteenth century (16). Figure 15 shows a typical Wedgwood, pierced, fish

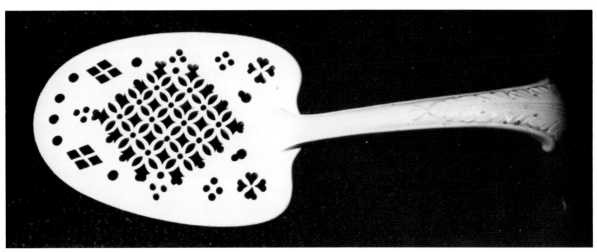

or pudding trowel, c. 1795, in English creamware. When their function was specified in contemporary catalogues, it was always to fish service. Peculiarly, for a reason not understood, all of the eighteenth- and nineteenth-century examples of the Georgian type that the author has seen (16) feature handle terminals in the Onslow pattern — even a late transfer-printed pearlware example of c. 1865 (Fig. 16). They are truly late in period and all the more remarkable since this finial does not occur in silver examples! The triangular form has persisted up through this century as smaller, usually unpierced and somewhat elongated ceramic cake or pie trowels. Contemporary long-oval ceramic shapes have not been seen, although earthenware survivals of the nineteenth-century scimitar shape are known. The latter are extremely rare; their omission from early catalogues suggest that they were not widely made or used, as is quite understandable considering the unsuitability of the ceramic implement for performing the cutting function.

A rather rare example of a wooden fish slice, complete with fish decoration, is presented in Fig. 17. The foliage and shell carving on the handle suggests a Scandinavian origin. The leaf shape, which is also anatomically complete on the carved underside of the blade, recalls the rococo forms of Continental servers of the last half of the eighteenth century (Chapter III). Undoubtedly, though, this example is of much more recent origin and can also be thought of as being a derived scimitar form. This lovely unpretentious piece is decorative rather than utilitarian and presumably represents an interest of the woodcarver rather than an example of an object intended for frequent or kitchen use.

Appropriately relating to the service of fish, examples have been noted of carved-shell, scimitar-shaped servers that have an attached handle also of shell material. A similar example in mother-of-pearl, with fish piercing, is given in Fig. 18. Figure 19 shows a small decorative shell trowel pastry server that is furnished with a brass stem handle. Large shell scoops with sterling handles were also made, in Britain at least. In Fig. 20 is seen a small shell fish-shaped server — perhaps for caviar.

An occasional nineteenth-century small cake or pastry trowel made from tortoise shell or horn may be encountered. Figure 21 presents a small horn tart or pastry trowel — believed early twentieth-century — having silver mounts and whose pierced decor and silver work suggests a Far East origin.

Figure 22 illustrates a turn-of-the-century ivory cake or pastry spatula. It has a sharpened front edge and blunt side edges. It is evidently a lifter. Slightly smaller ceramic servers of similar shape and purpose are common in the present century.

## Fakes, Defects, Condition and Repairs

It may be well to take up this subject early for the benefit of novice collectors, and to issue the general injunction that purchases should be made with restrained enthusiasm until serious study of one's field of collection has been initiated. Beyond that, however, a few early mistakes, *and* their contemplation, often have a salutary effect upon the later exercise of careful judgment — the *silver lining*, so to speak.

Fortunately, there seems to be very little deliberate faking of eighteenth-century slices and servers. And nineteenth-century articles are so abundant and relatively inexpensive as to make fakery quite unprofitable. What the buyer must be vigilant about is the detection of wear, damage and repair.

Trowel blades are particularly prone to cracking of the blade and to breaks in the pierced areas. Such damage occurs most often in the area around the boss junction but may be found anywhere on the blade. It is easiest to detect on the underside of the blade, where it is unobscured by surface decoration or engraving such as may be present on the topside. If repaired, scrutiny of both sides may be repaid; the added metal may interrupt decoration that has not been re-engraved or re-pierced. Breaks around the handle junction may be masked by a later-added strengthening cover plate, which was never provided as 'original equipment.' Evidence of new solder work in sloppy repair, and the occurrence of blanked piercing, are evident symptoms of such additions. Though not a structural defect, a highly polished or newly buffed blade, of whatever vintage, is not to be desired. More preferable is a blade that displays some evidence of a patina appropriate to its age. However, since these articles suffered hard usage it would be too much to expect examples of superior patina.

It should be kept in mind that a careful, leisurely half-hour examination with a loupe is sometimes necessary to discover repairs. It is best to take a piece on approval and to spend a relaxing period in its examination at home. Above all, beware of an article that is dirty and tarnished. A multitude of defects may be hidden under polishing compound, including holes and repair. Insist on seeing the clean article.

Obviously, cracks and, especially, crude repairs may drastically lower the value of an article. But an intrinsically fine or dramatic object should not be rejected merely because of a few relatively obscure breaks in the piercing. In the last decades of rapidly increasing scarcity of antique silver, the definition of excellence in quality judgements has changed markedly for all but the most wealthy.

A type of repair, which constitutes a marriage, is the replacement of one handle by another [see Fig. VII 38]. With regard to the whole handle, if done tastefully and carefully such substitution might be hard to distinguish from removal and restoration of the original handle during blade repair around the

17.    A wooden "scimitar" FISH SLICE, nineteenth century; length 26 cm. The function of the article as a nominal fish server, even though unpierced, is clearly revealed by the carved fish that lies in a bed of seaweed and greens. The edge of the leaf-shaped blade is serrated with a carving feature akin to feather edging. The underside of the blade has the carved anatomy of a leaf. The deeply carved handle is in a flower head and scrolling leaf pattern and attaches to the blade by a carved shell junction. The handle decoration suggests a Scandinavian origin. And although the blade shape is reminiscent *both* of the scimitar shape and of late eighteenth century Rococo trowel shapes [Figs. III 78,III 81], this purely decorative article is thought to be later dated; the shape also conforms with some late nineteenth century unpierced British, and especially American, fish and cake scimitar servers (Chapter V).

18.    A mother-of-pearl scimitar FISH SLICE, late nineteenth century; length 26.5 cm. The blade is decorated with a pierced, realistically-engraved fish in a reserve enclosed by six-pointed stars; it has a sharpened left edge. The handle (possibly a marriage) is decorated with opposed anthemion carvings. A split hollow brass junction embraces the blade; the junction area is set off by engraved semi-circles. This implement is essentially decorative, being insufficiently robust in either material or junction strength to withstand much usage; it is a one off. The name Balch is engraved in script lettering on the blade at the handle junction; presumably Continental.

19.    A shell spade CAKE OR PASTRY SERVER, early twentieth century; length 24 cm. The rod-like handle is hollow, of seamed and stamped brass sheet, and attaches to the blade by a sheet brass sandwich clip of fleur-de-lys shape that grasps the blade; the latter has sharpened edges. The junction is not strong; the article could not withstand frequent use and is largely decorative. Such servers were made in Britain among other countries.

20.    A small unpierced mother-of-pearl fish-shaped SERVER; length 14 cm. The blade is in the shape of a small, realistically engraved flat fish. The handle, which has turned ornament, is silver plated and attaches to the blade *via* a relatively long and narrow sandwich clip. The size and shape of the utensil suggests that it may be a server for fish paté or caviar. The clip and handle show wear; miraculously, the blade is almost unscathed.

21.    A pierced horn PASTRY TROWEL, early twentieth century; length 24 cm. Blade and handle are in one piece; the article has been steamed to give lift to the handle (see Chapter III, handles). The blade is of oval shape [compare Figs. III 31,III 42], has a scalloped edge, and is highly pierced with a central twin peacock or lyre bird design. Pinned to the terminal of the "Old English" shaped handle is a stamped silver mount which has a butterfly or flying insect design whose antennae go over into other scrolling features. The article is fairly robust and serviceable. It is seemingly Eastern in origin.

22.    An ivory PASTRY SERVER, late nineteenth or probably early twentieth century; length 30.5 cm. The spatulate blade is undecorated and has a broad, sharpened, slightly rounded front edge and rounded (unsharpened) sides. The server is made in one piece. The blade lifts to a plain straight handle that is decorated with two black inlay bands and a simulated twist and two mysterious, very deeply incised lines, on the top and underside of the twist, that cross. The implement cannot be easily used for cutting cake (except by somewhat awkward use of the front edge, and even then more suitably for flat pastry), but is mainly adapted for lifting. Because of its broad front edge, it cannot, in any case, be used for serving a round shape, such as a fruit pie.

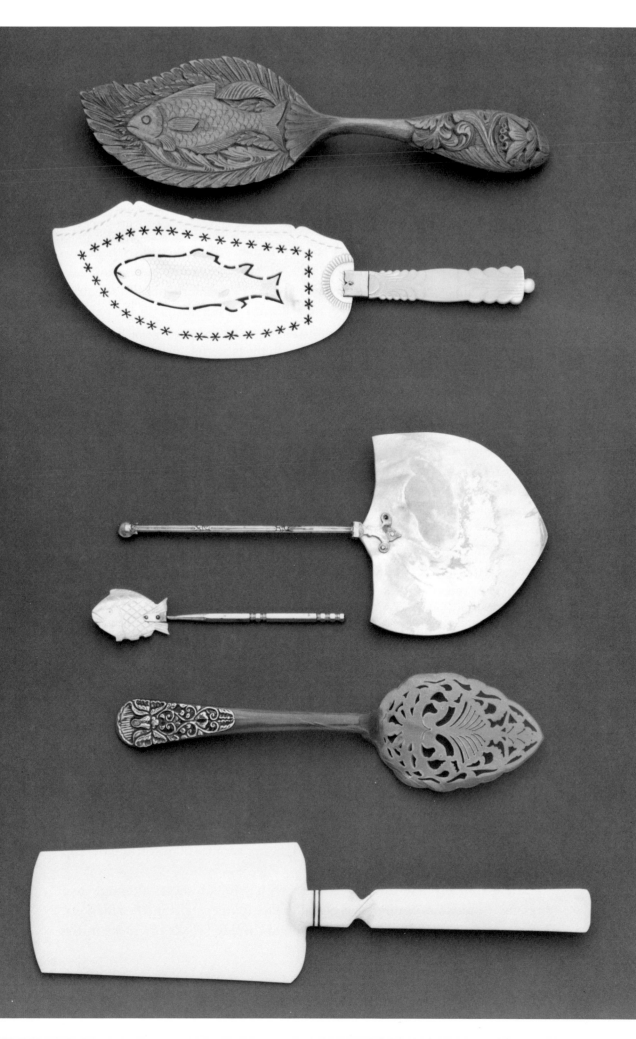

junction. If the latter is not evident then one may suspect handle repair *per se*, or replacement. Part of the handle, whether a wood or ivory component, may have been replaced and this may be detected in many instances by enlargement of the holes at the pin in the tubular socket, if any, or by crude pin replacement such as rough or projecting ends, or by an improperly sized pin. Hair-line cracking of the ivory portion is not of itself a serious defect; this is the nature of aged ivory.

A good set of marks is always a desideratum. Unfortunately, later piercing may have removed part of the marks. For highly pierced objects such as these, this defect simply becomes a fact of life and a reflection of the manufacturing and hallmarking custom of the time. This is not a real defect if the marks are still adequate for identifying the maker and date of manufacture. If not adequate, the value of the article is lowered by loss of such information. This is true also of erased and completely or partially indiscernible marks. In the latter instance, it is likely that the engraving decoration is also rubbed. Freshness, crispness, and clarity of decoration is one of the hallmarks of excellence. A weary piece is both a bore and a frustration. It is one of the burdens of 'study collection' that such articles or other defects must sometimes be accepted in order to illustrate some particular aspect of construction, or style, or other feature.

The remarks made with respect to trowels apply to long-oval servers as well. The latter are also susceptible to the same kind of blade damage, and similar caveats apply. However, strengthening plates at the handle junction were occasionally applied by the smith in the original construction and thus they are not necessarily later-added, cover-up repairs. A similar remark applies to scimitars. The most important difference between the two classes of servers relates to the filled silver or ivory handles — in any case, never solid silver handles — that the eighteenth-century long-oval British servers feature. It is desirable, but not a requirement, that a filled silver handle should have been "made" by the blade maker. Thereby, harmony of style and quality tends to be ensured. When the handle was evidently furnished by a handle maker — a permissible marriage — it is desirable (assuming good condition, of course), but not a requirement, that it feature the same date as the blade so as to help confirm it as the original handle. The condition of the ferrule (see Chapter IV), in the case of ivory handles, should also be examined; a good match to handle style is desirable in a quality piece. However, filled silver handles have proven so unsubstantial that their later replacement, like knife blades, is not considered as a defect. A weary or dented handle craves removal. More important is the quality and appropriateness of the replacement. It is most important that the size and shape of the handle-cum-ferrule match the tang shoulder well, avoid the appearance of misfit, and butt up without a gap.

Comparatively few difficulties arise with scimitar slices, although real 'dogs' may sometimes be offered, especially at temporary stalls and flea markets. These servers are quite robust and less often display breaks or cracks in the piercing or blade. Virtually all pre-1850, nineteenth-century scimitar blades, not part of a pair with a fork, were dished. In most instances, a planar blade indicates later flattening that may be confirmed by evidence of some greater or lesser attendant distress. Where filled or ivory handles have been employed then, of course, earlier remarks apply. One must distinguish, in the first instance, between articles that have substantial thickness and weight of handle and blade and lighter gauge implements, especially those that display very undesirable whippy blades. A gentle finger squeeze of the whole blade will suffice to confirm the latter characteristic, if present. The most common defect is probably weariness — a century or more of over-zealous polishing that has dulled the engraving and wearied the blade. Exhibition of fish, good and profuse engraving, or chasing, a novel piercing design, and substantial size and weight are features to be sought.

Not to be considered as fakes, are items of Chinese export silver (17). Although they sometimes reproduced the hallmarks of English silver by casting, including maker's marks such as those of Wm. Eley, the fuzzy marks were not intended to deceive. Chinese makers in silver, as well as procelain, were sometimes very literal in obeying their order instructions to reproduce a given object. Such pieces are nineteenth century mainly; most blades are scimitars. The workmanship and quality are very good and, somewhat paradoxically, such articles are now more valuable than their London counterparts.

A related category exists in the work of Canadian, American, Australian, and other colonial silversmiths who frequently used crude reproductions of British marks, such as the lion passant, or the sovereign's and leopard's head. Deception was not always intended. The use was a compliment, and these articles tend to be more valuable because of their comparative scarcity.

# References

1. G.B. Hughes, *Small Antique Silverware*. Bramhall, New York, 1957.
2. N.D. Turner, *American Silver Flatware 1837-1910*, Barnes, Cranbury, N.J., 1972.
3. R.F. Osterberg and B. Smith, *Silver Flatware Dictionary*, Barnes, New York, 1981.
4. a) M. Clayton, *The Collector's Dictionary of the Silver and Gold of Great Britain and North America*, World Publishing, New York, 1971.
   b) J.B. Himworth, *The Story of Cutlery*, Benn, London, 1953.
5. M. Girouard, *Life in The English Country Home*, Penguin, New York, 1980.
6. *Masterpieces of Cutlery and The Art of Eating*, Victoria and Albert Museum, London, 1979.
7. *Compact Oxford English Dictionary*, Oxford University Press, Vols. 1 and 2, 1971.
8. H.J. Kauffman, *American Copper and Brass*, Bonanza, New York, 1979.
9. J.S. Lindsay, *Iron and Brass Implements of the English House*, Tiranti, London, 1970.
10. H.O. Roberts, *Downhearth to Bar Grate*, Dawson and Goodall, Bath, 1981.
11. *The Kitchen Catalogue*, Castle Museum, York, 1979.
12. Caroline Davidson, *The Ham House Kitchen*, Victoria and Albert Museum, London.
13. G.B. Hughes, *Sheffield Silver Plate*, Praeger, London, 1970.
14. C.A. Peel, *British Pewter and Britannia Metal*, Peebles, London, 1971.
15. F. Bradbury, *History of Old Sheffield Plate*, Northend Ltd., Sheffield, 1968.
16. Further creamware examples include those in the Victoria and Albert Museum, London; the Buten Museum, Philadelphia (see G. Wills, *Wedgwood: Part I*, a Guiness Signature publication, London); the Norsk Folkemuseum, Oslo, Norway; *The Castleford Pottery Pattern Book*, Dunderdale, 1796; R. Haggar, *The Whitehead Catalogue*, 1798, D.B. Drakard, Milton Keynes, undated, which lists trowels as being available in two sizes; and *The Wedgewood Factory Shape Drawing Book*, Barleston, 1802.
17. C.L. Crossman, *The China Trade*, Pyne Press, Princeton, 1973.

# Chapter II

## FOODS AND DINING CUSTOMS

### *Foods and Eating Habits*

A SHORT INTRODUCTION to the foods and eating habits of the times, particularly in Britain, is desirable in order to clarify the context of the use of the utensils discussed here. The author acknowledges his indebtedness to the writings of the many authorities who are cited in the chapter references. The chapters that follow describe the implements used in the service of fish, pudding, pie, pastry, and so on. A discussion of vegetable, salad, and other servers is given also in Chapter VII, so that some general consideration of foodstuffs is useful. In addition to the food itself (1), the social customs of the people, and their political and economic conditions, are also relevant (2). These have changed and evolved with time and have affected the invention, alteration, and proliferation of the various silver articles used in the kitchen and dining room (3).

Some aspects of British food habits go back to Roman origins (1-3). Among other vegetables, the Romans introduced the later, omnipresent asparagus (sparagrass, sparrow grass) into cultivation (35), as well as the more widespread use of fish and poultry. And although the Saxons became heavier meat eaters (2), the love of some foods, e.g., fresh or potted eels and lamprey pies, never did diminish. The introduction of Christianity had as an indirect consequence the improvement of animal husbandry and agricultural practise, as carried on by the monks. Many of our common fruits and vegetables — apples, pears, grapes, peaches, mulberries, beans — were cultivated, as well as grains for bread. Dairy foods were favoured also. Saxons were bigger and better eaters than their more frugal Norman conquerors. Although the latter reverted to two meals a day, the later Normans began to develop those gastronomic propensities that later characterized some wealthy English as gluttons.

By the Middle Ages, the variety of foods available heavily overlap our present menus. Among fruits used in tarts and puddings were candied peel of various kinds, apples, plums, pears, strawberries, raspberries, dates and figs. Vegetables included garlic, onions, leeks, cucumbers, lettuce, parsley, cabbage, beets, and fennel. Added to the list of cereals were wheat, oats, bran, and rice. Nuts included almonds, chestnuts, and pine nuts. In addition to conventional wild fowl, such as swan, heron, crane, bustard, tern, bittern, and many small birds, and wild game, such as boar and deer, more exotic prey might include whale, seal, porpoise and bear. Fish ran the gamut from sturgeon, trout, mackerel, haddock, perch, cod, pike, turbot, sole and carp, not to mention salmon, to several varieties of the herring family, smelt, sprat, and other small fish, as well as shrimp, prawns, crab, lobster, oysters, cockles, and other mollusks. Spices and herbs were varied: cloves, mace, cinnamon, saffron, pepper, parsley, sage, mint, horseradish, vinegar, and salt, of course, and many others were represented. Sauces and relishes also improved the flavour. Flowers, sometimes candied, such as violets, cowslip, borage, dandelion, gillyflowers, primroses, roses, and broom buds, found favour, also, in salads (sallet or sallat) and confections. The latter evolved, on important occasions, into artistic sculptural creations in sugar, jelly, or paste. Tarts might include such things as primroses, rosebuds and marigolds as ingredients.

The supremacy of the English nobility as champion meat eaters was established in the sixteenth and seventeenth centuries, and Britons ate better than their Continental cousins (4-7). Wine gave way to ale and beer as the favoured alcoholic beverage. So important was gastronomic indulgence that the retinue of the wealthy included not only cooks, and bakers, and confectioners, but, also, cellarmen, plate-men and spice-men, among others (8). By the year 1700, the recently established vegetable market at Covent Garden in London featured melons and pumpkins, artichokes, asparagus, beets, beans, broccoli, cabbages, carrots, celery, cucumbers, endive, marrow, parsnips, peas, radishes, spinach and sweet potatoes. Potatoes were eaten by the gentry, but only became a staple for the poor during the course of the eighteenth century. Fruit included varieties of apricots, plums, cherries, currants, gooseberry, oranges, pears, quince, and pineapple — a native curiosity developed by Charles II. Billingsgate, destined to become world famous, was established as the premiere London fish market. In the homes of the affluent, many of the above items were cut preferably by silver blades, rather than iron.

Paradoxically, the incubus laid on wine drinking by the Puritan influence, together with a heavy tax on beer in the last part of the seventeenth century, fostered an even greater excess of consumption of spirits — notably gin — that was such a curse on the eighteenth century. On the other hand, from 1652 coffee (chocolate, tea) houses expanded and flourished through the next century. Queen Anne's own gustatory predilections helped to encourage the prominent role of eating as part of a way of life among the nobility that fluctuated between gourmanderie and gourmetism (9-16). It prevailed also, among the gentry and growing merchant class for the greater part of the eighteenth century. The great Samuel Johnson lauded himself both on his profound knowledge of cuisine as well as on *all* aspects of his oral capabilities (2,37). All of which contributed to what Nathaniel Hawthorne referred to as "an insolence of riches" (17), and the poet

Dryden in an earlier century had stigmatized as "the grossness of a city feast."

Although several classic cookbooks had appeared as early as the sixteenth century, the eighteenth century saw their continuing proliferation (*Mrs. Glasse's Art of Cookery*, in 1747) culminating, but not ending, in the middle nineteenth century with Mrs. Beeton's epics. Hundreds—thousands—of books were published on English food specialties, whether by type, or region, or special association of the authors—as even in the unlikely anthology by the Fellows of The Royal Society, London (18). But although the foods and social customs continued to change in the period covered by the present monograph, it is, perhaps, the more roisterous eighteenth century that is of greatest interest. The nineteenth century follows on more tamely, as does our present century, whose greatest gastronomic achievements — or failures — are the fast food chain, the appearance of plastic cutlery, and the bottling of vitamins.

What was eaten at meals when silver servers were in use? This of course evolved steadily. With regard to the period of interest here, the two-course dinner had been long established. But unlike today's custom, when a moderate meal might signify a light entree such as fish, followed by a main course, such as roast beef—the Englishman's specialty—the courses in Stuart or Georgian times were quite something else (9,12). A party dinner might consist of three to nine, or more, meat and fish dishes per course, plus additional side dishes. Dining was a labor-intensive exercise that extended over a period of four to five hours, of which at least the first two were heavily devoted to the work in hand, literally (although the increased advent of the fork by 1725-1750 also led to increased refinement in manners). The first course might include an array such as oysters, fish, patty of pigeon, fricassee of rabbit, leg or side of lamb, roast duck, pork brains. The second course might offer lobsters, roast chicken, anchovies, venison, beef, lamprey eel pie, and sundry puddings and pies discussed below. Both courses, especially the second, also might include custard, various sweet dishes, tarts, spiced and fruited puddings, and so on. The first course could be led into by soup or a pudding, and the second course was followed by, or included, sweeter fruit and cream concoctions. A list of eighteenth century "receipts" for cookery, puddings, pastry, cakes, creams and jellies may be found in Ref. (41); bills of fare—first and second courses — "for every season of the year" are provided.

The service followed the so-called 'French' style. All the dishes in each course were set out on the table and were accessed by cooperative exchange between diners or with the assistance of footmen or waiters when necessary. The meat was stewed, boiled and roasted, or made into elaborate savoury (spiced) pies, sometimes of considerable artistry, and all encased in a "coffin" of crust. Vegetables might include asparagus, cucumbers, beans of various sorts, spinach, potatoes, carrots, artichokes, peas, cabbage. Raw vegetables and, especially, fruit were neither popular nor considered healthful, although custom and belief changed for the better during the course of the century. This, together with the general proliferation of table silver described below, helps to explain the appearance of a number of articles of vegetable service in the second half of the century (Chapter VII). Sauces were made of, or flavoured by, gooseberry, borage, gillyflower, sage, currants. Sweet dishes included firm shortcakes, seed cakes, imbals (a fruit and nut cake), fruit and mincemeat tarts, "quaking" pudding, leaches (a gelatinous concoction of cream, spices, fruits, nuts and other ingredients), syllabubs. Cheeses of all kinds were served and during the eighteenth century became known by their place of manufacture.

Nor were the practitioners of these dining exercises surfeited by their excesses. If the dinner party went on into the evening, then a substantial supper followed at 10 or 11 o'clock. Admittedly, animal husbandry improved enormously through the eighteenth century; fowl and animals more than doubled their weight (15). On this account, diners of the early part of the eighteenth century, at least, were perhaps a little less excessive in their appetite than might at first appear. Nor did dining etiquette require them to sample all dishes.

Although food excesses tended to abate somewhat during the span of the eighteenth century, devotion to plentiful nourishment still remained a pastime of even the middle class. The *Diary of a Country Parson* by James Woodforde, cited by Hampson (2), reveals the good life enjoyed by this cleric. The diners at a dinner for nine "ate six pair of fried soal, a fine leg of mutton rosted, boiled ham and three chickens, beans, a boiled plumb pudding and new potatoes" for the first course, and "a couple of rost ducks and peas, berries charter (old English fruit fool?), raspberry cream, red currant and gooseberry tarts and black currant tartlets." There followed "Dessert: french olives, raspberries, cherries, three sorts of strawberries and white currants—." The meat-savory-sweet dish combinations of the eighteenth century — especially in the second course — led to juxtapositions of food stuffs that would today seem somewhat bizarre.

Needless to say, the lower classes — the vast majority of the population — ate only bare necessities, if that. A working man's diet at the end of the century, as cited in Eden's report on *The State of the Poor* (19), "consisted of bread, butter, cheese, pickled pork and a little butcher's meat" — and sweet tea if he could not afford beer. The unemployed and dispossessed suffered miserably from want and malnutrition. They scrambled for the orts from the rich man's table.

Notwithstanding Parson Woodforde's zeal for good eating, meals were becoming simpler by the end of the eighteenth century, while some improvement in transport reduced the need for highly spiced foods in order to cover the taint of decay. Although the Prince Regent was highly devoted to his gastronomic well being, he was as much gourmet as gourmand. The Victorian ethic that prevailed later in the nineteenth century de-emphasized indiscriminate indulgence of the appetite; overeating disappeared as a way of life (14,17). The improvement in transportation meant that fresh fish and foodstuffs could reach their destination; while the steamship even brought refrigerated beef from Australia.

The service at dinner also altered in several ways in the second quarter of the century. Each dish of a course itself constituted a course and these were served sequentially (20). Thus a modest dinner might be three-course; an elaborate one seven-course; while an important occasion, such as a state dinner, might double or triple that number. The mode of service became what is known as 'Russian.' The diner's plate was loaded in the kitchen, or the close-by butler's pantry, or at a sidetable, so that carving and serving implements were not required at table, although centerpieces, silver vases, cruets, sauces, boats, and glasses, still remained. A small dinner party might dine on turtle soup, whitebait, then grouse, followed by a sweet of apple fritters and jelly. Both French and Russian style are used today, with the popular buffet dinner being a type of do-it-yourself Russian service. An intermediate type of service, known as 'German' and still used, also occurred, whereby various dishes were presented in sequence by the waiter or servant who offered serving dishes and servers to each diner; soup is an exception, served by the hostess.

What about the foods themselves — especially those that would be served with a broad bladed server? The first to be considered is fish in its several forms. In earlier times, fish was eaten on as many as three days a week — Wednesday, Friday and Saturday in conformity with church ordinance (21). Henry VIII forgave all days as a papist custom, but Friday, especially, was reinstituted as a day of observance following his reign.

A large fish, such as salmon, might be prepared by boiling in a fish kettle — a long oblong copper pan furnished with handles and, sometimes, a strainer — and be then transported to the butler's pantry or to the side table (22,31). It could be transferred by means of a fish slice (of base metal of necessity in the early part of the eighteenth century) or large spoon to a platter, or charger, or to a pierced mazarine strainer set in a dish. The origin of the latter French article is somewhat obscure but by the eighteenth century it had come to mean a strainer and containing dish, particularly for fish — usually oval in shape, but sometimes round (3). George I owned more than fifty of these articles (36). Eventually the strainer itself was called a mazarine or fish plate. An early kitchen-style round Scandinavian brass example, dated 1716, is 38.4 cm in diameter; it has two loop handles and is pierced in a simple pattern of round holes. It is in the Nordiska Museet, Stockholm. Some later Georgian silver types are illustrated in Figs. 1 and 2. Old Sheffield examples were advertised as "fish plates" (30); ceramic ones are today called "drainers." Once placed on a platter or mazarine, after 1775 the fish could be carved with a silver fish knife.

Smaller fish could be lifted from a kettle or pot with use of a trowel or spoon, or from hot oil during the cooking process itself. Smart (23) has discussed in detail the preparation and service of white bait, the fry of the sprat and herring family. The term *bait*, itself, in addition to its conventional meanings of lure and snare, also signified a refreshment on a journey (26). Smart has described the celebrated

1.	An oval sterling MAZARINE strainer, Robert Sharp, London 1794; length 52 cm, width 36 cm. The mazarine normally sat on a fitted silver underdish that received the liquid. Many pairs have been separated by time. The plate is completely pierced over its whole surface in scrolling patterns; it has a central geometric diamond-shaped design which was machine press cut. A crest fills the center of the design. Most silver mazarines are oval in shape and are used for the service of fish and, less often, for meat. The surface of the plate bears a number of knife cut marks, indicating that at least one owner served from it and that it was not employed solely as a drainer.

2.	An oval sterling MAZARINE strainer, Paul Storr, London, 1806; length 42 cm, width 30 cm. The plate is pierced with diapers and scrolls and is circumscribed on the inside edge by a double line of circles and stars. There is a star-bordered central reserve in which are the arms of the Baron Foley with the motto Ut Prosim. Four bun feet have been added later so that the strainer can stand on a platter rather than in a fitted silver dish. The surface of the plate is marked with a few cuts.

ministerial sorties down the Thames from Westminster to Greenwich for the annual white bait dinners — a custom started in the eighteenth century and revived throughout the nineteenth century. White bait had been enjoyed at Greenwich, a holiday centre, as early as the first half of the century. The fish were cooked crisp straight from the nets after rinsing and flouring. They were dropped into boiling fat and then lifted out (7). A pile of cooked white bait was served with a trowel.

Fresh fish was rarely available to most people in eighteenth-century England. Raw fish was frequently tainted by the time of arrival at its destination. The affluent maintained fresh fish ponds on their estates, and, on occasion, travelled to the sites of the fresh catches. Preservation by salting, potting, pickling, and smoking was usually employed. To cover taint, and to vary the culinary form of presentation, a variety of other modes of cooking were also used. Fresh or not, fish was usually spiced and well seasoned by whatever mode of preparation; sugar also played a role as spice (1). Favourite recipes for both fish and meats included roasts, spicy pottages, stews, hashes, and fricassees; or the flesh was turned into bisques, jellies and blancmange — the latter a thickened gelatine puree rather than the sweeter custard of today. Fish pies were also popular in both the eighteenth and nineteenth centuries. In the earlier period, the fish might be incorporated with fruits, eggs, butter and spices in a strong coffin or crust made of flour paste. In time, the top crust cover, and later even the bottom, tended to disappear and be replaced by buttered bread crumbs. Depending on the artistry and disposition of the cook, something resembling a pudding might result. The so-called stargazey pie (7) made of a dozen or so small fish, herring or pilchards, a Cornish specialty, underwent similar transformation; the fish were arranged radially, or side by side, on a short crust pastry; the cover might disappear in the nineteenth century and the fish be covered with buttered bread crumbs and egg custard, and baked. Small fish became an article of breakfast fare only in the nineteenth century (4).

What passed under the title of pudding and pie? Of cake and pastry? Of

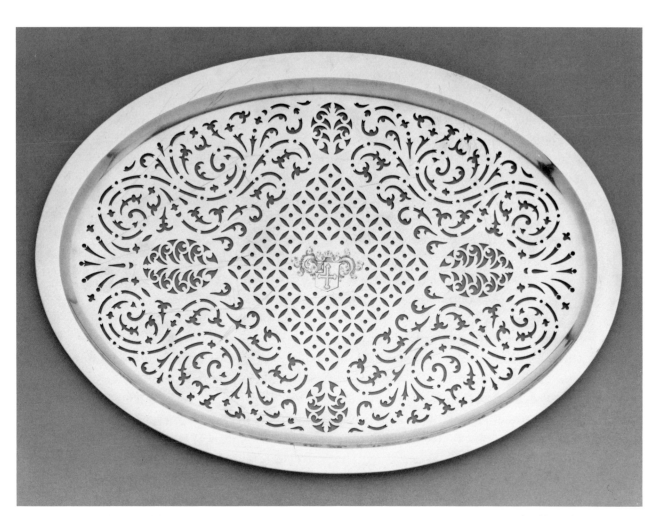

salads? Foods that were served with a trowel and other servers. Dinner time had been earlier called "pudding time" — the time at which a first dish, pudding, was set upon the table (24,25). Considerable indeterminacy attaches to the word *pudding*. Johnson's dictionary (26) includes the meaning of a meatless dish — a food made of meal, milk, eggs, sugar, spices, and other ingredients; as well as a stuffed animal gut. The stuffing itself, whether bloodless, meatless, or otherwise, took on the name of pudding, and other containers in addition to guts, including the pudding-cloth, were employed. Not the least of these was the pastry crust (coffin). Pudding making flourished and diversified in the seventeenth and eighteenth centuries.

For double emphasis, a savoury pudding with meat or fish baked in it might evoke the double-barreled name, *pudding pie*. But to confuse the nomenclature and our present-day understanding of terms, it may be noted that a Kentish cheesecake, made with currants and custard, was also known as pudding pie (12). Minced meat pies were very popular — a mixture of spices, dried fruits, suet, and ground or coarse meats. The famous variety, plum pudding, itself underwent notable evolution (24). The early version was a porridge made with meat broth, fruit juices and wine, with added raisins and spices and thickened to a semi-liquid with bread crumbs. By the middle of the seventeenth century it had stiffened to a semblance of the present pudding. The word *tart* tended to be restricted to the name for a covered pie made of fruit, but could include meat. Today, it signifies a small uncovered sweet (fruit) pie. Savoury meat and fish pies became more popular in the eighteenth century than sweetened meat pies. By contrast, mince pies tended to lose their meat, but not their suet, and became fruit pies; both varieties are made today.

The variety of puddings made in these times was impressive. They were steamed, boiled, baked and fried. Bayne-Powell (12) cites 67 recipes for these, including bread, rice, plum, cabbage, carrot, spinach, herb, oat and potato, to mention only some vegetarian creations; all suffused with numerous addends such as cream, eggs, suet, spices, sugar, wine, berries and currants. One perceives that the combinations and permutations possible by inclusions of meats and fish, in chunks or strips, ground, or pureed, might even lead to the evolution of the sixty-eighth variety! Indeed, civilization more than accepted the challenge and moved forward in the nineteenth and twentieth centuries. A well-known current cookbook (27), whose author's roots are confessedly Victorian, lists some 170 puddings. In the twentieth century, puddings fall mainly into the dessert category. Almost all are sweets: sweet custards, souffles, whips, creams, sponges, and the like. Blancmange has become a vanilla custard. No fish or meat ingredients are employed. A few puddings, such as baked plum and several steamed puddings, though sweetened are still of more solid consistency; Yorkshire pudding is now listed with dressings and breads.

In any case, it is clear from the brief descriptions given above that the term fish slice or trowel, for example, may imply both the service of fish *per se*, or of fish incorporated into a custard or pudding, or a fish puree or blancmange. Similarly a pudding slice or trowel might mean one that was intended for serving a savoury meat or fish pudding, or a vegetarian variety, or for some sort of sweetened variety, or a sweet. And if for the service of a fish pudding pie, say, is it to be called a fish trowel, or a pudding trowel, or a pie or pastry server? Evidently, as will be apparent in Chapters III-V, many such dilemmas tend to be artificial and have only a formal semantic basis.

As is recounted in Chapter III, some servers that were called pudding or fish slices were sometimes also designated interchangeably as cake or tart slices. What were those articles of food? Cakes in the seventeenth and eighteenth century were neither the light raised fluffy constructions that they evolved toward in the nineteenth century, nor the later nineteenth-century intensely sweet, many-layered pastries known as tortes. They were a form of enriched bread. In the homes of the wealthy, they tended to be large, rather firm short breads. A rich cake recipe (12) might include along with flour, 15 eggs, six pounds of butter and seven pounds of currents, or other dried fruits, together with sugar and other addends; the eggs served as leavener. Or the cake might be more like a wafer or biscuit made of batter (26) and used as an accompaniment to a jelly. Simnel cakes were made in two varieties — either a flat spiced fruitcake or a richer variety, like a bride's cake, and having an almond paste icing (25). Gradually, in the course of the eighteenth century and into the next, cakes tended to be less spicy and to become lighter, sweeter confections. So Mrs. Beeton (28), in the second half of the last century, prescribed baking powder (tartaric acid and baking soda) to leaven her cakes.

In the early eighteenth century, fruits were still often cooked or baked (in pastry tarts, say) rather than being eaten raw, for fear of harmful health effects. The cooked fruits could be sliced and eaten as a spiced compote, or be minced or crushed and become a constituent of a pudding, or be served in the second course as a creamy fool. The pastry designated as a tart was a pastry-cased fruit pie whose principal constituents might be citrus fruits such as domestic orange and lemon, apples, currants, pumpkin, plum, cherry, gooseberry, pear, prunes, quince, rhubarb and bananas. Spiced vegetable pies — such as potato, sweet potato, onion, and artichoke — were also popular; the fillings could be admixed with dried fruits, eggs, and various meats, and the whole served in a pastry coffin. In the course of time, tarts became sweeter and meat, if any, as in a mince pie, was omitted. The top crust might be a lattice, be replaced by a crumb composition, or disappear.

As pointed out by Wilson in her scholarly survey (1), raw salad vegetables, though considered suspect in the seventeenth century, did not come under quite the same severe health strictures as still affected fruit in the early eighteenth century. Salads might be simple, encompassing one or two green vegetables — such as lettuce, cress, endive, celery, cabbage, young leaves of many plants, and so on — dressed with oil, vinegar, and pepper or other herbs. In earlier times, some vegetables, such as spinach, were sometimes pre-cooked.

A boiled vegetable salad incorporating beans, carrots, potatoes, beets, and so forth, might be served hot. Pickled vegetables were also favoured — cucumbers, fennel, beans, and cabbage, to name a few; and, later in the eighteenth century, tomatoes. Asparagus was cheap, plentiful and widely used. In the seventeenth and eighteenth centuries, the "grand" salad, salmagundi, might include, in addition to an assortment of the above vegetables, various herbs and eggs, and sliced or diced meats, fish and anchovies. Berries and flowers such as nasturtiums, roses, violets, and primroses, candied or otherwise, were incorporated.

## Silver Dining Service

Economic factors and social customs dictated the living habits and practise in the homes of the wealthy with regard to the use of silver articles. These topics have been thoroughly developed in the monographs by Glanville (3), Girouard (8), and Gruber (29), among others. The arbiters of fashion in Western Europe and England in the late seventeenth and first half of the eighteenth centuries were Louis XIV of France, primarily, and his successor Louis XV. The seventeenth century was notable for an increasing elaboration and refinement of table furnishings and silver, which continued into the eighteenth century. The British spent much of that period trying to catch up, aided artistically by the immigration of skilled Huguenot craftsmen following the revocation of the Edict of Nantes in 1685 (33) and economically, as well, by the military successes of the Duke of Marlborough.

Actually, the whole of the eighteenth century was a period of great wealth — at least for the wealthy. The era provided them with the financial ability to follow the dictates of fashion as it affected dining and its accoutrements, among other things, and for the purchases of massive amounts of silver plate. Two developments brought about great changes in the middle eighteenth century (5,14,15). The first of these was the invention of agricultural machinery, such as the seed drill by Jethro Tull, and the introduction of innovative farming practises, such as Four-Year Crop Rotation by Viscount Townshend. The new methods could be most successfully applied to large acreages and provided a rationale and ostensible basis for the exclusion of rural populations from their historic, communal village farming plots. The Enclosure Acts enriched the large wealthy landowners and divested the rural populations of their land rights. They thereby facilitated the second development. Namely, it provided a new and plentiful source of cheap labour to staff the growing factories and population centres that attended the inventions and mechanization that characterized the Industrial Revolution. By 1760, the cotton, wool, iron and steel industries were being transformed. Foreign trade flourished. Manufacture and industry were greatly affected by the steam machinery of Matthew Boulton and James Watt that was also used in the rolling, stamping, and fly piercing of silver and silver articles and Old Sheffield plate in the Birmingham factory. The result was not only increased resources for the 'haves,' but the emergence as well of an affluent upper middle class of merchants, professionals, and tradespeople (15). All of this resulted in a great tide of new silver purchases to accompany the changes in living habits and social customs (8,31).

The principal innovations that are of concern here relate naturally to dining and dining practises. Prior to the eighteenth century, the dining room as we know it did not exist in England although already established in France (39). Stops-Jackson and Pipkin (31) credit Bess of Hardwick with the "first precocious step" in 1597 toward a permanent dining room, at Hardwick Hall. But a room set aside only for dining was first incorporated in 1722 in Sir Robert Walpole's Houghton Hall with, eventually, a permanent dining table. Prior to that time, temporary trestle or other tables were set up in a hall or parlour, as needed for a meal. By the end of the eighteenth century, a dining room, dining table, and sideboard, or side table or buffet, had become a standard feature of even relatively modest homes (34). Formal dinners became smaller affairs. Dining became a more intimate occasion; even a very large table usually seated only sixteen or so persons, and seating became more informal (9) [Figs. 3,4]. The walnut table of Walpole gave way to the polished mahogany table; the tablecloth disappeared and, to rectify its lack, napkins reappeared — having been banished earlier after the slow emergence in England of the fork and more fastidious table manners (10) in the early part of the century. However, the ewer and basin continued to be made in the first half of the century, as still required by hygienics and social grace.

During the century the dinner hour progressed steadily from 11 a.m. to 5-6 p.m. and toward 8 p.m. in the nineteenth century (9,13,14). This trend necessitated the introduction of the mid-day luncheon occasion and, eventually, a tea break; if a high tea was served in late afternoon, then a later light supper might follow. Early in the eighteenth century, dessert was served in the same room as the main courses without a break to another room; the surtout or epergne came into its own [Fig. 4].

Needless to say, these innovations demanded their own changes in the need for and placement of many items of room and table silver (3). The great court cupboard had already disappeared in the seventeenth century, and a decorative sideboard or table for silver, glass and other articles had taken its place in the dining room (4). A number of new articles of silver for the tea and dining tables appeared, such as teapots and caddies, dinner plates, tureens, sauce boats, and the later argyles, cruet frames, casters, skewers, milk jugs (as tea grew stronger), baskets for bread, cakes and fruit, epergnes that bore sweetmeats for dessert, and fish slices and related servers (3,32,33), not to forget table forks — although many diners continued to use their table knives as spoons until the end of the eighteenth century and, in America, in much of the nineteenth century as well (17,38). Instead

3.    Table setting for a more elaborate large dinner party of fourteen in the 1830s. The service of the flesh dishes is evidently 'French' in nature. The host and hostess divided the service function for the soup and fish dishes. It may be noted that only one fish slice is provided for the fish service; for an even larger party one fish slice and a fish plate or platter might be provided at each end of the table (V 12). In this illustration, asparagus would be served with spoons, as would the vegetables or salad. The diagram depicts other articles of dining table silver. From J. Williams, *The Footman's Guide,* Dean and Munday, London, c. 1836.
Courtesy of Victoria and Albert Museum, London.

of large ostentatious pieces on the side buffet, such as sets of bowls, pots, flagons, steeple cups and chargers, smaller and more useful articles for family dining took their place, including glass and ceramic pieces (3,6,13). Placed on the side board by the end of the eighteenth century, awaiting use, were items such as cruet stands, small waiters, a sugar basin, reserve spoons, and various plates such as for cheese and dessert. Glanville (3) and Gruber (29) have provided detailed accounts of these changes and the items themselves.

The mode of table service has been touched on earlier above and detailed descriptions have been provided by several authors (3,4,8,29). Even before the end of the nineteenth century, dining practises had assumed the style familar to us now in our own more formal occasions. It is ironic that the nature and mode of food service and of dining in the homes of the elite in these earlier centuries was much more of an unknown to the bulk of the contemporary populace than it is to historians today — notwithstanding the large gaps that do exist in our present-day knowledge as scholars attempt to piece out the details of the function of various articles and of social usages and customs from an incomplete record. The labouring classes and the poor simply lived in a different world. Present-day social mobility has done much to fill the chasm.

Stylistic changes in silver design were also greatly affected by the Industrial Revolution. This example is one of the most striking instances of the close interaction between style and technology. Notwithstanding the importance of the rediscovery of Pompeii and other historical influences of the mid-eighteenth century, there can be little doubt that the successful introduction of neoclassical forms and style in Britain around 1760 was also rooted in the development of easily rolled, uniform thin sheet and of die-cutting, forming, and stamping machinery and attendant economic aspects. It was these techniques, that could shape Old Sheffield sheet so well and efficiently, that compelled sterling makers to increase their own productivity and adopt similar fabrication methods. Labour intensive raising methods were replaced in much of the manufacture. Thin sheet was easily worked by bending and stamping. The Romans long ago had employed lathe spinning methods for raising sheet. The weight and cost of sterling and Old Sheffield articles declined markedly and silver entered the lives of many who could not previously afford it. Whereas a silver trowel by Boulton and

# DINNER PARTY OF FOURTEEN.

*Plate I. First Course.*

| | | | |
|---|---|---|---|
| 1.— Soup | 5.— Tongue | A.— Epergne | a.— 2 Wine Glasses |
| 2.— Fish | 6.— Chickens | B.— Wine Coolers | to each person |
| 3.— Vegetables | 7.— Asparagus | C.— Water Carafts | b.— Attendants, or |
| 4.— Melted Butter | 8.— Fish Sauce | D.— Branch Candlesticks | Waiters |

4.   Table setting for the dessert course of a more elaborate dinner party of fourteen in the 1830s. Cake, fruit, and nuts were served. The dessert epergne or centerpiece of the nineteenth century is a much simplified version of the George II article (3). The diagram depicts various articles of table silver. From J. Williams, *op. cit.*
Courtesy of Victoria and Albert Museum, London.

Fothergill cost around two pounds in 1780, Old Sheffield plate items were sold by them for one-third or one-fourth of that price (40).

## *References*

1.   C.A. Wilson, *Food and Drink in Britain*, Constable, London, 1973.
2.   J. Hampson, *The English at Table*, Collins, London, 1948.
3.   P. Glanville, *Silver in England*, Unwin Hyman, London, 1987.
4.   G. Brett, *A History of Dining in England 1400-1900*, Hart-Davis, London, 1968.
5.   C. Hole, *English Home Life: 1500-1800*, Batsford, London, 1947.
6.   C. Hole, *The English Housewife in the 17th Century*, Chatto and Windus, London, 1953.
7.   D. Hartley, *Food in England*, Macdonald and Jones, London, 1954.
8.   M. Girouard, *Life in the English Country House*, Penguin, 1980.
9.   E. Burton, *The Georgians at Home 1714-1830*, Longmans, London, 1967.
10.  J.A. Jeffreason, *A Book About Table*, Hurst and Blackett, London, 1875, extracted by H. C. Smith.
11.  F. de Rochefoucauld, *A Frenchman in England, 1784*, J. Marchand, ed., Cambridge, 1933.
12.  R. Bayne-Powell, *Housekeeping in the Eighteenth Century*, Murray, London, 1956.
13.  A.S. Turberville, *Johnson's England*, Oxford, 1933.
14.  M. and C.H.B. Quennell, *A History of Everyday Things in England, 1733-1851*, Batsford, London, 1933.
15.  J.H. Plumb, *England in the Eighteenth Century*, Penguin, London, 1950.
16.  M.D. George, *London Life in the Eighteenth Century*, Knopf, New York, 1925.
17.  E. Burton, *The Early Victorians at Home 1837-1861*, Longmans, London, 1972.
18.  N. and G. Kurti, *But The Crackling is Superb*, Hilger, Bristol, 1988.
19.  Sir Frederick Eden, *The State of the Poor, 1797*, abridged by A.G.L. Rogers, 1925.
20.  A. Brillat-Savarin, *Physiology of Taste (1825)*, Liveright, New York, 1948.
21.  *Oxford New English Dictionary*, ed. J.A. Murray, Vol. IV, Clarendon Press, 1901.

# DESSERT FOR FOURTEEN.

## Plate II.

| 1.—Pine Apple or Melon | 5.—Apples | A.—Silver Cake Basket or Epergne | a.—Finger glass & 2 Wine glasses to each person. |
|---|---|---|---|
| 2.—Grapes | 6.—Plums | B.—Wine Coolers | |
| 3.—Nectarines | 7.—Peaches | C.—Water Carafts | |
| 4.—Figs | 8.—Walnuts | D.—Branch Candlesticks | |

22. E. Perry, *Collecting Antique Metalware,* Hamlyn, London, 1974.

23. H.W. Smart, *Fishy Business for Ministers,* Country Life, November, 1974.

24. E.L. McAdam and G. Milne, *Samuel Johnson's Dictionary. A Modern Selection,* Gollancz, London, 1982.

25. C. Hole, *English Traditional Customs,* Batsford, London, 1975.

26. R. Whitlock, *A Calendar of Country Customs,* Batsford, London, 1978.

27. I.S. Rombauer, *The Joy of Cooking,* Bobbs-Merrill, New York, 1931.

28. S.O. Beeton, *Every-Day Cookery and Housekeeping Book,* Ward, Lock, London.

29. A. Gruber, *Silverware,* trans. by D. Smith, Rizzoli, New York, 1982.

30. G.B. Hughes, *Sheffield Silver Plate,* Praeger, London, 1970.

31. G. Stops-Jackson and J. Pipkin, *The English Country House,* Little, Brown, Boston, 1985.

32. R. Came, *Silver,* Weidenfeld and Nicolson, London, 1970.

33. J. Stone, *English Silver of the Eighteenth Century,* Cory, Adams and Mackay, London, 1965.

34. F. Trevor-Venis, *The Eighteenth Century English Dining Room,* The Israel Museum, Jerusalem, undated.

35. G. Wills, *Guinness Book of Silver,* Guinness Superlatives, London, 1983.

36. J.F. Hayward, *Huguenot Silver in England 1688-1727,* Faber, London, 1959.

37. A. Bryant, *Years of Endurance 1763-1802,* Harper, London, 1942.

38. N.D. Turner, *American Silver Flatware 1837-1910,* Barnes, Cranbury, N.J., 1972.

39. J. Fowler and J. Cornforth, *English Decoration in the 18th Century,* Barrie and Jenkins, London, 1974.

40. K. Quickenden, City of Birmingham Polytechnic, personal communication.

41. E. Smith, *The Compleat Housewife,* T.J. Press, London, 1968.

# Chapter III

# TROWELS

## *History*

ONE OF THE EARLY, specially designed silver serving utensils that came to the eighteenth-century English dining table was the elongated, triangular shaped slice called a trowel. The blade may or may not possess rounded shoulders. In British custom these implements were known as fish, pudding or pie trowels, among other names. Continental nomenclature for very early servers differs by country. The two most important of these are the Dutch designation for serving pieces, usually as fish slices or servers, "visschep," particularly if they exhibit a fish motif, or as pastry servers or trowels, "taartschep," if they do not (1-4); and the Scandinavian names for very early servers, namely as pastry-related cake spades or slices (kakspade or tårtspade) (5). For somewhat later articles, the German designation is primarily as "hebers," i.e., *lifters,* a very suggestive term, and the server name, fish or pastry or cake, is applied quite impartially even when the decor lacks fish or marine motif (6,7a).

The earliest and best known British slice of this genre, a fish trowel, is the famed one of 1741 by Paul De Lamerie (the spelling of whose name here follows the practise of his biographer (7b)) in the Farrer Collection of the Ashmolean Museum, Oxford [Fig. 1a]. It is one of five known trowels by this maker [Fig. 1], as well as the most celebrated survivor of the vicissitudes of the centuries. Some anomaly seems to attend this article, since it is neither triangular, as are virtually all succeeding English trowels, nor the earliest known European example of a fish slice. The mystery deepens a little when one encounters what seems to be the commonly held view that the invention of the fish slice was a French and English conception of the early eighteenth century and that other countries followed their example (8,9). Hernmarck (10) credits England with priority in the invention of

---

**Note.** Implements discussed or illustrated in this book that are derived from sources such as museums, collectors, or other works are described first of all by the names chosen by those sources; this helps to convey many opinions rather than solely those of the author.

1a.    FISH TROWEL, Paul De Lamerie, London, 1741; length 32 cm, weight 6.3 oz. This slice was once the property of the Earl of Howth; part of the Farrer Collection, it is now in the Ashmolean Museum, Oxford. It has many distinctions. It is the most famous of all British serving pieces, and both the first known by this maker and the earliest known British broad-bladed silver server. Although by definition a *trowel*, as defined later in the text, it is also the earliest English approach to a later shape that is called *near-elliptical* in Chapter IV. Moreover, it is the earliest known of the infrequent British examples of elaborate rococo blade decoration, other than those by De Lamerie himself. The simple Hanoverian handle is in pleasant contrast to the elaborately pierced blade which is engraved on both sides, and which shows some half-dozen fish, eel and dolphin avidly, and somewhat ill-temperedly, dining or disporting themselves in the reeds and weeds. The blade is almost plane with a slight "droop-snoot," and the edges are strengthened (thickened) and rise a little at the rear; there is no topside boss or junction to the handle. With use of only a little imagination, a resemblance to some of the early oblong fish slices and shovels illustrated in Chapter I may be perceived; this is discussed further in the text. Enlarged photographs of the blade are available in the literature (see Ref. I 4, Fig. 256 and A.G. Grimwade, *Rococo Silver*, 1727-1765, Faber, London, 1974, Plate 88b) and will not be displayed here again in favour of a less well-known De Lamerie example in Fig. 1b. The piercing has some repaired breaks and this "priceless" article is the ultimate example of the admonition given in Chapter I that a few minor repairs or breaks in the piercing do not vitiate an otherwise fine or dramatic object.
By kind cooperation and courtesy of the Ashmolean Museum, Oxford.

1b.    FISH TROWEL, Paul De Lamerie, London, 1743, with near-elliptical blade and length 35 cm. It bears the crest of Algernon Coote, Earl of Mountrath. It is in the genre of the Howth slice. It is engraved and decorated on both sides. Two central figures of mermen and two merchildren holding a net are displayed; also shown are fish (similar in attitude to the Howth slice) and a dolphin that have quizzical expressions. The leading edge of the blade has been slightly twisted, revealing that even such notable wares suffered from the sort of abuse discussed in the text. Detail of the blade is shown in the Frontispiece. A full dozen of fish, eel and dolphin are in evidence here amongst the weeds and leaves. The engraving again shows what seem to be rather unhappy sea life, quite unlike the depictions of frolicsome, rollicking dolphins by other artists, as for example, in Fig. V 112. Both sides of the blade are engraved.
By assistance of Jolyon Warwick James. From the Dawson-Damer Collection.

1c.    FISH TROWEL, Paul De Lamerie, London, 1744, with near-elliptical oval blade and Hanoverian handle whose stem is engraved "No. 2"; length 34.3 cm, weight 6.8 oz. As may be seen in the illustration, the maker's mark is lacking and has been lost in an old repair to the stem; the original weight was a little greater, as evident from the scratch weight of 7.3 oz. The resemblance to the slice of Fig. 1a and the quality of the piercing and engraving leave little doubt that this implement should be identified as a De Lamerie piece. The later crest is that of Lord Pettiward of Finborough Hall, Suffolk. The server was sold by Christie's, London, May 18, 1988. Detail of the blade is provided in the sale catalogue.
By kind cooperation and courtesy of Christie's, London.

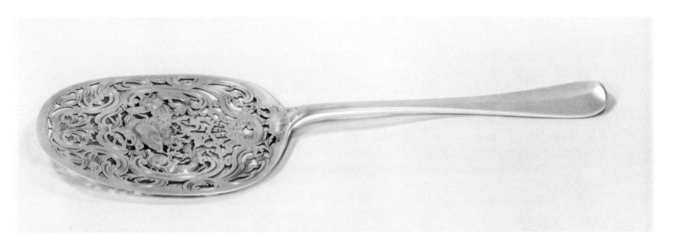

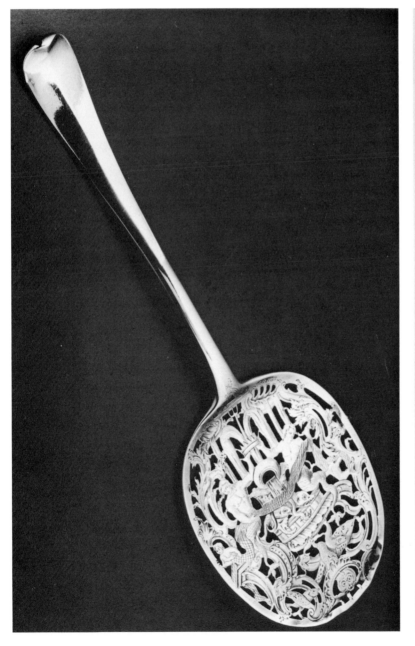

1d.    FISH TROWEL, Paul De Lamerie, London, 1746, with Hanoverian handle and near-elliptical blade; length 35 cm, weight 7 oz. This slice was originally made for Admiral of the Fleet George, Baron Anson. For a more detailed account of his life and as a patron of De Lamerie see Christie's catalogue, New York, October 27, 1987, Lot 429. The server has passed through the Lichfield and Swaythling Collections and was sold by Christie's, New York, on October 22, 1987. The blade is completely pierced and engraved on both sides with C-scrolls, scrolling foliage and flower heads, and two crossed dolphins amid seaweed and other fish life; the head of King Neptune is featured.
By kind cooperation and courtesy of Christie's, New York.

1e.    FISH/PUDDING TROWEL, Paul De Lamerie, 1748, with Hanoverian handle and near-elliptical shape; "tablespoon length" (i.e., 21-22 cm, estimated), weight 3.95 oz. The handle is engraved with a crest — a stag trippant — which has too many claimants (see J. Fairbairn, *Crests of the Families of Great Britain and Ireland*, New Orchard, Poole, 1986, Plate 68) to permit identification. The flat blade is pierced with scrolls and a central pattern of crosslets; it bears no engraving. This simple blade decoration, although not the shape, is in the style of the contemporary trowels shown in Figs. 16,17; but although these pierced servers are usually called fish trowels (see text), the contrast of this De Lamerie server with its more elaborate marine-decorated predecessors invites alternative description as a pudding trowel. Sold at Christie's, London, June 23, 1976.
By kind cooperation and courtesy of Spink and Son Ltd, London.

2.    CAKE SLICE or CAKE SPADE, Peter Henning, Stockholm, 1714. This is the oldest triangular server extant known to the author, although this does not foreclose the possible existence of an even older one. The unpierced flat blade is in late baroque style and is chased overall in a loose 'Rorschach' pattern of pouncing on which are superimposed regular foliate features. The flat handle, which has underblade attachment, is similarly, but more regularly, decorated and has a strong mussel shell finial feature. This heart- or spade-shaped blade is the prototype of all that follow in this period. This server is described further in *Svenskt Silversmide, 1520-1850*, by C. Hernmarck, Å Stavenow and G. Munthe, Nordiska Rotogravyr, Stockholm, 1963; see Vol. II, Senbarocken, Fig. 154.
By kind cooperation and courtesy of Nordiska Museet, Stockholm. Property of Mrs. Alice von Ehrenheim, Grönsöö, Sweden.

the fish slice. A survey was made of some seventy of the principal museums in Western Europe, for the moment excluding those of The Netherlands and Scandinavia, together with a small number of museums in Eastern Europe. The search failed to reveal any certain examples of a pre-1740 slice, and also provided an opinion that none such existed in Germany (9). No existing example of an early eighteenth-century French fish or pastry server or related implement has been discovered by the writer. Various compilations of early French wares provide no examples (11-14). It would, of course, be too brash to assert that there are none, and even more so that none had been made and been subsequently destroyed in the same manner that befell most early French silver. The latter is quite possible; although fish undoubtedly played a larger part in the diet of the British than of the French people (27).

Since the stylistic development of silver wares in Scandinavia depended heavily on French and German inspiration and sources, it is rather surprising to

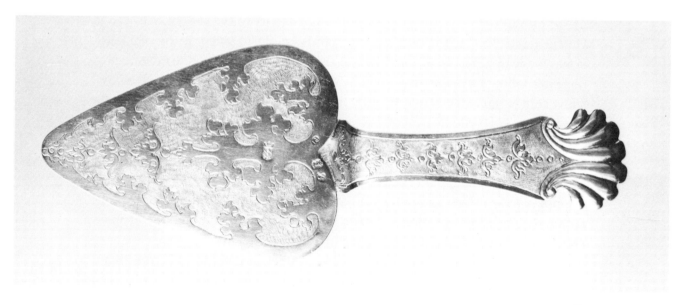

3.     CAKE TROWEL, Gottfried Dubois, Stockholm, 1723, with cannon-end handle; length 34.3 cm, weight 5.6 oz. The elongated, unpierced heart-shaped blade has slightly incurving sides and the surface is chased with Berain transitional baroque interlaced band and scroll style patterns that cast back to Renaissance themes. The cannon-end handle and finial cap is made in several pieces joined at ribbed junctions. The handle attaches under the blade to a spreading foliate cut-card junction which simultaneously decorates (although is unfortunately hidden) and strengthens the blade. The crests (a griffin erased and an etoile of eight points, each issuing from a coronet) have not been traced. Although cannon-end spoons and cut-card decoration of hollow ware are well known in British production at this and earlier date, neither of these features have been seen on broad-bladed servers.

4.     CAKE SLICE, Abraham Petersson Wirgman, Gothenburg, 1724. The spade-shaped blade is beautifully engraved overall with Berain style tracery and with heavy cut-card topside decoration designed to simulate a rat tail at the rear of the blade. The cannon-end handle has an octagonal cross-section and further decoration at the end near the fluted cap finial.
By kind cooperation and courtesy of Nordiska Museet, Stockholm.

5.     CAKE SLICE, Carl Zitski, Stockholm, 1731. Another fine example of Swedish silversmith work. The decoration and construction of the blade, flat handle and finial is very similar to that of Fig. 2, with the difference that Berain type strap patterns and scrolls are superimposed on the pounced background. This server is further described as Fig. 359 of *Svenskt Silversmide, Vol. II, Frederik I Stil* cited in Fig. 2.
Courtesy of Nordiska Museet, Stockholm. The article is in the care of Disponent Atle Lundström, Ludvika, Sweden.

6.     CAKE SLICE, Niclas Warneck, Karlstad, 1738. There is an evident close similarity between this server and those of Figs. 3 and 4. This server is further described as Fig. 358 of *Svenskt Silversmide,* cited above.
Courtesy of the National Museum, Stockholm.

discover that triangular Swedish cake slices date as early as 1714, not to preclude the possible existence of even earlier examples, and thus antedate the De Lamerie trowel by almost thirty years. Indeed, although its shape is unknown, at least one Dutch "tart trowel" (presumably triangular) is known to antedate the year 1702. It was made by Dirk van de Graeff, Haarlem, and is recorded in the inventory of his estate following his decease in 1702 (58). Of course, as will be taken up below, a few conventional triangular trowels may possibly have been made in Britain even before 1741.

Apparently, the oldest serving trowel extant is one by P. Henning, Stockholm, 1714, which has been designated (5) as a cake spade or cake slice [Fig. 2]. The blade of this beautiful example of baroque style is unpierced, as is also that of an example of 1723 [Fig. 3], again by a Stockholm maker, G. Dubois, that shows Berain style chased decoration, a cannon-end handle, and an underside leafy boss attachment that is very much in the cut card vogue of the time. The same Régence decorative style and features are manifest in the server by A.P. Wirgman, Gothenburg, 1724 [Fig. 4], also termed for cake (15). Two later Swedish servers,

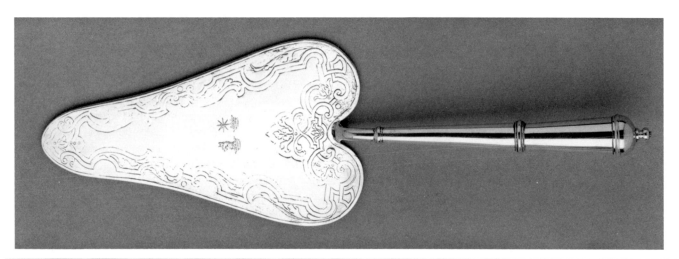
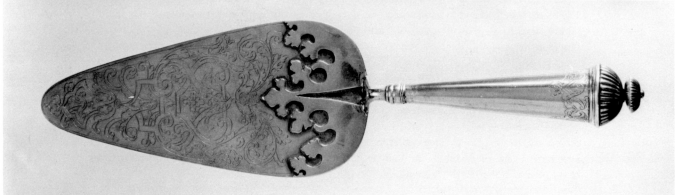

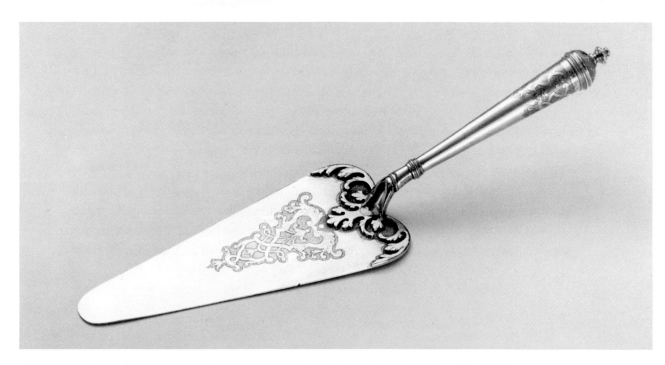

7.    STRAINING SPOON, Gustaf Stafhell, Sr., Stockholm, 1740. This spoon has a deeply cupped blade, pierced in transitional 'Frederik I' style. Its interest here revolves around its identification as a fish spoon by Å Stavenow in Fig. 356, *Svenskt Silversmide*, cited in Fig. 2. It bears a close resemblance to earlier olive and ecclesiastical skimming spoons. However, since fish engraving and piercing were at that time only then coming into vogue as decoration for fish servers [cf. Figs. 8 and 9], it is possible that the alleged function is correctly identified. Certainly, later large spoons of somewhat similar type *were* used for the service of fish [see Fig. 96 and accompanying discussion in the text]. Courtesy of the National Museum, Stockholm.

8.    FISH SLICE, Albert de Thomese, The Hague, 1737, Hanoverian handle; length 33 cm; weight 5.8 oz. This back view illustrates the underblade double drop junction and the crest on the handle. The blade is dished and has upturned edges so that it acquires the shape of a shallow ladle. It is totally pierced so as to leave a beautiful outline of Berain style interlaced bands and scrolls and also flower heads; it is fully engraved on both sides. This open work is well in advance of British decor [see Fig. 39]. This very early server has the traditional Dutch transverse oval shape of a fish slice and is so considered even though it lacks the conventional fish display [cf. Fig. 9].

9.    FISH SLICE, Jan Bot, Amsterdam, 1741. This splendid early Dutch example does display the conventional engraved fish symbolism, here in an artistically pierced net of quatrefoils and diamonds. The flat handle is attached to the underside of the blade by a panache of feathers and terminates in a baroque finial. The blade features very fine pierced work and the form of the fish is completely outlined by the piercing.
By kind cooperation and courtesy of the Rijksmuseum, Amsterdam.

dated 1731 and 1738, again reportedly cake spades or slices (5) and also unpierced, are shown in Figs. 5 and 6. Both are similar in style and decoration to the preceding examples. Although described as cake slices, these early servers could, of course, also be used for other delicacies such as sweetmeats, blancmange, meat or fish pies and puddings, slices of meat, and other related foods.

All of these trowels have flat, heart-shaped, unpierced blades and the attachment of the silver handles is made to the underside of the blade. The works by Hernmarck and colleagues (5,10) give detailed discussion of the stylistic styles and trends that characterize Scandinavian and European silver of the period. The variety of styles, which are all late baroque, is exemplified by the handles as well as the blades of these slices: the shell terminals of the flat handles are in more forceful baroque manner; the cannon ends are in Berain transitional style. English servers, it will be seen, started later as rather plain objects — always excluding the exceptional De Lamerie *opera* — escaping strong baroque influence ("undecorated" baroque) and becoming more ornate under rococo and particularly neo-classical sway.

It should be noted that the later four of the above servers, distinctly triangular in character and *having their major breadth in the rear half of the blade*, are quite elongated in character [Figs. 3-6]. Late nineteenth- and the more familiar twentieth-century cake and pie unpierced server blades bear an uncanny resemblance to these — at least in form if not in size. The sides of all four blades, from

44

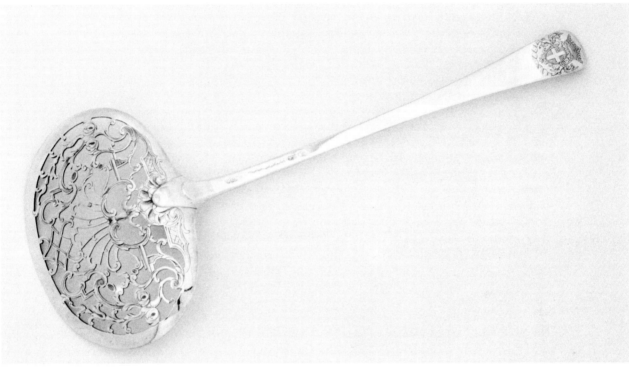

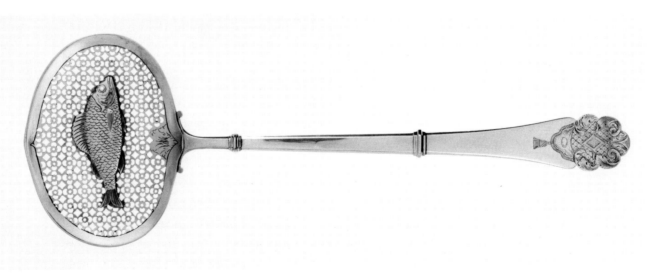

10.    FISH SLICE, Matthias Lotter, Cape Town, c. 1747; length 34.3 cm; weight 6.1 oz. The cast sheet blade is more crudely pierced and chased than its predecessor in Fig. 9; it features early, slightly stiff, rocaille chased decoration of the shaped handle. The blade is decorated on both sides; a fish is outlined by rococo C- and S-scroll work, along with transitional style diaper work on both surfaces near to the underblade double drop junction. The suggested date of c. 1747 seems appropriate. Lotter was an Augsburg silversmith who migrated to the Cape in 1733 *via* Amsterdam. He died in 1751, and his son J.C. Lotter, born in 1737 and also a silversmith, was too young to have used his mark; his succesor, Johan Hasse, could have. The server carries only the conjoined ML maker's mark for this maker (S. Welz, *Cape Silver*, Balkema, Rotterdam, 1976, pp. 136,150); this mark seems absent from Dutch listings; moreover the lack of assay or other marks make it unlikely that it has a Netherlands attribution.

11.    FISH SLICE, Arend Hoogland, Haarlem, 1760, length 36.2 cm. The blade is well chased and pierced with three fish amid scroll work. The rococo theme carries over to chased ornament on the handle and there is a cast rocaille and pendant feature at the finial. This lovely implement, with its slightly dished blade and curved handle, is strongly reminiscent of the attitude and shape of a ladle having an oval bowl.
Courtesy of the Frans Hals Museum, Haarlem.

12.    FISH SLICE with wooden handle, Lubertus Hendrik Bobbink, Amsterdam, 1798; length 37 cm; blade 14.5 x 10 cm; standard is 87.5% silver; there is a Paris mark for an object exchanged in commerce, c. 1800. The plain turned ebony handle is received in a silver tube that has a beaded rim and is attached to an imbricated flat strap stem *via* a rivetted and soldered split foliate junction; the stem attaches to the underside of the blade in a wide, very short drop. The engraved decoration, topside only, is early Empire and features three fish; one or three fish seem to be the statutory numbers on Dutch slices; two have not been seen by the author. The piercing, although not impressively refined in execution, is sufficiently refined in design so that it gives the impression of wire construction around the perimeter of the blade, rather than pierced sheet.

the near front end to the shoulders, are straight or very gentle arcs. The ratio of length of blade to maximum width is 1.4 for the Henning slice and rises for the latter four to the values 1.81, 2.16, 2.1 and 2.4, in chronological sequence. As will be seen, the last three ratios are considerably larger than occur in British examples and resemble the gross dimensions that appear much later for British long-oval slices.

Figure 7 shows a highly pierced oval Stockholm server by G. Stafhell, Sr., 1740. It is furnished with a Hanoverian terminal and is pierced in the late undecorated baroque style that carried over through the Régence period and corresponds in British parlance to the Queen Anne style. It bears a remarkable resemblance to an earlier French dog-nose design drawing of a spoon by Nicholas de Launay, c. 1700 (16), which is called an olive spoon by Hernmarck (10). But, interestingly, the Stockholm article has also been described (5) as a *fish* spoon; it is not unlike a spoon of similar pierced design such as an ecclesiastical wine-skimming spoon. Its rather small bowl and uncertain function contrasts with contemporary Dutch oval fish slices used for straining and lifting. The near-

46

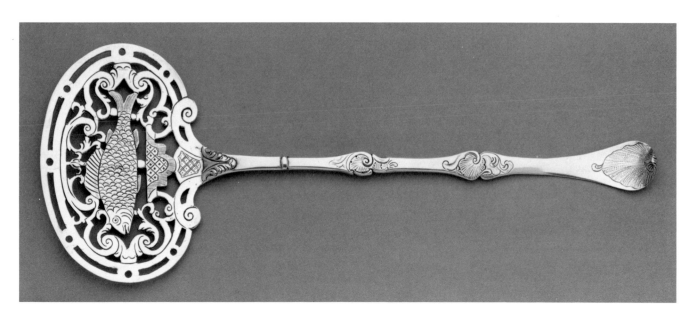

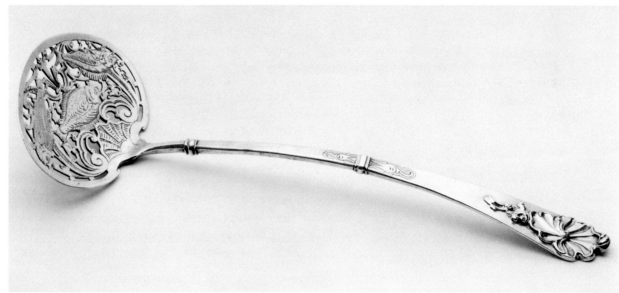

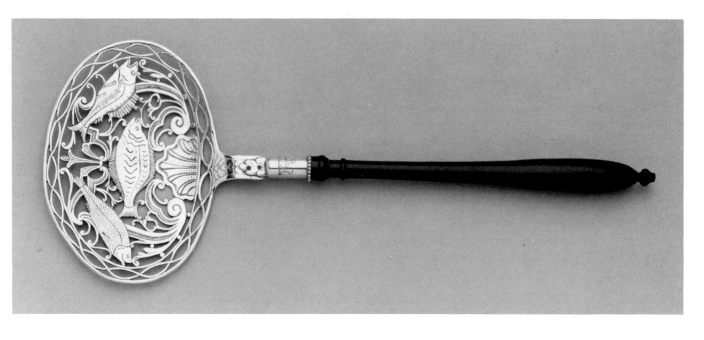

13.  CAKE/PASTRY TROWEL with wooden handle, Hans Atsma, Leeuwarden, c. 1732; length 19.4 cm, weight 2.2 oz. The starkly simple blade of isosceles triangle shape is relieved by a large well-engraved crest. The round wooden handle is attached by a rat tail to the underside of the blade by a simple rectangular S-cranked, wire stem and plain ferrule. Although this small server has been used as a ceremonial mason's trowel (17), the *ad hoc* use of fish or cake trowels for such purpose is not uncommon. This server is the prototype of the small pastry/tart trowels that followed in many countries in the eighteenth and, especially, nineteenth centuries.
By cooperation and courtesy of the Fries Museum, Leeuwarden.

14.  CAKE/PASTRY TROWEL, Jan van't Hofken, Amsterdam, 1734; length 28.5 cm. This is an exciting and strikingly beautiful early triangular trowel in late baroque style with incurving sides. The resemblance of the cast decorative features, including shell, acanthus leaf and flower heads, to the chased forms of Figs. 2,5 is obvious. The blade is highly pierced in a diaper and scroll pattern, but the difference in overall shape and handle of this implement from the conventional transverse oval fish slices lends support to its identification as a cake server.
By kind cooperation and courtesy of the owner, J. Van Loo, Epse.

15.  FISH/CAKE TROWEL, maker ICH, German, "c. 1730"; wooden handle. This late baroque decorated trowel of simple beauty and refinement has all-over crosslet piercing and diaper engraving. The blade has a flatly rounded front edge and cusped rear edge. The turned handle is attached to the blade *via* a conical tubular stem which rises from a circular boss attachment to the blade. The maker is presently unidentified and the date of making uncertain (see text). This server is Fig. 307 in A. Gruber, *Silverware*, Rizzoli, New York, 1982.
By kind cooperation and courtesy of Dr. Alain Gruber and of Office du Livre, Fribourg, Switzerland.

planar, or slightly dished, blades of the latter are placed with major axis transverse to the stem handle and usually carry one or more fishes embodied in the piercing and engraving decoration that announce their culinary association. Nor is the function of the Stafhell spoon as clear as that of the Dutch fish strainer spoon described below in the section on Function.

The early Dutch silver oval fish slices also precede the De Lamerie slice. They seem to represent a unique and original form. No precedent in silver wares is known to the writer, although the relationship to allied kitchen skimmers made of base metals is evident. The earliest known examples date from the 1730s. One of these, made in 1737 at the Hague by A. de Thomese, is shown in Fig. 8. The handle is plain Hanoverian in style. The blade, which is dished like a shallow ladle, shows very interesting Berain decoration, the contours of which are revealed in 'positive' by the piercing, as opposed to the conventional chasing and engraving on a silver background, as in Figs. 3 and 4. This very early fish slice, although of conventional shape, does not display the customary fish emblem. Another later rococo Dutch exception (W. Pont, Amsterdam, 1772), that displays only a floral theme, is illustrated in Ref. (56); Fig. 27b presents still another exception by F. Herle. The decoration of the handle of a slightly later 1741 server, which features the conventional fish motif on the blade [Fig. 9], is also baroque. A later example by M. Lotter, Cape of South Africa, c. 1747, provides an instance

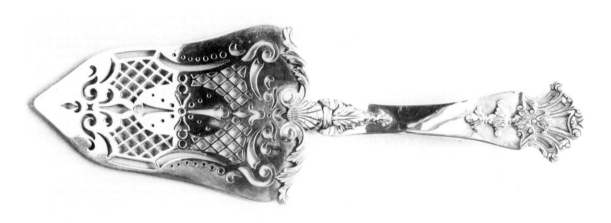

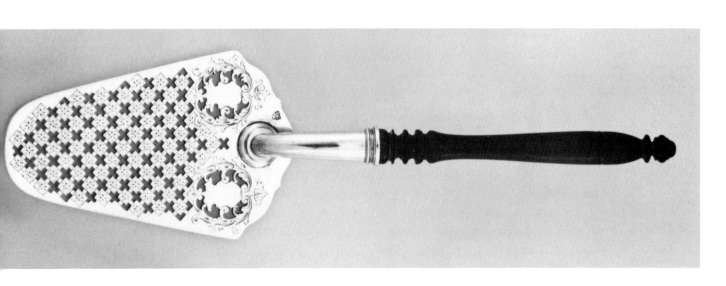

16.    FISH/CAKE TROWEL, unmarked, York (?), c. 1745; wooden handle; length 34 cm. The flat pointed cast blade has slightly curved sides. It is pierced with crosslets and scrolls. The rear edge is shaped with reentrant curves. The turned baluster handle is joined to the blade by a conical socket and rising cast stem and shell junction. The article is a rare example of a server that also serves as a 'momento mori.' Two inscriptions on the underside of the blade read "Henry Pawson, ob. 13 May 1742. Aet 16" and "Mary Foster, ob. 14 Junie 1744, AE 65;" Henry Pawson was buried in a York churchyard (27). The underside also carries a crest of a "Sun in Splendour" known to be that of Pawson of York (Fairbairn's Crests, Plate 162, cited in Fig. 1e). C.J. Jackson (*English Goldsmiths and their Marks*, Dover, New York, 1964) notes that "little if any plate was assayed and marked at York during the years 1716 to 1776."

17.    FISH/CAKE TROWEL, John Hugh LeSage, London, 1746; wooden handle; length 33.5 cm. The plain flat blade has straight sides. It is pierced in late baroque style with a central pattern of crosslets that is subtended at the vertices by pierced scrolling arcs and circles. The turned baluster wooden handle joins the blade *via* a conical tube, and a solid round rod to the cast raised shell. The rear edge of the blade makes two simple concave arcs. The underside of the blade is crested at the rear.

18.    FISH/CAKE TROWEL, John Harvey, London, 1750; wooden handle; length 31.5 cm. The small flat blade is pierced with foliate scrolls and a circular central cartouche which is engraved with a rubbed crest, and is otherwise plain. The rear edge makes two concave curves. The handle rises from a cast shell boss with lift to a conical holder for the turned baluster wooden handle. Obviously a lifter, the implement could serve as well for pastry as for white bait, although the latter designation may be considered as primary.

19.    TOY TROWEL, maker unknown, c. 1750; length 7.2 cm. A plain blade with straight sides and straight rear edge. The blade is pierced in a simple baroque design. Unfortunately, the crude chiselled piercing has infringed on the marks. The attachment of the turned wooden handle is *via* a waisted, balustered shank and shell boss. This is a very rare article.
Photograph by cooperation of Schredd's, Portobello Road, London. Courtesy of private owner.

19a.    FISH/PUDDING/PASTRY TROWEL, Samuel Herbert and Co., London, 1751; wooden handle; length 32 cm. The straight-sided flat blade is pierced centrally with quatrefoils, rather than crosslets, and with simple scrolls around. The rear edge is cusped and is curved forward. The handle shows growing rococo influence in the cast boss of flowing rosette design. The round stem lifts through a turned balustered section to a conical holder of a short, highly balusterd wooden handle. The underside of the blade is crested at the rear and divides the marks.

of early rococo chasing [Fig. 10]. The edges of these servers are blunt and have only modest parting capability. They may be regarded as a type of straining, lifting spoon or ladle, as is epitomized by the creation of A. Hoogland, Haarlem, 1760 [Fig. 11]. An early Empire example of 1798 by L.H. Bobbink, Amsterdam, has aquired a wooden handle and features three fish [Fig. 12].

Some examples of Dutch triangular trowels prove fascinating. A remarkable one by Hans Atsma, Leeuwarden, c. 1732, is seen in Fig. 13. It is the most severely triangular form that this writer has seen. The fact that the boss attachment of the stem from the handle to the blade is on the *underside* makes plausible that this

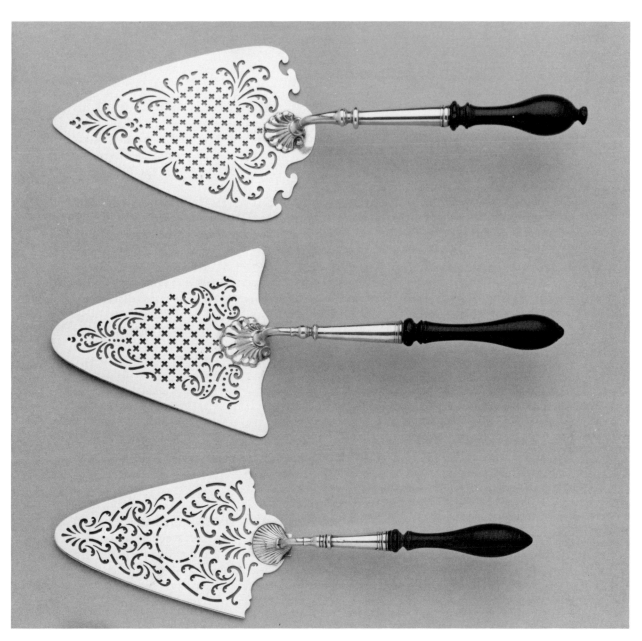

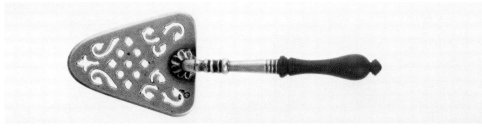

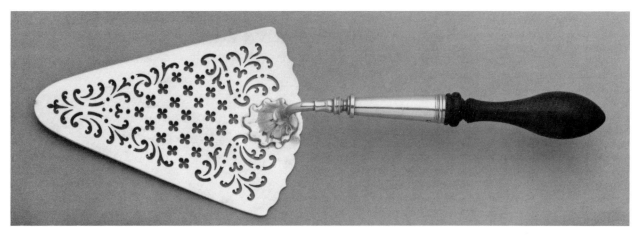

20.  FISH/CAKE TROWEL, Edward Aldridge and John Stamper, London, 1755; length 32.4 cm. The triangular blade has a rounded tip and curved cusped rear edge. It is pierced with foliate scrolls and inconspicuous leaf engraving and piercing guide lines. The handle is a stubby baluster shape of yellowed ivory joined to the blade by a wrythen tube and a cast dolphin junction piece — open mouthed and without seafoam.

21.  FISH/CAKE TROWEL, unmarked, London (probably), c. 1756; length 34 cm. The plain triangular blade has a waved rear edge and is highly pierced with scrolls, flowers, and pointed quatrefoils enlarged to leaf shapes. The heavy cast rocaille handle is somewhat disproportionate to the overall length; it represents the single, most definite statement of rococo style seen in a British server, other than by De Lamerie. It is decorated on both sides with flower heads and pods, leaves and matted shell work. The form and broad detail of this casting seems to have been rather extensively used at this time; examples differ in finer detail but not in size or design. It has been noted also as the finial of two ladles — one by John Jacob, London, 1753, and the other by Thos. Devonshire and Wm. Watkins, London, 1759. A later copy by Wm. Eley and Wm. Fearn, London, 1809, also exists.

22.  FISH/CAKE TROWEL, maker unknown, Dublin, 1758; length 33 cm. The triangular blade with curved waved rear edge is highly pierced with scrolling arcs, a basket that incorporates crosslets and with light branch and leaf, and flower engraving. The baluster wooden handle is joined to the blade by a cast shell and round stem rod. The date of making was determined by comparison with the manual by K. Ticher, I. Delamer and W. O'Sullivan, *Hall-Marks on Dublin Silver 1730-1772*, National Museum of Ireland, Dublin, 1968; the harp number is 22; the Hibernia mark is T. Irish (much less English) trowels of the mid-eighteenth century never show Chinese decorative influence, more common on coffee pots and other articles.

23.  CAKE/PUDDING TROWEL, Wm. Plummer, London, 1760; length 33 cm. The straight-sided unpierced plain blade, which is decorated only with a monogram, is a rather rare exception for this maker who is famed for his piercing. The fact may either confirm the alleged function of the title or simply be an accident of circumstance — a server that somehow got away before completion. The rounded back edge is cusped; the sides are straight. The baluster wooden handle is received in a conical tube that is connected to the blade by a cast, balustered round rod and a scallop shell bolster.

small article is a cake or pastry server, although it has seen service as a ceremonial mason's trowel (17). Ceremonial trowels made of silver date at least from the seventeenth century; examples made in 1649 (1) and 1696 (17) are known. It is of interest to note that they function as smoothers, tampers, and *lifters* of mortar. Still another early triangular slice is shown in Fig. 14. It was made by J. van't Hofken, Amsterdam, 1734 and is a strikingly beautiful example of Louis XIV baroque style. Moreover, although it has a highly pierced blade, it evinces no fish or marine motifs. Triangular Dutch cake trowels are much rarer than the oval fish trowels; a later example in rococo style is one by W. Angenend, Amsterdam, 1772.

Well-authenticated German trowels of the 1750s are known. Notwithstanding the negative results recorded at the outset of this section in the search for earlier German servers, two instances of claimants have been noted. A "fish or pastry lifter," by the smith Meister Wickert, Celle, ascribed as c. 1735, has been

24.    FISH TROWEL, Samuel Herbert and Co., London, 1762; length 34.5 cm. The straight-sided blade has a curved cusped back edge (which has cut off part of the assay office mark) and is pierced overall with a complex rococo scroll design. The top surface is delicately engraved with a leaf design, small scrolls, and piercing guide lines. The turned wooden handle is attached in the conventional way to the blade *via* a symmetrical raised rosette.

25.    FISH TROWEL, Wm. Tuite, London, c. 1762; length 3.18 cm. The very large (17.5 x 12 cm) plain flat blade has straight sides, a straight waved rear edge and rounded tip. It is pierced with a freely scrolled symmetric pattern. The rather elaborate handle starts from an asymmetrically swirled rococo floral junction which carries a vertical, shaped cast stem. The right-angle bend is decorated with a caryatid-acanthus leaf feature; the classical head was used both earlier and later. The tubular conical connector holds a bulbous balustered white ivory handle.

26.    FISH TROWEL, Wm. Plummer, London, 1762; length 34.3 cm. The straight-sided blade is highly pierced in a scrolling and flower design and the piercing is accented and guided by light engraving. The spiral twisted wooden handle has an oval cross section. It carries a spiral twist band silver ferrule and is connected to the blade by a matching spiral twist tube and a cast dolphin junction. The latter has been bent sideways by lateral pressure over the years; it can be regarded as an indication of an unintended function.

27a.   FISH SLICE, Thos. Heming, London, 1763; Hanoverian handle, bottom marked; length 31 cm, weight 5 oz. The shovel-shaped blade narrows slightly toward the front and has raised sides towards the rear. The front edge is sharpened and evinces many small dents. The handle stem is attached by a faceted long underside drop of contemporary ladle-spoon type. The blade is plain and is pierced in mixed early and later styles; a central diamond-shaped pattern of crosslets is surrounded by lunettes and scrolling work. The implement is reminiscent of the base metal spatulas and fish slices shown in Fig. I 1-5, and of the fish/pudding slice of De Lamerie in Fig. 1e; compare also the contemporary Dutch slice by Herle in Fig. 27b. The underside of the handle is crested. The article represents a literal refinement and adaptation of a kitchen implement to dining room use.

described as showing French and English influence in its design (6). It is a triangular trowel pierced in scrolling Régence style that has as its stem a rising curved conical tubular socket that is attached to the blade by a circular boss and that carries a shaped baluster wooden handle. However, another authority has estimated its date as later, post-1741 (18); if, indeed, it displays English influence, it is all the more reasonable to move back its date of manufacture, since even in England the fish trowel was not a widely used implement in the early 1740s.

The second German example [Fig. 15] that has been cited in the literature is also a trowel by an unidentified maker ICH of estimated date, "c. 1730," and assumed to be for fish service (19a). This lovely object, which features Régence diaper piercing, is of shape identical to the Wickert server blade, with similar rising conical socket stem, and ring boss, and a turned wooden handle. The estimated early date may be viewed with reservation. However, a rather early "pastry lifter" is definitely dated: this is an unengraved, scrolling-pierced, triangular server having a faceted baluster ivory handle, made by Elias Adam,

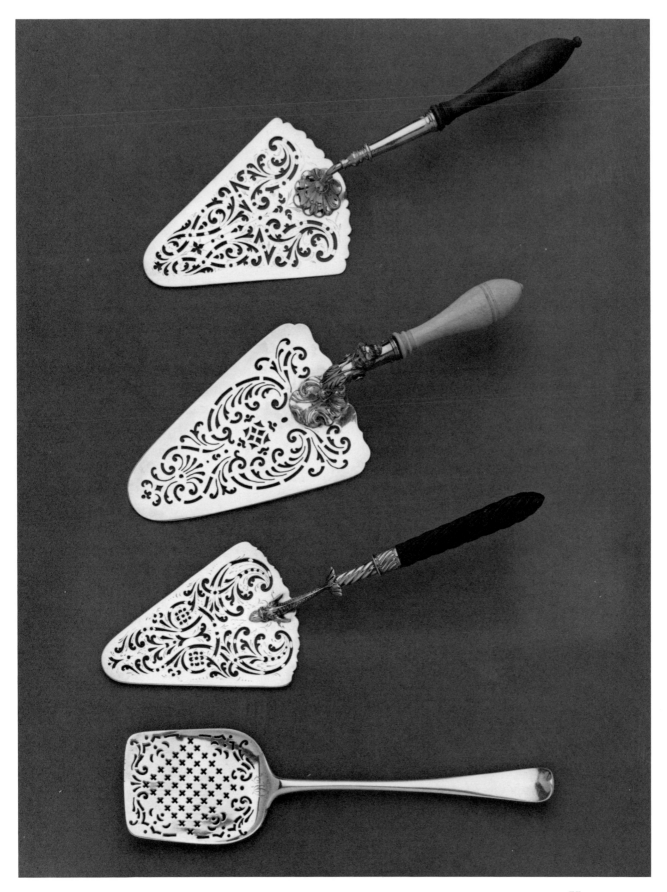

27b.   FISH SLICE, Franciscus Herle, 's-Hertogenbosch, 1770; length 33 cm. The flat spatulate blade of rare shape in silver has a late baroque piercing pattern. The rear of the blade bends upward in a shovel-like apron effect and leads into a long Hanoverian handle. The slice appears as Fig. 181 in *Zilver Uit s'-Hertogenbosch,* ed. A.M. Koldeweij, Noordbrabants Museum, 1985.
By kind cooperation and courtesy of Dr. A.M. Koldeweij and the Noordbranbants Museum.
Private owner.

Augsburg, 1741-1743 (19b). One may surmise, therefore, that even earlier examples may exist or were made.

As mentioned at the outset, no British trowels are known that precede the De Lamerie slice of 1741. Might earlier trowels have been made? Might earlier wares have suffered destruction? Although trowels are considered fairly rare present-day survivors, it is surprising that as many still exist as do. Apart from the De Lamerie servers, virtually all English trowels made in the period 1742-1775 had a triangular shape. Most of these implements had highly pierced, flat, rather fragile blades. The large number of repairs to silver in the records (20) of an early silversmith, George Wickes (of the damaged articles recorded many were of relatively robust character), suggest that the comparatively fragile trowel must also have been a frequent casualty. Wickes notes in 1748 the repair of a trowel for the Earl of Kildare even as he furnished two new ones. Since at such early date the damaged article must have been of fairly recent manufacture, this confirms the surmise that these implements suffered heavily. Indeed, they must also have been made in larger numbers than are presently credited for as many to have come down to the present day as have. Another indication of the correctness of this hypothesis is given by the records of the Goldsmiths Company (21): an extract from the minutes of a committee meeting of July 1751, acknowledges the receipt of "four curious silver trowels presented by Mr. Warden Pugh, two for fish and two for pudding, engraved with the company's arms." Of the gift, only two trowels (which have unpierced blades) have survived, and one of these shows evidence of cracking of the blade in the vicinity of the boss.

A frustrating indeterminacy results from an attempted interpretation of the adjective "curious" employed in the Company records. One of the meanings (I7) signifies *novelty*, as in the sense of strange or odd. This interpretation would obviously imply that trowels were not of frequent occurrence in the 1740s and that perhaps one need not look earlier than that decade for evidence of manufacture. However, a second contemporary meaning for the adjective was descriptive of an objective quality of things, in the sense that they were "made with care or art; skillfully, elaborately, or beautifully wrought." Examination of these servers shows, indeed, that they conform to this characterization. They exhibit the beautifully engraved arms of the Company on the top surface of the blade. The handles are of baluster shape, similar to contemporary turned wooden or ivory

handles, but are of silver; they have engraved floral decoration, and attachment to the blade *via* the stem is made by an ornate double shell boss. The articles are completely gilted. If the second meaning of the adjective, curious, is to be understood, then its relevance ceases as a negation of possible early date of manufacture of British trowels.

The Garrard ledgers contain a record of the business operations of George Wickes, who was personally active as a smith until 1748. They give the first documentation of his manufacture of a trowel as 1742, along with another made in 1745 (20). Apparently, Wickes made, on average, four per year to order during the early years, apart from any others sold without record (22). Roughly the same average prevailed twenty years later (60). However, such complete (or in most cases, any) accounts do not exist for other silversmiths and it seems quite probable that Wickes, De Lamerie, and their fellow craftsmen could have been engaged earlier in the production of these implements. On the other hand, it does seem unlikely, or at least very perverse, that any of these objects would have pre-dated the Dutch, much less the Scandinavian servers and still have disappeared without trace. A concomitant of a later appearance of silver servers and tablewares in England is the later date of advent of the dining room relative to Continental custom (Chapter II).

The earliest Irish examples of "pastry servers or pudding trowels" had flat pierced blades and are ascribed to the middle of the 1740s (23,24).

Although production of Georgian style ceramic trowels continued into the nineteenth century (Chapter I), virtually no silver London trowels were made in the eighteenth century after 1776. Provincial production continued somewhat longer, as would be expected. Some interesting data on fish slice production by the prominent Birmingham manufacturing partnership of Boulton and Fothergill (1762-1782) is provided by the researches of Quickenden (61). No silver "fish

28.    FISH TROWEL, Samuel Herbert and Co., London, 1763; length 32.5 cm. This trowel may be compared with Fig. 24 by the same maker. The blade is of the same shape, merely cut off slightly shorter at the rear; the cutting has taken an even greater toll of the marks that are arranged along the rear edge. The junction is a dolphin, its mouth buried in foam. The scrolled piercing is embellished with light engraved leaves and scrolls and piercing guide lines, as before, but a central pattern of crosslets has re-emerged.

29.    FISH TROWEL, Frederick Kandler, London, 1763, length 34.5 cm. The blade has curved sides, a straight cusped rear edge, and a sharply turned tip. The plain blade is pierced with arcs, scrolls and circles. The stained oak handle is joined to a cast scallop shell boss by a shaped stem which exhibits some lateral deformation. The underside of the blade is crested and also displays an earl's coronet. A minute (0.1 x 0.05 cm) workman's mark, IZ, in its own decorated reserve, is found close to the maker's mark; the latter has been impaired by the piercing.

30.    FISH TROWEL, maker's mark only, John Innocent or John Jackson II, c. 1763; length 33.7 cm. The blade is pierced with a basket of flowers that is shaped by crosslets, and by arcs and foliate scrolls; it is lightly engraved with leaves and accents and with piercing guide lines. The rear edge of the blade is a highly convex plain curve. The fluted, highly balustered green ivory handle and conical holder connect to the cast shaped stem via a gadrooned baluster feature. The scallop shell junction is single-pinned to the blade, which is crested on the underside. The handle and design make an even earlier date also plausible.

trowels" were made prior to 1771; from 1771 to 1777, the average (sporadic) production was 1 1/2 per year, including three in 1777; in the four-year period, 1778-1781, only one was made. The present scarcity of Old Sheffield fish trowels or fish spades is reflected by the seeming erratic production of these most prominent makers: namely (in an incomplete record), two in 1776, ten in 1780, and seven in 1781 are explicitly recorded. Some possible dearth of Old Sheffield production in these and other years is attributed by Quickenden, at least in part, to the expressed reluctance of the partnership to make these implements — "Fish trowels of plated metal will be bad things, let them be made ever so well, indeed we never recommend anybody to have plated trowels, silver ones being so much more durable..." Nonetheless some examples may be seen in Fig. 35b and in the illustrations of Ref. (26), as well as in Figs. IV 1, IV 2.

Other examples of later provincial production may be cited. One is a Scottish trowel [Fig. 53] by Peter Mathie, Edinburgh 1778. An Irish trowel by Carden Terry of Cork [Fig. 54] is dated by the author as c. 1780. A heart-shaped feather-edged example by William Bond is marked Dublin, 1780 (23). An elusive dating reference exists in the literature (25) to a triangular fish trowel by Richard Richardson — "probably Chester, 1784" (sic). Still later eighteenth-century articles that have come to the attention of the writer include two that are recorded in the Phillips sale of the Smart collection (26). Lot 125 describes a Scottish trowel, Edinburgh c. 1799; actually this article proves to have a long-oval blade (27). However, lot 109 of the sale refers to a trowel by Henry Chawner and John Emes,

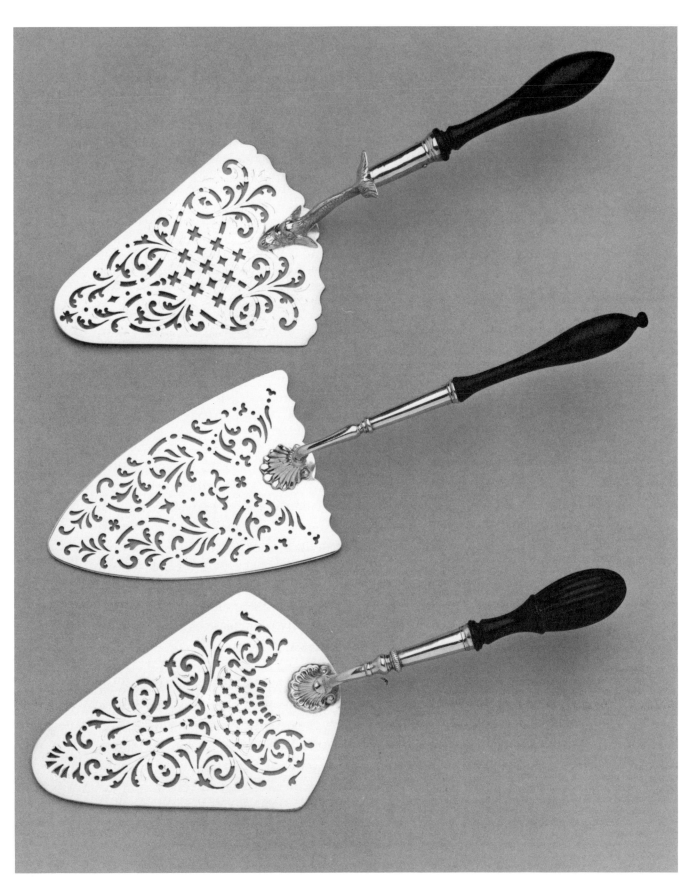

31.    FISH/PUDDING TROWEL, Isaac D'Olier, Dublin, 1764; Old English handle; length 30.5 cm; weight 3.7 oz (scratch weight 4 oz, 1/2 dwt). The plain small oval blade is doubly dished with respect to the principal axes, and has a cast pattern of scroll work around a central diamond pattern of quatrefoils. The long Old English handle has no underside rib. It is attached by a plain small underside flat drop. The server resembles a strainer ladle. The handle is crested.

32.    FISH TROWEL, John Kirkup, Newcastle, c. 1765; length 30 cm; weight 4.25 oz. The sterling mark is that listed by Jackson for the period, 1759-1769. The plain blade, which has a curved cusped rear edge and straight sides, is slightly dished, and is pierced in a floral scroll pattern. The handle is cast with an open-work pierced junction that is soldered and held to the blade by four pins. The beaded stem leads to a pierced scrolled finial.

33a.    PASTRY/CAKE TROWEL, Wm. Plummer, London, 1765; Hanoverian reeded handle; length 22.3 cm; weight 3.1 oz. The flat unpierced blade, which is completely covered by rococo C-scrolls and flower chasing, is both a rare English example of such overall decoration and of an early small trowel whose pastry/pudding association is evident; the Atsma trowel of Fig. 13 and the following figure should be compared. The handle is joined to the blade by a shell boss.

33b.    TART SPADE, Veuve Fritz, Strasbourg, 1773; length 18.2 cm. This silver gilt unpierced trowel is an early pastry server (pelle à tarte) at a time when a tart was a small covered pie of meat or fruit, although its present meaning is of an uncovered small fruit pie. The blade is decorated with an engraved frieze of small leaves and a large crest. The blade features an apron that leads to a conical holder for a turned ebony handle. See Fig. 198, *L'Orfèvrerie de Strasbourg*, by H. Haug, Éditions des Musées Nationaux, Paris, 1978, for further description. There is a strong similarity to the implement in Fig. 228 of Ref. 47, a cake slice by J.F. Kirstein, Strasbourg, c. 1795.
Courtesy of, and photography by, Musée des Arts décoratifs, Strasbourg.

London, 1796. These makers did produce smaller, pierced spade-shaped trowels with filled handles, which are the only post-1775 eighteenth-century English trowels that have come to the notice of the author. The type is illustrated in Fig. 57. The blade shape is similar to those of the earliest (1790s) double-bladed English servers that are discussed in Chapter VII. These are also the only English trowels having filled handles that have come to present attention; the shank has a slight lift. Filled handles are described in Chapter IV in the section on Handles.

Among known eighteenth-century American trowels are two in the Phillip H. Hammerslough collection: a fine pierced and engraved one having a shell boss by Meyer Myers, and a plainer example by John McMullen — both from the latter part of the century (28). Figure 55 illustrates a highly pierced trowel by J.W., c. 1790, identified as John Waite, New York (29). A heart-shaped fish slice by Joseph and Nathaniel Richardson, c. 1790, is pierced with geometric and floral shapes, has a turned wooden handle and a long rat-tail V-boss. In shape, it bears strong resemblance to the Irish server by William Bond (*vide supra*) and to many of the heart-shaped Continental trowels described in this chapter. It provides an illustration of the influence of Irish-Scottish-Continental style on American silversmithing. It is in the Garvan Collection (28). Another was made by Charles O. Bruff (30).

34.    FISH TROWEL, Wm. Reynolds, Cork, c. 1765; Old English handle, length 30.5 cm; weight 4.2 oz. The plain cast sheet blade is pierced overall with arcs and scrolls. The indented rear edge is only slightly curved. The Old English crested handle is ribbed underneath and joined to the stem by a scallop shell bolster. The twist stem is a not uncommon feature of Irish and Scottish silver of this period and was much admired by Victorian designers.

35a.    FISH TROWEL, Wm. Plummer, London, 1766; modified Hanoverian handle; length 28.5 cm, weight 4.7 oz. The flat straight-sided blade has a shaped rounded rear edge and a narrowly turned tip. It is pierced with scrolls, arcs, and circles around an inner triangular pierced central reserve that is set off by doubly chased lines. The surface is decorated with chased arcs, leaves and tendrils. The solid cast swirled husk boss is integral with a reeded stem and a cast double shell finial with pendant scrolls. The back side of the finial has a heavy raised cast multi-scroll cartouche and crest. The town mark is slightly cut by the piercing. This trowel is an illustration of rococo style in the British servers, and is another example of chased decoration. Lightly engraved decoration that is a little worn, with rounded edges, is very hard to distinguish from light chasing.

35b.    FISH TROWEL, Old Sheffield, 1765-70; length 31.5 cm. The blade has straight sides with a plain convex rear edge [cf. Fig. 30]. The pierced blade is engraved or finely flat chased with leafy tendrils, which are partially removed and infringed by the fly-cutting of arcs and scrolls. The estimated date corresponds to the analogous shapes and decoration of contemporary silver servers. There are no silver edges. The boss is a beaded pear shape and reflects early onset of beading decoration. A tubular socket-stem rises from the boss and holds a long, slim, turned, and green-stained, ivory handle.

36.    FISH TROWEL, Richard Williams, Dublin, 1767; length 31.8 cm, weight 6 oz. The flat blade has a rounded contour and tip and a waved straight rear edge. The blade is pierced with foliate scrolls and arcs and is scantily engraved with vine and tendrils worked into the design. The blade is crested in a central pierced cartouche. The unusual feature of this implement is its fish handle that holds in its mouth one end of a cast shaped rising stem that joins a stamped scallop shell bolster. The fish is composed of two soldered halves, embossed and chased and shaped quite realistically, if impractically.

Apart from an occasional example, to the author's knowledge the only significant instance of manufacture of British trowels in the Georgian tradition in the nineteenth century was a group made by the virtuoso London silversmith, Edward Farrell, in the late 1820s to the middle of the 1840s. The reason for this concentration is not known. The writer has encountered five of these so far. Farrell's slices are characterized by somewhat florid, exotic cast handles and imbricated, fish-like scale work. They include one that has a large ornate agate handle and another with a heavy twin dolphin boss that leads to an ornate cast hand and dolphin-head handle. The larger of the pair illustrated in Figs. 59, 60 is believed to be a representation of the Biddenden Twins, Mary and Elisabeth Chulkhurst, 1100-1134, whose memory is still actively preserved by their charitable bequest to the needy of the Biddenden, Kent, area and which now takes the form of a distribution of bread and cheese on Easter Monday. The two cast blades shown are identical in piercing design and superimpose exactly. However, the

36a.   FISH TROWEL, Wm. Plummer, London, 1767; Old English handle; length 29 cm; weight 5.1 oz. The straight-sided flat blade has a cusped, curved rear edge. The edge of the blade is decorated with a chased, meandering scroll that encompasses a scrolled, pierced triangular area. An inner chased triangular area encloses a pierced engraved region of flowers, leaves and a heron on a limb. The back of the blade (shown) is unusual in displaying some (lesser) engraved and chased decoration on the inner triangular areas, above a stork crest. The boss is an ornate raised, cast, scrolling rococo shell that lifts to a cast feather-edged handle having no underside rib (cf. Fig. 35a).

earlier and smaller one, and the least pretentious of the whole group, has the last series of piercings at the rear of the blade omitted. They were evidently made (cast) from the same mould.

Figure 60 is an instance of growing lavish Victorian display.

An unusual small 'trowel' blade, rather like an early pastry server, by A. and G. Burrows, London, 1813 [Fig. 58], is rather unique, also, in featuring a raised rear edge or gallery. Its shape is a subject of further mention in Chapter IV.

Further discussion of the historical evolution of trowels will be conjoined with the description of their blade shape and decoration. Small, pierced, so-called "butter spades" appear in the last quarter of the century. One by Henry Green, London, 1786, is shown in Fig. 56. Another example was made by Alexander Henderson, Edinburgh, 1790. However, these articles are so fragile that their use as butter servers, as frequently ascribed, appears improbable. Designation for more fluid foods, such as jam or jelly might be more appropriate. But more robust, often unpierced, small trowels of this or similar shape were made, and these do qualify as butter spades or as pastry servers, as discussed further in Chapter VII [Fig. VII 42].

The toy shown in Fig. 19, one of the products of a few highly-specialized smiths, appears to belong to the third quarter of the century. Unfortunately its marks have been mutilated by the piercing.

## Blade Shape and Decoration

A chronological display of British trowels is provided in Figs. 16-67. *The stated function-name(s) in each figure caption is to be understood as an important, but not necessarily exclusive designation.* Blade sizes vary usually between 12 to 17 cm in length, and 9 to 12 cm in width. A rare unpierced exception by W. Plummer, London, 1765 [Fig. 33a], is only 10 cm in length and 6.7 cm in width; it is a prototype of the small cake and pastry servers made a century later. In all of the discussion of trowels, the shape and decoration of the De Lamerie articles [Fig. 1] are exceptional, as will be understood without further reiteration in this section. Earliest English trowels of the 1740s and 1750s had flat blades of pronounced triangular form having straight sides and rounded tips. The earliest examples

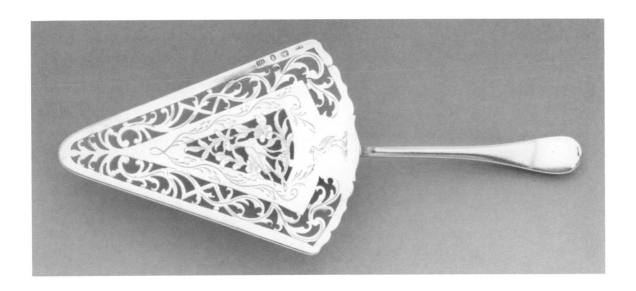

have concave rear edges [Figs. 16-18]. The rear edges of later blades are either flat or sweep forward in a convex outline; they may be smooth or, more usually, scalloped, cusped, or otherwise shaped and indented. The late baroque decoration favours heavy emphasis on large areas of pierced crosslet or diaperwork and simple arc patterns that frequently infringed on the handle junction. Fish or marine motifs were not featured. In most cases the piercing and engraving was carried out after return of the article from the assay office. A small minority of blades remained unpierced [Figs. 23,40] — whether by design in order to produce a cake or pudding slice, or by omission because sale or delivery of the article was not imminent. Instances occur of identical blades made by the same silversmith that are both pierced and solid [Figs. 39,40]. There is very little, if any, decorative engraving or chasing on the early blades. At that time, neither saw nor die-cut piercing was yet employed. Since ornamentation has frequently been employed to hide solder joints or defects, the lack thereof may be taken, perhaps, as a backhanded compliment to British craftsmanship. The small trowel by W. Plummer in Fig. 33a is also exceptional in another respect: the blade is competely covered with chased rococo decoration.

Inspection of the early examples makes it evident that the British trowel blades are considerably broader than the Scandinavian examples cited previously. For the implements shown here, the ratios of lengths of long axis to short axis lie usually between 1.2 and 1.6, as opposed to the four values quoted earlier for the Swedish implements, that fell between 1.81 and 2.4. In general, as will be seen further, British server blades tend to be relatively broader in construction than Continental counterparts in all periods right up to the cessation of their manufacture. The extrapolated angle at the blade tip is not necessarily a simple integral divisor of 360°, and it is believed by the writer that these servers were not

37.    FISH TROWEL, Chas. Aldridge and Henry Green, London, 1768; length 34 cm. The cast sheet blade has straight sides and a slightly rounded cusped rear edge. It has elements of Chinese fretwork in the pierced pattern and of neogothic in the pointed quatrefoils and circles. The arched pales have V-shaped ends, a piercing feature that persisted for the next seventy-five years. The turned baluster arborvitae handle enters a spiral twist connector that joins a two-piece cast twisted C-scroll and Y-junction to the blade.

38.    FISH TROWEL, Henry Bailey, London, 1768; length 31.8 cm, weight 4.5 oz. The blade has straight sides and a curved, wavy and toothed, rear edge. It is cast and shows residual flashing. It demonstrates the onset of finer pierced work in a chased trellis pattern with flower heads. The perimeter band is lightly chased with vine stems. The handle is cast. The pierced trilobate junction leads *via* a pseudo-gadrooned stem to a pierced leafed finial. This particular handle design appears on a number of servers and they were apparently purchased from specialist makers. The whole piece displays nascent neoclassicism.

39.    FISH TROWEL, Thomas Nash, London, 1770; length 28.7 cm, weight 4.1 oz. The spade shaped flat blade has a straight waved back edge. It has chased reeding around the perimeter and boss, and is feather edged. The blade and beautiful piercing are cast; every vertex of the piercing shows rounded retraction. The decoration is a good example of the change in neoclassic piercing style from silver-as-background to pierced spaces-as-background. There is very minor engraving of flower heads. The handle is an all-in-one casting with an anthemion-like bolster, an open-work scrolled finial and a feather-edged stem. The marks are in line along the right back edge.

40.    PASTRY/PUDDING TROWEL, Thomas Nash, London, 1770; Old English handle; length 27.8 cm, weight 4.4 oz. The flat spade-shaped blade provides an interesting comparison and contrast with its contemporary companion of Fig. 39 by the same maker. The two blades are of the same shape and have perimeter feather edging. But this one is unpierced; ostensibly, this is not due to inadvertence since the piercing of Fig. 39 was done in the casting and not by later saw cutting. The anthemion-like bolster is cast with a short shouldered shaft, which is soldered to an Old English terminal. The handle is feather edged, crested, and lacks the underside rib.

customarily made in sets of six or eight, cut from a circle, as has been suggested on occasion; in fact, any non-integral number from eight to 11 would be more apt.

As the century wore on, the piercing of the 1750s featured more rococo foliate scrolling with lesser incidence of simple crosslets and diaperwork [Fig. 19a], although overlapping decorative styles occur even into the 1760s [Figs. 27a,28]. Engraving decoration appears sometimes as the remnants between the pierced areas of the pattern guidelines and arcs cut into the blade surface [Figs. 26,28,30]. Blades themselves are sometimes strongly doubly dished (i.e., curved concavely around both major and minor axes). When this occurs, the blades tend to be pronouncedly rounded in the shoulders and tip and assume the aspect of "oval" trowels [Figs. 30,31,42,45,46,52a]. Nelson Dawson (31) likened such articles to a perforated spoon or strainer although acknowledging their use as fish servers. Irish silversmiths particularly seemed to favor this style, although the dietary or stylistic influences that led to this preference are not evident; service of pudding

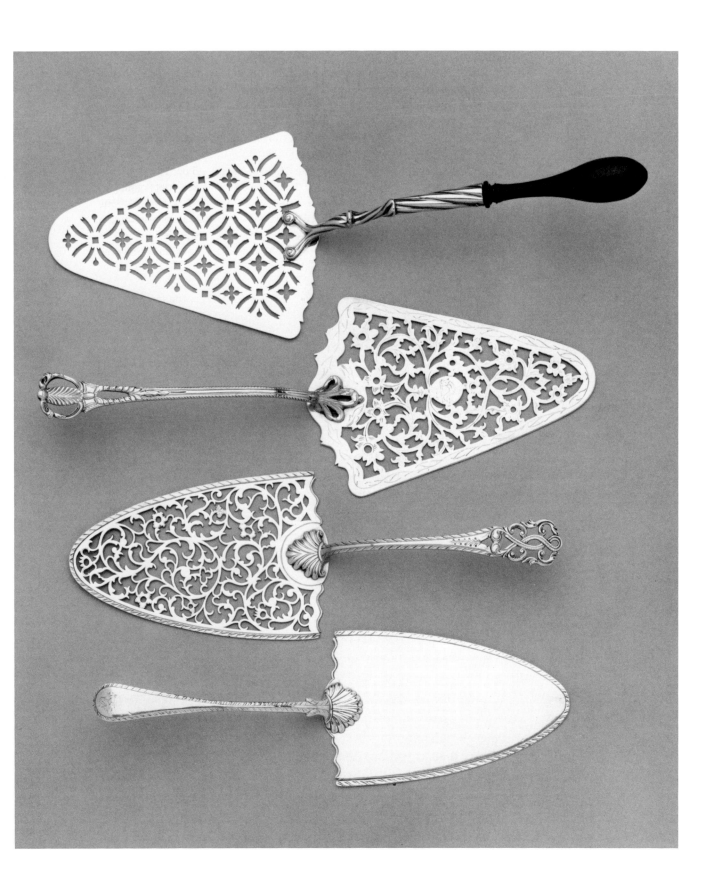

41.    FISH TROWEL, Wm. Plummer, London, 1770; modified Old English handle; length 28 cm, weight 4.4 oz. The spade-shaped blade is doubly dished and finely pierced in neoclassical style with chased scrolling foliage and flower heads around a triangular central reserve that displays three fishes and an eel in a pond, and a bird in the rushes. The rear edge is curved and cusped and part of a circumferential frieze that is chased with a continuous leaf and vine pattern. The cast handle has a pierced, scroll and lobe, chased Old English shaped terminal; it is feather edged. The boss is a shell with a ribbon border, on a cushion. The assay marks along the edge are slightly cut by the piercing.

42.    FISH/PUDDING TROWEL, Wm. Bond, Dublin, 1770; length 30.5 cm. The oval shaped blade is slightly dished and completely feather edged. It is beautifully pierced and engraved with foliage, flowers and feeding birds. The cast tri-lobate bolster is joined to a feather-edged handle of Old English shape, but which is rounded downward around the long axis. The finial is decorated with a shell, and with an asymmetric scrolled empty cartouche and pendant leaf tendril.
By kind cooperation and courtesy of S.J. Shrubsole, New York.

43a.    FISH TROWEL, Thomas Satchwell, London, 1771; Old English handle; length 26.5 cm, weight 3 oz. The straight-sided flat blade has a cusped, curved rear edge. It returns to the earlier rococo style of arcs, scrolls, and a central diamond-shaped pattern of quatrefoil piercing seen against a silver background. The pattern is accented by peripheral reeding, and by branch, leaf and flower engraving and residual pattern lines. The cast shell-on-pillow junction and shouldered shaft lead to a crested Old English terminal that lacks the underside rib; the handle is feather edged [cf. Figs. 36a,40]. The shaping of the rear edge has clipped part of the marks.

is one possibility. Indeed, it may represent nothing more than a wise design that greatly strengthens the blade.

Figure 27a is a server by T. Heming, London, 1765, of rather rare shovel shape. It resembles the earlier brass and iron spatulas or shovels, sometimes called fish slices, discussed in the Introduction and examples of which are shown in Figs. I 1,I 2,I 5. It is also related to the Dutch "visschep" by F. Herle, 1770, shown in Fig. 27b. It may have drawn some inspiration from the De Lamerie works. Modern nomenclature frequently represents current trade terminology and may not describe the original function correctly. No doubt these implements were also used for all purposes that could be served by a spatula and server.

The history of trowel decoration in the eighteenth century is a reflection in miniature of the constant struggle in ornamentation between geometric and naturalistic motifs that has found expression in other silver forms, in other art forms, and in other countries and other centuries. British rococo display came later and more weakly to servers than it did to hollow ware such as cups and coffee pots where its onset occurred already in the early '30s (32,33a). Examples of Chinoiserie are virtually absent [but see Fig. 37]. In fact, in contrast to Continental emphasis, British late-baroque, plain Queen Anne blades trended into the rococo style with only occasional strongly expressed flourishes. Usually, expression was limited to foliate scrolled and quatrefoil piercing of rather severely triangular blades; rococo feeling was most strongly incorporated in cast handle decoration

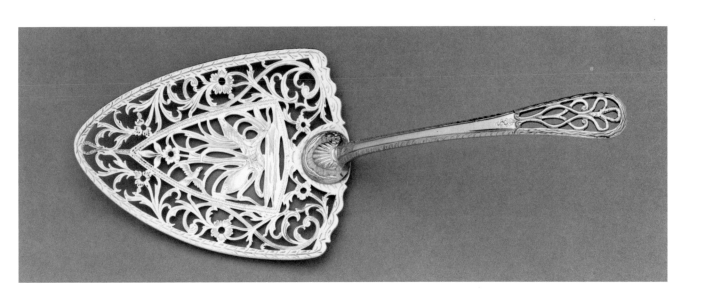

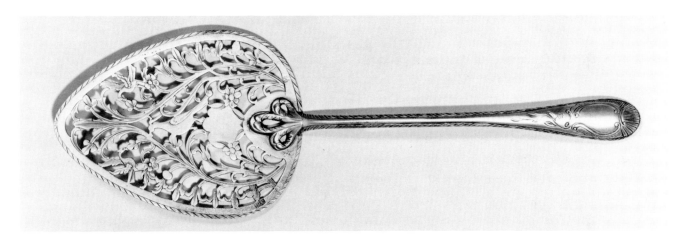

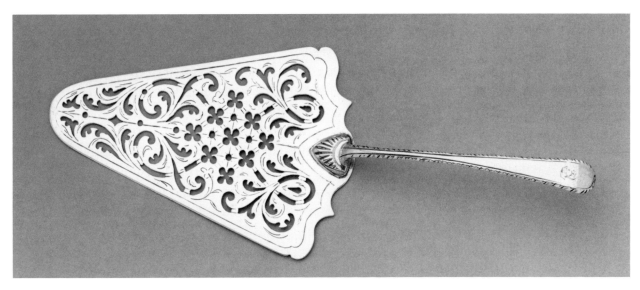

43b. CUTLERY CANTEEN, William Fearn, London, 1771; Old English finials, feather edged. The fish slice is part of the surviving forty-six pieces of this feather-edged spoon service, which was Lot 43 of Sale No. 26,404, Phillips, Blenstock House, London, 5 December, 1986. The blade is completely pierced with fretwork.
By kind cooperation and courtesy of Phillips.

[Figs. 21,25,32]. In general, the later 1760s were characterized by more elaborate invention [Figs. 35a,38], and neoclassical serving blades became even more artful in their engraving and piercing. In the 1750s and earlier 1760s, the scroll and foliate decoration was largely provided by the dark pierced areas as limned by the bright outline of more or less plain silver (negative and positive spaces). With the onset of neoclassical style in the later 1760s and 1770s, the pierced areas were enlarged so that the scrolling designs are provided by the (engraved) residual bright silver arcs and forms as seen against a largely pierced dark background. Blades were embellished with nascent bright cutting and engraving in neoclassical style. And although the piercing often came perilously close to the handle junction, the heel of the trowel blade never was provided with original reinforcement. The decoration frequently included fish, water bird and marine motifs after 1770 [Figs. 41,48,52b]. It often featured bough and leaf, flowers, scrolling foliage, and C-scrolling designs, as well as edge thread and line decoration [Figs. 39,50]. The rear edge was almost invariably curved and cusped, sometimes with fine structure. Moreover, trowels were rarely engraved or decorated on their unseen underside. One exception is the slice by C. Townsend, Dublin, 1773 [Fig. 46]; another is shown in Fig. 36a.

Serving trowels were sometimes ordered in pairs. Such luxury implied lavish dining appointments. George Wickes supplied "2 trowells" (not otherwise characterized) to the Earl of Kildare in 1748 (20). A pair of trowels were made, ostensibly by De Lamerie, in 1744, for Lord Pitteward of Finborough Hall, of which a single was sold at Christie's, London, in 1988 [Fig. 1b]. Surviving examples are rare. Of the two pairs received as gifts by the Goldsmiths Company in 1751 (vide supra), one pair only remains. Two rarities in one example have been seen: a pair of servers in rococo style by William Plummer, London, 1767, whose undersides are engraved with foliage and flowers that match the topside decoration.

Later blades were usually pierced by saw cutting; in some cases the drill and file might be used. Indeed, the chisel was also still employed in the 1750s and later, particularly by some ill-equipped craftsmen, even as it still is today in the Far East. Some blades show the characteristic pitted structure of cast silver. At this time, some sheet was still made in the time-honored manner by battery. More and more was fabricated by the use of rolling machines, which had been introduced in England at the beginning of the seventeenth century, and whose use became more

70

widespread in the latter half of the century during the Industrial Revolution. The original starting material could be an ingot, or the smith could short-cut the procedure by first casting, as in a skillet, and then further rolling or hammering a flat sheet. In some instances, this could explain the residue of pit structure in the sheet and, eventually, in the blades of some trowels [Figs. 31,51]. However, some highly skilled workers apparently even shorted the piercing process and cast a flat pierced blade, which was then touched up and finished. The pierced casting is revealed by some residual flashing [Fig. 38] or by the retraction and rounding that accompanies solidification of the liquid [Figs. 39,45,54,55,59]. Instead of sharp edges to the sides of the piercing being evident, a pronounced rounding occurs, which is all the more strikingly displayed at acute vertices of the piercing pattern. The inducement for casting a pierced blade might well also have been the high cost of piercing. In one example from the 1754 ledger of George Wickes, of a total charge of 2/13/6 for a fish slice, 18/0 was entailed for the piercing cost. In another

44.    FISH TROWEL, Chas. Aldridge and Henry Green, London, 1772; Old English handle; length 31 cm, weight 5.5 oz. The feather-edged straight-sided flat blade has a slightly rounded cusped rear edge. The piercing is older style with large silver background areas; the piercing pattern and chasing have mixed decorative elements. The cast shell junction has fine beaded stripes; it is joined to a feather-edged handle with Old English finial that is weakly ribbed on the underside. The handle is crested in a neoclassical cartouche.

45.    FISH TROWEL, Thomas Nash, London, 1772; Old English handle; length 28.5 cm, weight 4.6 oz. The plain cast blade is a pierced, doubly-dished, spoon-like oval; the cast nature is revealed clearly by residual flashing and rounded retractions at the vertices of the piercing. Nash has already been cited [Fig. 39] for his cast blades. The server is of mixed style. The pierced areas provide the background for the residual silver pattern of rococo scrolling. The cast palmette-like junction and shouldered stem appears integral with the cast crested Old English finial. The top of the boss is itself decorated with a crown and plume. The handle is feather edged and the finial lacks an underside rib; it is similar to that of Fig. 40. Nash may have cast his own handles or, more probably, purchased them from a specialist maker. The marks are slightly clipped by the piercing.

46.    FISH/PUDDING TROWEL, Charles Townsend, Dublin, 1773; Old English handle; length 35 cm, weight 4.6 oz. This is another rococo style ladle-shaped server with small dished oval blade. It is made in one piece from sheet silver. The blade and handle are feather edged. The blade is pierced with a basket of foliage against a silver background; the basket includes late baroque intimations in the crosslets and diaper work and a hint of neoclassical paling in the V-ended shallow arc paling. The blade is embossed with leaf and flower stems, and with an asymmetric scroll cartouche and pendant leafy tendrils on the finial of the Old English handle, similar to that of Fig. 42. The underside of the blade incorporates chased vine tendrils into the pattern. There is no underside rib on the finial.

47.    FISH TROWEL, Wm. Plummer, London, 1773; Old English handle, length 29 cm; weight 3.7 oz. The cast sheet blade is flat and spade-like in shape, with a rounded and cusped rear edge. It shows neoclassical influence. The blade is completely pierced, leaving a fret-work of interlaced C-scrolls separated by engraved flower heads. The rim of the blade is surrounded by a continuous frieze of engraved leaves. The cast handle is feather edged and the terminal is pierced with inter-laced scrolls and flower heads. The boss is a cast double shell. The underside of the blade is crested.

instance, although not so explicit, a January 10, 1748 entry for the making of two trowels reveals a disproportionately high cost of manufacture relative to other comparable objects, such as an orange strainer (20; entry August 13, 1747).

Later slices [e.g., Fig. 50] sometimes featured such incredibly detailed, refined and extensive saw piercing that was so free of evident fault or miscue as to suggest the best results of mechanical die fly-cutting. If Old Sheffield plated articles were pierced by saw cutting, the copper edge would be exposed thereby (see Ref. (33b) for an example). Extensive piercing of plated articles waited until the last half of the 1760s and 1770s following the introduction of technology that solved the problem by dragging a layer of silver over the cut as the cutting tool descended through the silver-copper sandwich into its bed (I 13,15). But unlike prospering silversmith firms such as that of Hester Bateman, the great majority of silversmiths could not afford the steam-driven equipment developed by

48. FISH TROWEL, Chas. Aldridge and Henry Green, London, 1773; length 28.3 cm, weight 5 oz. The spade-shaped blade is doubly dished and has a cusped curved reeded rear edge; a feather-edged band surrounds the sides. The neoclassical blade has extremely fine pierced and engraved (chased?) scroll work in an outer frieze, in which are displayed two fishes, and an inner triangular reserve of leaf and flower scrolling and flower heads. The pierced husk and gadroon-like feather edge of the triangular cast bolster leads *via* a decorated stem to a complex pierced, leafy and lobed finial very similar to that of Fig. 38, suggesting that both makers, or at least one of them, bought in their handles. The stem has a ridged imbricated structure at the top, which converts to a pendant laurel leaf neoclassical feature in the lower part.

49. FISH TROWEL, Basile Denn, London, 1774; Old English handle; length 30.8 cm, weight 4.6 oz. The double-dished spade-shaped blade is plain and pierced in a neogothic pattern of upspiked parallel pales and circles. The whole blade takes the form of an ogive. The cast fluted boss is of the same shape, as is the unpierced area surrounding it. The handle is feather edged and the finial has no underside rib. The marks along the left rear underside are clipped by the waved shaping. This maker made a number of servers in this style.

50. FISH TROWEL, Basile Denn, London, 1775; length 29.5 cm, weight 4 oz. The flat straight-sided blade is made from cast sheet. It has a cusped curved rear edge which is singly reeded. The sides of the blade are feather edged. The blade is beautifully and completely pierced with a basket and with foliage, leaves and flower heads. It is engraved with multiple short lines that accent the silver design. The cast handle has a palmette boss, a feather-edged stem and an open-work C-scroll and ribbon finial. Although neoclassical influences are evident, like other slices of the early 1770s, this one has transitional aspects.

51. FISH TROWEL, Wm. Cox III or Wm. Collings, London, 1775; Old English handle; length 32.5 cm, weight 4.2 oz. The elongated spade-shaped blade is made from cast sheet. It is slightly dished and has feather-edged sides and a waved, almost straight rear edge. The neoclassical blade is highly pierced with a basket, scrolls, swags, bell flowers and pendant husks. The surface is engraved with accent curves. The boss has a complex shell-husk-and-leaf structure. It is integral with the cast shouldered handle which has a bright cut peripheral band and an Old English finial with no underside rib. The length/breadth ratio of the blade is 1.64, somewhat on the high side relative to earlier British trowels. The marks are located along the upper left rear edge.

Matthew Boulton and James Watt (I 14) that was extensively employed in mass manufacture in the nineteenth century. Moreover, whereas a multi-panelled article, such as a basket, could utilize machine-pierced components to advantage, such was not the case for single-piece server blades of this kind. Nonetheless, some well-placed silversmiths did use mechanical piercing. Such is confirmed by consideration of Lots 13 and 132 of Ref. (26). The former is a finely pierced Old Sheffield trowel, the latter is silver by Hyland & Co., Sheffield, 1774; both have identical piercing and shape.

Saw piercing has continued without cease to the present day on the part of craftsmen who were not mass producers. There is abundant evidence from the nature of the pierced work, sometimes crude and irregular, that later-day irregularities are not merely the result of touch-up done on mechanically cut products.

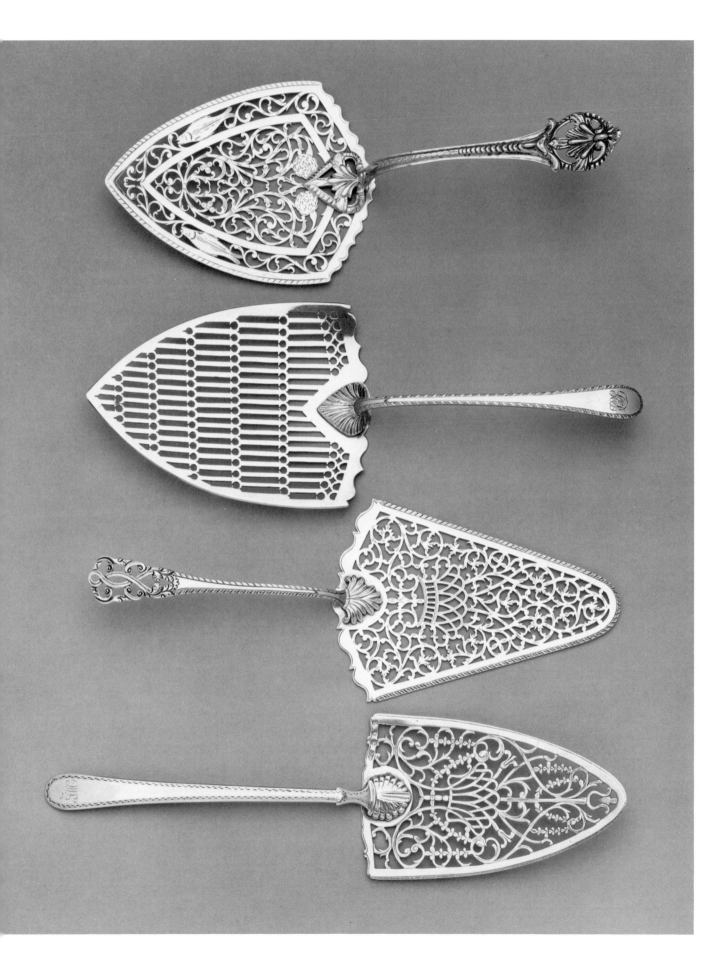

52a. FISH TROWEL, Charles Townsend, Dublin, c. 1775; length 33 cm, weight 5 oz. The oval blade is circumscribed by feather-edged and plain bands. Most of the blade is highly pierced and engraved with curved sweeping branches, flowers, and a large bird engrossed with an eel. The trilobate cast boss is attached to a feather-edged Old English handle that is concave downward around the long axis [cf. Fig. 42]. The finial is decorated with the same chased asymmetric scroll cartouche and pendant tendrils as are featured in Fig. 46; but unlike that slice, this one has no engraving on the underside. The marks are arranged along the upper left rear edge and Hibernia has been clipped by the piercing.

52b. FISH TROWEL, George Smith III, London, 1776; Old English handle; length 36 cm; weight 4.6 oz. The blade is nearly flat, has straight sides and rounded shoulders. The whole server is outlined by bright cut and zigzag bands. The blade is highly pierced with scrolling foliage and reeds and four fish among them; a heron holds an eel in its beak. The handle is attached by an underside long drop which is also denoted by topside bright cutting. The finial is engraved with a vacant oval flower-decorated cartouche and a pendant vine and leaf tendril. The length/breadth ratio is a remarkable 2.4, analogous to the proportions of newly introduced long-ovals (see Chapter IV). Another example of similar design and shape, also by George Smith, may be seen in Ref. (IV 18).

53. FISH TROWEL, Peter Mathie, Edinburgh, 1778; Old English handle; length 29.5 cm, weight 3.5 oz. The doubly-dished blade has rounded sides and shoulders and plain curved back. The perimeter of the blade is decorated with a laurel leaf frieze, as is a central triangular reserve. The two are separated by a plain band. The reserve is completely and, in one place, carelessly pierced with holes. The stamped or cast shell boss has alternating positive and negative lobes. The handle is feather edged and crested at the terminal.

54. FISH TROWEL, Carden Terry, Cork, c. 1780; length 35.8 cm. The plain blade is flat with straight sides, highly rounded tip and cusped, curved rear edge. The cast blade is pierced all over with scrolls, pales and circles, limned against the silver background. The shell bolster is cast, as is the stem and baluster feature that connects to the conical tube that grasps the turned baluster oak handle. The date of making follows the ascription by Jackson for this mark; the style of the server suggests an earlier date. The blade appears to be cast, from the evidence of the residual flashing in many of the vertices of the scrolls; however, it is remarkably free of pit marks, unlike the stem.

An example, of which a pair are coincidentally to hand, is the fork-slice by C. Eley, London, 1825, shown in Fig. VII 6. Comparison of the two, both 1825 and the same length and weight, having ostensibly the same pierced design, shows evidence of defects and multiple minor inconspicuous variations in the piercing pattern that makes evident their nature as handcraft from the shop of this scion of a family of distinguished and prolific flatware makers. What a smaller shop *could* afford were individual die cutters, featuring pales, stars, quatrefoils, and the like, which could be repetitively applied to the work, as in the Old Sheffield example of Fig. IV 40.

There is marked difference between the decoration of Continental and British servers, both with respect to baroque and rococo styles. With exceptions, as recounted above, the British articles display rather restrained and limited decoration. Early trowels are in simple Queen Anne taste and lack the rich engraving or applied ornament that is featured on early Scandinavian [Figs. 2,5] and Dutch baroque

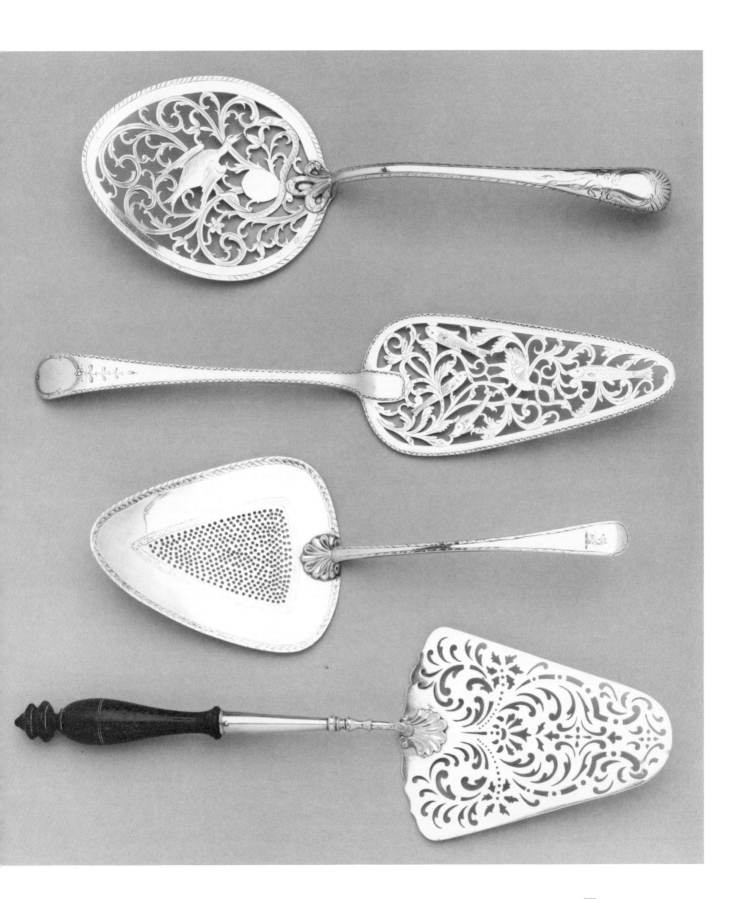

55.    FISH TROWEL, John Waite, New York, c. 1785; Old English handle; length 26 cm; weight 4 oz. The fairly thick flat triangular blade has straight sides and a cusped curved back. The server is cast, has many pits, rounded vertices with some flashing, and rounded contours to the overall piercing. The blade is feather edged and pierced in neoclassical style, including a guilloche frieze. The shell terminal and feather-edged handle appear to be cast in one piece; there is no underside rib.

56.    MINIATURE TROWEL, Henry Green, London, 1786, length 17.8 cm. The blade is spade shaped with straight rear edge. It has bright cut lunettes on the perimeter and a zigzag border. The central area is pierced with scrolls. A solid round stem rises from a drop junction to the tubular holder of a white ivory handle. As discussed in the text, it is believed that this is not a butter server or spreader.

57.    FISH TROWEL, Henry Chawner and John Emes, London, 1797. The spade-shaped blade is dished along the long axis. There are vestigial fish tail nubs, as described in Chapter IV for contemporary long-ovals. The surface is decorated with zigzag outlines, an empty laurel leaf cartouche, and a pierced lattice design in a triangular reserve. The simple decoration emphasizes the intrinsic beauty of the silver surface. The boss is a rounded Vee that leads to a reeded filled handle.
By kind cooperation and courtesy of Mrs. Michael Rossi; collection of Walter H. Willson.

58.    FISH/CAKE "TROWEL," Alice and George Burrows, London, 1813; fiddle handle; length 26.7 cm. The blade has peripheral floral vine engraving and a central doubly reeded reserve that is pierced with circles and a honeysuckle design. The unusual feature of this server is the raised side to the concave scalloped rear edge of the blade. Notwithstanding its appearance, the blade category is actually long-oval, as defined in Chapter IV. A plain English fiddle handle, which is attached by a V-boss, has the characteristic bevelled edges.
By cooperation and courtesy of Dr. Dale Bennett.


examples [Figs. 8,9,14]. Later British trowels lack the exuberant expression conveyed by the combination of elaborate engraving and fanciful rococo shapes of Continental blades, which exhibit swirling leaf, cusped and asymmetric contours [Figs. 73,75,79]. However, neoclassical server decoration did find rich expression in British decor, as seen in Figs. 41 and 48, and, especially, Figs. IV 1,IV 3-6, and other examples there.

A modestly restraining influence upon elaborate silver decoration at this time was the neogothic movement in which Horace Walpole was a leading influence (34). Although initiated in the 1750s, its effect upon silver server decoration was only seen in the following decades, initially as pointed quatrefoils [Fig. 37]. Figure 49 displays a fully realized gothic pattern — both the pierced circles, usually drilled out, and the paling have been cusped upward. The trowel blade is in arch form. As opposed to most other silver articles, which display gothic influence only in terms of their ornamentation or minor modification of form, the trowel server lends both its overall form, as well as its ornamentation, to a total expression of gothic sentiment. Another example of gothic style is found in a rectangular slice illustrated in Fig. IV 12. Obviously, the oblong shape does not lead to as convincing an expression of feeling as do the triangular trowel shapes, although

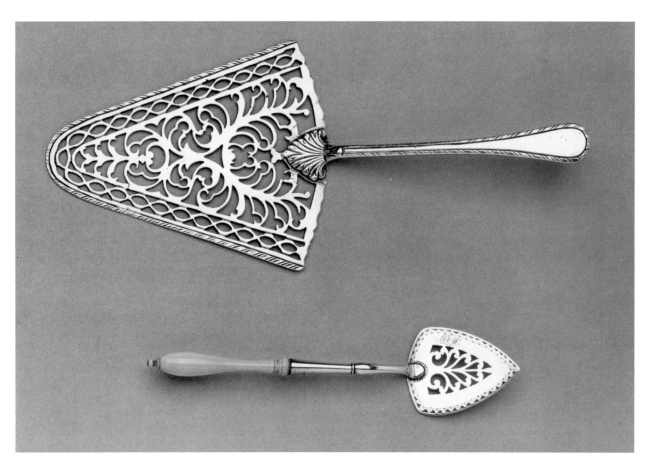

59.   FISH TROWEL, Edward Farrell, London, 1842; length 32.5 cm, weight 6.1 oz. The straight-sided blade has a curved cusped rear edge. The blade is outlined by double engraved lines. The all-over pierced design includes engraved scrolls, leaves and flowers. The cast anthemion boss has a surround of two engraved grimacing dolphins. The cast stem leads by a bolster feature to a scale-decorated cast finial that shows traces of gilding. This blade has piercing and shape identical with that by this maker in Fig. 60, apart from the fact that it lacks about 1 1/2 cm of the lower part of the latter. Moreover, the underside of the blade is quite pitted, indicating a casting. Since rolled sheet was readily available at this time, it is possible that Farrell cast a number of blades in the same mould to save the expense of piercing. Indeed, the silver scrolls are all rounded and the sharper vertices of the piercing show retraction and residual flashing. Among his other talents, it is evident that this virtuoso smith was a master caster.

60.   FISH TROWEL, Edward Farrell, London, 1844; length 38.5 cm, weight 8.5 oz. The slightly dished blade, seemingly cast, has straight sides and a curved cusped rear edge. A frieze around the perimeter of the blade is decorated with a dotted pattern of scales. It encloses a completely pierced area of engraved scroll, branch, leaf and flower designs that are much more detailed than those of Fig. 59. What was small leafage in Fig. 59 has now been ingeniously converted by the engraver to two feeding hummingbirds; and what was a junction reserve engraved with two dolphins has been converted to scrolling foliage. The junction is a cast bouquet of leaves and flowers from which springs a leopard that holds a tubular stem. The latter leads to a circular floral wreath and thence to an imbricated leaf section surmounted by the Biddenden Siamese twins, one of whom holds an out-pouring cornucopia in one hand and a long feather object in the other. The Maids are dated by local authority to the twelfth century. The rear view of the figures reveals an unshod foot, a bare leg and a knee. This server represents a series of puzzles. Why the twins? Why this date? Why Elizabethan dress? Or does this support a later date of birth as has been suggested? Why the reveal of bony knees and bare legs, especially of persons whose physical deformity must have caused considerable personal anguish and occasioned a high degree of modesty? Some casual research has not provided answers.

60a.   FISH TROWEL, John Figg, London (62), 1845; length 30 cm; weight 8.7 oz. The nearly straight-sided bevel-edged blade has a cusped curved rear edge. Save for a narrow peripheral strip, the whole blade is beautifully pierced and engraved with foliate scrolls and flowers. The cast handle is a dolphin-like sea monster that has a long flowing mane and dragon-like pectoral fins. It lifts from a tri-lobate leafy tail junction. The marks are laid along the top right rear edge.

the earliest English scimitar blade, shown in Fig. V1, is quite impressive in this respect. Paling continued in neoclassical decoration and through much of the nineteenth century. It was a form of piercing ideally suited to machine stamping.

A rather exceptional fish slice is seen in Fig. 67. It is an unmarked Old Sheffield piece in traditional fish-decorated Dutch transverse oval form. It is dated c. 1785, as accords with the beaded stem and handle edge, although it has a completely out-of-period dog nose terminal. It is affirmed as being of British manufacture (35) although it is not in the stylistic tradition.

Some Continental servers continued in the vein of the late baroque styles of the early eighteenth century up to [Fig. 69], and beyond [Fig. 27b] the middle of the century. At that time rococo influence began to make itself felt and persisted

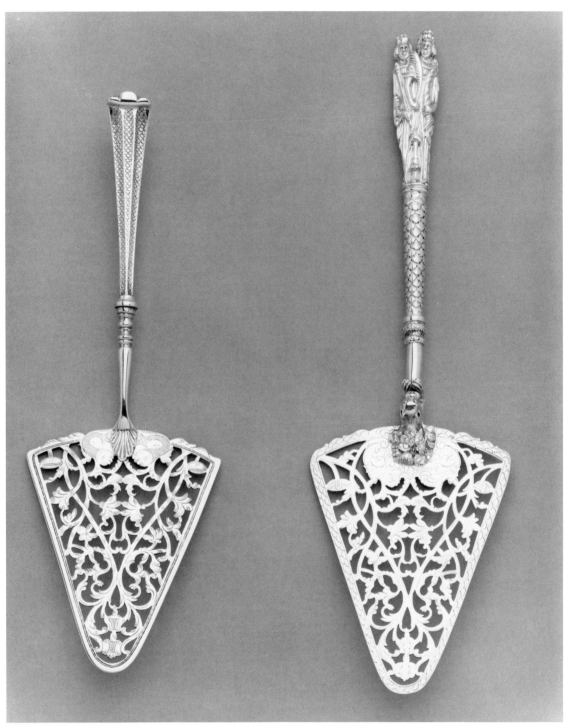
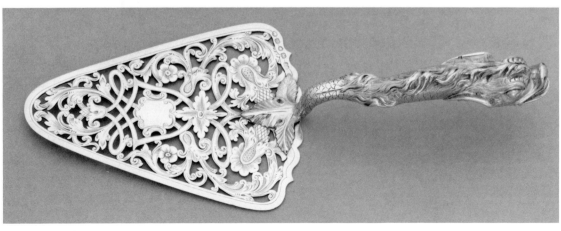

61.    FISH SERVER, Magnus Aase, Bergen, c. 1900; length 26.5 cm. The skate-shaped blade is pierced, embossed and repousée. Apart from the pointed tip, the waved sides are rolled up. The whip-like cast handle starts as a naturalistic tail that becomes a leafed vine. The whole has the flowing curves and sinuous form of Art Nouveau style.
By cooperation and courtesy of Dr. Dale Bennett.

62.    CAKE/PASTRY TROWEL, American maker unidentified, c. 1910; length 26.2 cm; weight 4.9 oz. The blade is stamped *handmade, sterling,* and has as maker's mark a gothic M in a trilobate rectangle. The long straight-sided triangular blade has a cusped straight rear edge and a sharply turned point. The blade is pierced with regular heavy J-scrolls and circles, and with asymmetric line scrolls. The handle, which is in line with no lift, is cast in two halves; it has a split spool boss that embraces the blade, which is strengthened on both sides with cut card leaves. The handle has a crudely modeled rib decoration and bud finial. The style is Art Nouveau.

63a.    CAKE/PUDDING SLICE, Omar Ramsden, London, 1921; length 27.8 cm, weight 5.9 oz. The plain flat oval pointed blade has a raised side that extends under the handle. A straight edge to the unpierced blade would has been clear evidence that this is a crumber; as it is, the highly rounded edge allows alternative interpretation. The handle is a heavy cast piece with a vaguely medieval vine and leaf pattern surmounted by a Tudor rose; its lower shank is ribbed and is pseudo-hammered in typical Ramsden style. Although extraordinarily robust, nonetheless the handle is reinforced along its whole length by an underside sheet rib which carries on as cut cart strengthening of the rear undersurface. The right underside edge of the blade is further strengthened by a narrow reinforcement strip along its whole length. Ramsden's work is recognized as part of, or an extension of, the Arts and Crafts movement. He is credited with being the force that reinvigorated the custom of individual craftsman commissions, as opposed to off-the-shelf purchases of 'machine made' work. But, paradoxically, some careless finishing detail on this piece shows something of the mass-production, entrepreneurial attitude he also brought to his establishment. His shop purchased many components and castings, and commissioned specialty work from other workshops. See P. Cannon-Brookes, *Omar Ramsden 1873-1939,* City Museum and Art Gallery, Birmingham, 1973, for a critique of Ramsden.

63b.    CRUMBER, Henry Birks, Montreal, patd. 1891; length 27.5 cm; weight 3.8 oz; solid handle. The sides are raised all around save, of course, along the straight working edge. The raised sides and handle are stamped with C-scrolls. The modified fiddle terminal is crested; the same handle pattern is illustrated for a jelly spoon on p. 197 of Ref. 57.

in vogue through most of the rest of the century; compare Fig. 8, Ref. (18), described immediately below. It was accompanied in the last part by neoclassical influence, which persisted into the nineteenth century and itself intermingled with Empire style. The intention here, however, is neither to discuss the stylistic evolution of silver serving pieces on the Continent intensively, nor extensively, nor by country. The present purpose is more restricted and is intended to illustrate some differences in the history of British and Continental server wares. The discussion centers on style and blade shape.

It has been seen that at least some early Continental servers displayed much more ornate baroque ornament than did the British servers that followed. But still another striking difference in stylistic evolution was the extent and importance of

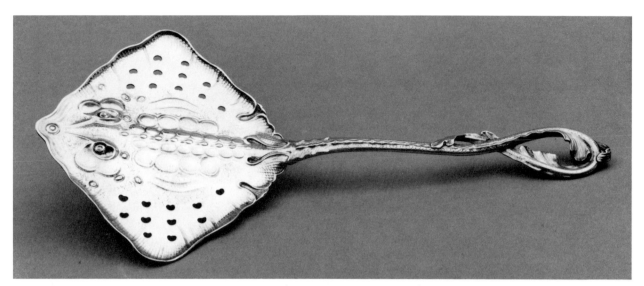

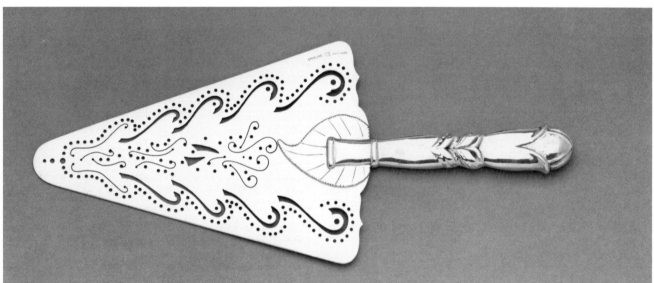

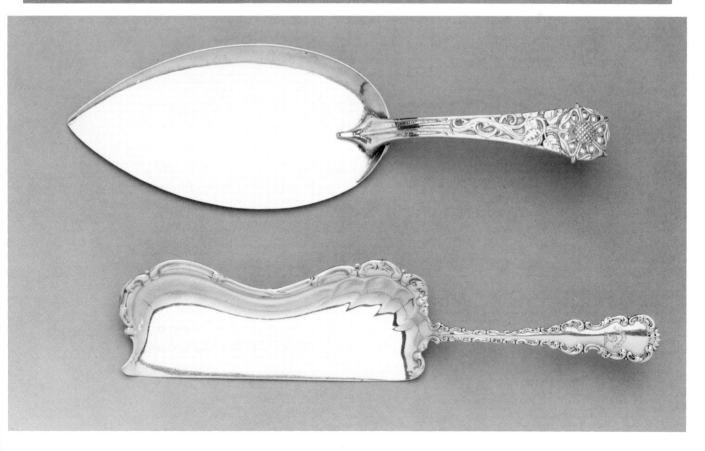

64. FISH TROWEL, Benton Seymour Rabinovitch, Seattle, 1980; length 34.3 cm; weight 11.8 oz. The pierced hammered blade is in the form of a ray, with chased fins. The boss follows the blade shape as a small ray. The stem ends in a hammered fish tail finial. Great makers such as De Lamerie and Storr made their products good and they usually made them heavy; this smith has made this implement good and heavy.

65. FISH TROWEL, Rod A. Kelly, London, 1988; length 34 cm; weight 10.5 oz. The trowel blade is pointed and has sharply turned shoulders on a generally rounded contour. The blade is sharply domed and is dramatically chased with a sinuous enveloping fish riding on the pierced swirling foam. The handle, with fish-tail finial, shows a fish half-buried in the swirling sea. The chased design is reminiscent of the fluent flowing curves of Art Nouveau style, while the horizontal angularity of the hollow handle, the vertical boss attachment, and the overall shape carry intimations of the Art Deco.

66. CAKE TROWEL drawing, Malcolm Appleby, Banchory, Scotland, 1990; length ~28.5 cm; weight 14.7 oz. Design for a pierced, heart-shaped server that is beautifully and whimsically engraved with an earthy, gluttonous queen. The handle rises on a forward curving loop. The intended function is clearly defined by the quotation engraved on the handle, "Let them eat cake"! Note. The completed server features minor variations.

rococo influence on Continental implements. It was noted earlier that the Régence example in Fig. 15 and the related fish server by Wickert resemble early English servers of the 1740s. Figure 8 of Ref. (18) illustrates a similar trowel by Georg Carl Brenner, post-1754, but here rococo vine decoration was introduced on a blade whose shape and thematic style of V-band border diaper piercing is still late or transitional baroque. The Danish slice of c. 1750 [Fig. 70] also shows overlapping styles. By contrast, the trowel server in Fig. 73 by A. Lüring, Hamburg, post-1756, provides, in its boss attachment and asymmetric swirling, an expression of free rococo feeling that was rarely attempted by British silver server makers. It is matched and surpassed by the lavishly decorated Swedish slice of J. Pettersson, 1764 [Fig. 75]. Indeed, Scandinavian silversmiths were amongst the vanguard in venting rococo expression in silver servers. Figure 68 shows an even earlier cusped-edge, modestly pierced trowel (called "fish slice" (36)) by J. Kahrs, Bergen, 1747. It may be noted in passing that 'cake spade' might seem a more suitable designation for this article. Figures 71,72 display slices by P. Pettersson, Stockholm, 1756, and P. Julin, Köping, 1757, that demonstrate highly developed rococo decoration, even as the blade form of the first and the shell terminal of the second reveal remnants of baroque influence. These several servers illustrate a remark made earlier, namely, that Scandinavian silversmiths of the time seemed to have been remarkably *au courant* with developments further south and their expression, in this case, of rococo style. Indeed, Swedish archives are a great storehouse of French patterns (10).

Figures 74,76 show two Danish trowels, one by B. Jonsen, Copenhagen, 1763,

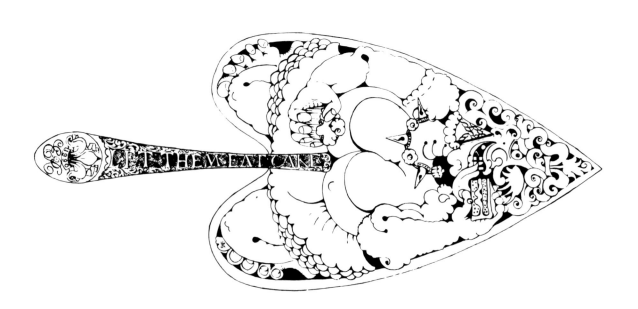

the other by J. G. Høderich, Copenhagen, 1779, both with all-silver handles. The former exhibits modestly imposed rococo influence in the engraving and rippled edge of what is otherwise a severely triangular shape. The latter, with rounded shoulders and oval contour, moves on in time and exhibits an intermingling of rococo shape with neoclassical engraved decoration. Another example of later mixed style may be seen in Fig. 77. This lovely "fish lifter" by Jens Sveistrup, Copenhagen, 1781, has a fully developed cast rococo handle and a blade that has a curvy, cusped trowel edge, but with a central oval engraved neoclassical motif. A server [Fig. 80] by J.H. Kemerer, Copenhagen, 1783, divides into two styles: a neoclassical blade and a rococo handle.

Among German examples, the cake slice shown in Fig. 78 by G. Lütkers, Augsburg, 1779, exhibits a clean engraved leaf shape. Another leaf shape by B.W. Heer, c. 1780 with plain engraving is displayed in Fig. 79. Figure 81 illustrates a later "fish lifter" by H. J. Berg, Lübeck, 1789, with a well developed rococo swirling trowel blade, also in leaf form. A more restrained symmetrical cusped leaf blade is revealed in a "fish" trowel by Jacob Steen, Christiana, 1790 (38). Rococo style was obviously alive and well on the Continent throughout the eighteenth century.

A common feature of later eighteenth- and nineteenth- century Continental servers that is rarely, if ever, seen in British servers is the provision of an (sometimes raised) 'apron' at the rear of the blade to which the handle is attached [Figs. 27b,33b,69,70,82,83; other examples may be found in the figures]. This structural feature was sometimes differentiated sharply in contour and decoration from the rest of the blade, and more so in later wares. Some nineteenth-century American slices also show this influence [Figs. V 112,V 113].

A remarkably expressive oval blade form occurred in the Nordic double-fish trowel design. Perhaps the earliest example is that by J.J. Smidt, Strømsø, post-1746 (39). Norwegian examples of this imaginative design occur throughout the last half of the eighteenth century. Figure 84 displays one such made by S.S. Brandt, Drammen, post- 1764. The blade is a flat fish, such as halibut or sole, of general contour that is not easily differentiated from that described in Chapter IV as *long-oval*, and has decorative scale work and piercing. Its tail is held in the jaws of a smaller eel-like fish, such as a snake mackerel, which serves as the handle. The body of the snake fish has been placed by different makers either in the plane or, as in the illustration, perpendicular to the plane of the flat fish, a somewhat more comfortable orientation for the user. A later example is the beautifully decorated one by P.C. Beyer, Bergen, 1787 [Fig. 85]; a Copenhagen, 1779, example is found in Ref. (37). Still another late example by Githard Möbus, Kragerø, c. 1790, is in the Norsk Folkemuseum, Oslo; here, the snake fish is in the plane of the blade. The piercing is restrained on these servers and usually takes a lunette, scale-like shape. The Smidt slice may well be the earliest fish-shaped server that has survived.

Although not as striking as the double-fish conception, the occasional fish-shaped blade furnished with a conventional contemporary handle style of the time was also made in the late eighteenth century, as in an example by M. Pettersen, Bergen, 1794, that has an Old English type beaded handle [Fig. 86]. Additional examples occur throughout the nineteenth and into the twentieth century and in many other countries, although more rarely in Britain as a realistic fish [see Fig. IV 41]. Other instances are shown in Fig. IV 50 and Figs. V 112, V 114, V 126. Still another permutation of the possible combinations of blades and handles is evident in the Dublin trowel in Fig. 36. Here a fish handle is attached to a conventional flat trowel blade. Since the fish is provided with a suitable complement of sharp fins, it proves impossible to grasp the handle firmly — at least not without considerable discomfort.

Following on the rococo period, other influences also operated in the evolution of the trowel server in the late eighteenth century. Neoclassical style, called Louis XVI on the Continent, favoured more restrained symmetrical blade shapes. Actually, the simple trowel shape derived from the earliest Scandinavian forms never did disappear. As is discussed further in Chapter IV, unlike the British experience wherein the server having greatest breadth in the *rear* half of a broad blade rather suddenly gave way at the end of the third quarter of the century to a long-oval slice having greatest breadth at the *middle* or in the *front* half of the blade, no abrupt changes in form took place on the Continent. This may now be illustrated by a few examples.

The double-fish design, whose blade approximates the later British long-oval shape (Chapter IV), is described above. In Fig. 69 is shown a Norwegian trowel — "fiskespade" — dated from post-1750. The sides of the blades are now well rounded and the maximum width (transverse diameter) has moved forward somewhat on the blade; the length-to-width ratio is 1.7. Still another Danish fish trowel, which has restrained blade shape, is seen in Fig. 70; the rounded blade contour of this bold, sturdy server is not only pronouncedly oval in shape, but quite long in its proportion; length-to-width ratio of blade being 2.1. A later Danish example by J. Friis, Randers, post-1770 [Fig. 87], featuring a geometric piercing pattern, is somewhat stubbier in proportion than the preceding example but nonetheless also presaged things to come. Moving along, an illustration of a transitional shape is provided in Fig. 80 by a "fish slice or cake spoon" by J.H. Kemerer, Copenhagen, 1783. This server, which exhibits mixed rococo and neoclassical ornamentation, is formally a trowel, inasmuch as the major width is slightly to the rear of the transverse center line of the blade; but it lacks shoulders and takes on the aspect of the long-oval servers described in Chapter IV. Its designation, whether as trowel or long-oval, is almost a 'judgement call,' as is that of the even more ambiguous Danish implement shown in Fig. 88. Their resemblance to British and Continental long-oval servers is unmistakable. Yet another judgement call is the later French "fish" server by A.C. Clérin, Paris, 1809-1819, in Fig. 89. Further transitional examples continue in Chapter IV.

67.    FISH SLICE, Old Sheffield, unmarked, c. 1785; length 33 cm. This apparently standard Dutch-type of fish server is anomalous, both in its English origin (35) and in the style of its dog nose crested finial. The beading on the handle is appropriate for its estimated date by the source cited below; however, the flowing asymmetric pierced decoration and engraving suggest an even earlier date, say 1765-1770, at which time beading on other related items such as ladles had already appeared. The engraved fish certifies its intended function. See J.D. Davis, *English Silver at Williamsburg*, University of Virginia Press, Charlottesville, 1976, Fig. 264.
By kind cooperation and courtesy of The Colonial Williamsburg Foundation.

68.    FISH SLICE, Jens Kahrs, Bergen, 1742; length 23 cm. This early Norwegian trowel has been designated as a fish, rather than cake, server despite its minimal piercing and relatively small size. Both the handle and the piercing and engraving of the blade are in late baroque style; the blade proportions resemble those of Fig. 2. The cusping of the blade edges into something reminiscent of a leaf shape is an indication of early rococo influence in server decoration. The blade tip has suffered maltreatment.
Courtesy of the Rana Museum, Mo, Norway.

69.    FISH SLICE, maker unknown, c. 1750, South Norway; Hanoverian handle. The narrow pointed blade could serve well for cake or pastry. This implement is contemporary with that of Fig. 70 and both have the same general shape. However, this one has a plain surface and simple late baroque piercing. The server is constructed in one piece; there is no junction; the rear of the blade rises as a narrow apron. See J. Fossberg, *Norsk Solv-Skjeer*, C. Huitfeld Forlag, Oslo, 1974, p. 60.
Courtesy of Norsk Folkemuseum, Oslo.

Notwithstanding the appearance of new long-oval and scimitar shapes of fish and pastry servers, Continental production of a variety of trowel shapes continued into the nineteenth century and has not stopped to this day. A few more examples will suffice here in addition to those in Figs. 82,82 and 89. Figure 90 is an elongated long triangular Netherlands server, c. 1820, while Fig. 91 is a heart-shaped fish slice by J.M. Voigt, Lübeck, 1827. And a spade by the maker, L.K., Prague, 1828, is shown in Fig. 92. Examples of straight-sided, severely triangular trowels, having scrolling or geometric piercing, are contained in the catalogue of Le Musée Historique de l'Ancien Évêché, Lausanne (40). A number of illustrations [cf. Fig. 93] from the periods 1780-1800, 1790-1800, 1800-1810, many with raised rear aprons and most with wooden handles, are shown along with a heart-shaped, highly scroll-pierced trowel, 1820-1830, and several very plain, unpierced spade shapes, 1830-1840; they are all named "pastry shovels" (pelle à patisserie) whether pierced or not, except for a lone unpierced scimitar, 1800-1810, called "pelle à tartelette."

Figure 94 illustrates a waisted Norwegian fish trowel of the latter half of the century. Figure 99 is a late reproduction of a very early cake blade shape [cf. Fig. 6].

Later, post-1850 British trowels usually have small, narrow, unpierced and frequently undecorated blades, similar in shape to the earliest Scandinavian trowels but only one-half or two-thirds of their size. They differ somewhat from

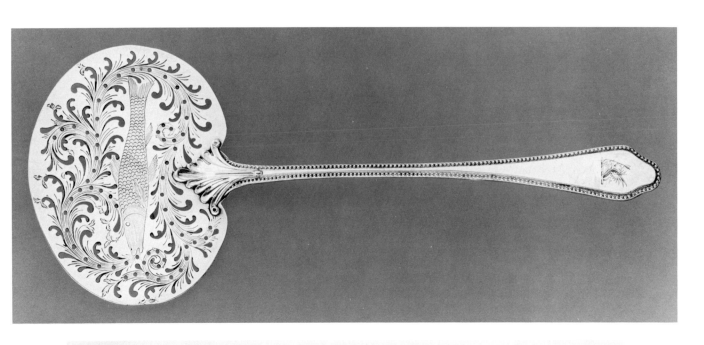

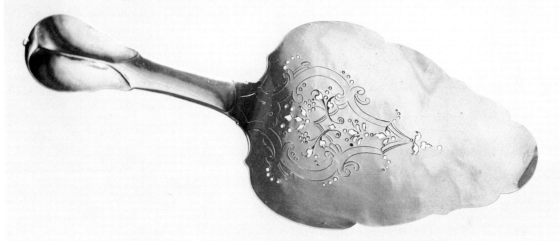

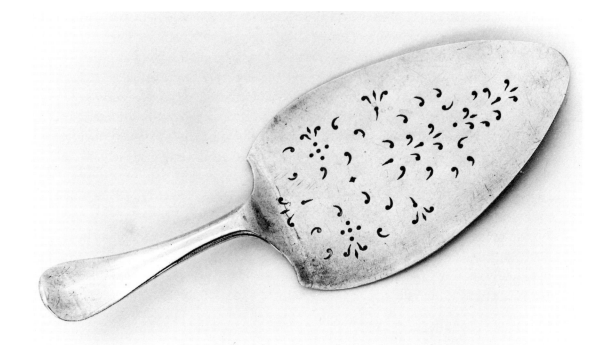

70.   FISH SLICE, maker's mark illegible; Copenhagen, c. 1750; length 27.3 cm. This article is part of the Rosenborg Palace collection. This sturdy server, of imposing clean design of continuous blade and handle, has mixed stylistic elements of blade shape and handle and scrolled piercing with a naturalistic vine theme. Like Fig. 69, the narrow pointed blade could serve for cake or pastry. See Erik Lassen, *Knives, Forks and Spoons,* Høst, Copenhagen, 1960, p. 70, for further discussion of this implement.
Courtesy of Høst and Sons Forlag.

71.   CAKE SLICE, Petter Pettersson, Stockholm, 1756. This trowel demonstrates beautifully engraved rococo motifs on blade and handle finial, although the blade has the somewhat severe, elongated form of the earlier baroque Swedish examples [Figs. 3-6]. It is delightfully engraved with swirled scrolls, shell, and pendant vine tendrils. The finial of the flat handle is a scrolled shell. The article is further described as Fig. 639 of *Svenskt Silversmide, Vol. II, Rokokon,* cited in Fig. 2.
Courtesy of Nordiska Museet, Stockholm. Private owner.

72.   CAKE SLICE, Petter Julin, Köping, 1757. In addition to all-over scrolls and shells on blade and handle, the blade shape with its gently scalloped edge is more free than that of the preceding example in Fig. 71. Nonetheless, the mussel shell finial of the handle, which has underblade attachment, casts a look back to the bold baroque feature of Fig. 2. The implement is further described as Fig. 638 of *Svenskt Silversmide, op. cit.*
Courtesy of Nordiska Museet, Stockholm. Private owner.

73.   FISH SLICE, August Lüring, Hamburg, post-1756. This server, which might just as well be used for cake or pastry, has only a modest pierced asymmetric pattern of scrolls, but the blade leaf shape is an exuberant swirled expression of rococo style. The boss is a large shell form that is tastefully pierced with a scrolled opening. From W. Scheffler, *Kunst und Antiquitaten,* Part 2, 1976, page 24, Fig. 9.
By kind cooperation and courtesy of Dr. W. Scheffler. Private owner.

their Georgian forebears in shape; they are narrower than the small W. Plummer slice of 1765 shown in Fig. 33a, although of similar length. They resemble more the earlier slice by A. and G. Burrows [Fig. 58]; and the distinction between a small variant of these and some butter servers (see Chapter VII) even becomes a little tenuous. They were used as pastry (pie, cake) servers, and have continued in shape and function into present day manufactures that are found in every kitchen in the form of small, frequently unpierced, triangular pie and pastry servers.

Small oval trowels, some flat and many dished, were commonly made in American manufacture from 1830 on through the century, and were usually called (57) pastry or pie servers [Figs. 95-97]. They are of overall length 20-25 cm and a little wider in proportion than their Continental and British counterparts. They are usually unpierced but may be lavishly decorated with engraving and engine turning. The side edges are often very fancifully shaped, especially toward the rear of the blade. To anticipate the section that follows, the handles may be of standard English pattern, but more often exemplify the plethora of American styles (57). They are usually continuous with the blade rather than being joined to it by a junction piece.

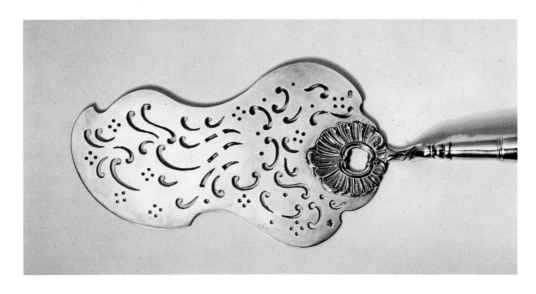

74.   FISH SLICE or CAKE SPOON, Brandt Jonsen, Copenhagen, 1763, fiddle handle, length 28 cm. This Danish trowel has a characteristically broader-shouldered blade than the preceding Swedish contemporaries, and is reminiscent of the Norwegian example of Fig. 68. The fine, streaming, filamental curvilinear vine decoration is unusual. The plain waisted fiddle handle has underblade attachment. For further description see G. Boesen and C. A. Bøje, *Old Danish Silver*, Hassing, Copenhagen, 1949, Fig. 487. Note the variable usage suggested by these authors and their allusion ("spoon") to the etymological origin of the word *trowel*.
By kind cooperation and courtesy of Gudmund Boesen. Private owner.

75.   CAKE SLICE, Johan Pettersson, Norköping, 1764. If there are more beautifully decorated servers than this they are very few in number. It represents a total expression of rococo style, both in its swirled blade shape and intricate flowing engraved decoration, as well as in its handle decoration and curved shell finial. It maintains the narrow shape of Swedish cake servers. See Fig. 640, *Svenskt Silversmide, op cit*, for further description.
Courtesy of Nordiska Museet, Stockholm.

76.   FISH SLICE or CAKE SPOON, Johan Georg Høderick, Copenhagen, 1779; Hanoverian handle; length 28.2 cm. This server exhibits mixed stylistic elements, namely, a late Hanoverian handle with underblade attachment, a cusped shaped edge, and the onset of neoclassical (Louis XVI) engraved decoration. For further description see Fig. 488, G. Boesen and C. A. Bøje, *Old Danish Silver, op cit.*, Fig. 488; note again the indefinite choice of title by these authors.
By kind cooperation and courtesy of Gudmund Boesen. Private owner.

77.   FISH SLICE, Jens Sveistrup, Assay Master F. Fabritius, Copenhagen, 1781; length 27.8 cm. This server shows mixed stylistic elements. The ornate cast and chased handle is in full-blown rococo style, as is the blade shape. The decoration on the blade is mixed. At the rear, where the handle attaches underblade, is a chased asymmetric shell and pendant drop. The centre of the blade features a swirled, pierced neoclassical rosette. This server is described as Fig. 355 in M. Meinz, *Schönes Silber*, Klinkhardt and Biermann, München, 1964.
Courtesy of Dr. Manfred Meinz; photograph by the Worshipful Company of Goldsmiths, London. Private owner.

Very few large trowels have been made in the twentieth century [Figs. 61-66]. They tend to follow the traditions of the resurgent craftsmanship that became prominent at the start of the century. They reflect the individuality of the artist-craftsmen who looked to their own Muse for inspiration, rather than to the past [see also Fig. IV 51].

## *Handles*

The earliest Continental trowel handles were made of silver, as were those of the De Lamerie trowels [Figs. 1-10]. The handle might be forged, soldered along a lengthwise seam, or cast in one piece, and connected directly to the blade either by an underside boss connection at the rear end of the blade, or in a manner continuous with and as an extension of the blade [Fig. 1]. Unlike the early Swedish servers [Figs. 2-6], most British handles attach to a boss on the rear topside of the

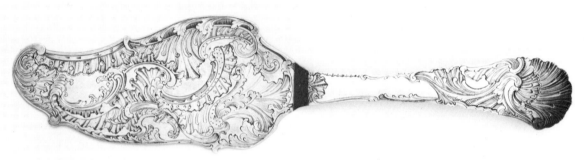

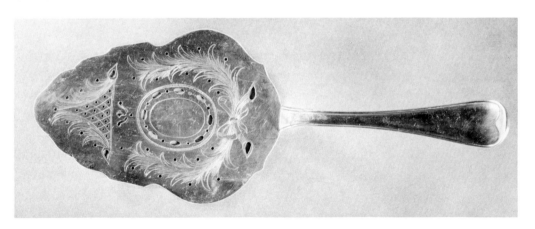

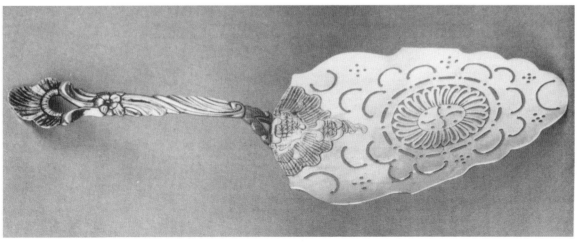

blade. Occasional underside attachment occurs [Figs. 27a,31,52b], and Scottish makers sometimes used this arrangement in later scimitar slices (Chapter V). Alternatively, if the handle proper was a separate piece, called a *haft*, such as the cannon-end handles of Figs. 3,4, attachment to the boss junction was made *via* an intermediate stem piece. The number of very early examples is very limited and no pattern of construction details or characteristics emerges.

British trowels possess two types of handles: either non-silver, favoured prior to the middle 1760s, or all-silver, favoured thereafter. Most early handles are of highly balustered turned shape, either of wood or ivory [Figs. 16-20]. So-called "ebony" handles refer to the wood stain color and not the material. Ivory handles are either natural white-yellow, or green-stained with copper or chromate salts. Occasional handles of bone or other materials, such as an agate one by Richard Mills, London, 1774 (53) and mother-of-pearl by William Chatterton, London, 1775 (26), were made. The handle fits into a hollow conical silver socket that connects *via* a stem or shank to the silver boss or junction at the rear of the blade. The stem has an S- or crank-shape so that the handle is lifted markedly (several inches) above the plane of the blade; it is usually angled gently downward, although occasionally it may be positioned parallel to the blade plane [Fig. 25]. The boss itself is frequently a stamped shell, or anthemion, or husk form of one sort or another. Less often, it is a rose or other floral or animal form [e.g., Figs. 20,24,25,44,45,60]. The boss may be cast and may be pierced, i.e., have a floral loop design [Figs. 38,42,56], and is sometimes riveted to the blade for additional strength as well as being soldered [Figs. 30,32].

Exceptions can occur. One such implement, described as c. 1745 and by an unknown maker (41), eliminates the shank, the S-crank, and the boss attachment; instead, the straight conical tubular socket connects directly at a relatively steep angle with the rear of a diaper-pierced triangular blade. Still another feature, whose purpose is obscure, is the detachable handle of a trowel by Samuel Courtauld, London, c. 1750, illustrated in Ref. (26). Speculation has been offered (27) that this arrangement would have facilitated cleaning or, alternatively (and less likely), transport, i.e., the article was a personal server. In any case it seems to be unique among British servers. The same feature occurs occasionally in Continental slices with a handle on a screw attachment. By contrast, detachable "convertible cutlery" had a more obvious rationale (Ref. 19, Fig. 301).

A popular form of stem and boss that occurred in the late 1750s and 1760s and persisted in the occasional later scimitar slice, as well as in the nineteenth-century trowel creations of Edward Farrell, is a combined dolphin stem-boss. In such devices, the conical socket attaches to the tail of a small dolphin whose mouth, often buried in spume, constitutes the blade junction on the top side of the blade [Figs. 20,26,28].

All British silver handles are of two types. The first are cast or partially cast forms and are frequently unique in style, although repetitions do occur [Figs.

38,48,60]. These almost certainly represent purchases of individual servers that were joined to a table service that was of different style. The handles might represent anything from ornate rococo, the most fully developed of any aspect of rococo influence in British servers [Figs. 21,35], to later examples of neoclassical influence [Figs. 47,50], as well as other unusual shapes such as the fish handle mentioned earlier [Fig. 36]. The second type is a standard forged or stamped cutlery form (33a); the De Lamerie trowels and Fig. 27a feature Hanoverian style; later examples have a type of Old English handle, sometimes with feather edging and other engraving or chasing decor of the time. Trowels, however, disappeared from the scene before many examples [Fig. 52b] featuring bright cutting cumulated. Most English examples of Old English terminals are flat and lack the conventional underside longitudinal rib, e.g., Figs. 43,46,51,55. Old English style Irish handles tend to be long and flowing [Figs. 31,46] — a not uncharacteristic feature that is echoed in Irish ladle handles; the handle is sometimes convex downward (dished) along the long axis so as to describe about one-quarter of a circular arc [Figs. 42,52a]. The silver handle is never in the plane of the blade; it always features a lift, in the manner of sauce ladles that have handles of comparable length.

The writer has never encountered an example of a British cannon end handle, analogous to the early Scandinavian examples described above and to early English ladle spoons c. 1700. Nor has he seen an Onslow terminal, which he assumes were, at most, only infrequently made (contrast the ceramic examples of Chapter I). Nor have examples of French fiddle or, even rarer, very early English fiddle terminals been found, although both appear very occasionally in contemporary spoons and ladles. The rare incidence of a filled handle was mentioned in the History section, and a design drawing is shown in Fig. IV 1.

Undoubtedly, most trowels represented individual cutlery acquisitions. As revealed by the Earl of Kildare's account in the Garrard Ledgers (20, Appendix II), although it included four fish plates, not even the "superb" Leinster dinner service incorporated trowel servers; those were part of another order to George Wickes. However, the development of complete flatware service canteens did progress to the point that at least some surviving trowels were originally part of a complete set. One instance [Fig. 43b] is a canteen of cutlery by W. Fearn, London, 1771 (42).

Later Continental trowels have handles that are similar in principle to the British wares. They feature turned wooden [Figs. 78,79,93], ivory [Fig. 90], an occasional agate, and all-silver handles, again either forged in contemporary cutlery styles [Figs. 27b,69,86] or cast [Figs. 61,77]. Expected differences include the pointed Old English handles, familiar in British production in their Irish and Scottish (Celtic point) influence [Fig. 88], and Continental style fiddle handles, particularly the waisted fiddle [Figs. 74,80]. Although the stem is usually applied to the top of the blade [Figs. 93c,d], or to the apron [Figs. 93a,b], there is more

78.   CAKE SLICE, Gottfried Lüttkers, Augsburg, 1779. This server offers a well-developed leaf shape with branch, leaf, and fruit line-engraving superimposed upon an all-over asymmetric pattern of scrolled piercing. The cast trilobate leaf boss and branch stem lead to a carved handle. This item appears as Fig. 308 in *Silverware* by A. Gruber, Rizzoli, New York, 1982.
By kind cooperation and courtesy of Dr. Alain Gruber and Office du Livre, Fribourg. Private owner.

79.   FISH/CAKE TROWEL, Bernard Wilhelm Heer, Kleve, c. 1780, length 29 cm. The blade has a fully developed leaf shape in rococo style, and a beveled edge. The surface is engraved with a simple tree outline and is pierced with small tilde scrolls. The boss is a cast, realistically textured, lopped branch. It has two leafed branches that give it a three-point attachment to the rear surface of the blade. A small conical socket is pinned to a turned multi-balustered wooden handle that terminates in a ivory bead.

80.   FISH SLICE or CAKE SPOON, Johan Henrick Kemerer, Copenhagen, 1783; length 27.2 cm. This article is formally a trowel, since it has its maximum breadth in the rear half of the blade. But its highly rounded contour also gives it the appearance of a near-elliptic server (Chapter IV). The pierced blade is decorated with well-developed neoclassical motifs of bows and ribbon bands, while the feather-edged waisted fiddle handle features an asymmetric shell boss and finial, and pendant leaf and flower engraving. See Fig. 489 of G. Boesen and C.A. Bøje, *Old Danish Silver*, Hassing, Copenhagen, 1949.
By kind cooperation and courtesy of Gudmund Boesen.

frequent occurrence of under-blade attachment [Figs. 72,77] as well as instances where the shank is an extension and continuation of the blade with the elimination of the boss junction [Figs. 69,70,83]. Figure 99 illustrates an unusual late nineteenth-century example of a filled handle.

## Function

The mode of employment of trowels presents two aspects: the first is the question of *how* the trowel was physically used. The second is the question of for *what* service it was intended. These matters will be taken up in order.

British serving trowels were not intended to be used as cutting implements. It is true that because of the comparative thinness of the sheet of silver that comprises the blade, it automatically has some cutting edge whether bevelled or not. However, the physical construction of trowels and the very thinness of the blade makes immediately evident that they could not serve such a purpose. Effective use of a (knife) edge for cutting requires application of a force in the plane of the blade and directly in the direction of the cut — as in slicing a loaf with a bread knife. As trial immediately reveals, efficient force may *not* be applied along an axis that is displaced at an angle some six inches behind and several inches to the side of the cutting edge, which, in any case, is itself steeply angled and which presents its rear edge to the work. In practice, such attempted misuse develops a torque on the blade, which leads to bending and ultimately to splits in the

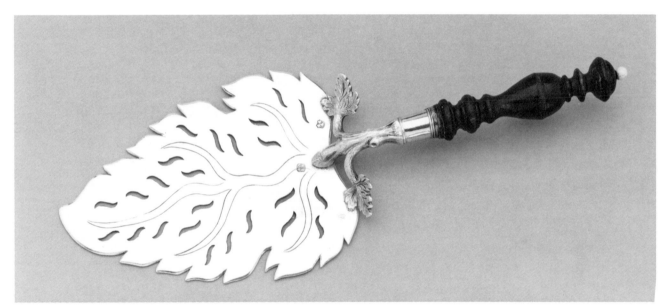

81.    FISH LIFTER, H. J. Berg, Lübeck, 1789; length 33 cm. A later, leaf-shaped, swirled-edge blade with simple pierced circle and comma design and with flower and foliage engraving. The blade is grasped, mainly underblade, by a simple stem that leads to a Hanoverian handle. Comparison with Fig. 78 makes evident that one man's cake slice may be another man's fish slice. This item appears as Fig. 26 in B.R. and M. Kommer, *Lübecker Silber, 1781-1871,* Verlag Max Schmidt-Römhild, Lübeck, 1978.
By kind cooperation of Dr. Ulrich Pietsch and courtesy of Schmidt-Römhild.

82.    PASTRY/CAKE SLICE, Hans Caspar I Wüest, Zurich, c. 1800; length 27.5 cm. Although the trowel blade is heavily pierced around the perimeter with a frieze of interlaced geometric bands and flower heads — thus combining both decorative elements — the small size and shape of the blade conforms to the assigned title. The blade extends into a rear apron from which a flower boss and flat stem rise to a conical socket that hold a turned wooden handle. It appears as Fig. 313 in E.-M. Lösel, *Zürcher Goldschmiede Kunst,* Zurich, 1983. There is a close resemblance to a similar article by J.F. Kirstein, Strasbourg, c. 1795, in Fig. 228 of Ref. (47), as well as to the implement of J.F. Buttner in Fig. 83.
Courtesy of, and photography by, Swiss National Museum, Zurich.

83.    Large TART SPADE (Grande Pelle À Tarte), Jean Frédéric II Buttner, Strasbourg, 1809-1819; length 37.4 cm. This implement was named "Grande" in comparison with the server of Fig. 33b. The silver-gilt, spade-shaped blade is pierced and engraved with a neoclassical palm leaf motif and surrounded by an waved line border. From the raised rear apron, which has some engraved lines, a tubular stem-socket rises without a junction boss to a turned wooden handle. For further description see H. Haug, *L'Orfèvrerie de Strasbourg,* Éditions des Musées Nationaux, Paris, 1978.
Courtesy of, and photography by, Musée des Arts decoratifs, Strasbourg.

piercing. Of course, a dished trowel could not in any case function properly as a cutter. Thus their physical structure dictated that trowels should be used mainly in their capacity as lifters and strainers. Smart (see Chapter II) has described in detail the importance of white bait in the diet of the English nobility and gentry and its associations with social and political custom. The pierced trowel was well adapted in both of its capacities for such employment.

With regard to the first application, highly pierced blades, and indeed all thin blades, are susceptible to stressing and cold working when used to lift heavy portions or to handle or remove tenacious foods and crusts from a pudding dish. Notwithstanding paeans of praise to the ingenious artfulness of the piercers who allegedly managed to maintain the strength of the blade while enhancing its decorative aspect, it transpires that a trowel blade, especially a pierced one, will tolerate little force that is directed perpendicular to its plane. It has strength only for forces in the plane of the blade; but this is a situation that was almost never realized, except in later and modern cake trowels in which handle and blade are often in the same plane [e.g., Fig. 62]. Their usage was most successful when applied to relatively fluid or light amenable materials such as jelly, mousse, blancmange, or white bait; blancmange, it will be recalled, was a gelled spiced puree of fish or meat at that time. When subjected to frequent hard usage, trowels

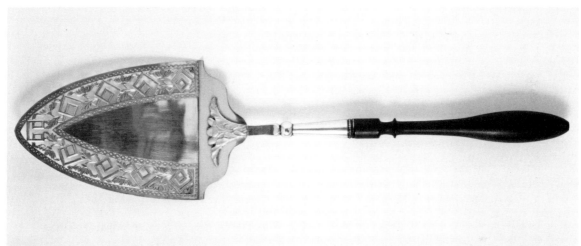

84.    FISH SLICE, Sören Samuelsen Brandt, Drammen, post-1764; estimated length c. 28 cm. This realistic server — a fish handle biting the tail of a fish blade — is almost of the long-oval type (Chapter IV). The blade is a large flat fish. Many (most) fish shapes of, and engravings on, servers do not correspond to well-identifiable species. The blade is engraved with scales and pierced with scale-like lunette openings. The fish seems unjustifiably jovial in mien in light of the attack on its tail by the smaller snake-like fish handle. The tail of the flat fish serves as an apron that carries the handle.
By kind cooperation and courtesy of Kunstindustrimuseet i Oslo.

85.    FISH SLICE, Peder Christiansen Beyer, Bergen, 1787. A beautifully engraved fish-on-fish in wonderfully pristine condition. The piercing in this case is an array of small circles intersecting the central fish scale pattern that is surrounded by a double frieze of smaller scales and of fine fins.
By cooperation and courtesy of Vestlandske Kunstindustrimuseum, Bergen.

86.    Fish slice, Mathias Pettersen, Bergen, 1794. This server, still of realistic fish form, now displays neoclassic influence. Inside a frieze of engraved fish scales and of chased and pierced arcs, engraving and piercing are combined in a central pattern of vine and leaf bands. The beaded Old English handle has underblade attachment. This article might well be included in Chapter IV [cf. Figs. IV 31,50].
By cooperation and courtesy of Vestlandske Kunstindustrimuseum, Bergen.

could be expected to fail. Even unpierced blades were evidently tested beyond their capacity in dealing with some puddings, or solid or crusty foods. Examination of the unpierced Goldsmith Company trowels (*vide supra*) reveals evidence of hard wear in the form of dents, as well as rubbed, marked and abraded edges, and a crack in the blade at the tip of one boss junction. Two of the gift trowels are no more. Small wonder then that surviving, relatively fragile, highly pierced blades show clear evidence of distress in many cases. Cracks in the piercing are frequently found. Examination of several of the figures presented gives clear evidence of extreme abuse. Figure 26 pictures one of the Plummer slices; it is evident that it *was* used as a cutter and that a pronounced lateral deformation of the dolphin stem has occurred. Similar evidence may be seen in Fig. 28. Rough and inappropriate usage has undoubtedly carried off many more of these objects than survive today. Since they were sometimes used at the dinner or banquet table by individuals to help themselves, their casual employment at the hands of a hungry horde could not help but be hazardous. Nor, despite the esteem in which they are held today, should it be supposed that such modest items of their time were carefully preserved or held in reverent regard in the manner of more monumental pieces. Assuming, for example, that the Goldsmith Company's trowels were actively used for fifty years or less, then two in poor condition might well have been disposed of for the benefit of a charity or other worthy cause (43).

The second application, use as a strainer, is a very plausible one. Recourse to the dictionary (17,44) is again helpful. The word 'trowel' is derived from the Latin, *trulla*, and French, *truelle*, and has among other meanings that of a culinary ladle

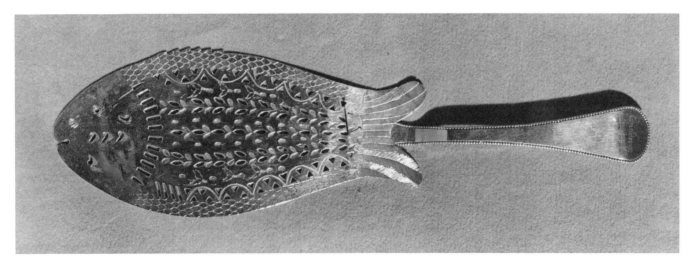

87.     FISH SLICE, Jørgen Friis, Randers, 1770-1780. This slice with waisted fiddle handle is clearly a trowel. But the highly rounded shoulders lend the impression of a skewed elliptic blade. The central piercing and engraving possibly suggest some neogothic influence along with a touch of the neoclassical in the surrounding bright-cut lunettes; the latter point to the later part of the suggested date span. The handle has underblade attachment. Further description may be found in E. Lassen, *Knives, Forks and Spoons*, Høst, Copenhagen, 1960, p. 70.
Courtesy of Høst and Sons Forlag.

88.     FISH SLICE or CAKE SPOON, Meyer Nathan Levy, Copenhagen, 1805; length 28 cm. Although formally a trowel, this server has the feeling of a long-oval. The slightly ovoid blade has neoclassical piercing and engraving. The engraved pointed Old English handle is attached by a decorated floral boss. See Fig. 490, G. Boesen and C.A. Bøje, *Old Danish Silver*, op. cit. for other description.
By kind cooperation and courtesy of Gudmund Boesen.

89.     FISH SLICE, A. C. Clérin, Veuve Lecour, Paris, 1809-1819. This pointed oval trowel has a repetitive, pierced, circumferential bright-cut band of bell flowers and engraved pincer-like (ice-tongs) scrolls, together with an inner, minor pierced pattern of pales. The turned wooden handle is connected *via* a conventional conical socket, faceted stem and Vee-boss. The article might as well be called a cake slice. See R.W. Lightbown, *French Silver*, Victoria and Albert Museum, London, HMSO, 1978, Fig. 103, for further description, as well as Fig. 108 where another slice (1819-1838) by this maker, which is of long-oval shape, is shown.
By cooperation and courtesy of Victoria and Albert Museum, London.

or scoop. Thus the server should perform a function related not only to a lifter but also to a straining spoon. Their relationship to the etymological Latin root word *trulla*, a spoon or ladle, is strikingly illustrated by the splendid Dutch server in Fig. 11 and by the Irish trowels cited earlier [Figs. 31,46]. Perhaps the most direct literal relationship in fish service is exemplified by a large Dutch straining spoon, Rotterdam, 1794 [Fig. 98]. This is of the size of a large basting spoon, in bright cut pointed Old English style. The bowl of this one, which is 10 cm long, is completely pierced and engraved with a fish and rushes. It totally symbolizes a strainer spoon function; for example, specialized to remove small cooked fish from the attendant liquid, as from a fish kettle. Although "water fish spoons" are mentioned repeatedly in Dutch records of the first half of the eighteenth century (58,59), it is still not clear (59) whether this refers to the oval fish slice, or indeed means that fish spoons of the Rotterdam type were made much earlier [cf. Fig. 7; another later example by Johannes Verloove, Rotterdam, 1782, has also been cited (59).

With respect to some implication, otherwise, in the literature, when a pair of trowels was part of a service there is no reason to believe that they were ever used together — one in each hand.

To this point we have exempted the De Lamerie servers from much of the discussion. What are they? The oldest [Fig. 1a] is of slightly dished oval trowel shape. They all bear a strong resemblance to the long-oval or elliptic servers in Chapter IV. As such they represent not only the first English silver servers but are

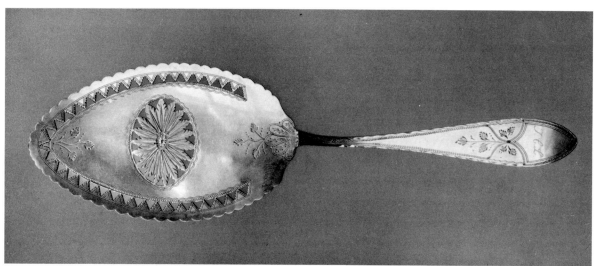

93a. PASTRY SHOVEL (SLICE), unmarked, Switzerland (?), 1780-1800 (?); length 29 cm; wooden handle. This is the first of some severely triangular trowels shown in Ref. (40); it displays casual pierced rococo scroll work. The turned wooden handle is attached by a cylindrical holder to a raised rear edge, or sharply up-turned apron.

93b. PASTRY SHOVEL (SLICE), Phillipe Vernet, Lausanne, 1800-1810; length 34.2 cm; wooden handle. The severely triangular trowel is pierced obliquely with pales that, in an English fish slice of this period, might be called a fish bone pattern. The stem rises from a ring boss on a rear apron to a turned, balustered wooden handle. The server, as well as the preceding one, would do as well for fish.

93c. PASTRY SHOVEL (SLICE), Gely Frères, Lausanne, 1820-30; length 34.4 cm; wooden handle. The heart-shaped blade is highly pierced in a looped scroll design. The stem rises from a rosette boss and the turned, balustered wooden handle is held in a conical holder. Comparison with companion servers in this series, especially the following, makes one wonder at the uniformity of the assigned names.

93d. PASTRY SHOVEL (SLICE), Gely Frères, Lausanne, 1830-40; length 32 cm; wooden handle. This unpierced spade-shaped blade seems best to deserve the described function. A large ornate floral boss proceeds to the oval turned handle via a cranked stem and conical holder.

Servers 93a-d are the property of the Association of Vieux-Lausanne and the Community of Lausanne. They are in the Musée Historique de L'Ancien-Évêché, Lausanne; see Ref. (40) for further details.
By cooperation and courtesy of the Museum and of the publishers, Editions du Grand-Pont, Lausanne.

motif may even be associated with an obviously irrelevant function, as in the instance of the fish-shaped cover for a set of farrier's horse lancets that have sickle-shaped blades (45). A mason's trowel in the Los Angeles County Museum of Art by James Le Bas, Dublin, 1824, and used to lay the cornerstone of new premises for Rundell, Bridge and Rundell, has two engraved fish on the blade – but in this case it is a reference to the shop sign displaying two salmon. The second criterion is that if the server blade is unpierced (or, to push the rule, has small or inconspicuous piercings), then it is intended for the service of cake – or tart, pastry, pie, and pudding – i.e., other than for fish as such. Again, if the object is highly or effectively pierced, the implication is that it is intended for fish, as a strainer or lifter from oil or liquid, i.e., a hand-held drainer as opposed to a fixed place strainer or mazarine, which would automatically perform the straining function. The invariable use of the description, fish server, as applied to large, pierced plain ceramic trowels [Fig. I 15] in the catalogues of the late eighteenth century (I 16), supports the rule in British custom, at least. The extreme of this view would hold that a fish server *must* be so pierced. The Garrard Ledgers designate as "fish trowels" objects that are only *sometimes* specified as "pierced" (60); but this lack of distinction may be only a matter of carelessly succinct entries. In his research on the output of the Boulton-Fothergill partnership, Quickenden finds no mention of broad-bladed servers other than fish (61). Still another criterion that

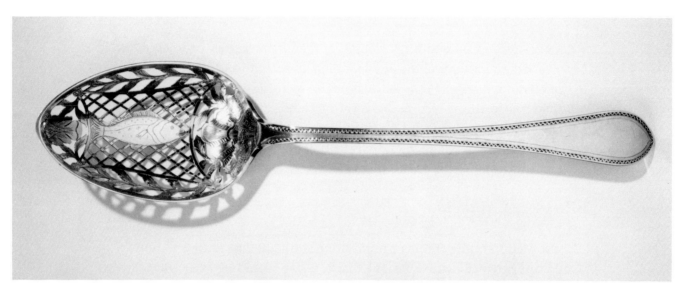

Finally, the highly pierced Strasbourg trowel by J.F. II Buttner, dated 1786 [Fig. 83], is called (52) "grande pelle à tarte"; its length is 37.4 cm. A smaller trowel (length 18.2 cm) with unpierced gilted blade [Fig. 33b] and dated 1773 (maker unknown) is called "pelle à tarte." This latter is another forerunner of the small trowel pastry or sandwich servers of the later nineteenth and twentieth centuries (another possible ascription will be made in Chapter VII) with regard to function. Both of these implements are furnished with rear aprons. A closely similar pair, c. 1780, illustrated in Ref. (47), are designated there as *fish slice* and *cake slice*, respectively.

The following limited propositions seem reasonable. If a trowel server displays fish or marine motif, then, whether pierced or not, it is most likely to be a fish slice. An unpierced server of suitable shape and having no marine motif may be assumed to be a pudding, cake, or pastry server. Application of these statements to pies or puddings cannot be made generically or unequivocally because of the highly variable connotations of those terms as discussed in Chapter II, even though Warden Pugh's gift argues for inclusion of the term *pudding* with cake and pastry. In any case, both the various kinds of implements, as well as the nomenclature, have been employed by owners and writers as has suited their wishes and custom, whether correctly or not; rarely was a versatile implement used for only one purpose. This theme will be resumed in Chapters IV and V.

## *Marks and Makers*

Notwithstanding frequent implication in the literature to the contrary, it would appear that, with foresight that a blade would be later pierced after hallmarking, the London assay marks tended to be stamped along an edge on the underside of the blade, in order to minimize subsequent mutilation. Earlier trowels often have the marks divided along both sides of the rear edge. On later trowels the marks were usually applied in a line, either on a side edge near the back of the blade or along the rear edge itself. It is, of course, true that the very high regard that now attaches to the preservation of a good set of marks was lacking at the time. Fortunate placement of the stamps so as to avoid mutilation might have been associated with personal pretensions or with commercial aspects.

Of course, not all placement was sufficiently providential as to avoid all hazard. In some cases, not only the piercing [e.g., Figs. 19,28] but the later shaping and cusping of the rear edge [e.g., Figs. 23,27] has (partially) obliterated the marks. Some marks have been boldly or carelessly stamped in the center area of the blade and have suffered accordingly. Irish servers, and some provincial pieces, tend to have the marks placed on the rear top side of the blade, on either side or sometimes divided on both sides. Servers having cutlery style silver handles were most frequently marked in conventional manner on the back bottom side of the stem, although some implements were marked on the blade.

Represented in the present gallery of early British trowels are three from Dublin, two Cork, one Edinburgh, one Newcastle, one York, and one from New York, if a cuckoo be included. The forty-odd British antique trowels shown in the figures were made by more than twenty silversmiths. Well-known early makers include John LeSage, John Harvey, Frederick Kandler, William Cripps, Edward Aldridge and Joseph Stamper, William Tuite, S. Herbert and Thomas Heming. The names of William Plummer, Thomas Nash, Basile Denn, and the firm of Charles Aldridge and Henry Green recur several times, especially the first and last of these. Certain later "B•D" marks (Chapter IV) do not correspond exactly to those recorded for Denn or Burrage Davenport, as replicated in Grimwade's treatise (54); as is well known, some relevant record books of marks of the Goldsmiths Company have been lost and the identification remains uncertain. William Plummer's name is particularly associated with the crafting of pierced objects; baskets were a favorite. Surprisingly, no trowels appear to have been made by Hester Bateman although she is well represented after 1775 in the long-oval category; this may be a side-light on the emergence of her family firm as a strong independent enterprise (55).

## References

1. J. de Bree, *Zeeuws Zilver*, Interbook International B.V., Schiedam, 1978.
2. M.L. Wurfbain, *Museum de Lakenhals*, Leiden, personal communication.
3. J.S. Fredericks and M. Nijhoff, *Dutch Silver*, The Hague, 1958.
4. N.V. Druk, *Fries Zilver*, Catalogue Fries Museum, Leeuwarden, 1968.
5. C. Hernmarck, A. Stavenow and G. Munthe, *Svenskt Silversmide, 1520-1850*, Nordiske Rotogravyr, Stockholm.
6. M. Meinz, *Schones Silber*, Klinkhardt und Biermann, Munich, 1964.
7. a) H. Domdey-Knodler, *Silver*, Battenberg Antiquitaten Kataloge, Battenberg Verlag, Munich, 1979.
   b) P.A.S. Phillips, *Paul De Lamerie*, Holland Press, London, 1968.
8. Dagmar Thormann, German National Museum, Nurenberg, personal communication.
9. Gerhard Dietrich, Kunstgewerbemuseum, Koln, personal communication.
10. C. Hernmarck, *The Art of the European Silversmith 1430-1830*, Vols. I and II, Sotheby-Parke-Bernet, New York, 1977, and personal communication.
11. J. Guiffray, *Inventaire Generale de Mobilier de la Couronne sous Louis XIV*, Paris (1885).
12. S. Brault and Y. Bottineau, *L'Orfèvrerie Francaise du XVIIIᵉ Siecle*, Presses Universitaire de France, Paris, 1954.
13. F. Dennis, *Three Centuries of French Domestic Silver*, Metropolitan Museum of Art, New York, 1960.
14. R.W. Lightbown, *French Silver*, Victoria and Albert Museum Catalogue, HMSO, London, 1978.
15. Teje Colling, Nordiska Museet, Stockholm, personal communication.
16. R. Came, *Silver*, Weidenfeld and Nicolson, London, 1961.
17. C. Boschma, *Catalogus*, Fries Museum, Leeuwarden, 1985, and personal communication.
18. W. Scheffler, *Fischheber*, Kunst und Antiquitaten, Part 2, 1976, and personal communication.
19. a) A. Gruber, *Silverware*, translated by D. Smith, Rizzoli, New York, 1982; and personal communication.
    b) C. Overzier, *Deutsches Silber*, 1550-1850, Klinkhardt und Biermann, München, 1987.

20. E. Barr, *George Wickes: Royal Goldsmith 1698-1761*, Rizzoli, New York, 1980.

21. J.B. Carrington and G.R. Hughes, *The Plate of The Worshipful Company of Goldsmiths*, Oxford University Press, 1926; see also the exhibition catalogue, *The Sterling Craft*, The Worshipful Company of Goldsmiths, London, 1966.

22. Philippa Glanville, Victoria and Albert Museum, London, personal communication. See also, Philippa Glanville, *Silver in England*, Unwin Hyman, London, 1987.

23. *Irish Silver 1630-1820. An Exhibition*, Irish Printer Limited, Dublin, 1971.

24. D. Bennett, *Collecting Irish Silver*, Souvenir, Dublin, 1984.

25. E. Lassen, *Knives, Forks and Spoons*, Høst, Copenhagen, 1960.

26. Phillips (Blenstock House) London, Sale No. 24,737, Nov. 30, 1983.

27. Henry W. Smart, *Country Life*, December 1974, and personal communication.

28. K.C. Buhler and G. Hood, *American Silver*, Yale University Press, New Haven, 1970, Vol II.

29. S.G.C. Ensko, *American Silversmiths and Their Marks*, Cracker Barrel Press, New York, 1937, p. 55.

30. K.M. McClinton, *Collecting American Nineteenth-Century Silver*, Bonanza Books, New York, 1967.

31. N. Dawson, *Goldsmiths and Silversmiths Work*, Methuen, London, 1907.

32. C. Oman, *English Domestic Silver*, Adam and Charles Black, London, 1968.

33. a) G. Taylor, *Silver*, Barnes and Noble, New York, 1964.
    b) I. Pickford, *Silver Flatware*, Antique Collectors Club, Suffolk, 1983.

34. S. Calloway, M. Snodin and C. Wainwright, *Horace Walpole and Strawberry-Hill*, London Borough of Richmond upon Thames, 1980.

35. C.J. Shrubsole, S.J. Shrubsole Limited, personal communication.

36. T. Krohn-Hansen and R. Kloster, *Bergens Gullsmedkunst fra Langstiden*, Vestlandske Kunstindustrimuseum, Bergen, 1956.

37. G. Boesen and C.A. Boje, translated by R. Kay, *Old Danish Silver*, Hassing, Copenhagen, 1949.

38. J. Fossberg, I.-M. Lie, J-L, Opstad, *Oslo Solv I 400 ÅR*, Kunstindustrimuseet, Norsk Folkemuseum and Oslo Bullsmedlaug, 1979.

39. A. Polak, *Norwegian Silver*, Dreyers, 1972.

40. M. Grandjean, M.C. Jecquier and M. Panicali, *L'Argenterie du Vieux Lausanne*, Editions du Grand Pont, Lausanne.

41. H. Wykes, Antiques Magazine, Vol. 10, No. 2, 1926.

42. Phillips (Blenstock House) London, Sale No. 26,404, Dec. 5, 1986, Lot 43.

43. Rosemarie Ransome-Wallace, Goldsmiths Company, London, personal communication.

44. E. Klein, *Comprehensive Etymological Dictionary of the English Language*, Elsevier, London, 1967.

45. E. Bennion, *Antique Medical Instruments*, Sotheby-Parke-Bernet, London, 1979.

46. Captioning of exhibit at Victoria and Albert Museum, London, November 1986.

47. H. Brunner, *Old Table Silver*, translated by J. Seligman, Faber and Faber, London, 1967.

48. J.D. Davis, *English Silver at Williamsburg*, University Press of Virginia, Charlottesville, 1976.

49. M. Clayton, *Christie's Pictorial History of English and American Plate*, Phaidon, Avon, 1985.

50. J. van Loo, Epse, private communication.

51. *Irish Silver*, Smithsonian Traveling Exhibition, 1982.

52. H. Haug, *L'Orfèvrerie de Strasbourg*, Editions des Musées Nationaux, Paris, 1978.

53. Sotheby Parke Bernet, New York, Sale No. 4039, October 1977.

54. A.G. Grimwade, *London Goldsmiths 1697-1837*, Faber and Faber, London, 1976.

55. D.S. Shure, *Hester Bateman*, Doubleday, 1959.

56. V. Brett, *The Sotheby Directory of Silver*, Sotheby's Publications, London, 1986.

57. N.D. Turner, *American Silver Flatware 1837-1910*, Barnes, Cranbury, N.J., 1972.

58. K.A. Citroen, Haarlemse Zilversmeden, 1988, and personal communication.

59. G. Goedhard, *De Stavelij*, vol. 4, pp. 3-6, 1989.

60. H. Clifford, Ph.D. Thesis, Royal College of Art, London, 1988, and personal communication.

61. K. Quickenden, City of Birmingham Polytechnic, personal communication.

62. John Culme, *The Directory of Gold and Silversmiths, 1838-1914*, Antique Collectors Club, Woodbridge, Suffolk, 1987.

Chapter IV

# LONG-OVAL SERVERS

## *History*

THE FLAT-BLADED, long-oval or near-elliptical British server apparently first appeared in 1775. It thus overlapped the triangular trowel for only a few years. No earlier examples have been seen by the writer. When such is alleged, the example may be considered suspect and likely will be found not to possess a date letter. Why the long-ovals appeared in England as abruptly as they did and why they took the elongated blade form are both something of a mystery. The reader is reminded that the chapter title is merely conveniently descriptive. These pierced wares continued to be known at the time as fish (or pudding) slices, trowels, and spades (1), while the name, *fish knife*, for these (and the later scimitars) also came into use around this time (2). The latter term may lead to confusion with fish eater place cutlery of the latter half of the nineteenth century. One well-known auction house has currently used the terminology *cake knife* to designate these early servers (3).

Another difference from the trowel exists also with respect to the historical sequel of these articles. That a new implement of cutlery should appear in response to a perceived need, real or cultivated, is not surprising. That the silver trowel almost disappeared completely at this time in English manufacture, apart from occasional reproductions in the nineteenth century, is more startling. In any event, such was not to be the fate of the long-oval server. Although losing in popularity to the scimitar, which shortly became the preferred blade shape, the manufacture of the long-oval never did cease and it continued in intermittent production through the first half of the nineteenth century, albeit in slightly reduced size. It shared in the later Victorian eclectic resurgence of earlier styles, with greater frequency of appearance in the pairs of fork and slice that became modish toward the latter half of the nineteenth century. At that time, when a family owned an eighteenth- or early nineteenth-century server, sometimes a fork was ordered in matching pattern in order to bring the service up to latest fashion [Figs. 21, V 41]. This was certainly a more provident practice than the centuries-old custom of melting down old silver and remaking it.

As was discussed in Chapter III, and is considered again below in later sections, the Continental long-oval server appears to be simply an evolutionary form of the elongated round-shouldered oval trowel, with less well-differentiated physical dimensions and having no pronounced difference in service function. Very few long-oval American servers were made in the late eighteenth and early part of the next century.

Both trowel and long-oval shapes persisted together on the Continent for longer periods and more abundantly than did the British wares. Contemporaneous long-ovals appeared in Holland alongside the unique transverse oval servers; the latter reappeared in the later nineteenth and early twentieth century as crudely modelled cast articles. All competed with the more common scimitars in the nineteenth century.

## *Blade Shape*

British trowels, even those having rounded shoulders or sides, are always easily differentiable by type from the later long-ovals. They are distinguished by either, and usually both, of two criteria. First, whereas the triangular blades of Chapter III have their greatest breadth in the rear half of the blade, the long-ovals (which are only occasionally near-ellipses) have their maximum breadth at the middle, or, usually, in the front half of the blade [Figs. 3-41]. Second, the relative dimensions of the two types of servers differ. Unlike the British trowel, whose ratio of lengths of major to minor blade axes is almost invariably less than 1.75 and usually less than 1.6, ranging down to 1.2, the new blade shape possessed axes whose ratio of major to minor dimension was usually greater than 2.0, ranging up to 2.7. The earlier British eighteenth-century long-oval blades conform to the general dimensions of 16-19 cm in length and 5.5-8 cm in breadth. In the later 1780s and 1790s, the long ovals tended to be shorter, 14-16 cm, and relatively wider, 6.5-9 cm.

No long-oval examples may violate both of these tests, although some near-pathologic exceptions exist [cf. Figs. III 89, III 93 and 43], and the De Lamerie trowels come close. An interesting variant is the elongated trowel by G. Smith, London, 1776 [Fig. III 52b], for which the above ratio has risen to 2.4; it seems plausible that this smith was influenced in its design by the new long-ovals. He made a number of slices having this shape and decor at this time (18). Its designation as a fish slice is clearly manifest by its delightful fish motif. The Burrows slice of Fig. III 58 is an example of a long-oval that has a trowel feeling. A contrary kind of near-exception is found in the Old Sheffield Pattern Books of Boulton and Watt (1): Volume 1 of that series for the years 1761-1790 displays [Fig. 1] a *drawing* of a cake trowel that is almost long-oval in shape; the junction boss is an applied acanthus leaf and connects to a turned wooden handle. Still another example shown is a trowel that is also almost long-oval in shape and is fitted with

1.    Drawings from the Old Sheffield Pattern Books of Boulton and Watt, Vol. I, 1761-90. The slices are approximately 30 cm in length. The four upper long-ovals bear fish engraving, and one (uppermost right) has the abstract fish shape; they all have filled handles in-plane with the blade. The next two lower servers (one on each side of the illustration) are actually trowels whose maximum diameter is just back of the center point of the blade; the near-elliptic one on the left clearly qualifies as a judgement call; the one on the right, with wood or ivory handle and acanthus leaf boss is unpierced and may be called a cake slice. The lowest slice (right side) is a George II style trowel, completely pierced with crosslets — quite out of period.
Courtesy of Birmingham City Library.

an oval 'split-penny' boss (*vide infra*) that leads to a filled handle; the filled handle fixes the date of the illustration as post-1775. Interesting at this late date is an illustration of a conventional trowel of baroque George II style. Figure 2 shows another example of a 'judgement call.' These articles, which may never have entered manufacture, are the sole British examples that the writer has so far seen that are reminiscent of the transitional eighteenth-century Continental trowel shapes illustrated earlier in Chapter III.

Figures 3-41 provide a chronological display of the stylistic evolution of British long-oval servers. A cut-off date of 1800 has arbitrarily been applied; unlike Continental articles, British servers of this type, in the first half of the nineteenth century, tend to be utilitarian rather than highly decorative, and are interleaved chronologically with scimitar slices in Chapter V [see, for example, Figs. V 14, V 37].

It should be noted that despite the choice of name, i.e., near-elliptical or long-oval, some of these servers have straight sides. But they still conform to the second criterion and reference to Figs. 10,17 shows how easily recognizable they are as being of the present type. Apart from some modest asymmetry displayed by a few very early long-ovals described in the section on Function and termed *knife shapes*, these slices are symmetrical with respect to the long axis of the blade. However, they are usually not symmetrical with respect to the short axis. The base of the blade to which the handle is attached is frequently truncated, and the curvature of the sides at the back or heel of the blade departs from that of the forward half of the blade. The back edge can be flat [Figs. 10,11,20,37], concave re-entrant [Figs. 16,22,39], or convex [Figs. 15,17], or virtually non-existent [Figs. 24,27], with or without cusps or scallops. However, a few examples do exist of servers that are completely symmetric about both major blade axes [Figs. 17,40] and some are almost elliptic [Figs. 24,27,46]. These near-elliptical servers are a doubly-symmetric form of the long-oval server. Those with pointed ends are sometimes described as being of navette form. The De Lamerie servers *approach* these types in shape, but are of broader proportions and just slightly wider in the rear half of the blade, as characterizes the trowel shape.

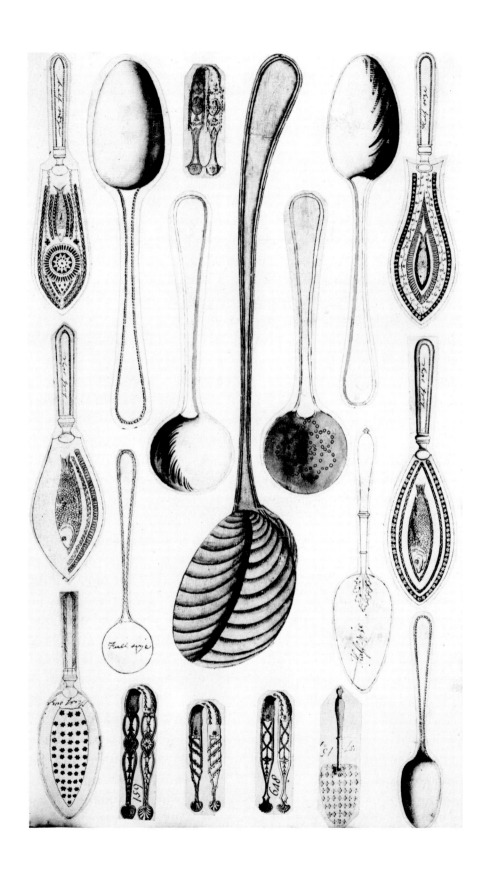

Later slices, starting around the mid-1780s, tended to be broader than the earlier ones. They were sometimes given an abstract fish influence with tail-like projections or nubs toward the rear end of the blade [Figs. 22,27,32,38]. This style was continued sometimes in almost absurd appeal, as witness the tabs at the base of the nineteenth-century modified (acorn shape) long-oval in Fig. VI 13. An example of imaginative realism in a long-oval is shown by the fish-shaped Inverness example in Fig. 41. Several near-replicas of this rare shape, including Old Sheffield, exist (15,16). They post-date the earlier Scandinavian fish-shaped blades [Fig. III 84].

Some long-ovals were made in the shape of rounded-corner oblong rectangles, particularly in the period 1790-1830 when many *transient* shapes occurred alongside the more familiar scimitar shapes of that period; these are discussed in Chapter VI. The rounded-corner oblong blade actually made a very early appearance. Examples for the years 1778 and 1780 are shown in Figs. 12,15. The blade of the 1780 implement is highly and symmetrically engraved and decorated on both sides; the 1778 server is not engraved and is a later example [cf. Fig. III 49] in a server of the rarer and plainer neogothic style extolled by Horace Walpole and his associates (III 34.) These slices are unique in several ways. They are some of the very earliest oblongs and also some of the very earliest examples of servers having a soldered raised side; and, in these particular cases, they also have a scalloped or wavy edge to the raised side. An early long-oval by Hester Bateman, London, 1778, with raised wavy edge, is shown in Ref. (17). The raised edge obviously defines both the top side of the blade and the left edge as the cutting edge. The destruction of the symmetry of the flat blade by the raised right edge identifies the server as being 'right-handed.' Left-handed ones have not been seen. This, in itself, is not surprising; until recently, left-handed persons have usually been expected to conform to right-handed custom. Nor were bladed servers used in pair, at least in the early nineteenth century, as revealed in accounts of the social etiquette of the times (4). Rather, serving spoons were conveniently placed to hand in table setting in order to facilitate any required two-handed operation.

Servers with a raised right rim ostensibly exhibited an improved serving function, i.e., to lift and retain the serving portion. However, unlike the later nineteenth-century table crumber, the raised edge scarcely seems necessary for the performance of the basic function of this implement. The crumber required its edge because it could replace *two* early articles — the narrower voiding knife and the

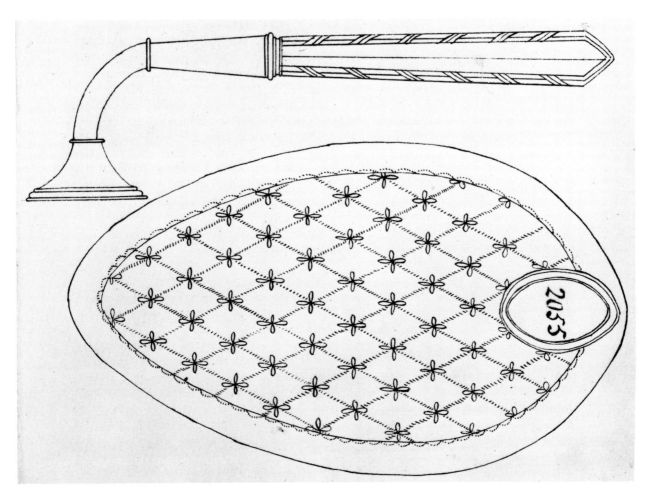

2055

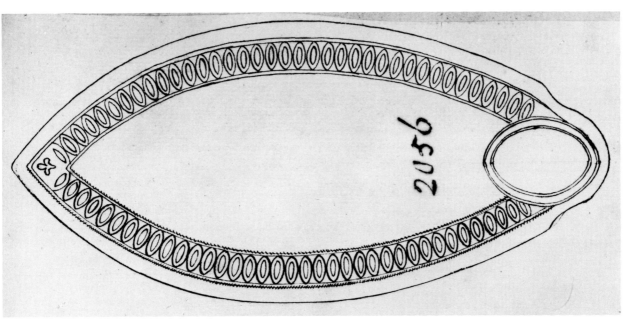

2056

121

3.     Long-oval FISH SLICE, Wm. Plummer, London, 1775; length 30.5 cm; handle, rubbed W.S. (?), no date mark. The flat blade is engraved on both sides. The blade has a frieze of laurel leaves. It encloses an engraved pierced area of scrolls — foliage, reeds — in which are found four fish and a dolphin. It is sharpened on both edges. The blade is held by a split penny junction at the rear edge, below an unpierced area of engraved leafage. Although the pierced area was removed from the junction, the concave curves at the heel of the blade make that area very narrow and prone to cracking at the boss. The latter is integral with a short, oval, waisted shank that connects in the plane of the blade to a crested reeded octagonal filled handle. This date represents what is believed by the author to be the earliest British long-oval servers.

4.     Long-oval FISH SLICE, Chas. Aldridge and Henry Green, London 1775; length 30 cm; handle, CA and HG, no date mark. The flat blade is singularly unadorned for this early period. It is lightly engraved on both sides with flower accents within the simple piercing of circles, scrolls, quatrefoils, and a star. The split boss and short oval waisted shank connect to a reeded oval filled handle. This implement could well be a cake server, as could its companions.

5.     Long-oval FISH SLICE, Wm. Plummer, London, 1776; length 30.3 cm; handle, rubbed W.S. (?), no date mark. The flat blade is undecorated around a central, pierced engraved reserve of scrolling foliage and two fishes at right angles. The split penny boss and waisted shank lead to an octagonal beaded filled handle with stamped shell terminal.

6.     Long-oval FISH SLICE, Robt. Hennell I, London, 1776; length 29.7 cm; handle, W.S., no date letter. Grimwade lists several possibilities for this W.S. mark, who is also the presumed source of the handles in Figs. 1 and 3. The rather broad flat blade has a bright-cut dash dot circumferential frieze which encloses a totally pierced, highly engraved area of neoclassical motifs — laurel leaf swags, an urn, a starburst, a lobed flower — and scrolling foliage, and two crossed dolphins. This underside photograph illustrates the complete decoration of *both* sides of the these early long-ovals. The blade and piercing were cast but also later worked over in some areas with a saw. The rear end of the blade is curved so concavely as to leave only a narrow tongue to which the handle is attached. The split penny boss and short round waisted shank lead to a filled octagonal feather-edged handle with double-shell finial ornament.

7.     Long-oval FISH/CAKE SLICE; Robt. Hennell I, 1776, length 31.5 cm; handle, rubbed W? mark, no date mark. The flat blade has a circumferential frieze of bright cutting and double wrigglework lines around a pierced engraved area of laurel wreaths, swags, and a central star burst. The unpierced area is bright cut with a floral bouquet. The split penny boss is outlined by bright cut flutes. The waisted shank connects to an octagonal, beaded, crested, filled handle having a shell ornament [cf. Fig. 5]. The narrow tongue to which the handle is attached makes the blade susceptible to cracking at the boss, notwithstanding the absence of piercing in this area (unlike trowels). The term *cake* is a summary designation that includes pudding, pie, tart, and pastry of various sorts; it is a designation favored by Continental scholars.

8.     Long-oval CAKE/FISH KNIFE, Wm. Plummer, London, 1776; length 31.5 cm; handle W.S., no date letter. This flat blade appears to be cast and is more highly decorated than that in Fig. 9 of similar asymmetric shape. The rear edge is blunt. It has a circumferential frieze of oak leaves and engraved decoration that carries to the rear of the blade. The center of the blade is pierced and engraved with a basket and scrolling foliage and flowers. The absence of the fish motif of Fig. 9 encourages a variable designation of function. The split penny boss and short baluster stem lead to another hollow handle similar to that of Fig. 7.

9.      Long-oval FISH KNIFE, Chas. Aldridge and Henry Green, London, 1777; length 31.2 cm.; handle, CA and HG, no date mark. The asymmetric blade helps explain why these long-oval slices were also known as fish knives; the rear edge is quite blunt and has no cutting function. The plain perimeter encloses a pierced, engraved scrolled area on which a fish is stiffly posed. The split penny boss and short oval shank connect to an octagonal beaded filled handle with shell terminal [cf. Fig. 7]. The blade and handle have matching crests and monograms.

10.     Long-oval FISH SLICE, Burrage Davenport, 1777; length 31 cm; handle, CA and HG overstamped, undated. The heavy flat blade is cast. It has parallel sides and the familiar neoclassical frieze of laurel leaves. The central area is pierced and engraved with scrolls and a heron with a fish in its bill, and a second fish above passively awaiting its fate. The split boss is oval in shape and proceeds *via* a short oval stem to the crested and beaded filled handle which was either supplied to BD or is a later replacement.

11.     Long-oval SERVER, Thos. Daniel, London, 1777; length 31 cm; handle W? rubbed, no date letter. The blade is cast with incurves to a flat rear edge [cf. Fig. 10]. There is a peripheral bright-cut zigzag band that surrounds a highly pierced and engraved Tree of Jesse bearing fruits and flowers. The oval split boss leads *via* a short, waisted stem to a beaded handle having ribbon and tie borders.

12.     Oblong SERVER, Wm. Plummer, 1778; length 28.4 cm; crested handle, maker rubbed. The oblong, slightly double-dished blade is cast or made from cast sheet. The rear blade edge is a cusped convex curve. It has peripheral bands of bright-cut and engraved zigzag. There is a very minor row of stamped cross-hatched circles at the base of the piercing, and floral engraving on the split penny boss. There is no decoration at all on the underside — the first instance of such omission in the present collection. The piercing takes the form of vertically cusped pales, in neogothic mode. This is one of the earliest slices to display an applied raised side. It clearly defines the implement as a right-handed server. The top edge of the raised side is waved, and has some minor engraved decoration on both of its sides. The boss, round stem, and beaded filled handle are analogous to the preceding examples.

13.     Long-oval CAKE/FISH KNIFE, no makers mark, Edinburgh, 1780; length 32.5 cm; crested handle completely unmarked. This server appears to be a copy of the earlier London articles [cf. Fig. 9] in shape, engraving and piercing design. Some differences are the oval split boss and beaded pointed handle; also the marks appear on the upper surface here, but on the undersurface in Fig. 9.

14.     Long-oval CAKE/FISH SLICE, Hester Bateman, London, 1780; length 30 cm; handle, rubbed ?S mark. The flat blade shows both neoclassical and neogothic influence. The pierced longitudinal arched pales are separated by pierced circles. Apart from a small vacant reserve, the whole surface is embellished by bright cutting and zigzag adornment. The split-penny boss proceeds to a very short, waisted turned stem and a filled handle that is decorated with beading. This blade pattern, with other handles including ivory, was made by the Bateman firm over a period of approximately ten years.

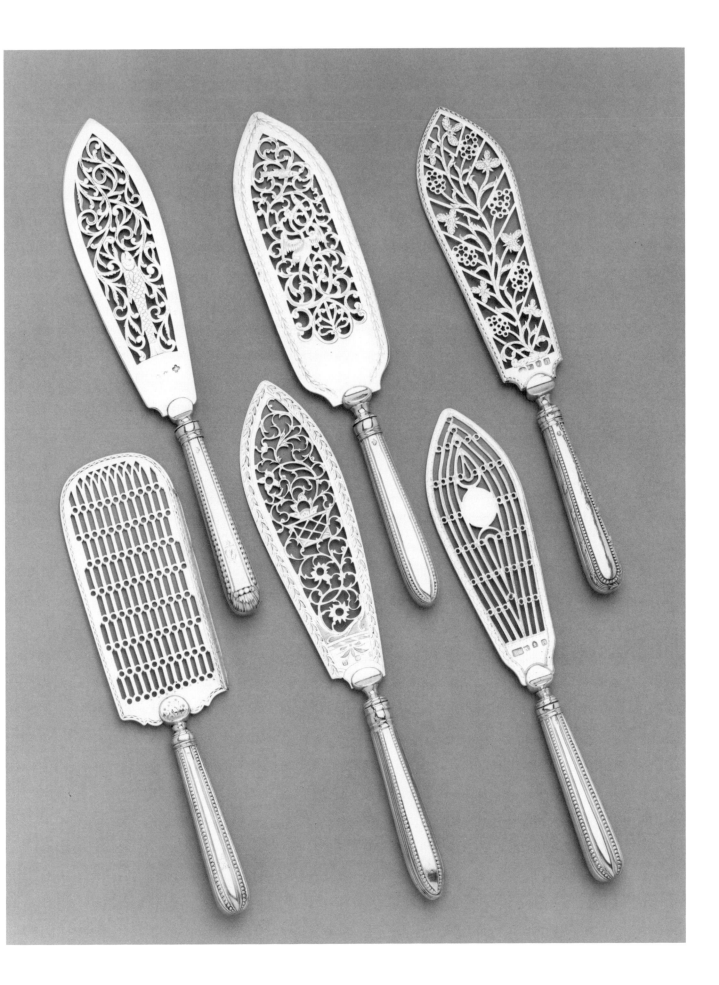

15.   Oblong SERVER, Wm. Plummer, London, 1780; length 29 cm; handle, W.S., undated. This raised side, cast blade server is very similar in shape and structure to the earlier one by this maker [Fig. 12]. However, the decoration is completely neoclassical. Apart from the reserve around the handle junction, the surface is completely pierced and covered with bright cutting and engraving and zigzag work in familiar frieze, bell-flower, scrolling and rayed motifs. The decoration on the underside is fully as elaborate. The bright-cut and engraved split-penny boss proceeds *via* a short, waisted balustered stem to a crested beaded filled handle.

16.   Long-oval FISH/CAKE SLICE, Jas. Waters, London, 1781; length 31.8 cm; handle, rubbed marks. The flat blade is of great weight and thickness, and is made by soldering two sheets together, the top of which appears cast. The blade edge is strongly bevelled all around. The blade is highly pierced with engraved scrolls, flowers, and palmette bouquet in an urn, and with a peripheral, bright-cut zigzag band. The simulated penny boss and rising stem are a cast one-piece assembly, and represent the first example of a stem with lift in the present chronology. Another first are the marks which are laid along the right rear side edge — rather than across the rear (usually underside) edge of the blade as in all the preceding examples. The filled handle is reeded and has two vacant laurel leaf cartouches, top and bottom.

17.   Long-oval SERVER, Chas. Aldridge and Henry Green, London, 1781; length 33.5 cm; handle by same. The flat blade has double symmetry and is of 'race track' shape, with parallel sides. The front three-quarters of the blade is completely pierced and engraved with neoclassical motifs; the underside, by contrast, has only minimal engraving. A band of bell flowers completely encircles the blade and contains a horseshoe band of twisted ribbon. The boss is an applied pear shape that rises by a flattened solid stem to a filled handle similar to that of Figs. 9 and 10. A similar shape by these makers has fish engraving and a raised side.

18.   Long-oval FISH SLICE, Old Sheffield, unmarked, c. 1780; length 31 cm; ivory handle. The flat crested blade is fly cut with a frieze of ten stylized fish and a central pattern of engraved scroll work; it is decorated equally on both sides. The edge of the blade is heavily bevelled with no applied silver edges. The crest is not set in. The oval split boss leads through a short, oval, split-soldered stem to a ferrule socket that holds the green-stained fluted handle.

19.   Long-oval PUDDING SERVER, Wm. Plummer, London, 1781; length 30 cm; handle, W.N.?, undated. The plain blade is undecorated apart from a large central crest. The blade is unpierced and strongly dished in the forward half so as to become somewhat spoon-like. Hence its designation as a pudding — pie, cake — server. The same blade shape by Plummer, dated 1782 and pierced with a floral pattern, has been seen. The rear edge is cusped. The split-penny junction is connected to the completely fluted, ovate filled handle by a waisted short stem. A simulated ferrule is defined by a double band of beading.

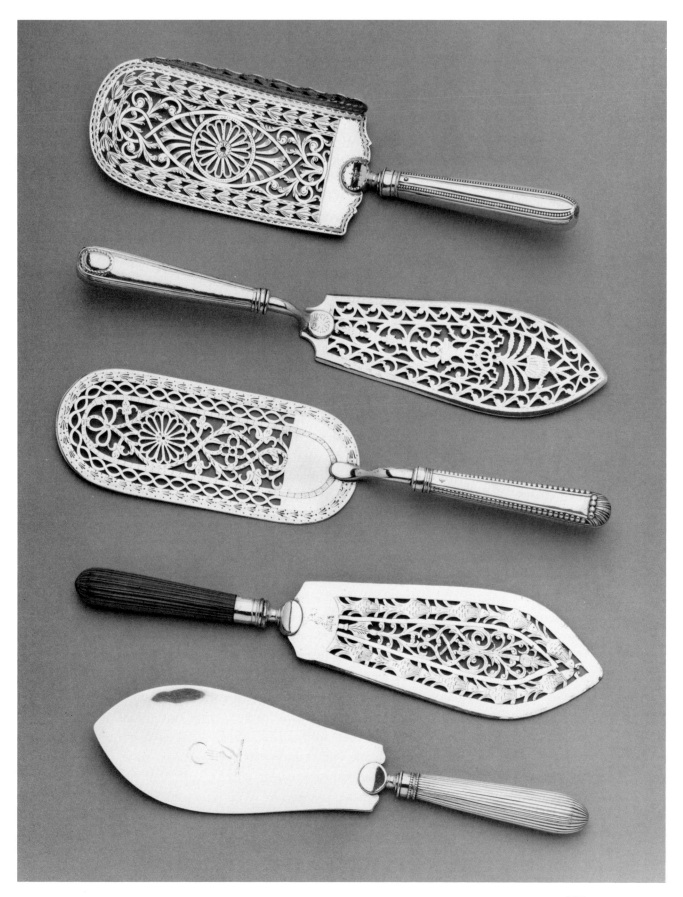

voiding dish (5,6). Undoubtedly, the scalloped decorated side rim strengthens the server blade and adds to the total decorative effect. In any case, the later nineteenth-century table crumber should not be confused with the raised side server. The former nearly always features a perfectly straight or slightly curved left side and a sharply raised edge rim that embraces virtually the rest of the blade [Fig. III 63b].

The raised-side long-oval server occurs more often in the early 1780s and 1790s and particularly in examples made by R. Hennell [Fig. 25] and the Batemans [Fig. 37]. The proportion of raised-side pre-1800 servers is small, being on the order of 20% in the present collection (with the largest percentage for those of the 1790s and much less later for scimitars). Toward the end of the century, the raised side sometimes took on the form of a stamped, or hammered, rolled right edge [Figs. 34,35].

Long-oval blades were invariably flat in the first five years of their history, and frequently so in the 1780s. During that decade and the next, however, blades that were dished either around the short axis, or double dished with respect to both axis, also appeared. The resulting nonplanar conformation gives an apparent lift to the stem and handle even when such does not actually exist [Figs. 27-29,31,32]. This theme is resumed below in the section on Handles. Such dishing makes the server much stronger and able to withstand deformation; more spoon-like and able to hold a serving of fragmentary nature more securely; and slightly less adaptable as a cutting instrument. Strengthening might well have been the primary motivation for dishing such servers since they were susceptible to cracking of the blade or the piercing; this is considered below. One robust, thick-bladed slice by Jas. Waters, London, 1782, is unusual in that the flat blade is a sandwich of two thinner sheets soldered together [Fig. 16].

The same facility for distinguishing long-oval and trowel types described at the outset of this section does not apply to Continental servers. As was seen in Chapter III, these are much more difficult to categorize in some instances. Some servers have a shape and feeling that are intermediate between that of the trowel and the oval ellipse, or are otherwise difficult to discriminate, particularly when the shoulders are highly rounded [Fig. 43]. In such cases, it is a discretionary call [Fig. 46; cf. Fig. III 89]. In any case, by the last quarter of the eighteenth century, long-oval servers resembled their British counterparts very closely; highly orna-mented wares with neoclassical or Empire decoration were more persistent and continued well into the nineteenth century. Like the trowel, some Continental and American long-ovals also featured rear aprons [Fig. 45] as well as structural continuity between blade and shank with elimination of the boss, as in the Amsterdam example of 1804 by Jan Buysem (7). It will be sufficient here to provide a few illustrations of all of these. In order to avoid later repetition, their presentation is reserved to the following sections [Figs. 42-50].

## Handles

Long-oval servers before 1800 were not provided with solid silver handles. The most common type was the filled silver knife handle made mainly by the Sheffield and Birmingham haft makers. These were stamped from thin sheet in halves, in a variety of cross-sections, and might incorporate impressed decoration such as beading, fluting, and shells. The halves were joined by a miracle of virtually invisible soldering. The handles did not necessarily carry their original maker's mark. By contrast, it may be remembered that, with one or two later exceptions, trowels were not equipped with filled silver handles but had either a solid silver handle or a baluster wood or ivory handle that was connected to the blade *via* a silver bolster shaft, frequently cast and of ornate design.

Early filled handle attachment to the long oval blade was made via a short, straight, waisted [e.g., Figs. 3-8], and sometimes balustered [Figs. 27-29] stem of circular configuration that had a flat face and a tang at the handle end. An early stem was 3-5 mm in length; a later one by 1790 might be 1-2 cm in length. It was attached to the blade at its other end by a wedge-shaped concave-sided split penny boss, 4-5 mm in thickness at the forward thin edge and 6-10 mm at the rear. The boss is approximately 15-20 mm in diameter and grasps both sides of the blade. It was round in plan, at first [e.g., Figs. 3-8] but, shortly, oval contours also appeared; the long axis of the oval was placed parallel to the short axis of the blade [Figs. 11,23,28] and is 18-25 mm in length. The boss itself was sometimes decorated with bright cutting, engraving, or dot-dash and wriggle work. In size, it is smaller than the junctions employed with trowel blades. This corresponds in some measure to the comparatively narrow rear ends of the elliptical blades. Unlike the trowel blades, whose pierced decoration frequently encroaches on or even encompasses the handle junction, the earliest long-ovals usually reserve up to an inch or so of the heel surface of the blade free of piercing; and in later models as much as two or more inches may be left solid. As a consequence, the near-elliptical servers were somewhat more free of the curse of blade cracking along a transverse line at the front of the boss than were trowels. However, because of its use as a cutter, and as occurred also in the case of the even more robust scimitar blades that could be employed with powerful force, both of these types often do exhibit evidence of cracking of the blade. The more fragile tracery of the long-ovals, like the trowels, also frequently give evidence of previous abuse by cracks in their piercing. Unlike the trowels, whose blades were never reinforced by a heel plate at the junction in order to prevent cracking, the occasional long-oval slice was so treated as part of the original design, as opposed to later repair and reinforcement. Such original strengthening was also occasionally, if a little more frequently, a feature of scimitar construction; the work of the Batemans in particular seems to exhibit this feature, as in a 1797 long-oval [Fig. 37].

20.   Long-oval FISH SLICE, Hester Bateman, London, 1782; length 30.3 cm; handle, marks rubbed. The flat crested blade has a circumferential band of zigzag and bright-cut ornament. A highly pierced area in the forward three-quarters of the blade displays vines, leaves, a flower bouquet in an urn, and a pair of crossed dolphins diving into the briny. The boss, stem and handle are of standard type [cf. Fig. 14]. The same piercing pattern is shown in another slice of this date but with ivory handle; see M. Holland, *Silver,* Octopus, London, 1973, p. 65.

21.   Serving pair; long-oval SERVER, Robt. Hennell I, London, 1782; length 30 cm; handle, ?B, rubbed; FORK, W. and J. Barnard, London, 1883; length 25 cm; handle Francis Higgins, London, 1883. The server has a flat crested blade that is lightly decorated on both sides with bright cutting and zigzag engraving and is pierced with lunettes, pales and circles. The split penny boss, stem and handle are similar to Figs. 9 and 10. The fork, made 100 years later, has matching crest, decoration, piercing pattern, and filled handle. The split boss is oblong, while the flattened stem, of different design from that of the server, is elongated, shaped, balustered and multiply waisted. The combination of articles reflected the changed situation — labor and manufacturing costs exceeded the value of the silver and it was quite uneconomical to melt down old silver in order to conform to a new style (see Chapter V, Pairs).

22.   Long-oval FISH SLICE, Burrage Davenport, London, 1782; length 31 cm; handle, Moses Brent (?), rubbed, London, 1808. In usual fashion, the marks lie across the rear underside edge of the blade and one is clipped by the (later) shaping. The plain blade shows what may be called incipient fish tail nubs [cf. Figs. 27,32,38]. The surface is plain, apart from pierced bands of longitudinal pales around an urn with sprouting foliage and central star burst. The rounded V-boss rises on an integral flattened stem to a filled handle that is fluted on its rear half. There are mismatched crests on blade and handle; a good example of the many later handle replacements.

23.   Long-oval FISH SLICE, George Smith III, London, 1783; length 30.5 cm; handle, CA and HG, rubbed. The thick flat blade has a circumferential band of interlaced zigzag, accentuated by bright cutting. The upper two-thirds of the pierced work represents a potted flowering tree with scrolled embellishments; the lower third, a fish trapped in seaweed. The surface is freshly engraved and chased on both sides. The saw piercing is crudely irregular. The edges are strongly bevelled. The top surface exhibits a bold well-executed contemporary monogram. The split oval junction and short, waisted stem lead to a clearly original, octagonal filled handle that has a double shell stamped terminal on both sides.

24.   Long-oval SERVER, Wm. Abdy, London, 1784; length 30 cm; handle, Wm. Abdy. The doubly symmetric, elliptical or navette blade is double dished, and is pierced with bands of horizontal and vertical pales and circles. It has a bright-cut central vacant reserve. There is a little bright-cut zigzag and laurel leaf decoration, with lesser embellishment on the underside of the blade. A V-boss and flattened stem rises with lift to the filled beaded handle. The marks lie across the rear underside of the blade. The article does very well as a pudding or pie server among other possible uses. Abdy seemed to favor this shape.

25.    Long-oval SERVER, Robt. Hennell I, London, 1785; length 30.5 cm; ivory handle. This somewhat weary article is of interest in illustrating several newer features: an applied raised side; engraved and bright-cut decoration only on the top surface; a pierced area of urn and scrolling foliage which has moved well forward onto the blade; and marks laid along the rear left underside edge of the blade. The V-boss lifts to the natural colored handle. Hennell made quite a number of this type during the decade.

26.    Long-oval FISH SLICE, Robt. Hennell I, London, 1785; length 31.5 cm; carved ivory handle. Another server by Hennell similar in spirit to Fig. 25: moderately engraved only topside, the pierced area well forward; and the marks along the right rear underside edge of the blade. The vertical fish and dolphin signify that this is a fish server; that in Fig. 25 may be thought of as a cake or tart slice.

27.    Long-oval FISH/PUDDING SLICE, Wm. Plummer, London, 1786; length 29 cm; handle, Moses Brent, London. The near-elliptic, unpierced blade is completely undecorated save for a large central monogram. It escapes ellipticity by virtue of two weak rear nubs, called fish tail here [cf. Figs. 32,38]. The small blade is double-dished and eminently spoon-like for serving puddings, but more specific function is confused by the weak, abstract fish allusion. The split-penny boss leads *via* an extended, double-waisted and balustered stem to a crested, in-plane reeded hollow handle. The marks are placed underside on the front part of the right edge — an unusual position. This smith, renowned for his pierced work, is responsible for a surprising percentage of unpierced blades.

28.    Long-oval FISH SLICE, Hester Bateman, London, 1788; length 29.7 cm; handle, Moses Brent, London, undated. The relatively short, broad, slightly double-dished blade is in the form of an abstract fish. The blade has a frieze of engraved zigzag swags and an inner horseshoe band of pierced and bright-cut flower heads. A central elliptical band of bright-cut lunettes and dot engraving enclose a decorated bouquet of foliage. The underside is unadorned. The split oval boss goes over to a double waisted, balustered beaded stem and in-plane reeded filled handle. The marks are laid underside along the rear right edge, as now occurs most frequently. The double-waisted stem evidently became popular at this time [cf. Figs. 27,29].

29.    Long-oval SERVER, no makers mark, London, 1790; length 28.3 cm; handle, Moses Brent, undated. The blade is slightly dished around the short axis only; it is another short broad blade that illustrates a diminished area given over to piercing — in this case a band of interlaced ribbon with internal floral structure, and a central area of scrolling with a starburst. The engraving is somewhat perfunctory — mainly wavy and straight bands of dot wheel-engraving, and some bright cutting and an oval cartouche. The underside is plain. The small split-penny boss leads *via* a doubly waisted and balustered stem to an in-plane reeded filled handle. The marks are laid along the right rear under edge.

30.     Long-oval SERVER, Henry Chawner, London, 1790; length 32.5 cm; handle, R.T. The doubly dished blade of this article has reverted to earlier dimensions and shape, but the pierced area is still relatively reduced and well forward; it depicts an engraved and bright-cut flowering shrub in a two-handled vase. The periphery of the blade is decorated with a continuous line of bright-cut swags and exterior and interior double arcs of dot and wrigglework. A bright-cut octagonal cartouche holds a crest. The V-boss has an engraved star and the stem has lift to a reeded filled handle. The implement has been used for heavy cutting, as is revealed by the lateral distortion of the stem.

31.     Long-oval PUDDING/FISH SLICE, Wm. Plummer, London, 1790; length 28 cm; handle, John Tatum, London. The small plain undecorated spoon-like blade is doubly dished. It features a central pierced fish net design. The split-penny boss and short waisted stem carry to a reeded filled handle. The marks lie along the central right underside edge.

32.     Long-oval FISH SLICE, John Blake, London, 1792; length 28.,5 cm; handle, W.G. & Co., Sheffield (?). The short broad blade is of stylized fish shape. The blade and small pierced area are heavily bright-cut and engraved with bands of foliage, flowers, scrolls, and central starburst, together with an oval cartouche and contemporary monogram. A double line of hit and miss wheel work surrounds the double-dished blade and the decorated, applied, simulated split-penny boss [cf. the boss of Fig. 16]. A flattened stem lifts to a stamped reeded handle with additional wrigglework lines. The underside is plain with marks on the right rear side edge.

33.     Long-oval SERVER, no maker's mark, Edinburgh, 1793; length 30.5 cm; handle unmarked. The shape and size of the blade is similar to Fig. 26 and earlier types. But the decorative pattern has moved on to a style common in the next several decades; namely, a horseshoe shape of pierced and bright-cut packed acanthus leaves, as the main feature. The doubly-dished blade is outlined with double dot engraving and bright cutting. A central, pierced and bright-cut floral burst is now a minor feature. A bright-cut rectangular cartouche, held by ribbons, is vacant. The underside is plain. An oval split boss is soldered and held by two rivets. The in-plane filled fluted handle is attached by a very short waisted stem. The marks lie across the rear under edge.

34.     Long-oval SERVER, Thos. Watson & Co., Sheffield, 1795; length 30 cm, handle, marks absent. The blade is similar in shape and ornament to the preceding figure although dishing is mainly with respect to the short axis. It differs in having a rather unique sharply-raised, scalloped right edge which has been turned up rather than being applied. The split oval boss leads by a short, waisted round stem to an in-plane reeded filled handle. The marks lie across the rear under edge.

35.    Long-oval SERVER, Old Sheffield, c. 1795; length 31 cm; ivory handle. The blade shape and decoration is similar to that of the preceding and following figures; slightly dished around the short axis. The right edge is now simply rolled up in a gentle curve. The blade has silver edges. A topside simulated, engraved, semi-elliptical boss holds an underside boss of similar shape that is soldered and pinned on. The flat stem lifts to a ferrule and natural colored handle.

36.    Long-oval SERVER, Crespin Fuller, London, 1797; length 30 cm; handle, John Tatum Sr. and Jr., London, 1797. The blade is similar in shape and decoration to the preceding slice and is pierced and engraved with bright-cut flower heads and swags. It is double-dished, but mainly with respect to the long axis and has a narrowly rolled up right edge. The V-boss and stem lift to a fluted filled handle.

37.    Long-oval SERVER, Peter and Ann Bateman, London, 1797; length 29.5 cm; handle, Moses Brent, London, 1797. The bright-cut flower heads and engraved circles are in horseshoe pattern, together with dotted ornament curves similar to preceding examples. But the sharply raised right side is once again an applied soldered edge; the rear edge is flat and scalloped. The rear underside of the double dished and abstract fish-shaped blade is strengthened by an applied incurved Vee plate that appears to be original equipment, not uncommonly supplied by this company. The faceted V-boss lifts to a reeded filled handle. The marks lie underside along the rear left edge.

38.    Long-oval FISH SLICE, William Doyle (?) overstamp, Dublin, 1798; length 32 cm; handle unmarked; provincial makers appear to have bought in handles that were unmarked and left so [cf. Figs. 33 and 34]. The blade is of the abstract fish shape. It is double dished and decorated with double horseshoe bands of bright-cut swags, leaves, pales, and pendant flowers; and with peripheral bands of dots and wrigglework lines with a round, bright-cut cartouche and crest. Like the preceding articles, the underside is undecorated. The shaped V-boss lifts by a long flat stem to the reeded filled handle. The marks are divided topside on either side of the boss.

39.    Long-oval SERVER, Thos. Wallis, London, 1799, length 28 cm; ivory handle. The small spoon-like double-dished blade is now centrally pierced with geometrical horizontal pales characteristic of many servers made in the next two decades. It has a double reeded border along the blade edge and around the pierced reserve. There is no engraving, save a laurel leaf cartouche — another not uncommon feature of the first decades of the nineteenth century. The faceted V-boss lifts to a ferrule strengthener for the rectangular natural colored handle.

The earlier shanks as well as all later servers equipped with the split penny boss, were straight and the whole article lay in one plane. The handle filling was usually some resin such as shellac, together with other weighting and binding material of a siliceous nature. The handle enclosed, and was sometimes pinned to, the tang and butted snugly up against the flat face end on the bolster. London handles often carried the marks of specialist haft makers such as those of W.S. and, later, Moses Brent and John Tatum, Sr. and Jr. (8). Some implements of more elegant quality had filled handles that were not made, but at least marked, by the blade maker, and which complemented or conformed to the design of the blade or stem [Figs. 8,23]. They were usually decorated with reeding, beading, or shell (near the handle end) ornament.

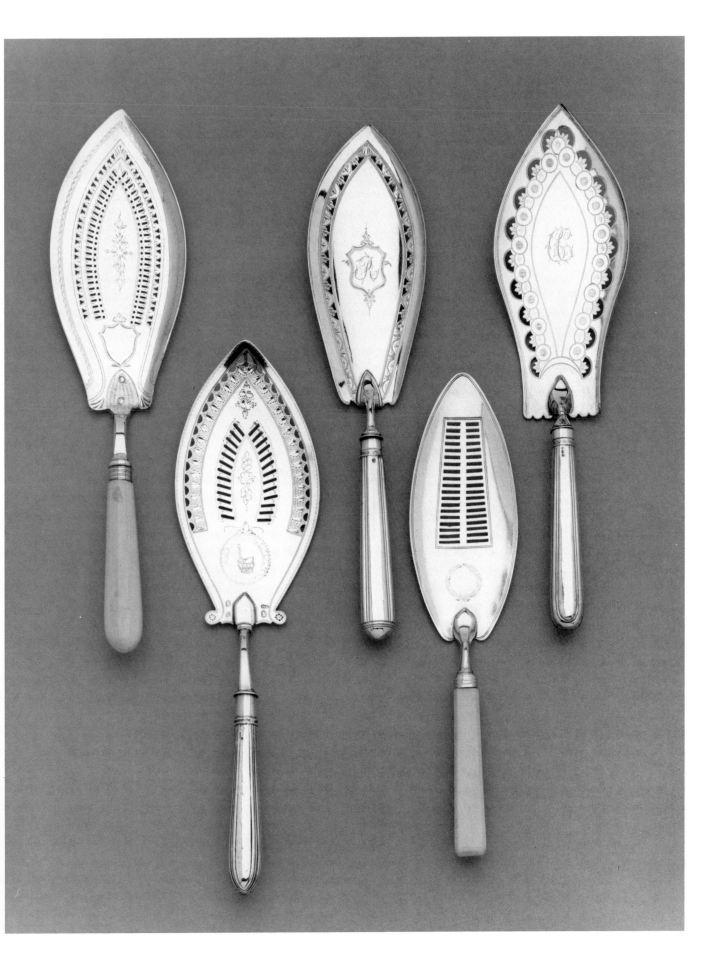

Ivory was the most frequently, almost exclusively, used of alternative handle materials. An occasional bone, mother-of-pearl or agate handle is found (9a). Ivory was either stained green with copper salts or with chromate, or was left in its natural color. At the front end where the tang entered, the handle was strengthened and decorated by a silver ferrule, either plain, reeded, engraved, or of more elaborate invention. These handles might be plain, or are frequently reeded longitudinally or otherwise shaped in decorative fashion [Figs. 18,26]; occasionally they are furnished with a silver cap [Fig. 49].

Later junctions added various shapes. Application to the top-side of the blade in the early 1780s was also made by a V-boss [Figs. 22,24], or less often by another shape such as a simulated split-penny [Fig. 16] or pear shape [Fig. 17]. Continental junctions tended to be more imaginative and venturesome [Figs. 42-50]. In a few instances, the boss was applied to the underside of the blade, more often by provincial makers [Fig. 35] and more often on Continental servers [Figs. 43,46,50]. With the advent of the V-boss that tended to replace the penny attachment on British blades in the latter half of the 1780s and in the 1790s, the stem became longer, acquired an inch or so of lift by an S-bend, and lost its rounded contour, becoming flattened or faceted [Figs. 22,30,36-38]. The lift to the handle was not as exaggerated, however, as in the earlier trowel; the handle tended to lie more or less parallel to the blade or angled downward slightly toward the blade. The V-boss itself also was frequently faceted, especially in the last decade of the century. It also occurred with rounded top, or with convex sides, or as a half-ellipse, or with cut parallel sides to make a four-sided figure, or even altered to oval-like contour and other occasional shapes. Inspection of the figures illustrates these several variables of stem and boss characteristics.

Hollow handles persisted on long-oval slices right through the eighteenth century and continued to appear with greatly reduced frequency in the next, but with a resurgence in the later half of the nineteenth century. The first all-silver handles, analogous to those on scimitar slices and frequently as part of a complete flatware service canteen, only appeared after the turn of the century but then became predominant. These handles were most often the rather new English fiddle, or a later variation such as reeded fiddle or King's pattern, and, more occasionally, Old English or reeded Old English. But all styles of flatware cutlery handles (9b) were employed (see Chapter V). A long-oval of 1786 by Henry Chawner described in a Phillips sale (III 26) as being furnished with an Old English silver handle proves to be a later marriage (10).

## *Function*

Enjoyment of white bait, and traditional pies and puddings, did not cease in the seventh decade of the eighteenth century, but continued actively in social custom through the nineteenth century, as described in a previous chapter. The change in British social and dining customs that occasioned the change in silver slice design from triangular to long-oval, or obviated the need for the older lifters, remains a puzzle for which no conclusive answer is yet apparent. Perhaps the change was an unrelated and belated aspect of the rather abrupt switch (19) that took place in England from rococo to neoclassical design. That the Georgian-style trowel, labelled as a fish server, persisted for another hundred years in English ceramic ware manufacture (Chapter I) only compounds the conundrum. Clayton (I 3) has suggested that double-bladed slices (Chapter VII) were for the service of white bait; however, they did not appear until the 1790s.

That the long-oval slice was intended for cutting and parting as well as lifting is evidenced by several facts, as well as the sometime use of the term, "fish knife" at this time. Both sides of the blade were frequently beveled to a sharpened edge, although the occasional right edge was left somewhat more blunt by the maker. Articles that lie in a plane have no intrinsic handedness. Moreover, the design of the earliest servers, having no lift to the shank so that the handle and blade lie in the same plane, clearly encouraged the use of the blade for cutting. Indeed, despite the relatively short, stout nature of the stem, occasional evidence of deformation of the article due to the pressure applied in its use as a cutter gives further indication of its function, as well as of abuse. Thus, the utensil was well adapted to separate the skin from the flesh of the fish, the flesh from the bone and to divide the soft flesh into portions. As well, it was probably also applied to more arduous duty such as severing the back bone of smaller fish. The narrower blade shape also made long-oval servers well suited for tarts, cake, and shallow puddings and pies; or in the case of savoury puddings, to sunder, on occasion, a tough pastry coffin of the contents. As needed, their use could be assisted by a spoon in the other hand.

Within a year of their advent in 1775, an asymmetrical long-oval blade resembling a knife appeared [Fig. 8]. Unlike the double-edged server, however, this knife-shaped blade by Aldridge and Green is sharpened only on the knife edge and is quite blunt on the back edge. Nonetheless, contrary to this example, the Edinburgh knife [Fig. 13], made a few years later (1780), is sharpened on both edges, although more so on the normal cutting edge. Evidently, generalizations made on the basis of only a few examples are hazardous. In any case, despite its early appearance, and evidently useful knife-shape for performance of the cutting and parting function, this variant of the long-oval server was of very infrequent occurrence, notwithstanding the fact that the blade was flat and could perform any serving requirement just as well as the more symmetric blades. In both

40.    FISH/CAKE/PUDDING SERVER, close plate, c. 1790. This is both an example of a completely symmetric long-oval server and of repetitive hand-operated press piercing. The placement of the members of the two horizontal exterior rows of quatrefoils is slightly irregular. The missing handle was obviously not solid metal.
Gift of Henry W. Smart.

41.    FISH SLICE, Chas. Jamieson, Inverness, c. 1790. This delightful long-oval server is in the realistic shape of a fish with appropriate piercing and engraving to enhance the effect. The shape is rare and the few existing English examples in silver or Old Sheffield were made by Northern smiths (see Refs. 15,16). All of these examples are closely similar in date and in the detailed arrangement of design features and decoration, as though inspired by a single source. The handle is hollow and is attached *via* a waisted stem and split oval boss.
By kind cooperation of Mary Cooke Antiques, London. Property of Dr. Dale Bennett.

42.    Long-oval SERVER, F.W. script sole mark, Continental, c. 1800; length 35.5 cm. The flat blade, rather rare at this time, has an applied, raised, cusped right edge. It is pierced with parallel, arched pales and circles and is lightly engraved with bands of dashes, zigzag, and ties in Louis XVI style. There is a central, vacant bright-cut oval cartouche with pendant flower heads. The applied elliptic boss, engraved as an acanthus leaf, is continuous with a stem of rectangular cross-section that lifts to a conical socket that holds a turned and multi-balustered wood handle.

43.    FISH SLICE, C.A. Mordt, Christiana 1802. This is a trowel by definition, but suggestive of a waisted long-oval server in total impression and in proportions of the blade; compare Fig. III 94. Although called a "fiskespade", it would do as well, or better, for cake or pie service. The pierced decoration is neoclassical. The pointed Old English handle has bright cut decoration and cartouche. See J. Fossberg, I-M Lie and J-L. Opstad, *Oslo-Sølv 1400 ÅR*, Kunstindustrimuseet, Oslo, 1979, p. 43, for further discussion of this server.
Courtesy of the Norsk Folkemuseum, Oslo.

instances, however, because of their blade length, narrow blade area, and the absence of a pronounced lift to the shank, their use as a lifter, in the sense of the use of the trowel as a white bait lifter or blancmange server, was less convenient, especially where entry into a pot or bowl might be involved.

That long-oval slices decorated with dolphins, fish, and marine motifs are associated with the service of fish seems undoubted, notwithstanding the wide use of such motifs in contemporary and earlier rococo decoration. Whether similar articles not so decorated had the same purpose is somewhat more speculative. Nonetheless, they are commonly so designated in present-day British nomenclature, and, with reverse emphasis, as cake servers in Continental custom. Somewhat interestingly, in a sale catalogue of one auction house (3) there is found a long-oval (pointed) slice by Robert Hennell, London, 1779, designated as a cake knife, while a near-elliptical server devoid of pointed tip, by Aldridge and Green, London, 1781 [Fig. 17], is named as a fish slice. Neither carry marine symbolism and both are pierced. How and when any or all of these servers, pierced or not, were used for the presentation of foods, other than conventional service of fish itself or pastry, is uncertain. Above all, it must be kept in mind that,

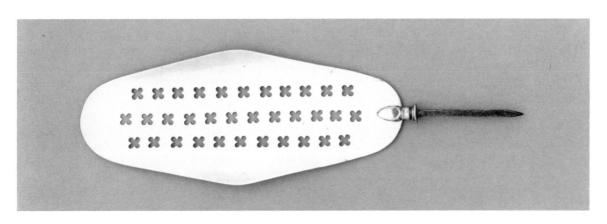

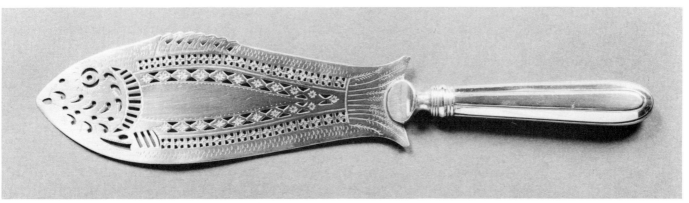

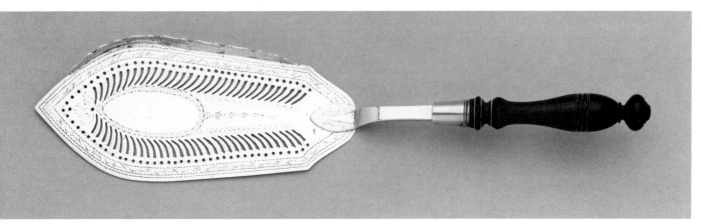

44.  Long-oval FISH SLICE, maker overstamped, unidentified Continental marks, c. 1810 (?); length 38 cm. This blade is about as realistic as an abstract fish shape can get. The blade is pierced with an engraved horseshoe band of oak leaves and a central leaf burst. The junction is a cast curled acanthus leaf that connects to a long socket-stem that holds a plain turned wooden handle.

45.  CAKE/PASTRY SHOVEL or SLICE, Jean-Baptiste Engel, Paris, ante 1824; length 33 cm. This long-oval server of abstract fish shape is nonetheless described as a "pelle à tarte". It is highly pierced with a flower and leaf design. A raised rear apron carries a flower junction, and a silver stem and conical holder rise to a turned wooden handle. It appears as Fig. 208 in H. Haug, L'Orfèvrerie de Strasbourg, Musées Nationaux, Paris, 1978.
Courtesy of Musée des Arts Décoratifs, Paris; photo Sully-Jaulmes.

46.  FISH SLICE and CAKE SLICE. Drawings of two unpierced servers, part of a design for a set of cutlery by G. Belli, Italy, c. 1800. The surface of the first is represented as extensively engraved with a neoclassical flower and foliage design, together with a fish inside a laurel wreath; that of the second is undecorated, apart from a laurel wreath cartouche. Both servers are of long-oval type; one is a completely symmetric navette elliptical shape; the other is more of a judgement call. Their differences in shape do not distinguish their function, however. It is the fish decoration on the one — even though it is unpierced — that supports the designation of *fish slice*, as opposed to *cake slice* for the other.
Courtesy of the Cooper-Hewitt Museum, The Smithsonian Institution/Art Resource, New York.

within limitations, people do what they want — knives and spoons universally continue to be used, sometimes, as screwdrivers! Undoubtedly, therefore, even though the piercing was unnecessary as well as harder to clean when used for the service of sticky foods, and flat unpierced blades perhaps very marginally do not release liquid quite as well as pierced servers, both types have been used interchangeably as has served their owner's wishes.

Continental usage with respect to long-oval servers again illustrates very well the dilemma presented immediately above. The conclusions reached there and in Chapter III remain unchanged. A few examples will suffice. A long-oval, highly pierced, raised-edge server by an unknown maker, Leiden, 1793, is illustrated in Fig. 47. It is chased and engraved with flowers and vine tendrils. But it is highly pierced and of the form designated here as abstract fish, thus a fish slice, although it has been labelled as a pastry slice ("taartschep") (11); however, J. van Loo calls it a fish server (12). Figure III 88 displays a nearly symmetric server by M.N. Levy, Copenhagen, 1805, which is impartially named "fish slice or cake spoon." The piercing is in geometrical horseshoe pattern around the edge, together with a central transverse oval motif in an ill-defined neoclassical/ Empire style. A Swiss "pastry shovel" by Gely Frères, Lausanne, 1820-30, is so-called (III 40) despite that it is of abstract fish form and is pierced around the edges; it has an engraved central floral spray. Another more highly pierced example [Fig. 48] by F. Lecomte, Lausanne, 1833-1845, having fish tail nubs, is reasonably termed a fish lifter by Gruber (13), who applies the name cake shovel (slice) to a

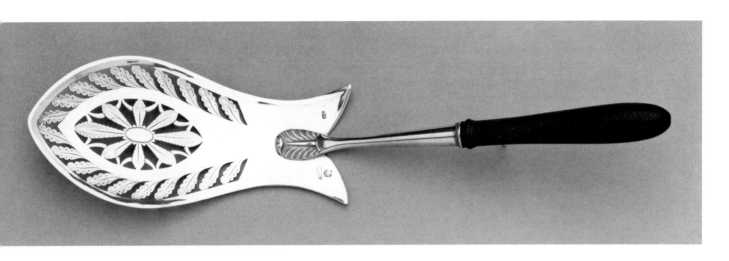

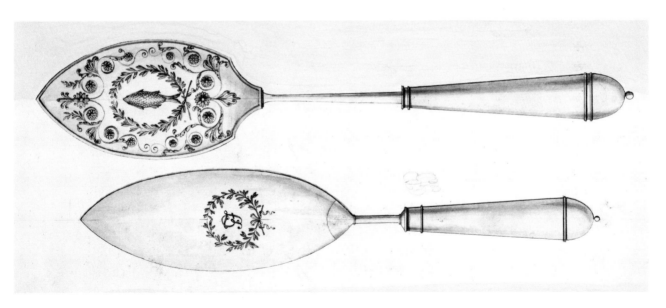

143

47.   FISH SLICE, maker unknown, Leids, 1793; length 36 cm. The abstract fish-shaped blade has a raised right edge, and is completely decorated with pierced neoclassical radial loops around a central reserve that is engraved with flowers and vine tendrils. The trilobate junction is attached at the rear edge of the blade and the stem leads to a cylindrical holder and turned wood handle. The server has been designated as a cake or pastry slice ("taartschep") in a catalogue, *Leids Zilver*, Stedelijk Museum de Lakenhals, Leiden, 1977. Both the author and the server's owner prefer to think of it as a fish server.
By kind cooperation and courtesy of J. van Loo, Emse.

48.   FISH SLICE, Ferdinand Lecomte, Lausanne, 1833-45; length 32 cm; turned wooden handle. This highly pierced, engraved, long-oval server has a rosette boss rising *via* a faceted stem and conical socket to the handle. It has an abstract fish shape with tail nubs that accords with its designated function and contrasts with that of the following illustration. See *Silverware,* by A. Gruber, Rizzoli, New York, 1982, translated by D. Smith, Fig. 309.
Courtesy of Swiss National Museum, Zurich.

49.   Long-oval FISH SLICE, unmarked, nineteenth century, length 32.7; ivory handle. The long-oval blade is slightly double dished, and is pierced and simply engraved with a sinuous fish in stylized lily pads. The octagonal socket stem grasps the blade, and is reinforced on top by a cast skate junction and on the bottom by a transverse elliptical heel plate and by a small superimposed trilobate decorative junction piece. The natural ivory handle is also octagonal, and is engraved with interlaced scrolls that match the pattern on the silver cap. The article has been claimed to be of Austrian manufacture but the eye structure of the fish suggests an Indian or Eastern origin.

50.   Long-oval FISH SERVER, Norway, last half of the nineteenth century; length 29 cm; weight 3.4 oz; solid handle. The realistic, fish-shaped, stamped blade is unpierced, but this is surely a fish slice nonetheless; the underside is plain. Figure III-86 has long preceded it in shape [cf. also Fig. 41]. The underblade rat tail junction is decorated with a shell that matches the finial of the single-struck waisted fiddle handle. The blade is identical with one by Gottlied Frederik Middlethon, Trondheim, 1850-60; that slice is termed "half-manufactured"; it has a filled fluted handle and is privately owned.

pierced contemporary (c. 1830) German long-oval slice of closely similar shape but without tail nubs [Fig. 583, ref. 13]. Figure 46 shows two long-oval *unpierced* elliptical Italian server designs by G. Belli, c. 1800. One of these is called a fish server by virtue of a rather modest engraved fish inscription at the blade center, amidst a densely engraved, overall floral scrolling flower pattern; the second has only a simple central engraved laurel cartouche and is named a cake slice (III 19). Finally, Fig. 45 illustrates a French long-oval, abstract fish shape, made by J.-B. Engel, Paris, pre-1824, that has been described as a tart shovel; it displays a rear apron.

In all of the above speculation it is worth reiterating an earlier admonition. The names presently assigned to antique silver articles of all kinds do not necessarily correctly portray their original titles or functions; also, titles may change their meaning; in addition, national custom varies. Many current names became part of trade or professional parlance long after the article in question disappeared from production. The variability and ambiguity in the assignment of

144

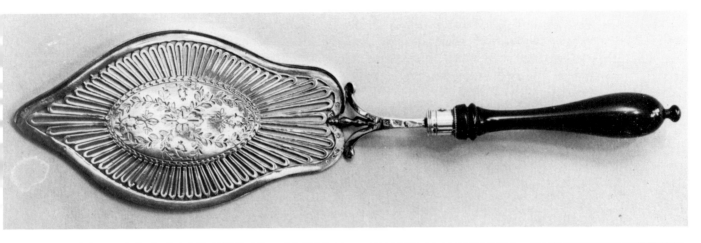

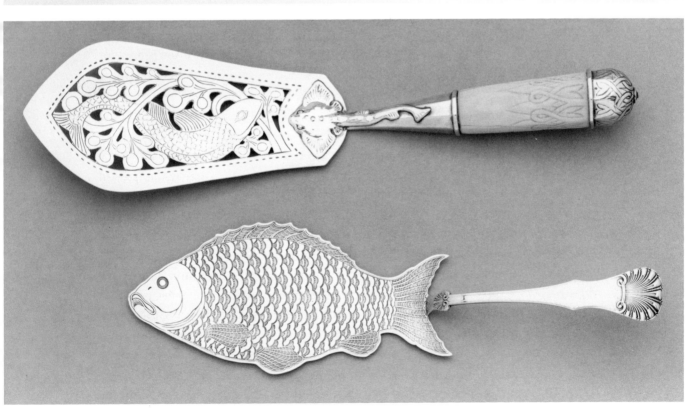

145

51. FISH SLICE, T.H. Saakes, The Hague, 1919; length 32 cm; weight 6.0 oz. The long-oval blade is doubly dished. It takes the shape of a flat fish, with gills and a gently upcurved right side that stands in for fins; the front end and left edges are bevelled. The blade is completely hand pierced with a pair of mirror image fishes — or a split fish — and has a central bed that is decorated with crosslets. It is lightly engraved and bright cut. The upturned heavily reeded handle is integral with the blade. In its beautifully simplistic artfulness of design — its directness and honesty — this server stands with the best of twentieth, or any, century productions.

names for various servers, is a continuing and somewhat time-wasting problem throughout the record of the eighteenth century and even into the next (see Chapter V). Only an incomplete history of the times exists, and that record still has not been completely uncovered.

## *Decoration*

The rococo style was virtually gone in Britain when the long-oval shape first appeared, although that style persisted much longer on the Continent. For the first decade of their production, the long-oval servers were highly decorated, being pierced and also bright cut, and engraved or chased on both sides equally. The most common motifs showed neoclassical influence, including urns, baskets of flowers, crowns, flower heads and swags, and floral and foliate scrolling [e.g., Figs. 6,7,8,11,15], and, of course, fish, water birds and other aquatic and marine symbolism [e.g., Figs. 3,5,9,10]. Toward the latter half of the eighth decade, however, the decoration — piercing, chasing, and engraving — became more perfunctory and was confined largely, or almost entirely, to the top side of the blade and to a smaller area forward on the blade [Figs. 24-26,28]. This trend continued through the 1790s [Figs. 31-33,39], and such ovals as continued to be made in the nineteenth century were engraved, if at all, on one side only, in a manner similar to the more abundant scimitar shapes.

Why were the early ellipses decorated on both sides? A plausible, if un-proven, rationale for this and the later trend in decoration may be adduced. Unlike trowels, whose lift and handle dictated a topside, and the underside of whose blade was never seen, the flat servers that succeeded them had no imposed orientation. These slices could be used interchangeably with either side of the blade upward, which called for two-sided blade decoration. As lift was added to the handle in the 1780s, decoration of the unseen underside was not needed and eventually disappeared. In the nineteenth century, with the introduction of the solid silver handle, the long-oval simply became a variant of the dominant scimitar shape and was decorated in like manner.

An exceptional example (9) was made by William Eaton, London, in 1841. Its flat blade rivals the nicest of the early long-oval servers and is indistinguishable

146

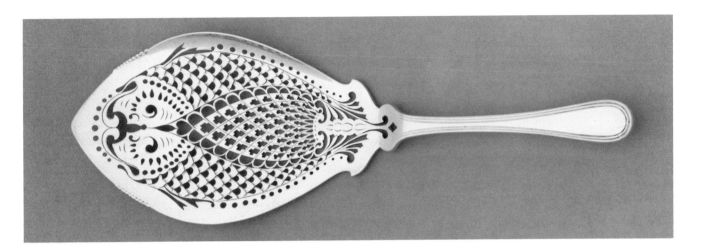

from those. It is of the same shape and size as are they and is completely pierced, engraved and bright cut on both sides of the blade. There is no lift to the handle and it lies in a plane. Most peculiarly, the split boss that grasps the blade is asymmetrical, being 'penny' on one side and 'Vee' on the other!

Eventually, in the second half of the nineteenth century, long-oval knives, in pairs with forks, became more ornately decorated again. This was part of a trend that was facilitated by prosperity, by mass production, and by the use of sophisticated machine technology for pseudo-engraving, chasing, and piercing of less expensive articles; and which was accentuated also by a reversion of style to the flat-bladed, planar conformation [Figs. V 99, V 100]. Figure 40 is an example of a symmetric plated blade that demonstrates an earlier intermediate technology. The lines of pierced quatrefoils have been punched with a die and were not sawn or filed. But the non-uniform alignment and spacings of the piercing reveals the hand of the smith's apprentice.

With avoidance of invidious comparisons, scrutiny of the figures in this chapter reveals that Continental long-oval slices of the eighteenth century were also attractively and tastefully decorated. A difference between Continental and British examples becomes more apparent in the following century. Whereas British servers tended to be plainer and more utilitarian in character in the first twenty-five years (Chapter V), Continental slices in Empire style are evidently quite ornate in their piercing and decoration. Other examples may be found in the references of Chapter III, including the article by Scheffler (III 18).

## Marks and Makers

The hallmarks on long-oval servers usually appear on the underside of the blade; the latter is defined for flat servers as being the reverse of the crested side. The early English slices were marked along the rear under edge. In the 1780s, the marks began to appear along an under rear side edge, and very frequently so in the later half of the decade; marks were only occasionally stamped on the upper surface, and more frequently on Irish wares. Amongst the very earliest makers of long-oval slices were William Plummer and Burrage Davenport. Charles Aldridge and Henry Green made many of the earlier slices. Numerous examples of Plummer's craftsmanship persist to the early 1790s, when his son, Michael, also became represented among makers of servers. Robert Hennell I was another early maker who continued to display abundant inventiveness for some time. Hester Bateman was a prolific and continuing maker of several piercing patterns and blade shapes, frequently repeated. Her first long-oval server so far noted (14), a highly pierced vase of flowers, is dated 1777. The above makers are responsible for the majority of early long-oval servers extant. Their work is uniformly distinguished by the elegance of its piercing, engraving and bright cutting. William Abdy, Thomas Daniel and George Smith III also contributed superior articles, although less frequently.

Also well represented in later, somewhat less ornate production were William Abdy, Henry Chawner, John Emes, Peter and Ann Bateman, and Thomas Wallis; their work emphasized fine engraving and bright cutting. The great majority of all production was from London, with Dublin being the next most productive silversmithing center.

## References.

1.  *Pattern Books of the Firm of Boulton and Watts*, 1762-1836, Soho Works, Birmingham.

2.  a) Advertisement by silversmith Thomas Daniel, The Daily Universal Register, London, January 1, 1785.
    b) K.C. Buhler, *Mount Vernon Silver*, Mount Vernon Ladies Association, 1957.
    c) W.S. Prideaux, *Memorials of the Goldsmith's Company*, Vol II, H.M.P., 1896.

3.  Christie's East, New York, Sale March 21, 1980.

4.  J. Williams, *The Footman's Guide*, Dean and Munday, London, c. 1836.

5.  M.A. Greenwood, *The Ancient Plate of the Drapers Company*, Oxford University Press, London, 1930.

6.  E. Wenham, *Old Silver for Modern Settings*, Knopf, New York, 1951.

7.  J. Verbeek, *Nederlands Zilver 1780-1830*, Tijdstrom Antiek Wijzers, Lochem-Gent, 1984.

8.  See A.G. Grimwade, *London Goldsmiths 1697-1837*, Faber, London, 1976 for this plausible identification of the mark MB found on filled handles.

9.  a) F. Bradbury, *History of Old Sheffield Plate*, Northend, Sheffield, 1968, p. 392 illustrates an OS long-oval by John Kay & Co., 1798, with a pearl (fruit-knife) handle; it is assumed that the handle is original, else the original illustration loses point.
    b) I. Pickford, *Silver Flatware*, Antique Collectors Club, Suffolk, 1983.

10. Henry W. Smart, personal communication.

11. *Leids Zilver*, Stedelijk Museum de Lakenhal, Leiden, 1977.

12. J. van Loo, Epse, personal communication.

13. A. Gruber, *Weltliches Silber*, Katalog der Sammlung des Schweizerischen Landesmuseums Zürich, Verlag Berichthaus Zürich, 1977.

14. R.R. Wark, *British Silver in the Huntingdon Collection*, Castle Press, 1978.

15. G.B. Hughes, *Sheffield Silver Plate*, Praeger, London, 1970.

16. G. Wills, *Silver*, Arco, New York, 1969.

17. F. Trevor-Venis, *The Eighteenth Century English Dining Room*, The Israel Museum, Jerusalem, undated.

18. E. Delieb, *Investing in Silver*, Transworld, London, 1967.

19. J. Stone, *English Silver of the Eighteenth Century*, Cory, Adams and Mackay, London, 1965.

Chapter V

# SCIMITAR AND RELATED SERVERS. PAIR SETS

## *History*

THE SCIMITAR SWORD or knife is an ancient Oriental weapon. In one form it is a long curved narrow blade of roughly constant breadth, with pointed end and sharpened edge. In another mid-Eastern form it broadens somewhat from the base of the curved blade and narrows again toward a sharp tip that reverts to the rear unsharpened edge *via* a short concave contour. This is the form signified by use of the term here. The designation *sabre* will here arbitrarily signify the turned-back, rounded, and broadened-end shape, demonstrated by the table knife of the late Stuart period (which was allegedly adapted as a spoon for the purpose of eating peas and other foods, whether in the absence of forks or because they could not be retained by early two- or three-tined forks). The scimitar blade differs markedly in shape from the symmetric long-oval of Chapter IV, which also broadens before narrowing toward the tip. The scimitar server is an asymmetric shaped knife that is clearly a cutting instrument. Nonetheless, the tasks to which it was properly applied never called for the more arduous duties of a steel knife.

The earliest English silver scimitar slice known to the writer is a flat-bladed implement dated 1780 by Joseph Steward II, London [Fig. 1]. It is of classic weapon shape and impressive size. It is much larger, and made even more imposing by its neogothic piercing, than similar contemporaneous scimitars made by Hester Bateman, an example of which, shown in Fig. 2, is dated 1783. An earlier prototype by her, dated 1780, is known. This is another example of the multiple reproduction of a few piercing patterns and blade shapes by the Bateman firm in the 1780s. Additional examples of this prototypical classic formidable shape do not recur until the mid-nineteenth century, principally in some spectacular, highly-pierced examples (1) by Francis Higgins and by George Adams, made as part of pair sets (*vide infra*) [Fig. 3a], as well as later copies [Fig. 3b].

The earliest Continental scimitar server encountered by the author (but surely not the earliest made) is the splendid bright-cut Dutch example shown in Fig. 4, made by J. Keeman, Dordrecht, 1782. Its bold shape is unlike the weapon

150

forms of Figs. 1 and 2 and antedates the later less-martial British examples of the 1790s.

It is not known what influences occasioned the early appearance of these scimitar shapes or why an interval of approximately ten years elapsed before British scimitar servers, in somewhat more pacific form [Figs. 5-7], came into regular and expanding production to fill a perceived culinary need. Henry Chawner was one of the earliest of these makers and quite a number of his servers, including some from the very early 1790s, have survived. The production of asymmetric servers (presently described by dealers as "shaped") has continued without a break to the present time, often in modified and sometimes fanciful forms. Although the scimitar shape is pronouncedly knife-like, especially in its prototypical weapon form, another connotation has sometimes been ascribed to the 'softened' form of the 1790s implement; namely, a likeness has been found between it and the shape of a headless fish, thus emphasizing its fish-service association. Individual British scimitars, whether decorated with a marine motif or not, are invariably known as fish slices. Later pair knives usually have flat blades and lend themselves more obviously to alternative description. American, and especially Continental, asymmetric servers that lack marine decoration are frequently designated for cake or pastry, even when dished. The smaller size of many American slices of the second half of the nineteenth century favors such allusion. Nomenclature is obviously heavily influenced by national custom and semantics, in addition to considerations of function.

In the late 1830s, the slice (still often, and even more appropriately, called a fish *knife*) paired with a fork began to appear concurrently with the conventional single blade. A Phillips (London) sale of 26 October 1990 records an early cake pair by Wm. Sansom, Sheffield, 1837. Fish carver and cake serving pairs came into use in the second quarter of the nineteenth century and proliferated markedly in the third quarter. A date as early as 1820 has been claimed (2). An early example by W.J., Aberdeen, and estimated as c. 1820 has also been cited (3). By contrast, a catalogue by a well-known Savory firm (4) of the 1830s lists fish knives (slices) in a variety of styles but no companion forks. A very early, one-off example of a "cake serving pair" by Paul Storr, London, 1813, is illustrated in Ref. (22). The pair have cast handles, one as huntress, the other as hunter. The fork is two tined; the knife is sabre shaped and has a silver blade.

The individual broad scimitar slice persisted in extensive manufacture until approximately 1850, after which time pairs greatly predominated. Worthy of mention is an impressive and massive early American pair by R. and W. Wilson, Philadelphia, who worked in the period 1825-1850; the knife is 36 cm long, the blade in the shape of a dolphin; the fork is 32.5 cm long. An early single slice was sometimes reinvested as a fashionable pair set by later creation of a matching fork [Fig. 41]. The long-oval slices of the eighteenth and nineteenth centuries went through a comparable evolution into pairs. One pair [Fig. IV 21] has a matching

1.	FISH SLICE, Jos. Steward II, London, 1780; length 37 cm; handle, Moses Brent, undated. The asymmetric blade, possibly cast and then cleaned up, is of impressive size. The plain blade is sharpened on the left arc. It is pierced with parallel, vertical, V-notched pales that, together with the elongated tip, introduce a gothic appearance. The concave curve is nearly vertical at the tip and leads down to a marked positive cusp and thence by a gently concave curve to the waved straight rear edge. There is an applied crest topside; the marks lie along the underside rear edge. The split penny boss connects by a very short waisted stem to a highly reeded filled handle.

2.	FISH SLICE, Hester Bateman, London, 1783; length 31 cm; handle, ?C, undated. The blade has a sharpened left edge and the vertical tip hook turns ninety degrees to an unusually pronounced positive cusp. The blade has symmetrical negative cusps and waist at the rear end. The blade is highly pierced and engraved and bright-cut with a peripheral frieze of bright-cut swags, a scrolling S-band and enclosed vine, scrolled foliage and a crested reserve. The underside is also decorated but somewhat more perfunctorily. The beaded and reeded filled handle is attached *via* a short waisted stem and split penny junction.

3a.	FISH SERVER PAIR, George Adams, London, 1861; knife, length ~37 cm; fork length ~28 cm. The impressive fork and knife are one of many pairs in this style made (sold) by this maker, and by Frances Higgins, for some dozen years before, and for some time after, this date, and with some variations in blade, or fork, or in handles. Who bought what from whom is not clear since both firms were suppliers of cutlery. The four-panelled, highly pierced and engraved, scalloped blade has a cast boss. It features shells, scrolls, and fish schooling in the reeds and foliage, as does the five-panelled fork which is pierced into the four tines in similar mode. The filled handles are stamped in matching patterns and decorated with fish, crabs, and shells. Another example (George Adams, 1850) may be found in the Victoria and Albert Museum, London, and other illustrations seen in Refs. (7) and (III 56); see also Christie's, New York, Americana sale, Oct. 21, 1989, Lot 84.
By kind cooperation and courtesy of Phillips (Blenstock House), London.


fork made a century later. Transient shapes of blades (Chapter VI), including the oblong rectangulars already mentioned in Chapter IV, did not survive beyond 1840; the trailing chronological end occurs more often in Irish (provincial) examples, and transient shapes rarely occur in later pairs (a very exceptional acorn-shaped blade has been seen).

The large serving pairs — excluding meat and poultry carvers — most often described in later nineteenth-century manufacturers' catalogues, and in greatest detail, are fish carvers. Other pairs featured are cake servers, pie servers and melon carvers. With a few exceptions and intrusions, British scimitars have been arranged chronologically in Figs. 1-106; American and Continental examples follow.

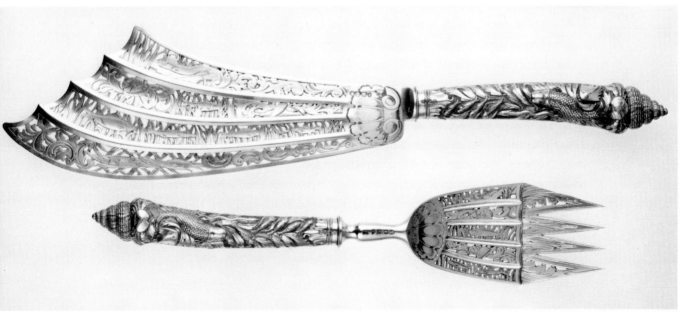

153

3b.   FISH SLICE, Alexander Clark Manufacturing Co., Sheffield, 1905; length 34.5 cm; handle, R.F.M. (overstamped) Sheffield, 1905. Here is a pattern that has persisted for over fifty years. This server is less impressive than those of Higgins and Adams, having only three panels of piercing and engraving of a total of seven fish in the reeds and rushes. The blade is engraved only on the top surface, which also bears the marks in a tri-shell engraved cartouche. Each panel is outlined by fine double reeding. Only the leading left arc is sharpened, and the absence of underside decoration makes this asymmetric server right-handed. A split oval boss and butt plate — with no intervening stem — holds a filled handle stamped with fishes, leaves and shells in rococo style.

4.   FISH SLICE, Johannes Keeman, Dordrecht, 1782; length 34 cm; filled handle. This lovely blade is the earliest Continental scimitar blade so far seen by the author. It is pierced along the right edge and, notably, and in contrast to British custom, is also heavily pierced along the cutting edge. It is engraved and bright cut with neoclassical motifs. The blade has a single positive cusp and a straight right edge. The split penny boss and short balustered stem are in line with the hollow handle. Although designated by its owner as a fish slice, perhaps this is also a cake slice, since (most) Dutch fish servers are transverse ovals.
By kind cooperation and courtesy of J. van Loo, Epse.


## Blade Shape

        The formidable weapon-like implements, as oriented in Figs. 1-3, display a concave hook leading down from the tip to the right side of the flat blade, giving rise to what is termed here as a *positive* cusp at the top end of the right side of the blade [Fig. 8A]. The left curved edge is sharpened and the maximum in the arc of the knife edge occurs below the top cusp. The right edge of the blade is blunt; the occasional exception has been sharpened [Fig. 5b and Ref. (10)]. Since, for these examples, the handle is in the plane of the blade, there is no intrinsic handedness to the articles; the situation is similar to that described in Chapter IV for early long-ovals. The quality, handedness, appears only when the stem is given lift and the handle is above the plane of the blade, or when an edge is raised; the slices are then invariably right-handed [see Fig. I8].
        The blades of the 1790s have at least one positive cusp as in Fig. 8A, and frequently two [Figs. 6,9], as in Fig. 8B — the second arising if the bottom right edge breaks suddenly toward the handle stem or heel edge of the blade, rather than flowing more or less continuously into it. Although Types A and B — positive cusps — virtually disappear (for fifty years) in English manufacture by 1800, the basic shape continued in many nineteenth-century Continental servers [Figs. 128,129,132-138] and in many later nineteenth-century American fish, cake and pie servers [Figs. 108,113,122], and more occasional English ones [Figs. 3,100,101].
        It may be well now to anticipate other blade shapes and to define the several principal types that occur [Fig. 8]. The Steward [Fig. 1] and Bateman [Fig. 2]

154

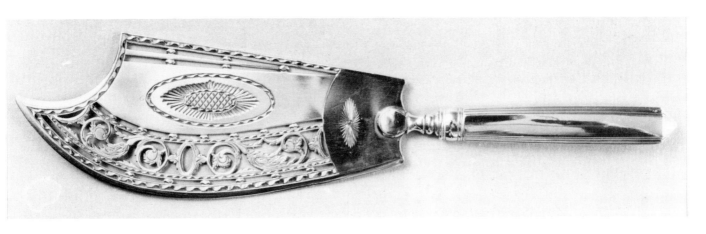

servers, as also the Higgins/Adams designs [Fig. 3], are of type A; they exhibit only a single positive cusp; the right edge flows smoothly into the heel of the blade. Type C shows a single *negative* cusp that is formed by an indentation at the position previously designated for the leading positive cusp. Examples will be found in Figs. 49,97. Type D of Fig. 8 proves to be the most common British shape and displays two negative cusps and a straight right side. Sometimes the left edge of the blade may also turn concavely inward toward the rear edge [Figs. 7,56,61]. Most examples below conform to type D. Finally, type E is a representation of a fluid blade shape whose back edge tends to be of rather amorphous form, sometimes in almost tortured variation, and may display no well identifiable cusps, or many. Later nineteenth-century blades [Figs. 38,98,103], especially American ones [Figs. 111,115,117,119] and more occasionally Continental ones [Fig. 138], sometimes display this character. Variations and combinations of these features also occur, including, as may be seen [Fig. 121], other mutations such as multiple cusps, edge scallops, and so on. Although the right sides of the blades have been drawn as near straight lines in Fig. 8A-D, in a small minority of cases the edges are actually concave; a high degree of concavity is unusual in British

5.    FISH SLICE, Old Sheffield, c. 1790; length 32 cm; ivory handle. The blade has a double positive cusp, as do most scimitar slices of the 1790s. It is pierced with a key pattern, enclosed in a double thread outline, along the right edge. There are no silver edges despite the estimated date. The boss is split and pinned together — but, peculiarly, it is oval topside and reverse pear-shaped underside. The hollow stem lifts to a green stained handle.

6.    FISH SLICE, Henry Chawner, London, 1795; length 32 cm; handle, John Tatum Sr. and Jr., London, 1797. The small, rather plain, narrow blade is slightly doubly dished. It has a double positive cusp with a straight side between; the latter feature, in contrast to the preceding Old Sheffield example, is the most usual construction. Double hit-and-miss lines encircle the blade; a pierced row of flower heads and half-circles lie along the right edge. A bright-cut laurel wreath on the rear surface contains a later monogram. A split V-bolster connects through an integral flattened stem to a reeded filled handle. This early example is a rare instance of an in-plane extended flat shank. The marks lie along the rear of the underside left edge. Chawner made scimitar shaped blades at least as early as 1792.

7.    FISH SLICE, John Denziloe, London, 1796; length 29.5 cm; handle John Tatum Sr. and Jr., 1796. The blade is very unusual for an English scimitar in having two double sets of positive cusps on the right edge; it might almost belong with the modified long ovals in Chapter VI. It is almost planar and has a double dot surround with light, worn, inner engraving. The central pierced reserve, of blade shape, is reticulated with net tied with bows, with engraved floral scrolling around and horizontal paling above. A split penny boss leads by a short, waisted and balustered stem to the reeded filled handle. The marks lie along the rear of the underside left edge.

8.    Idealized versions of five different styles of scimitar server blades. Variations on these occur, as well as other styles: A, a single upper positive cusp on the right side; B, two positive cusps on the right edge; C, a single upper negative cusp on the right edge; D, two negative cusps on the right edge; E, an amorphous and highly variable outline of the right edge. Other variables in blade shape included the position of the maximum in the arc of the cutting edge relative to the top cusp; concavities or convexities in the side edges of the blade as they approach the rear edge; the vertical location of the blade point relative to the boss or to the right edge; the shape of the rear edge of the blade, whether straight, curved, waved, or cusped. The common shape of the right lower edge of D is the concave arc shown; frequently, it is even more so such that the curve has a reentrant angle with an attendant 'kick' at the heel. Prior to 1850, virtually all blades are single dished around the long axis, and many/most are not engraved or chased, or only slightly, apart from reeded or engraved lines.

slices [Fig. 29] although not so in American [Figs. 110,115,118] or Continental ones, particularly Dutch [Figs. 132,133]. Particular modifications were favoured by some smiths, but variations do occur even in the products from a single shop.

The blades of the 1790s tend to be small and relatively narrow [Figs. 6,9,12]. The length of most blades lies in the range 15-17 cm, with the breadth being 5.5-6 cm. Some early blades are flat [Figs. 5,7,9]; others are dished around the long axis [Figs. 6,10-13], *as are virtually all later slices* [for exceptions, see Figs. 22,30,67]. Two negative cusps (Type D) begin to appear in the blade design [Figs. 10,12] later in

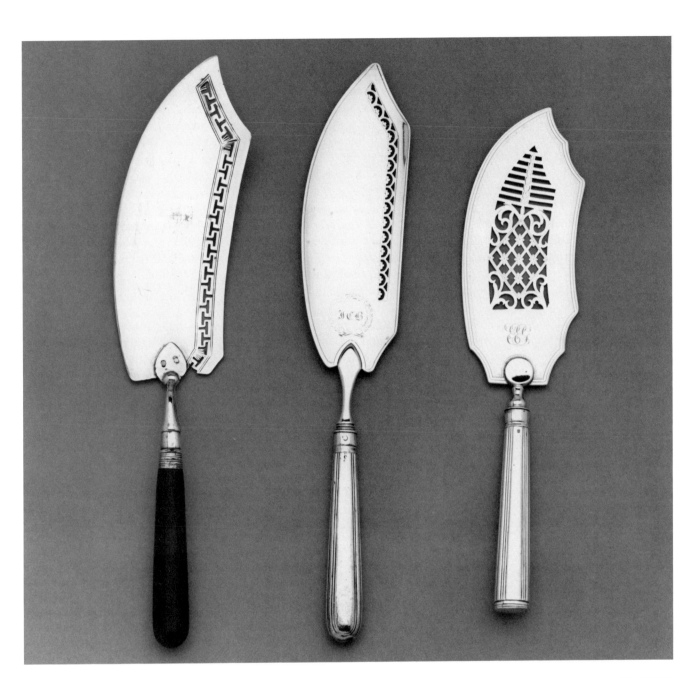

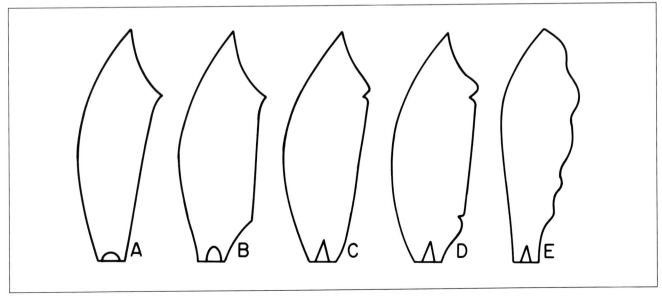

9.     FISH SLICE, Duncan Urquhart and Napthali Hart, London, 1797; length 30 cm; handle, Moses Brent, London, 1796. The rather small narrow blade is flat and has two positive cusps and a gently concave right side. The blade has a zigzag and wavy band surround, and band of bright-cut flower heads, interspersed by fine scribed lines, along the right side. The central pierced panel is similar to (much of) that of Fig. 7. The rounded V-bolster lifts on a flattened stem to a reeded filled handle. The marks lie underside along the rear of the right edge.

10.     FISH SLICE, Wm. Eley and Wm. Fearn, London, 1799; length 30 cm; ivory handle. Another small narrow blade that is dished around the long axis and now has two negative cusps on the straight right edge. A double thread line runs along the right edge and around a narrow pierced band of net along the straight right side. The oval junction and flattened faceted shank lift to a reeded ferrule that binds a natural ivory handle of diamond cross-section. The marks lie underside along the rear of the right edge.

11.     CAKE/FISH SERVER, John Emes, London, 1800; length 30 cm; ivory handle. The small narrow blade is very slightly dished around the long axis. It has an applied raised right edge and an unusual transitional combination of two positive cusps on the right of the blade and two corresponding negative cusps on the raised side. The crested blade is unpierced and lightly decorated with dotted lines. The faceted, pointed oval boss rises on a rounded stem to a green-stained reeded handle. The marks lie underside along the rear of the right edge.

12.     FISH SLICE, Thos. Wallis, London, 1800; length 30 cm; ivory handle; The small narrow blade has two negative cusps and is dished around the long axis. There are lines of hit-and-miss design around the blade and the pierced area. The pierced floral reserve is a little unusual at this time in being purely naturalistic — an early touch of Regency. A laurel leaf cartouche holds a contemporary monogram. The faceted pointed oval boss lifts on a bevelled stem to a flattened hexagonal natural colored handle. The marks lie underside along the rear of the right edge.

13.     FISH SLICE, Wm. Eley and Wm. Fearn, London, 1801; length 30 cm; solid fiddle handle; weight 4.6 oz. A late example of the small narrow blade, with single dishing again, and two negative cusps. There is a line of double reeding along the right side and around a pierced reserve of blade form with abstract fish skeletal paling. The crested English fiddle finial is attached by a conventional bevelled and shouldered stem and bevelled V-junction. The marks have now moved in line from the blade to the back of the handle finial.

14.     Long-oval SERVER, Stephen Adams II, London, 1801; length 29.7 cm; handle, John Tatum, London, 1801. This is one of the last of the eighteenth-century style British ovals until the advent of reproductions after a lapse of close to fifty years. The blade is only singly dished around the long axis and has circumferential dotted bands and hit-and-miss lines around the central pierced and engraved decoration and a monogram reserve. The rear edge is cusped. The piercing is a horseshoe band of opposed lunettes separated by a bright-cut and scribed band and a central bright-cut, pierced floral burst and other bright-cut touches. The underside is undecorated. A stepped V-boss rises on a waisted faceted stem to the stepped rectangular filled handle. The marks lie underside along the rear of the right edge.

15.    FISH SLICE, Abstainando King, London, 1802; length 30.5 cm; handle, John Tatum, London, 1801. One of the last of the narrow scimitar blades, dished mainly around the long axis, and with two negative cusps. There are fine bands of hit-and-miss around the blade; and a bright-cut and scribed waved oval band around a central pierced fish. There is a vacant engraved wreath cartouche. The pointed faceted oval-shaped boss and waisted bevelled stem lead up to a filled handle identical with that of the preceding handle. The marks lie underside along the rear of the right edge.

16.    FISH SLICE, Robt. Keay, Edinburgh (Perth), 1802; length 29.3 cm; filled handle, unmarked. This provincial blade has a mix of negative and positive cusps. However, like most of the preceding and following slices, the blade has a straight right edge between top and bottom cusps. The blade is well decorated with notched hit-and-miss lines, a frieze of engraved laurel leaves along the left cutting curve, a band of pierced, engraved and bright-cut leaves along the right edge and a laurel wreath cartouche with erased monogram. The elliptical bevelled boss and short stem rise to the plain filled cannon-end rounded handle, which is formed from relatively heavy sheet and may well have been made by Keay. The underside of the rear edge of the blade is strengthened by an original, half-ellipse plate, shaped to the waved edge. The marks lie underside along the rear of the left edge.

17.    FISH SLICE, Thomas Freeth (?), London, 1804; length 31 cm; handle, maker rubbed, London, 1805. The blade is of transitional shape and has a straight rear edge. It is unengraved and has double negative cusps and double reeded lines along the right edge and around an oval pierced toroidal fretwork design. The large V-boss is attached underblade and lifts through a topside bevelled stem to a hollow reeded handle that has been soldered to the butt plate. The marks lie underside along the right rear side.

18.    FISH SLICE, Alice and George Burrows, London, 1804; length 29 cm; ivory handle. The blade, like most succeeding scimitars, has two negative cusps and is singly dished around the long axis. Lines of notched hit-and-miss circumscribe the blade and pierced areas. A wavy band of interspersed bright cutting and scribed lines lies along the left edge. An asymmetrical horseshoe shaped band of pales encloses a vacant laurel wreath. The pointed faceted boss and faceted waisted stem lift to a natural colored, twist-fluted handle. The marks lie underside along the rear of the right side of the blade.

19.    FISH SLICE, Old Sheffield, c. 1805; length 3.4 cm; ivory handle. The blade has a double line of reeding along the right edge. It has silver edges. The blade resembles somewhat the preceding example of Fig. 18 in blade size and shape, piercing pattern, and boss shape and shank; the blade decoration is simpler, although not more so than many contemporary and later wares. The natural ivory handle is of stepped rectangular shape similar to the filled handles of Figs. 14 and 15.

20.    FISH SLICE, Alice and George Burrows, London, 1804; length 29.7 cm; weight 4.5 oz; solid handle. The blade now has proportions of length and breadth that are quite common for the slices of the next fifty years. It has a straight edge between upper and lower negative cusps. The lower cusp breaks to the rear edge on a straight line; the more usual shape is a concave curve. The periphery of the blade and pierced area is decorated by machine engraving of notched hit-and-miss lines. A band of alternating pierced S-curves and bright-cut S-shapes lie along the right edge. There is a vacant bright-cut elliptical cartouche. The shaped V-boss rises by a bevelled stem to a plain fiddle handle. The marks lie in line along the underside of the finial.

160

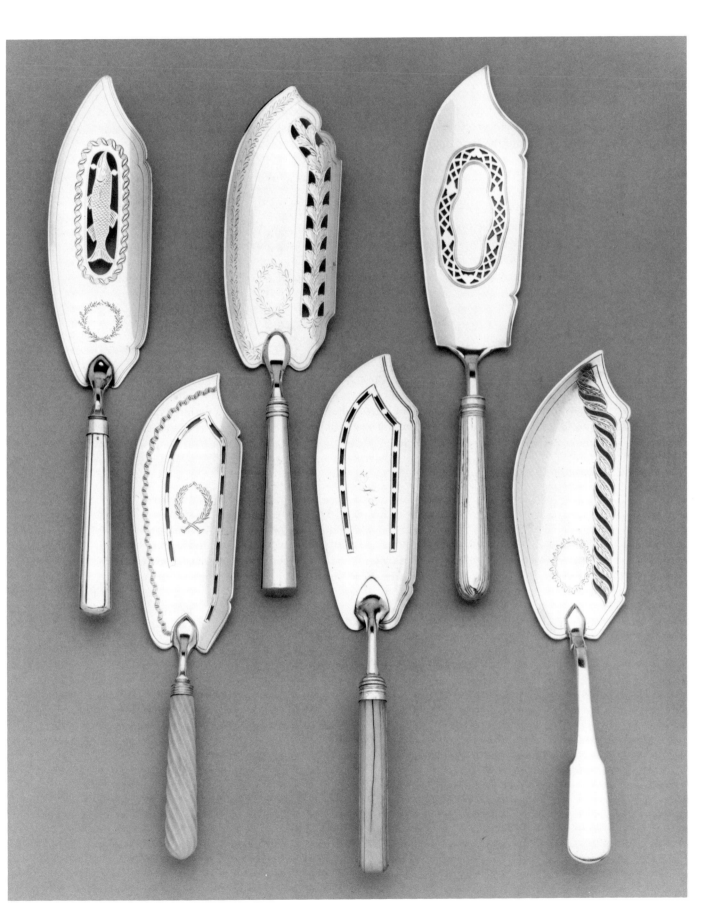

21. FISH SLICE, no makers mark, London, 1805; length 30.5 cm; ivory handle. The dished blade is decorated with dotted lines. A band of small bright-cut leaves and stippling lies along the right edge, outside of a parallel pierced band of notched pales. An oval cartouche with an engraved Greek key surround holds two monograms. The back of the blade is strengthened by an original applied curved rib shown in the photograph. The faceted pointed boss and shaped stem lift to a natural ivory handle of elliptical cross section. The marks lie underside along the rear of the left side.

22. FISH SLICE, Richard Morton, Sheffield, 1805; length 30.7 cm; ivory handle. The flat blade has a positive cusp and a rolled stamped right edge. The cutting edge is decorated with a pierced engraved frieze of acanthus leaves and the right edge with a scrolled zigzag border around a pierced strip of lattice work. The one-piece hollow oval boss and rounded tapering tubular stem show the influence of Old Sheffield manufacturing techniques; compare the analogous structure of Fig. 19. The natural ivory handle is of bevelled rectangular cross-section. The marks lie across the top left rear of the blade.

23. FISH SLICE, Solomon Hougham, London, 1808; length 29.7 cm; weight 3.6 oz; solid handle. A plain conventional scimitar blade, double reeded along the right edge and the shaped central pierced reserve; the latter in a paled fish bone pattern. The V-boss lifts to the monogrammed Old English finial, and the marks lie in line on its underside.

24. FISH SLICE, Stephen Adams II, London, 1808; length 28 cm; ivory handle. The singly dished blade is decorated with dotted lines and interlaced rope around the edges and central piercing; the latter is a shaped, pointed U-band of scrolls and reflects a growing tendency in the next decade away from geometric and toward naturalistic motifs. The V-boss and flattened faceted stem lift to a reeded ferrule and a natural ivory handle of elliptical cross-section. The marks lie underside along the rear of the left edge.

25. FISH SLICE, Thos. Hayter, London, 1808; length 30 cm; weight 4 oz; solid handle. The dished blade is doubly reeded along the right edge and around a central pierced area that is somewhat disconcertingly cusped toward the rear. The piercing takes the form of waisted squares that follow the outline of the blade, and with notched comma scrolls at the base of the reserve with an engraved floral surmount. The V-boss lifts to an Old English handle. The marks are in line under the finial.

26. FISH SLICE, John Steward (?), London, 1809; length 28 cm; ivory handle. The blade edges and pierced band are outlined by machine-notched hit-and-miss lines that give the *appearance* of zigzag lines to the casual eye. The band of opposed lunettes along the right side is interspersed with engraved and bright-cut leaves. The faceted boss and waisted stem lift to a natural ivory handle of bevelled rectangular cross-section; it is monogrammed. The marks lie underside along the rear of the left edge.

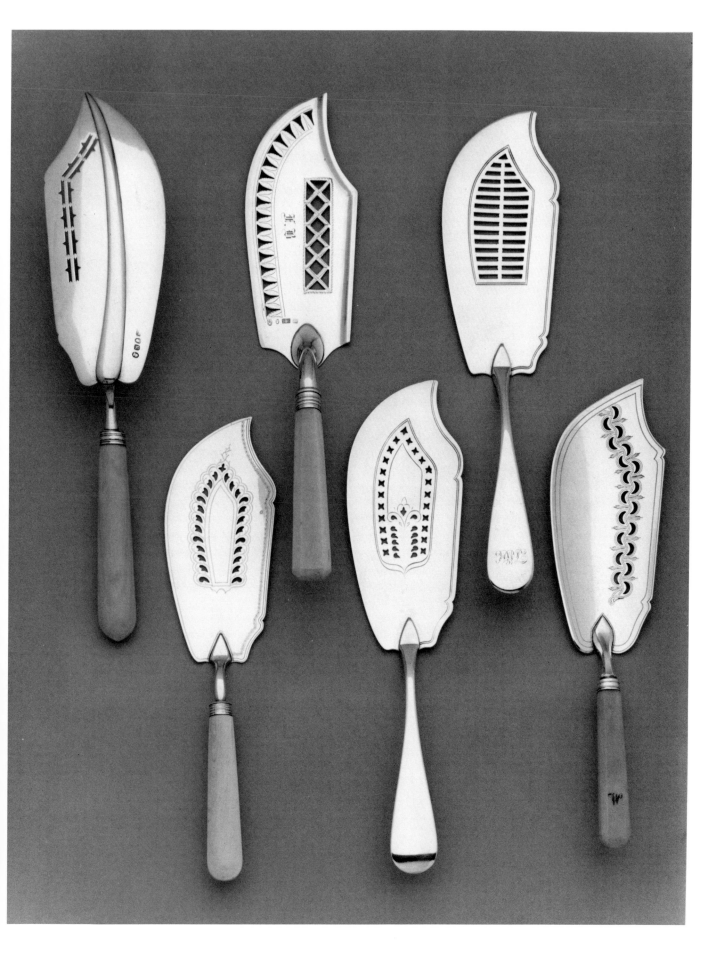

27.    FISH SLICE, Wm. Welch, Exeter, 1811; length 27.2 cm; weight 4.7 oz; solid handle. An example of a bashful Exeter slice. The small plain, highly dished blade lacks any reeding or engraving. The negative cusps are barely perceptible sawn notches. A band of Greek key piercing decorates the right edge. The V-boss and shouldered bevelled stem lead to a crested fiddle finial. The marks are in line on the underside of the finial. Obviously, Exeter makers could fabricate more sophisticated articles [Fig. 40] and these plain objects probably say as much about the clientele as about the smith.

28.    FISH SLICE, William II and Samuel Knight, London, 1811; length 30.5 cm; weight 4.6 oz; solid handle. A conventional blade shape with small negative cusps. The right side of the blade is engraved with straight and wavy dotted lines; the left side features two lines of notched hit-and-miss lines. The server is unusual for the remarkable fine piercing of an engraved coach and four drawn up at a toll gate. The part-elliptical boss and bevelled shouldered stem lift to a fiddle handle. The marks are in line along the underside of the finial. This slice is also shown on p. 65 of Ref. (7).

29.    FISH SLICE, Stephen Adams II, London, 1812; length 28 cm; weight 4.6 oz; solid handle. The shaped blade is unusual for its highly concave hook and concave right side; the blade tip is in line with the right side cusps. The dished blade is decorated with dotted and hit-and-miss lines along the edges and around a central reserve, and with finely dotted and scribed lines in the bright-cut pierced reserve and around a long narrow V-boss. A bright-cut band of small vertical scrolls parallels the right side. The piercing pattern is a 'Christmas tree' of crescents and cusped hexagons. Here is another shouldered and chamfered stem and fiddle finial with marks in line on the underside of the terminal.

30.    FISH SLICE, Old Sheffield, c. 1810; length 29.6 cm; ivory handle. This article incorporates several contradictions. The large size and exaggerated concave shape of the right side of the flat blade (cf. the preceding illustration) resembles some Dutch and French slices [Figs. 128,132,133], but the negative cusps and quality of this plated article indicates its English origin. The highly pierced and ornately chased blade, as well as the split oval boss and short stem, suggest a pre-1800 date of manufacture; but the width and size of the blade indicate a later date. The blade has silver edges. The natural ivory handle is of stepped rectangular cross-section, similar to several preceding ones [see Fig. 19].

31.    FISH SLICE, William II and Samuel Knight, London, 1812; length 30.5 cm; weight 4.8 oz; solid handle. A conventional blade having double reeding along the right edge and around a plain pierced reserve of scrolled lunettes and arranged as pendant ribbons. Variations on this theme, wherein the ribbons are no longer separated, occur for the next twenty years (spray or wave pattern). The small half-elliptical boss and shouldered bevelled stem lift to a chamfered fiddle terminal. The marks lie in line under the finial.

164

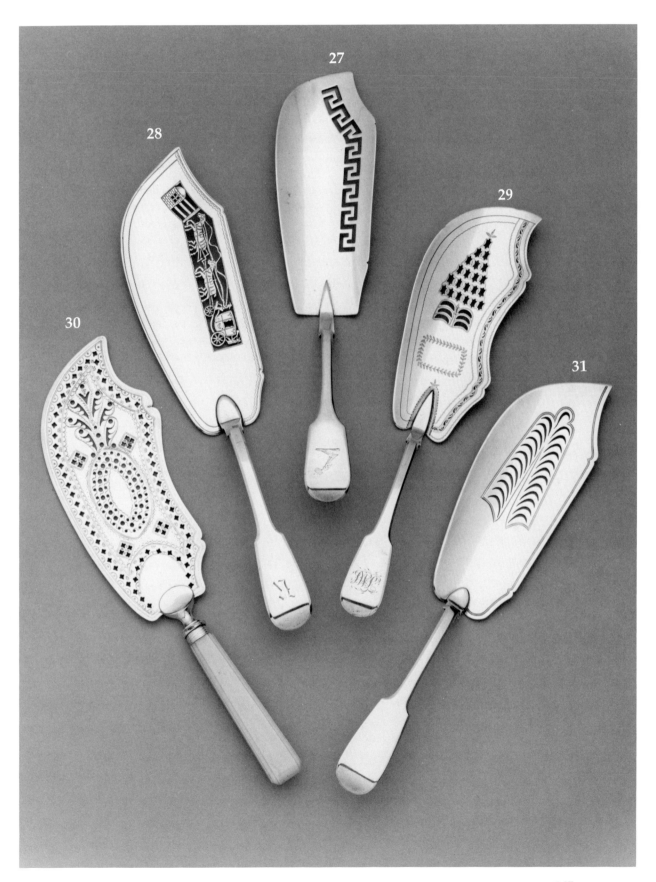

32.   FISH SLICE, Thomas Freeth (?), London, 1813; length 32 cm; weight 4.8 oz; solid handle. This dished scimitar blade is unusual in that it has no cusps and the handle is attached underblade by a long Vee, almost a rat tail [cf. Fig. 17]. The solder joint is masked by a band of zigzag. The periphery is decorated with dotted and hit-and-miss lines. A band of dotted braided rope outlines the right edge and a rectangular empty cartouche. The center is pierced with a pattern of holes defined by hit-and-miss notched arcs as a twelve-petalled flower head with small stippled leaves around. The bevelled stem shoulders are rounded in Continental style. The marks lie in line on the underside of the fiddle finial.

the decade.

After 1800, the blades increase in size and become a little longer and wider. The blade length of the period 1800-1840 averages around 17 cm, with maximum breadth being a little greater than 7 cm. Blades with double negative cusps greatly predominate. Other variations between scimitar shapes arise *via* the following variables: a) the position of the blade tip relative to the vertical long axis of the blade as located by the position of the handle boss; b) the concavity of the right hook at the tip, which may vary from the conventional gentle arc, seen in a majority of the examples, to a highly curved hollow, depending somewhat on the position of the blade tip relative to the right of the center line [Figs. 47,66,70,82]; c) the position of the maximum swell in the arc of the cutting edge, which was usually close to the centre point of the blade length (i.e., below the topmost cusp), or opposite the topmost cusp [Figs. 55,60,77], or, rarely, above the topmost cusp, i.e., toward the blade tip [Fig. 82].

Most London slices locate the blade tip a little to the right of the vertical axis, and, more occasionally, in line with the right edge of the blade. They exhibit a gentle hook that makes an angle of roughly 30°- 45° with respect to a vertical line dropped down from the tip. Occasionally, when the hook is stronger, the top of the hook arc may be close to the vertical or the angle may even become negative in the top portion so that the hook is reentrant [Fig. 52]; in such case the tip of the blade may line up close to the right edge [e.g., Figs. 66,77].

Provincial slices, particularly Scottish and Irish, yield more examples of blade tips that are displaced more strongly toward the right edge, feature more concave sickle-shaped hooks, and place the maximum swell of the cutting arc opposite or above the topmost cusp. In an extreme case of a sickle-shaped hook, the tip of the blade might not even be its most forward point [Fig. 66]. Of course many variants may be found in all categories. Some Edinburgh slices are short and broad [Fig. 47] and may exhibit only a single negative cusp [Type Fig. 8 C]. The correlations described represent only a general tendency; still other features may be seen in Figs. 61 and 69.

Some variations also occur in the shape of the heel of the blade — whether the blade occasionally comes over from the lowest negative cusp to the rear edge

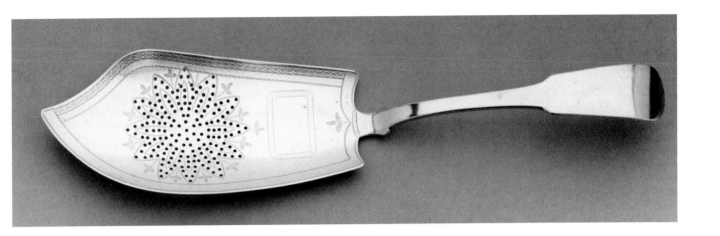

in a smooth convex arc [Fig. 83] rather than in the more customary concave curve; or displays a little 'kick' at the rear right corner as featured in a Paul Storr article [Fig. 46, also Figs. 64,68]; or very occasionally exhibits remnants of fish tail nubs, found more frequently on long-ovals (Chapter IV) or related shapes (Chapter VI).

Continental nineteenth-century scimitars differ in a number of respects from their English counterparts. Those (e.g., Danish, Austrian, Russian) of normal (British) size tend to show both positive [Figs. 129,135,136] and negative cusps [Figs. 139,145]. There is a greater incidence of flat blades, particularly those of Austrian origin [Figs. 143,144]. There is also a group of earlier servers of very large size, typically Dutch [Figs. 132,133] but also including French examples [Fig. 128], and those of other nationalities. These tend to display positive cusps predominantly, and feature greatly exaggerated curvature of the hook, such that the tip of the hook is vertical; also, the tip of the blade may line up with the right hand-edge or extend even further to the right (see also Ref. (21)). The writer has seen a 'deformed,' nineteenth-century, probably German blade, maker unknown (script BB or RB), c. 1825, with pearl handle, whose canted tip end and hook comprises half its length, and which terminates fully 3.5 cm. to the right of the right edge. It manages to achieve the aspect of a tipsy jester wearing a fool's cap. Some of these implements are of rather light weight and incline toward whippiness. Not all Continental divergences from English style tend to gigantism, however. The stubbiest scimitar shape ever made may be the double negative-cusped Norwegian implement by F.J. Brinck, Christiana, 1838, illustrated on page 43 of Ref. (III 38). It is so nearly oblong as almost to appear as a tapered oblong or kidney shape. The maximum swell of the knife edge lies forward of the topmost cusp [cf. a later slice by J. Bryde in Fig. 141b]. Intermediate between the last two servers mentioned is the slice shown in Fig. 138 by T.J. Lange. Its tip serves no function as such, and the end of the blade is rounded in the manner of the oblong servers described in Chapter VI. Later (post-1850) Continental slices seem to display negative cusps most frequently [see Fig. 139 and following illustrations].

33.    FISH SLICE, Wm. Eley, Wm. Fearn and Wm. Chawner, London, 1813; length 32 cm; weight 7.2 oz; solid handle. The dished blade is of conventional type with double reeding around the right side and the central blade-shaped reserve. The piercing of pales and lunettes was probably the most common design and was used over a long period; it is sometimes called the sea-foam pattern and is an abstracted representation of a fish in the sea. It first appeared shortly after 1800 and continued to appear in London and, especially, provincial and colonial production for the next fifty or so years, with every variation of cutlery handle including plain and reeded fiddle, plain and reeded Old English, King's and Queen's and many variations thereof, and ivory. The V-boss and heavy reeded stem, without shoulders, rise to a double struck Queen's pattern finial. The marks lie along the blade right under edge; the back of the finial has room only for a small crest. The underheel of the blade is plain.

34.    FISH SLICE, close plate, J. Gilbert, c. 1813; length 30.5 cm; ivory handle. By contrast with the heavier, relatively expensive sterling implement of the preceding example, this (smaller) article was the kind of silver that could also be enjoyed by those having more modest means. The iron body, with its solid stem, resisted hard usage in a manner not feasible for Old Sheffield wares. Decoration followed sterling custom: double reeding of the right edge and central pierced reserve, in the sea-foam pattern here. A V-boss rises, *via* a waisted bevelled stem, to a reeded ferrule and natural ivory handle of rectangular cross-section. An unusual feature is the double crest—a reflection of the fact that close plate and, especially, Old Sheffield articles were used also by the gentry.

35.    FISH SLICE, William Welch, Exeter, 1814; length 28.7 cm; weight 3.5 oz; solid handle. Another example by this maker [cf. Fig. 27] of a small plain provincial article that has no reeding or engraving, and with a simple geometric pattern of diamond paling that casts back a few years stylistically. The handle is of standard type — a V-boss and chamfered stem, and a fiddle finial with the marks in line on the underside.

36.    FISH SLICE, Peter and Wm. Bateman, London, 1814; length 29 cm; weight 4 oz; solid handle. The perimeter of the highly polished, dished blade and pierced reserve are outlined by a line of hit-and-miss. The pierced pattern is oval. The blade is decorated with bright cutting and fine scribing over much of its area with a pattern that has Eastern touches. Another V-boss and bevelled stem and fiddle finial.

37.    Long-oval SLICE, Peter and Wm. Bateman, London, 1814; length 28.6 cm; weight 3.5 oz; solid handle. The dished blade has peripheral bands of wheel-inscribed notched hit-and-miss and central decoration lines. The oval, parallel-scrolled piercing pattern is bright cut and finely scribed and interspersed on the perimeter with finely scribed leaves. The V-boss and bevelled, shouldered stem and fiddle handle are standard. The marks are in line underneath the finial. This slice by the same makers is similar in decoration, handle and size to its companion in Fig. 36. Articles made by the Batemans tend to be somewhat more elaborately decorated than those by other contemporary makers.

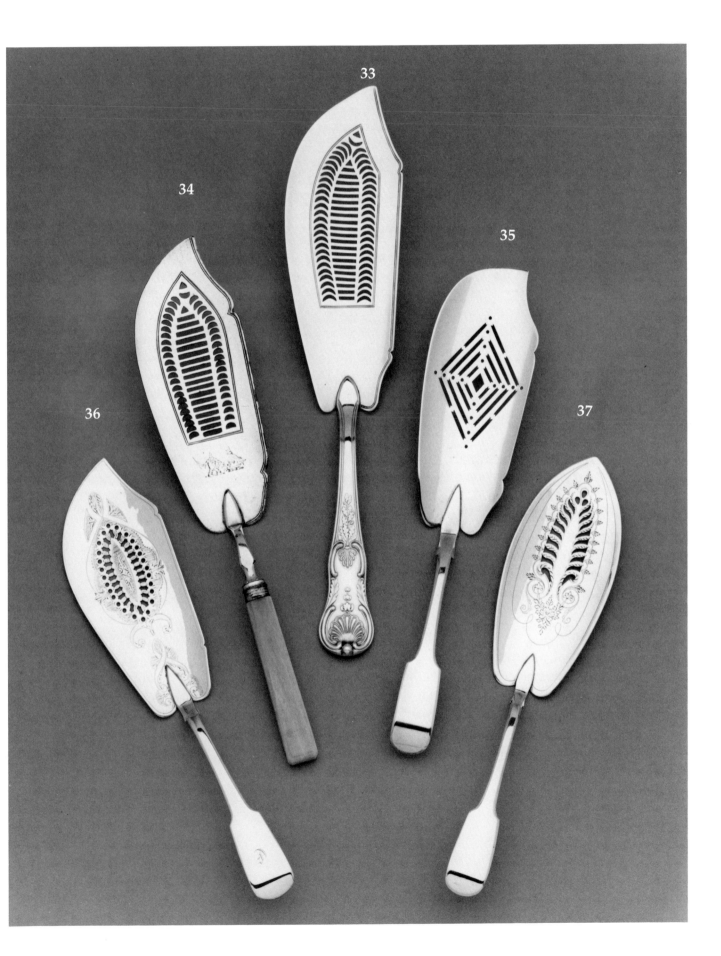

38.　FISH SLICE, Benjamin Smith, London, 1814; length 29.7 cm; weight 7.4 oz; solid handle. This unusual slice has a multiply waved right edge outlined by four chased and engraved scrolls and interspersed arcs. A double reeded central reserve is engraved with leafy vines pierced with circles. The boss is a cast shell with leafy surround. The handle with reeded raised edge is decorated with eight graduated husks on a pounced background. The marks lie underside in line along the middle of the right edge.

Figure 134 displays a rather fragile French miniature scimitar that is very closely similar in shape to its normal counterparts, and in size to the "tart server" of Fig. 129. Its use and survival, say as a tart server, is unclear and it will be thought of here as a jelly or mousse server, or as a trade sample or masterpiece.

No specific mention has yet been made of examples that have a raised right side to the scimitar. Such feature is of less frequent occurrence in English slices than is found with long-ovals or oblong rectangular slices, but does occur in British and, especially, American [Figs. 111,118,121] and Continental servers, as in illustrations already cited. When it does occur in British servers, the cusps are frequently positive, although the raised rim edge may itself show one or two dips at the cusp positions, i.e., negative cusps [Fig. 11]. Instances of soldered, sharply-raised right edges exist [Fig. 11], as are found with long-oval slices, but more often a type of degenerate raised rim occurs in the form of an up-rolling stamped or hammered curve of the right edge of the blade [Fig. 22]. The Brinck/Bryde slices just described also display this feature. This was the type of edge first illustrated by the enamelled iron scimitar implement of Fig. I 11 . Sometimes the raising is supplied merely by a heavy pressed gadrooned edge [Fig. 40] or other ornament [Fig. 39].

American (and Canadian) scimitars in the early part of the nineteenth century are similar to those of British style [Figs. 107-109]. However, by 1820 and continuing to the end of the coin silver (1860-1870), and into the later sterling period, a systematic difference in American blade size and shape occurs. Many unpaired blades are smaller than their British counterparts, being of the approximate size of the first scimitars that appeared in the 1790-1800 period, i.e. 2-3 cm shorter and ~1 cm narrower; they also tend to be of thinner gauge [Figs. 113,116,121-123]. In addition, the scimitar shape becomes much more amorphous, varied and fanciful [Type Fig. 8 E]; the right edge of the blades demonstrate any and every combination and number of negative and positive cusps, swirls and curves, as well as indented and protruding shapes [Figs. 115-117,121-123]. Many are only vaguely scimitar in feeling. At least half of them have a somewhat rolled-up right edge. Some show a stepped-in strip along the bottom 2-3 cm of the left cutting edge. The tip of the blade is very frequently along the line of the right edge of the blade so that the topmost concave hook is more or less vertical. A high percentage of the blades — estimated at 60-70% — are flat. Some of the slices, in particular those

170

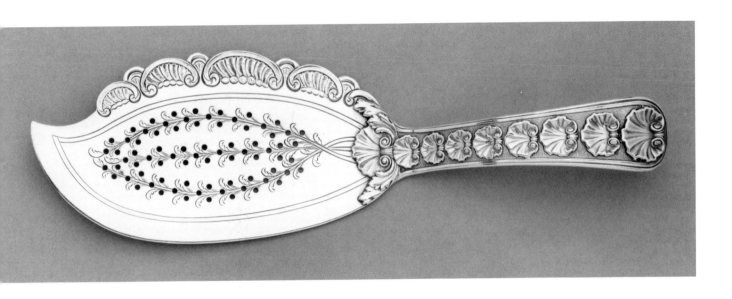

made by Wood and Hughes, New York, flare toward the rear of the blade and have a narrow raised alate portion that is reminiscent of acorn slices (Chapter VI). Later sterling servers continued these styles, but tended, if anything, to become shorter and highly dished — sometimes quite spoonlike. Quite surprising is an English pair by George Adams, London, 1845, whose slice has this late, American spoon shape and which is quite out of character with its contemporaries described below.

Following the appearance of knife and fork pair carving serving sets in the 1830s, the British scimitar pair-knife shape underwent further variation, becoming more elongated and narrower [Figs. 96-100]. Typical dimensions are 16-18 cm in length and 4-6 cm in breadth of blade. These narrower blades may exhibit positive cusps; alternatively, they may retain the topmost negative cusp on the right edge, but the second lower cusp frequently has disappeared [Figs. 96,97,99]. They are almost invariably flat, rather than dished like their earlier counterparts. Long-oval blades in pair sets also became of more frequent occurrence at this time and especially in the second half of the century [Figs. 102,104]. The better quality implements have blades of size and shape similar to eighteenth-century examples, although exhibiting a higher proportion of more symmetric, near-elliptical shapes. Standard, mass-produced implements tend to be smaller and of narrower shape. The forks are always decorated in matching style to the knives. The heel and even the tines of the fork may be pierced in better quality sets. Four is the usual number of tines [but see Figs. 105,106,124]; they are usually straight, but spread tines also occur [Figs. 114,115].

39.    FISH SLICE, close plate, J. Gilbert, c. 1815; length 29.7 cm. The dished blade is outlined by two dashed lines and a wavy zigzag band. The blade is pierced with an engraved fish, paling, and petals. The right edge is raised by virtue of an applied scrolled shell and scrolling foliage. The V-boss and bevelled shouldered stem rise to a crested fiddle finial that has another scrolled shell. The engraved eagle crest bites through the thin silver layer. The following example may be compared.

40.    FISH SLICE, Simon Levy, Exeter, 1817; length 28 cm; weight 6.9 oz; solid handle. The dished blade has a cast raised gadrooned right edge. The dished blade is pierced in a conforming paled shape. The short, hefty, reeded stem and crested handle is double struck with the Hourglass pattern; with shoulders and cast shell boss. The marks are in line under the stem. This Exeter server is of unusually high quality [cf. Figs. 27 and 35].

41.    FISH SERVER pair. Slice, Jas. Scott, Dublin, 1818; length 31.5 cm; weight 5 oz; solid handle. Fork, C.B., Sheffield, 1896; length 23 cm; weight 2.5 oz; solid handle. The slice is in the style of an earlier one by Wm. II and Samuel Knight [Fig. 31]. The plain matching fork was made eighty years later. Both fiddle handles have the same, later monograms.

42.    FISH SLICE, Wm. Knight II, London, 1818; length 29.7 cm; weight 4.6 oz; solid handle. The dished blade is double reeded along the right edge and around a pierced reserve that is cusped to the rear analogous to Fig. 25. The piercing is now more naturalistic with parallel S-curves surmounted by foliate scrolls. This pattern recurs for the next dozen or more years [cf. Fig. 30]. The handle is the conventional one; a V-boss, bevelled shouldered stem and fiddle finial. The marks are in line under the terminal.

43.    FISH SLICE, Wm. Knight II, London, 1818; length 28.5; weight 3.8 oz; solid handle. The blade is double reeded along the right side and around a conforming reserve that illustrates a combination of geometric and naturalistic piercing by its parallel pales, flower heads, and surmounting leaf scroll. It has a short broad V-boss, shouldered, bevelled stem and a plain monogrammed fiddle. The marks are in line underneath the terminal. Variations on this pattern occur for the next 15-20 years.

## Handles

Remarks made regarding handles in Chapter IV apply here also. Early scimitars of the 1790s had filled, ivory, or bone handles, ferrules, and stems similar to the long-ovals, with or without lift in the stem. An occasional mother-of-pearl haft is found [Fig. 50]. Attachment to the scimitar blade was usually by a Vee or other rounded junction [Figs. 9,10]. A split-penny applicator still occurred as, for example, in a slice of 1796 [Fig. 7]. A rarer split-V boss also occurs [Fig. 6]. After the turn of the century, the solid silver handle with plain English fiddle terminal and champfered edges became most common. But filled, ivory, and other handles still continued to appear throughout the century, particularly in provincial manufacture [Figs. 19,22,30,44,57,84], although in reduced proportion up until c. 1840 and with increased frequency thereafter [Figs. 86,98,103,104,106].

44.     CAKE SLICE, Wm. Eley and Wm. Fearn, London, 1818; length 26 cm; ivory handle. The small double reeded blade has two negative cusps and is unpierced; it is crested. The boss is a throw-back to the split penny; a round balustered stem leads to a reeded ferrule and an in-line green-stained ivory handle. What is this implement if it is not a fish slice? It could be a cake or pastry server, or possibly a melon knife.

45.     FISH SLICE, G. Turner, Exeter, 1819; length 28.5 cm; weight 3.8 oz; solid handle. A small plain dished blade with no engraving and with reeding only around a tapering, quadrangular pierced reserve of geometric parallel circles and pales in earlier style. The handle has a crested fiddle with V-boss and bevelled shouldered stem. The marks are in line under the fiddle.

46.     FISH SLICE, Paul Storr, London, 1819; length 30 cm; weight 5.7 oz; solid handle. This is a solid, but not outstanding, piece by this celebrated maker. The right edge of the blade and large pierced central reserve are double reeded. The inner reserve is outlined by a band of alternating circles and quarter-moons with an inner abstract pattern of scrolled stem, leaves and petalled flower burst. The right bottom edge has a little kick. A heavy rounded V-boss goes to a conventional bevelled shouldered stem and plain fiddle terminal. The marks are in line under the finial.

47.     FISH SLICE, D.G., Edinburgh, 1819; length 29.3 cm; weight 3.7 oz; solid handle. Despite much fine work from Edinburgh, this article has the character of provincial work. The dished blade is lightweight, and is unengraved and unreeded, with only a rudimentary pierced fish. Its rather broad leading proportions and short hook are distinctly atypical. The only extra adornment is the cusping of the lower breaks from the right edges to the rear. The boss is the simple waisted drop used on spoons and ladles; the bevelled stem has no shoulders; the plain fiddle is monogrammed. The marks are in line along the back of the finial. The maker's mark appears to be that given by Jackson for David Greig, Canongate.

48.     FISH SLICE, Wm. Knight II, London, 1819; length 29.5 cm; weight 3.7 oz; solid handle. Geometric themes are disappearing, as in the piercing of this stylized potted shrub, or else continue but intermixed with naturalistic motifs. The plain blade has a double reeded edge and single reeding around the piercing. The V-boss lifts to a later monogrammed, fiddle terminal, marked in line underneath. The handle shows some lateral distortion that has accompanied heavy use as a cutter.

49.     FISH SLICE, Wm. Bateman I, London, 1820; length 29.5 cm; weight 4.2 oz; solid handle. This server shows the extra touches associated with the wares of the Bateman firm. The shaped blade has a single negative cusp and two idealized fin-like projections on each edge; the acorn forms of Chapter VI should be compared. The blade has a line of wheel notched hit-and-miss around the blade and arched and looped hit-and-miss and dotted arcs and cusps in the central area. An asymmetric shaped array of pierced triangular forms is adorned by bright-cut ovals, scrolls and two bands of scribed flower heads. It has a standard handle with long slim V-boss, shouldered and heavily chamfered stem and monogrammed fiddle. The marks are in the usual place under the handle.

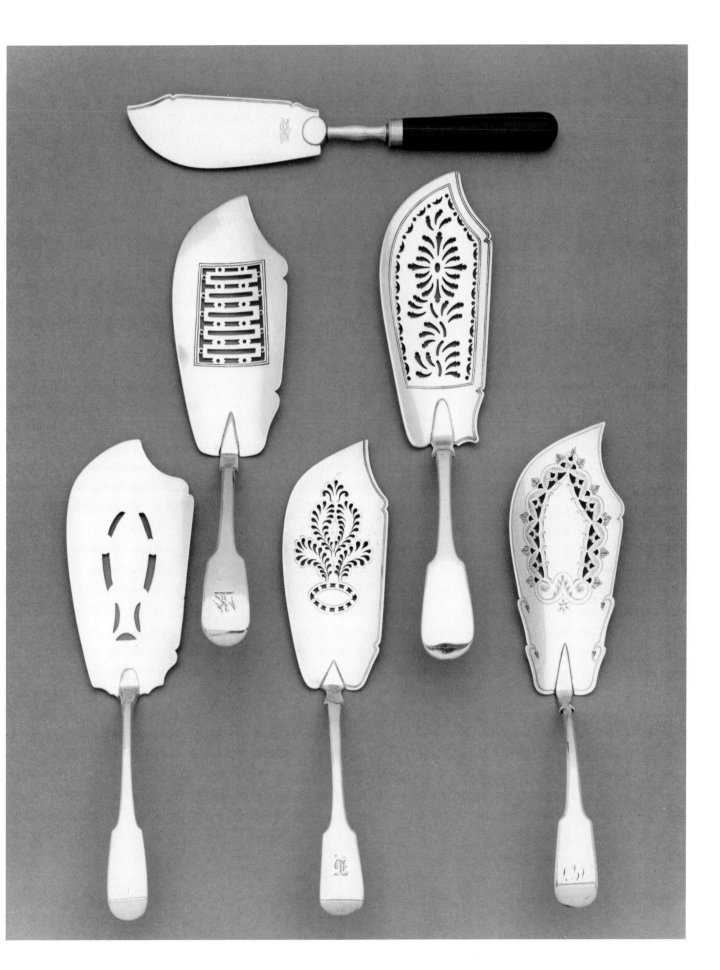

50.  FISH SLICE, close plate, Savory, London, c. 1820; length 29.7 cm; mother-of-pearl handle. The blade is of conventional size and shape. This example is in about as pristine condition and with as high quality handle as one can expect to find in a close plate server. The right edge and shaped reserve are doubly reeded and pierced with a stylized leafy vine pattern. The faceted V-boss and stem lift to a stepped butt plate. The reeded ferrule binds a rectangular handle that is carved in a palmette and bead design, with a diamond-shaped cartouche and engraved contemporary monogram.

51.  FISH SLICE, Wm. Knight II, London, 1820; length 30.3 cm; weight 5 oz; solid handle. Conventional scimitar blade reeding, with shaped reserve pierced with loop and lattice design surmounted by foliate scrolls. The fiddle handle has a V-boss and shouldered stem, and marks that lie in line under the finial.

52.  FISH SLICE, Jonathan Hayne, London, 1821; length 28.5 cm; weight 4.7 oz; solid handle. A conventional blade with double negative cusps; the hook with reentrant angle and tip close to the right edge. Several lines of pricked border and wheel notched hit-and-miss circumscribe the blade and the oval, doubly cusped reserve. The latter is pierced with bright-cut and scribed foliage around a circular, spoked, engraved motif. Conventional monogrammed handle with marks under the finial.

53.  FISH SLICE, Jonathan Hayne, London, 1823; length 29 cm; ivory handle. The blade is of standard shape and size. It is outlined by notched hit-and-miss, and the conforming central reserve by a double line of wrigglework. A frieze of leaves bounds the right edge. The central reserve pierced pattern has a double row of arcs and flower heads, now separated by a spine of pierced scrolls in contrast to the geometric pales in the 1818 example of Fig. 43. The whole is adorned by dot engraving and attached engraved leaves. The faceted boss and stem lift to a reeded ferrule and bevelled, rectangular, natural ivory handle. The marks are in line on the rear underside of the left edge.

54.  FISH SLICE, Wm. Traies, London, 1823; length 31.5 cm; weight 4.6 oz; solid handle. A conventional cusped dished blade with wheel-notched hit-and-miss around the blade and conforming central reserve. The right edge has a frieze of scribed scrolling leaves. The reserve is pierced, engraved and bright cut with leaves and flower symbols of Britain, a theme evidently admired by this smith [see Fig. 55]. A short V-boss and shouldered bevelled stem and fiddle are crested. The marks, as usual, lie in line on the underside of the finial.

55.  FISH SLICE, Wm. Traies, London, 1824; length 31 cm; weight 4 oz; solid handle. The principal decorative themes remain the same as in Fig. 54: a frieze of engraved leaves along the right edge and a pierced engraved central oval reserve displaying the four flower symbols of the United Kingdom with each quadrant separated by scrolled jumping salmon. It is interesting to note, however, the variations that occur in the work of a smith: the handle is much less robust; the reserve is now oval; the blade shape was altered by moving the maximum in the arc of the cutting edge forward opposite the first negative cusp; the blade tip is now rounded; the V-boss is now elongated (and engraved with bands of cross-hatched dotting).

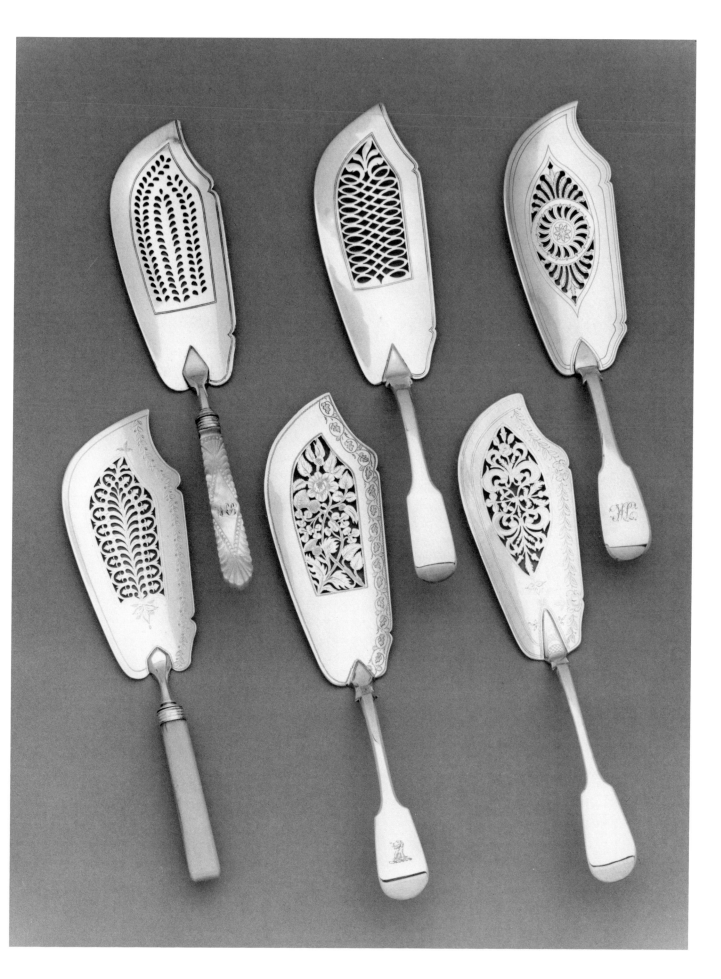

56.    FISH SLICE, Chas. Marsh and Edw. Twycross, Dublin, 1824; length 31.5 cm; weight 5.6 oz; solid handle. This Irish server has a bevelled edge right around the blade. The vertically angled hook is sharpened — possibly for cutting through the backbone of the fish (10). The left curved cutting edge is a little unusual in the concave arc feature as it approaches the heel; this is usually a characteristic of the right side [Fig. 8D]. The blade is highly decorated with straight and wavy lines of dots and notched hit-and-miss, together with a guilloche border on the right edge. The center of the blade is occupied by a pierced engraved dolphin and branch and leaves. A wavy hatched leaf-shape surrounds the V-boss that leads to a shouldered stem and crested fiddle handle. It is marked on the back of the stem and on either side of the boss. As may be seen in the following several illustrations, fish motifs were particularly popular at this time.

57.    FISH SLICE, Jos. Taylor, Birmingham, 1824; length 29 cm; ivory handle. Birmingham slices are surprisingly rare. For some reason they did not engage the interests of these prolific smiths. This one is of standard shape and size apart from an extra wave along the rear of the right edge. The blade is circumscribed by conforming lines of wheel-notched hit-and-miss pattern. The right edge has a frieze of engraved and scribed acorns and oak leaves. A central pierced fish has finely worked dotted scales. The V-boss and flattened stem are bevelled and lead to a reeded ferrule and natural, bevelled rectangular ivory handle. The marks lie underblade along the middle of the right edge.

58.    FISH SLICE, Jonathan Hayne, London, 1825; length 29.5 cm; weight 4.4 oz; solid handle. The blade and central cusped oval reserve are outlined by lines of dots, notched hit-and-miss, and zigzag. The reserve is pierced and bright-cut with two engraved fishes, a water bird, leaves and acorns. This design is widely repeated in other years and other wares (e.g., a slice by Thos. Death, London, 1829) not merely in spirit but in replication from a common pattern. The leading hook is highly reentrant [cf. Fig. 52]. The shaped V-boss and shouldered stem and fiddle, with underside marks, are conventional.

59.    FISH SLICE, Wm. Jamieson, Aberdeen, c. 1825; length 30.5 cm; weight 4.3 oz; solid handle. The blade and central elliptical reserved is outlined with zigzag and dotted lines. A band of leaves is parallel to the right edge. The reserve is pierced with peripheral triangles and a vertical fish decorated with engraved scribed and bright-cut lines. The oval boss lifts through a shouldered bevelled stem to a fiddle terminal with contemporary monogram. The marks lie in a line underneath and consist of four WJ marks and the letters ABD.

60.    FISH SLICE, Wm. Traies, London, 1826, length 32 cm; weight 4.8 oz; solid handle. The blade has an extra-long almost straight hook that places the maximum of the cutting arc opposite the leading negative cusp. Lines of waved dots and notched hit-and-miss outline the blade and conforming central reserve. An engraved frieze of vine leaves and bright-cut floral motifs lies along the right edge. The reserved is pierced, bright cut, and engraved with a fish laid on oak branches, leaves and acorns, and with other neoclassical motifs. The pierced work has expanded to cover more of the blade, as happens more frequently for the next twenty-five years. This same pattern, although differing in minor piercing detail and in blade shape, reoccurs in the work of several smiths in this decade. A banded, engraved long V-boss is the only refinement of an otherwise standard fiddle handle.

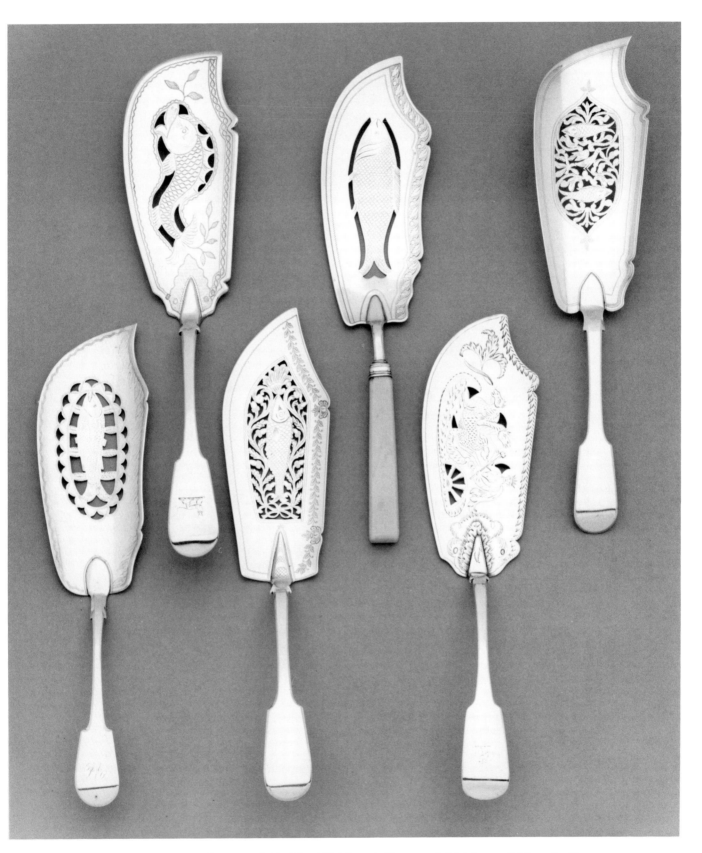

61.   FISH SLICE, Chas. Marsh, Dublin, 1826; length 31 cm; weight 4.4 oz; solid handle. The blade is of standard size and shape but with two incurves at the bottom of both edges. It is covered with engraved and bright-cut leaf frieze along the right edge and is pierced, also, with Neptune in a chariot *with wheels* that is drawn in the sea by two hippocampi. The blade is further decorated with engraved and bright-cut leaves and scrolls and with V-boss peripheral ornament. The crested fiddle handle and marks are standard.

62.    FISH SLICE, Wm. Knight II, London, 1828; length 30.5 cm; weight 4.3 oz; solid handle. A plain blade double reeded along the right edge and central reserve. The pierced pattern is a late London display of mixed geometric paling and scrolled anthemion or palm leaves arranged in three parallel groups. The V-boss, bevelled shouldered stem, fiddle terminal and underside marks are standard.

63.    FISH SLICE, Thos. Cox Savory, London, 1828; length 30 cm; weight 4.4 oz; solid handle. A conventional blade, although a little shorter and broader than most, with the usual reeding and fiddle handle. The unengraved piercing pattern of anthemion, S-scrolls and lunettes now has begun to change to the rather open, coarse scrolling that characterizes much of the production of the next twenty years. The handle has been slightly deformed by lateral stress.

64.    FISH SLICE, Chas. Shipway, London, 1828; length 31.5 cm; weight 5.5 oz; solid handle. The elongated blade shape is a little unusual. The hook is vertical and slightly reentrant; the cusps are token and the leading cusp is much displaced rearward, opposite the maximum of the cutting arc, and the lower right side has a pronounced kick at the heel. The blade and central reserve are outlined by many straight and waved lines of dots and notches. A frieze of flower heads runs along the right side. The reserve is pierced with three horizontal fishes on a bed of oak leaves and acorns. The V-boss is banded and outlined by zigzag, and the crested handle is a conventional marked fiddle.

65.    FISH SLICE, Wm. Elliot, London, 1829; length 31 cm; weight 5.1 oz; solid handle. The plain blade of conventional shape is double reeded along the right side and the reserve. The latter is pierced with scrolled anthemion and circles and stars. The V-boss and crested fiddle handle are conventional.

66.    FISH SLICE, Hamilton and Co., Calcutta, c. 1830 (?); length 33.3 cm; weight 7.8 oz; solid handle. This strikingly large and heavy slice has conventional double reeding and conforming reserve pierced in late sea-foam pattern. The hook of the tip is so severely reentrant and so displaced to the right that the server lacks a useful pointed tip. The right edge is blunt. The handle is shell, thread and fiddle. The boss is a reeded drop. This colonial company functioned from 1815 to post-1870 (see S.R.T. Wilkenson, *Indian Colonial Silver*, Argent Press, London, 1973). The marks under the top of the stem correspond most closely to those of the company in their later period. The suggested date is consistent with the cutlery style used by the company at that time.

67.    FISH/CAKE SLICE, Wm. Chawner II, London, 1830; length 33 cm; weight 8.1 oz; solid handle. A heavy server with a remarkable, original flat blade. The plain blade is double reeded on the right edge and around the reserve. The pierced open-work pattern has a notched scroll fish spine surrounded by palmettes and crescents. The heavy double-stamped, fiddle thread handle is marked in a line on the underside. Fiddle handles became more elaborate in the second quarter of the century.

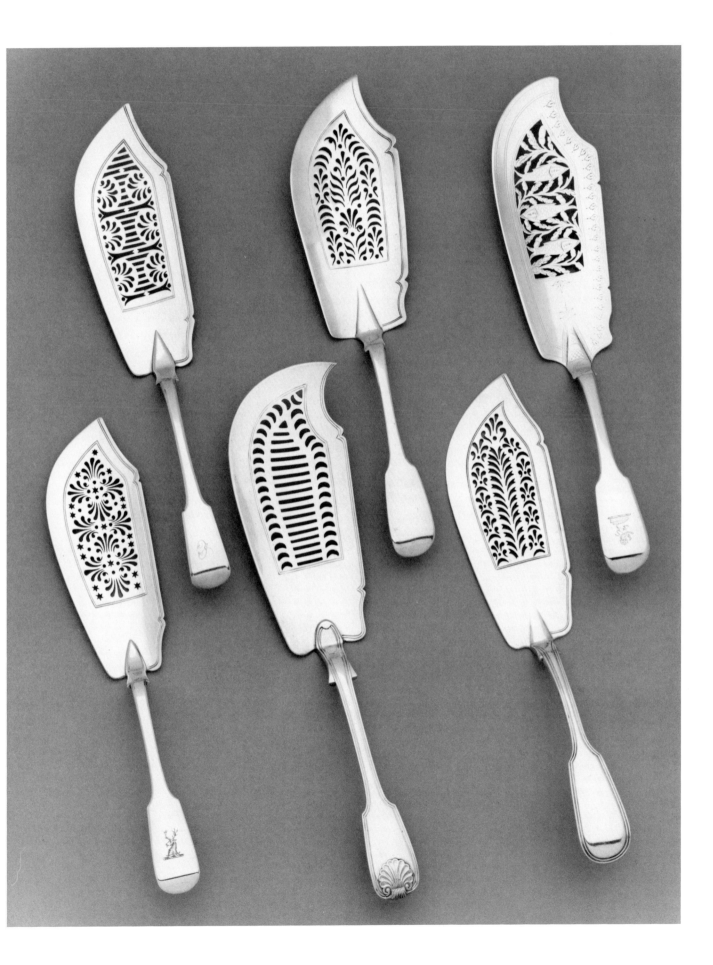

68.    FISH SLICE, Jonathan Hayne, London, 1830; length 30.3 cm; weight 6.3 oz; solid handle. The heavy blade is plain with a sharpened kick to the right edge. The plain blade is double reeded in the familiar manner. The conforming reserve is enlarged to cover most of the blade. It is pierced with a central column of anthemion and parallel arrays of flower heads and arcs, similar to Fig. 43 with anthemion replacing geometric pales, cf. Fig. 53. The very robust handle is double stamped in the King's Husk pattern. There is no real boss; the shoulders constitute a micro-apron and the stem attachment is strengthened (thickened) by the husk shell and leaves at the heel and on the underside of the shoulders by small scrolls and acanthus leaf. The marks lie near the rear under the left side of the blade.

69.    FISH SLICE, Robt. Gray and Son, Glasgow, 1830; length 31.5 cm; weight 5.8 oz; solid handle. The plain unreeded blade is a real provincial throwback — surprising for this productive manufactory. It is pierced simply with six small squares lying between the two negative cusps. It has what is not uncommon for this (and other Scottish) maker, namely, an underblade waisted drop of the spoon type, and rounded French shoulders and single stamped Scottish Bastard King's finial (5). The marks lie underneath the bottom of the stem. Gray made a number of servers in this style.

70.    FISH SLICE, Jonathan Hayne, London, 1832; length 29 cm; ivory handle. The plain blade has a slightly reentrant hook and is double reeded in the usual way. The conforming reserve is pierced with a central scrolled rib like several preceding examples, but is now surrounded by rows of circles and stars. A contemporary monogram lies in front of the shaped V-boss and stem that lifts to a bevelled rectangular natural ivory handle. The marks are placed along the middle underside of the left edge.

71.    FISH SLICE, Wm. Traies, London, 1832; length 32 cm; weight 6.5 oz; solid handle. A standard double reeded blade with conforming central reserve that is pierced with a fretwork pattern reminiscent of Fig. 51 but with added foliate scrolls. The heavy crested, chamfered handle has a V-boss, shoulders, and a double stamped fiddle shell terminal, but plain heel; the marks are in line on the underside of the fiddle.

72.    FISH SLICE, Peter Arthur, Glasgow, 1833; length 29.5 cm; weight 4.3 oz; solid handle. Double reeding along the right edge, but none around the open-work pierced pattern of scrolled spine and surrounding bands of stars and crescents, in somewhat cruder and simpler replication of several earlier English patterns illustrated above. The waisted drop is applied top-side, the bevelled handle has rounded shoulders. The marks lie under the fiddle finial.

73.    FISH SLICE, A. Walker (?), Edinburgh, 1834; length 31 cm; weight 5 oz; solid handle. A conventional double reeded blade with a central unelaborate pierced pattern, not unlike Fig. 72, but with its own simple arrangement of scrolls, arched lunettes, circles and stars. Servers in this style and that of Fig. 72 were also made at this time by J. and W. Mitchell, Glasgow. The heavy handle with V-boss and wide shoulders is single struck with King's pattern. The marks are underside at the top of stem and a contemporary monogram is engraved above that.

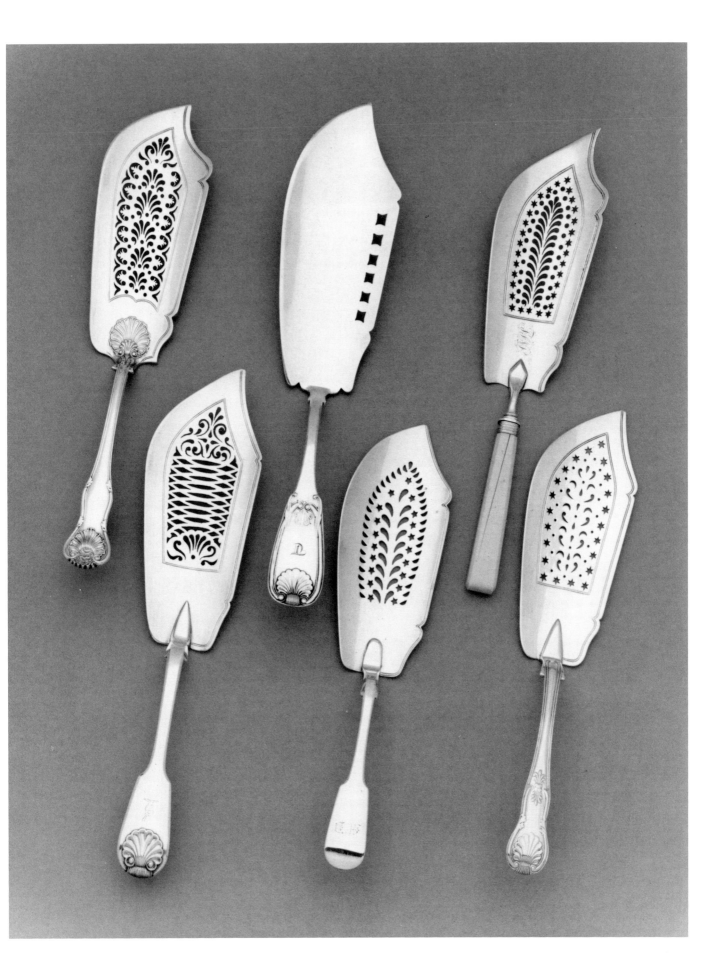

74.  FISH SLICE, Mary Chawner, London, 1836; length 31.3 cm; weight 5.7 oz; solid handle. A conventional pattern that has now persisted and evolved for some 20 years [cf. Figs. 43 and 53]. The handle is more unusual; the V-boss attaches to a rare Hanoverian Thread Drop pattern handle (5). The marks are underside at the top of the stem.

75.  FISH SLICE, Charles Lias, London, 1836; length 32.5 cm; weight 6.9 oz; solid handle. The blade is of standard shape, double reeded in the usual way. The reserve clearly shows the coarse open foliate scrolling characteristic of this later period. The heavy V-boss leads to an equally massive, crested Old English Thread handle. The marks lie under the finial.

76.  FISH SLICE, Wm. Traies, London, 1837; weight 7.7 oz. A school of fish disport themselves on the pierced and highly engraved ornamental blade. The right edge is amorphously shaped by cast leaves and reeding. The blade is grasped by an aged gnarled lopped staff that intertwines with a cast grim-visaged dolphin handle. It is quite a superior article.
The original photograph was a gift from the late Henry W. Smart; the original source is not traceable.

The solid silver handle is constructed so that the stem or shank provides lift and is integral and continuous with the handle proper. The solid handle-blade combination is a very robust one that permits strong force to be developed on the cutting edge even though the handle and blade do not lie in the same plane, as for an optimally designed cutting instrument. The blade junction is made, as described previously, *via* a boss that, apart from early split types, is usually soldered to the top rear end of the blade. The boss is usually V-shaped or modified as described earlier in Chapter IV, with more occasional employment of other devices such as shells, husks, and rosettes, or even more ornamental junctions such as a dolphin. V-bosses are made smoothly continuous with the bottom surface. Scottish [Fig. 69] and other provincial makers [Fig. 87], as well as the occasional London maker [Figs. 17,32,81], applied the stem to the underside of the blade, usually by a Vee or a simple short spoon-type drop. Less frequently in the British Isles, and more frequently on the Continent and in the United States and Canada, especially after 1830-1840, the slice was made in "one piece" with no boss and no special strengthening at the rear of the blade, although sometimes it was provided with a rear apron. In a few cases a strengthening plate at the heel of the blade is a feature of original construction [Figs. 16,21] and not a later repair. Such construction can represent a tastefully decorative as well as useful addition; the Batemans also sometimes employed such a device.

Apart from the common simple fiddle pattern, and particularly in the later 1820s and thereafter, the handle itself might feature some more elaborate variation such as Thread, Husk, King's pattern, Queen's pattern, Hour glass, and a host of others, including Old English and its variations; in short, most of the cutlery patterns as described in references such as Pickford (5). Better quality handles, such as Albany, Coburg, or Albert, are sometimes complemented by other

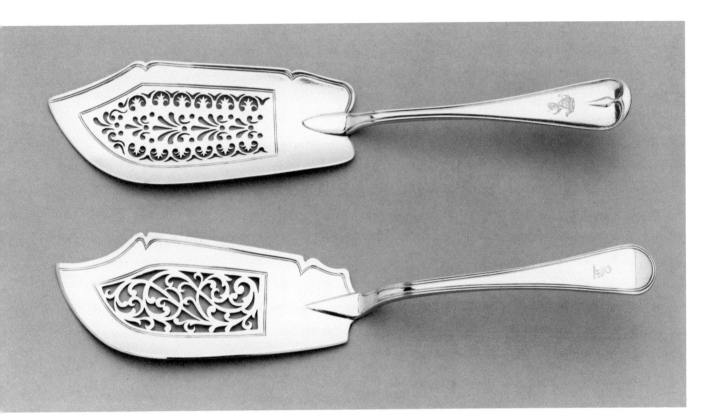

185

77.  FISH SLICE, Benoni Stephens, London, 1838; length 30.5 cm; weight 5 oz; solid handle. The hook is vertical and the blade tip is in line with the lower cusp; the maximum in the cutting arc is opposite the top cusp; the left edge breaks sharply at the rear edge; the right edge has a vertical concavity at the heel. The blade and reserve are outlined by wavy lines of zigzag and notched dots. The pierced pattern of oak branch, leaves and acorns is finely engraved with dot work, scribing and bright cutting. The engraved reserve approaches the V-boss. The latter is outlined by dot and zigzag lines and is decorated with dotted bands of diamonds. The bevelled shoulders and fiddle handle are monogrammed. The marks are on the underside of the finial.

78.  FISH SLICE, Benoni Stephens, London, 1838; length 31 cm; weight 4.7 oz; solid handle. The blade is a little different, in the manner described in Fig. 77. The piercing is open scroll work in which the word FISH is cunningly hidden. The boss and handle have a lovely bit of zigzag bright cutting all around the border, with a starburst and empty oval cartouche on the Old English finial. The marks are in line underneath.

79.  FISH SLICE, Wm. Eaton, London, 1839; length 32 cm; weight 5.4 oz; solid handle. The conventional double reeded blade has a conforming reserve that has expanded to cover the surface above the boss. It is engraved and pierced with foliate scrolls and flower heads. The V-boss lifts to the Old English Thread handle which is double crested; the marks lie under the finial.

80.  FISH SLICE, Mary Chawner, London, 1839; length 31.5 cm; weight 5 oz; solid handle. The blade is of conventional shape and single reeded only along the right side. The whole surface of the blade is pierced with scrolls of various shapes, quatrefoils, arched lunettes, circles, and the like — a picture of busy, open work. Standard V-boss and crested fiddle handle.

81.  FISH SLICE, Wm. Eaton, London, 1840; length 32.5; weight 7.8 oz; solid handle. The blade is the standard one in shape and reeding. The conforming reserve is pierced in a coarse open scrolled pattern. These patterns appeared regularly for the next twenty years [Figs. 86,88], but they differed usually in arrangement and detail, in part or in whole, whether made by the same or by different makers. The handle is Albany pattern (5) with a heavy long threaded drop under the heel of the blade. The marks lie along the back of the stem.

82.  FISH SLICE, John or James Osmont, Exeter, 1840; length 31 cm; weight 4.4 oz; solid handle. The blade has a slightly reentrant long hook; the negative cusps are rather closely spaced. As a relatively rare example, the maximum in the cutting arc lies above the negative cusp. One might think that this pattern, first noted here for 1823 in Fig. 53, is simply a late provincial survival. But George Adams, London, used the same pattern in exact detail (although slightly different proportions) at least as late as 1849. It has appeared frequently in the thirty-year interval [e.g., Fig. 68]. A long V-boss and spread shoulders lead to the crested fiddle handle; the marks are placed under the finial.

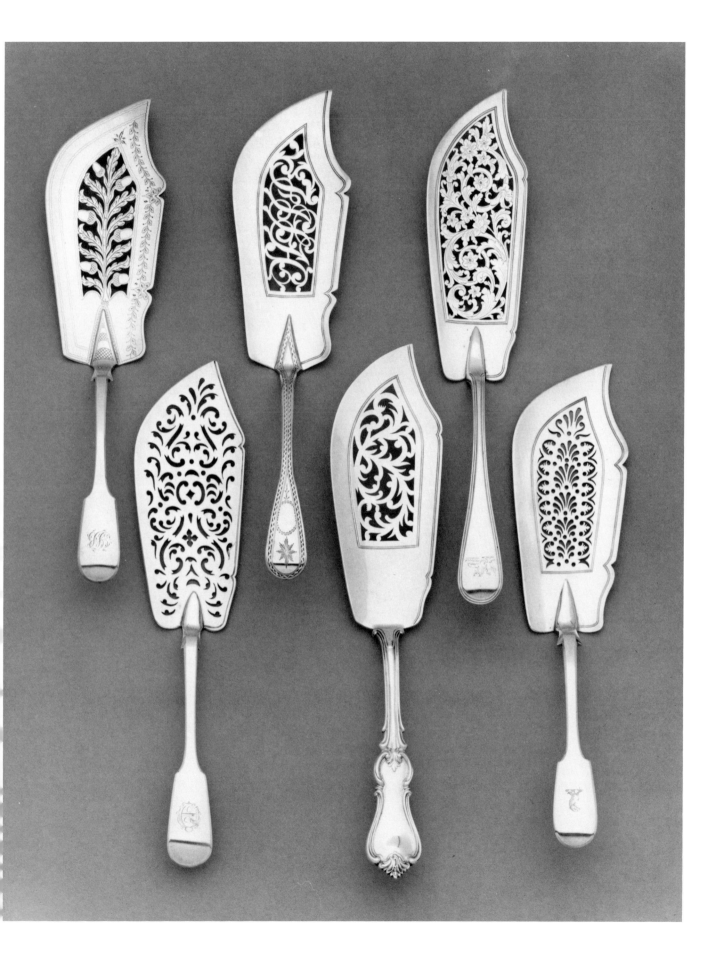

83. FISH SLICE, Robt. Wallis (?), London, 1841; length 32 cm; weight 5 oz; solid handle. The blade is standard in shape except that the bottom of the right side is straight rather than concave. The blade and reserve are outlined by wheel notched hit-and-miss lines and dots. The reserve is pierced and highly engraved and bright cut with a bird in an oak tree, leaves and flowers. A dotted undulating frieze lies along the right edge. The V-boss is outlined by a bright-cut, scribed band and accentuated by a leaf cluster. The handle is a plain monogrammed fiddle. The marks lie under the finial.

84. FISH SLICE, D.D., Edinburgh, 1841; length 31.7 cm; ivory handle. A plain provincial blade with double reeding only along the right side. The piercing is a simple, naive pattern of horseshoe lunettes and central stylized scroll flowers. An elongated V-boss lifts on a solid rectangular stem to an integral box holder of the natural rectangular ivory handle. The marks are topside along the rear of the left side. Top marks appear frequently on Irish servers and less frequently on Scottish ones.

85. FISH SLICE, Wm. Eaton, London, 1841; length 31 cm; weight 5.3 oz; solid handle. The blade has standard shape and reeding. The central conforming reserve is pierced with scrolled paling in the bottom half and foliate scrolling above in (originally) a transitional pattern that goes back, with intermittent repetition, to at least 1818 [Fig. 42]. The boss, fiddle handle and marks are also conventional.

86. FISH SLICE, Samuel Hayne and Douglas Cater, London, 1842; length 29 cm; ivory handle. Plain standard blade and reeding. The reserve is pierced with coarse open scroll work. Beneath is a contemporary monogram that is in transitional style between Georgian/Regency and later Victorian. The faceted, shaped pointed oval boss and stem lift to a fluted ferrule and bevelled rectangular natural ivory handle. The stem, of narrower cross-section than all-silver handles, shows pronounced lateral distortion due to applied cutting pressure. The marks are placed along the left under edge.

87. FISH SLICE, John Walton, Newcastle, 1843; length 30.5 cm; weight 6.5 oz; solid handle. This is a fine piece but the blade shows provincial idiosyncrasies. It is reeded only along the right side, which has double leading negative cusps and only a slight wave where the lower cusp would normally be. The handle is attached by an underblade V-boss. The large pierced conforming reserve has its own distinction with its enclosed, and enclosing, circle and lozenge incorporating scrolled flower heads and foliage. The handle is a short heavy broadened version of single struck King's pattern. The marks lie under along the bottom of the finial.

88. FISH SLICE, WE in a double lobe, London, 1844; length 30.5 cm; weight 4.9 oz; solid handle. A standard blade in shape and reeding. The piercing is a coarse, open work but pleasant pattern of stylized flowers and scrolls. The boss, fiddle handle and marks are standard.

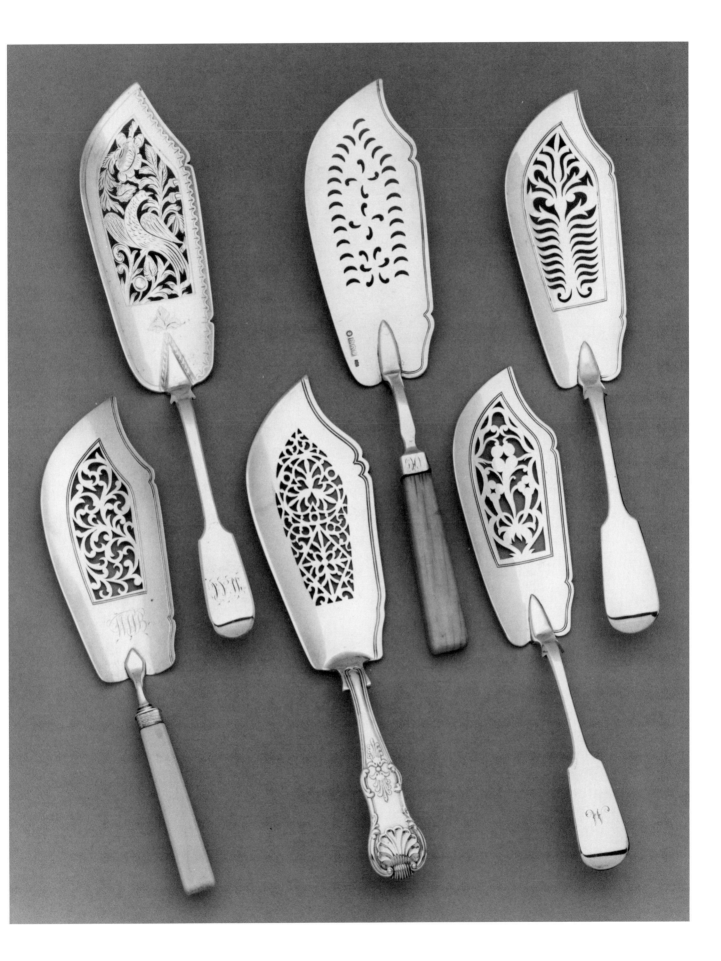

89.    FISH SLICE, Wm. Eaton, London, 1844; length 32.5 cm; weight 6 oz; solid handle. A standard reeded blade with a lightly pierced anthemion and scroll pattern. The V-boss leads to a heavy fiddle thread crested handle, with marks conventionally placed. This pattern is a continuing one.

90.    FISH SLICE, A. Walker (?), Edinburgh, 1844; length 31 cm; weight 5.2 oz; solid handle. The blade is crisply decorated with dotted lines and zigzag around the blade, central reserve, and V-boss, along with a frieze of scribed leaves and densely dotted twigs with a central pierced and engraved vertical fish. The whole pattern is reminiscent of the Scottish blade by Jamieson [Fig. 59]. The handle is a conventional bevelled shouldered fiddle and shell handle, with marks under the finial together with a later name.

91.    FISH SLICE, George Adams, London, 1844; length 32.5 cm; weight 7.4 oz; solid handle. A standard blade with single reeded right edge. The whole blade is marvellously pierced and engraved with a crest, a coat of arms, and the helmet of a gentleman. The whole, with scrolls, flowers, and formal motifs is in rococo style. The crest is a double spouted water pot, with sprig above, on a ducal coronet. The V-boss goes to a double-struck shouldered Albert pattern handle with an applied leaf shape. The marks are low on the back of the shaft.

92.    FISH SLICE, Lattey Brothers and Co., Calcutta, c. 1848; length 32.5 cm; weight 6.3 oz; solid handle. The blade is of standard shape. It is unusual, among other ways, in that the right edge is not reeded whereas the conforming reserve is. The right side has a pronounced kick at the heel. This plain colonial server is pierced in the seafoam pattern, which thus has appeared for almost fifty years [Fig. VII 17]. The semi- elliptical boss rises to long shoulders on a highly bevelled stem with a fiddle terminal. The maker's mark under the finial corresponds to the earlier phase of the operation of these makers between 1843-1850 (W.R.T. Wilkinson, *Indian Colonial Silver*, Argent Press, London, 1973).

93.    FISH SLICE, George Adams, London, 1850; length 32.5 cm; weight 6.1 oz; solid handle. The blade is standard in shape and reeding. The large reserve has a coarse open scrolling pattern typical of the period. The V-boss lifts to a heavy reeded Old English handle. A monogram is in typical later Victorian style. The marks lie in line under the terminal. Adams was one of the largest producers of silver flatware of Victorian times.

stamped decoration on the underside of the blade heel. Provincial, especially Scottish, handles tend to be single-struck, i.e. the pattern is stamped only on the topside. A variety of handles were employed over the years in conjunction with the popular sea-foam blade style. Needless to say, from time to time some special and creative handles were fabricated by the better smiths. One famous slice by Paul Storr has a dolphin handle and weighs over 10 oz (6a); it was offered for sale at Sothebys (London) in 1972. William Traies later made a similar one in 1837 [Fig. 76]; Fig. III 36a should be compared. An unusual Canadian article by H. Polonceau is shown in Fig. 126. Edward Farrell also did his part (Chapter III). In general, although some particular piercing designs were frequently repeated by many smiths, blade piercing and decoration tended to be much more inventive than were server handles. The figures provide many examples of this proposition.

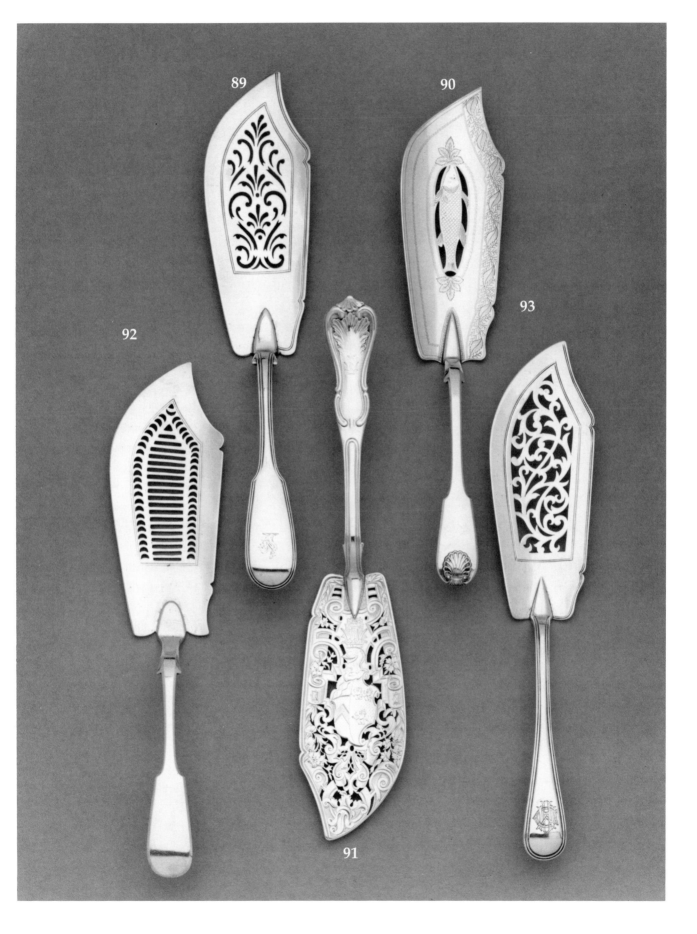

Later Victorian handles of higher quality knife carvers became more elaborate [Figs. 101,102,124]. Use of more sumptuous materials such as mother-of-pearl, agate, or porcelain was more frequent, although solid, filled and ivory handles still dominated production. Staghorn was a not-uncommon material; ebony and shell also served. Long-oval servers often have solid handles; the latter always feature a lift to the stem [Figs. 100,105], and sometimes with continuous extension of the blade into the stem, rather than a boss attachment. Of course, junction bosses do not disappear, whether for oval or scimitar blades, especially in the case of higher quality items. Most of the scimitars have hollow or non-silver ornamental handles that lie in the plane of the blade [Figs. 102-104,106]. Quality items equipped with silver handles, whether hollow or not, or with ornamental handles of ivory or other material, feature silver blades rather than steel; the latter tended to be confined to dessert cutlery (4).

As revealed by the catalogue literature and the articles themselves, the handles of inexpensive British fish carver pairs of lower or standard quality — especially those made by the larger plated-silver/silver manufacturers in Sheffield and Birmingham (15-19) — exhibit the following trends. Scimitar blades are fitted commonly, although not invariably, with synthetic ivory handles — Ivorene, Ivoril, celluloid (Xylonite) and so forth, — or with hollow handles that are sometimes filled, but in later production are hollow and hard-soldered to a very short stem leading onto the blade. The handle may butt against a thickened splayed plate that terminates the blade. Silver plated handles usually conform to plated blades; however, the ferrule on an ivory handle may still be of sterling silver — a feature frequently dwelt upon in urgent salesmanship of these articles.

Continental handles of wood, ivory, or hollow handles, are similar to, but possibly a little more ornate than, British prototypes. They occur much more often than the latter in (earlier) nineteenth-century production. Almost all of the examples cited in Figs. 127-138 are of these types. Handles are sometimes of the waisted fiddle Continental type [Fig. 139], but these wares sometimes show very novel shapes [Fig. 148].

The boss junctions of Continental servers tend to be more ornate and varied than those of British servers. The Vee and oval shapes also occur, but acanthus leaves [Fig. IV 44], as well as anthemion [Fig. 131], rosette, or husk [Fig. 137], and animal [Figs. 133,143] shapes also occur. The handles (e.g., ivory) of a few slices were made to unscrew from the silver stem on a left-handed thread — whether for ease of cleaning, or storage, or other reason, is not clear.

American bosses are often of the conventional V-shapes. They differ sometimes from their London counterparts of the earlier half of the century, resembling Scottish examples more in that they may be applied to the top rear of the blade with the joint at the rear edge being left exposed, rather than the blade being drawn smoothly into the stem joint without evident discontinuity [e.g., Fig. 108

and Chapter VI examples]. Incidence of under blade attachment occurs also in American [e.g., Fig. VI 19] and Continental examples [Figs. 140,141,146].

More Continental scimitars feature a continuous junction between blade and handle than do British servers. Later American slices also usually dispense with the boss. The blade passes to the stem continuously *via* a larger or smaller apron that usually breaks upward from the plane of the blade. Hollow handles of Continental and American (coin silver and sterling) servers of the nineteenth century are almost invariably hard soldered to the stem rather than filled.

## *Blade Decoration*

Like contemporary long-ovals, the scimitar of the 1790s carried only a modest amount of engraving or decoration on its top side. With some trailing influence of earlier naturalistic decoration [Figs. 7,9,10,12], the piercing patterns before and around the turn of the century tended toward the geometric. Overall piercing gave way to more limited geometric designs that tended to take either of two shapes: a shaped U- or horseshoe frieze that retains the outlines of the blade [Figs. 14,18]; or a band in-line along the right side of the blade [Figs. 20-22] that would be called Empire, in Continental notation. Apart from provincial servers, particularly those by Exeter and Glasgow makers, which are often singularly plain and unembellished [Figs. 27,40,47,69], many slices carry a double line of reeding along the right edge of the blade and around a pierced reserve of shape that conforms to the blade shape. Other dot or dash engraving, or chasing, or reeding (single band sometimes), sometimes circumscribes the pierced reserve or even the whole blade, including the region around the junction.

Almost all pre-1850 slices are pierced. The occasional blank blade is found (Figs. 11,44) — often a kidney-shaped server (Chapter VI). During the first years of the nineteenth century, the pierced area tended to enlarge and move into the forward central part of the blade, inside a reeded surround that is a sort of foreshortened replica of the blade shape (headless fish). The piercing design still remained largely geometric in character although naturalistic floral designs — whether a late trailing remnant from the period preceding or an early precursor of the trend to follow shortly — do occur [Figs. 24,32]. Applied decoration is frequently of simple zigzag, dot, hit-and-miss, or other wheel-applied type. Bright cutting also appears. The decoration was sometimes applied to the top surface and perimeter of the boss [Figs. 55-58,60,61]. The latter also served to mask solder work. The pewter example [Fig. I 6] illustrates this well, in addition to rare underside decoration.

In time, other reserved areas or pierced designs — oval [Figs. 17,36], quadrangular [Fig. 45], or other shapes [Fig. 25] — also appeared, sometimes with detriment to the appearance of the whole in the conflict generated between the shape of the blade and the shape of the design or reserve.

94. FISH SLICE, George Adams, London, 1850; length 32 cm; weight 6.6 oz; solid handle. The blade is standard in shape and reeding. The piercing is yet another repetition [see Fig. 70] of the earlier patterns of anthemion sprays with stars and circles disposed around. The Old English handle is in the rare, crowned fouled anchor Admiralty pattern. The marks are under the stem; a broad arrow struck with the marks indicates Navy issue. A crest under the finial is probably that of the officer who purchased the set (5).

95. FISH SLICE, George Adams, London, 1855; length 30 cm; weight 4.8 oz; solid handle. This is a relatively small, standard reeded blade for an Adams production, with another large, open-scrolled pattern. The V-boss handle is a standard crested fiddle. Adams made a wide range of pieces from very ordinary to outstanding. This slice is probably one of the last of the single slices, as judged from its shape. Pairs occur almost exclusively after this time and pair slices are characterized by narrower flat blades, as in the following figures.

96. FISH/CAKE SERVER PAIR, Elizabeth Eaton, London, 1847. Knife, scimitar, length 33.3 cm; weight 5.6 oz; solid handle. Fork, length 26 cm; weight 5.3 oz; solid handle. As discussed in the text, pair knives became narrower and flatter than the single slices but this example seems too much, too soon. This flat scimitar blade is as narrow, or narrower, than they will ever get; one is led to think that the smith was not making a fish slice at all, but rather a cake or pastry knife. In any case, this pair article is not for pudding! The knife blade is double reeded in the usual way along the right edge and around the central reserve, which is pierced with a contemporary coarse scrolling pattern. The blade has a single negative cusp forward and a waved suggestion of a rear positive cusp. There is a little stamped floral chasing or engraving on the heel of the blade. There is no boss. The blade and handle are stamped in one piece, with sharp lift to shoulders on a rare double struck reeded waisted fiddle handle called King's Shape Double Thread (5). The four-tine fork has a pierced heel and a stamped vine-leaf-and-flower pattern with a rococo touch. The shoulder handle matches the knife; both with Georgian style initials. The marks are on the backs of the stems.

97. FISH/CAKE SERVER PAIR, Wm. Robt. Smily, London, 1849. Knife, scimitar, length, 32.5 cm; handle, W.R.S., 1849. Fork, length, 24 cm; handle, W.R.S., 1849. The flat heavy blade has one negative cusp and a single thread line only around the pierced reserve which occupies most of the area. A frieze of foliate scrolling runs along the narrow right edge. The reserve is highly pierced to leave a residue of foliate scrolls engraved on both sides, and a central plaque inscribed with Georgian style initials MJGS on one side. A scimitar blade engraved on both sides is highly unusual; but this server has only a pseudo-boss and a filled handle in line with the blade and, hence, no handedness. The marks lie topside along the rear of the cutting edge. The filled handle is stamped in the Victoria pattern (5). The heavy fork is similarly totally pierced and engraved — on both sides and including the four tines! — leaving a central topside initialled plaque. The engraved stem leads to a matching filled handle.

195

98.   FISH SERVER PAIR, John Hilliard and John Thomason, Birmingham, 1851. Knife, scimitar, length 35 cm; hollow handle. Fork, 27 cm; hollow weighted handle. The flat blade is of amorphous shape. It is unpierced and might also be named a cake knife were it not chased/stamped with several fish swimming among lily pads and flowers that cover the upper top surface of the blade from tip to heel; the underside is plain. A simulated split boss of lily pads grasps the blade and is soldered in a line to a hollow weighted handle stamped in the form of lily flowers, pads, stems, and buds. The marks are in the pattern on the top rear surface. The style is known as the Lily pattern. The four-tine fork is highly shaped and is connected to a matching handle by six-point attachment of a double open-work twisted cord stem. The marks are placed on either side of the top rear surface of the fork. A like set is in the City of Birmingham Museum. Designated, formally, for fish, here, only because of its ornament.

99.   FISH/CAKE SERVER PAIR, George Adams, London, 1854. Knife, scimitar, length 32.5 cm; weight 5.1 oz; solid handle. Fork, length 25.8 cm; weight 3.7 oz; solid handle. This is a rather pedestrian pair. The flat narrow blade has one negative cusp only. It is single reeded along the right edge and the conforming central reserve, which is coarsely pierced with foliate scrolls. The handle and boss are of conventional fiddle type with marks under the finial. The four-tine fork is pierced in similar style. The handle is a matching up-turned fiddle.

100.   FISH SERVER PAIR, Thos. Stone (?), Exeter, 1865. Knife, scimitar, length 32.5 cm; weight 5.2 oz; solid handle. Fork, length 25.7 cm; solid handle. The flat narrow blade has two shallow positive cusps. It is single reeded, only along the right edge. It is coarsely pierced and engraved (top side only) over the whole surface with foliate scrolls and has a central engraved reserve with a fish and water scene. A V-boss and shoulders lift to a crested fiddle with marks under finial. The fork is pierced on the heel and on the four-tines, and is engraved in matching foliate style. The blade and long upturned fiddle handle are stamped in one piece. The marks lie under the top of the stem. Designated for fish, only because of the engraving.

With advance of time, more and more floral scrolling and curved arc influences tended to modify the simple geometric piercing. Combinations of styles in a single design appeared [Figs. 42,43,53], until in the 1820s scrolling motifs became most common and blades were more highly embellished by fanciful piercing, engraving, and bright cutting. Fish and marine forms were also introduced more frequently: one, two, three, or even four fishes in various patterns and configurations — vertical, horizontal, intersecting, and so on — were used [Figs. 15,39,55,58,64]. Dolphins also had a role [Figs. 56,76]. In Continental terms the Biedermeier style was becoming more prominent; later Victorian servers show a resurgence of rococo and baroque forms [Figs. 101,143,144]. Slices were occasionally lesser decorated on the underside.

Many of the piercing and engraving designs find frequent repetition. These include basic elements such as paling, dashes and circles, scrolls, lunettes (crescents), and stars (popular from the contemporary Egyptian influence), or whole patterns such as the sea foam and fish back-bone patterns, much used by Eley, Fearn and Chawner, and others [Figs. 13,23,33], and which were also made in

197

101. FISH SERVER PAIR, Henry Holland (?), doubly marked, Birmingham, 1855, London, 1872; cast handles; total weight 23 oz. This set is of very high quality. The scimitar blade has two negative cusps separated by a positive one on the right edge and one rear negative cusp on the cutting edge. The decoration on this server is a mix of styles that embrace the whole eighteenth century. A neoclassical/rococo frieze of engraved shells, scrolls and flowers lies along the right edge. The large central reserve is highly pierced with scrolling foliage. A bold cast baroque shell boss provides the tail of a cast, highly carved, and detailed "dolphin handle" [cf. Fig. III 60a]. Two sets of marks lie along the top rear of the blade, including a set of London assay marks for 1872. The four-tine fork is in matching style.
By kind cooperation and courtesy of Phillips (Blenstock), London.

close plate; or the spray pattern of William Knight and brother Samuel [Figs. 31,41]. The acorn motif is a common feature and may have patriotic allusion to English 'hearts of oak.' The thistle, shamrock, and rose appear more occasionally [Fig. 55]. Such repetitive usage of a few motifs and patterns, with little variation, appears throughout the history of the scimitar slice, as may be confirmed by reference to the many individual figures; thus, the sea-foam pattern is represented for almost a half-century [Fig. 92] in the products of British and colonial makers. This pattern book usage and some lack of innovative artistic talent — half of all servers seemingly fall into this group — clearly label many silversmiths of the period as technical craftspeople rather than decorative artists, as they are trained today. Nonetheless, a surprising number of novel designs and blade shapes do keep surfacing, so that despite close attention to the subject for many years, the writer is still constantly being stimulated by the discovery of yet another new feature or example.

Among the imaginative and elaborate motifs that have appeared is the scene of the sea god Neptune in his carriage (equipped with wheels!) being drawn over the foamy deep by his hippocampi [Fig. 61]. In other variations he is drawn by dolphins. Some elaborate devices are quite unrelated to any culinary association, as witness the coach-and-four drawn up to the toll gate in Fig. 28, and a similar illustration in Fig. VII 5. Patriotic themes, such as Prince of Wales plumes, after the beginning of the Regency in 1811, also occur (6b).

As is evident from the specific examples cited and by reference to the illustrations in this chapter, the decoration, whether piercing, chasing or engraving, was not necessarily restrained within the confines of a specific or delineated reserve. Also, as noted above, piercing reserves varied considerably in shape. Engraved or chased decoration, including floral motifs and vine and leaf themes, appears in, around, and outside of the reserves. The decor of the 1825-1850 period, especially, incorporated larger reserves, as well as more all-over blade decoration [Figs. 64,68,79,80,87,91]. Figure 147 of Ref. (5) illustrates another example, by William Traies, London, 1842, in which no part of the blade surface has been left untouched.

198

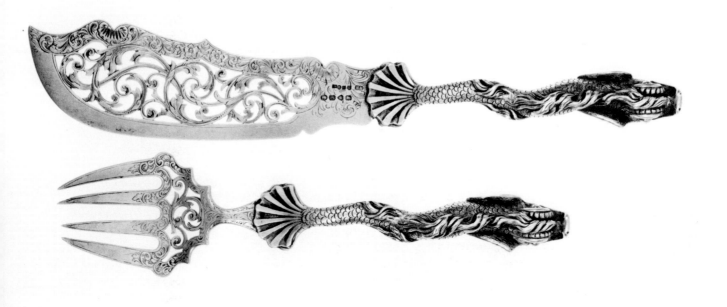

In the 1830s and 1840s, the scrolled piercing began to degenerate in quality and detail, and rather coarse, open, repetitive patterns [Figs. 63,75,80,96] appeared. The advent of server pairs and of machine technique somewhat paradoxically turned the trend in *quality* articles in the second half of the century back toward more interesting and detailed work. Forks and knives were decorated in matching designs that were sometimes more free and fanciful than those of the Regency period and might feature two-sided engraving [Fig. 97]. Much of the piercing, and some embossing and engraving, was still done or assisted by hand. An effort for over-all striking effects was frequently demonstrated. The scimitar servers by Higgins and Adams [Fig. 3] are a case in point. The example shown here, dated 1861, is very similar in design to others by Adams and to those of Francis Higgins. The piercing is extraordinarily detailed and intricate, but the numerous small, yet significant differences in detail shows that they were not struck by a die. Much hand-sawing was involved in the fabrication of these articles. In contrast to Russian and Scandinavian work as the most notable, enamel and niello decoration was not much employed in British or American manufacture of silver articles in the nineteenth century.

At the same time, in the last quarter of the century, cheap, mass-produced silver and silver plate sets began to appear in quantity. These lower quality implements had little, or only cursory, stamped piercing and decoration [Fig. 103]. In general, stamped 'chasing' replaced piercing as the principal form of decoration of inexpensive or silver plated sets, but it was often so perfunctory as to discourage interest. Mass production sounded the death knell of the broad-

102. FISH/CAKE SERVER PAIR, Martin Hall & Co., Sheffield, 1876. Knife, long-oval; length 32.7; handle RM and EH, Sheffield, undated. Fork, length 26 cm; handle RM and EH, Sheffield, undated. This is a quality pair. The blade has zigzag lines around the blade and a pierced frieze of engraved lozenges and circles. The oval reserve is pierced and stamped in a formal pattern with lion mask below a crest. The blade is chased and engraved and crested on both sides. Marks are in line along the length at the rear of the underside of the blade. It has no boss but butts against a filled beaded handle stamped with a matching diaper pattern. A crest shield holds a Victorian monogram on the top side. The fork is pierced and decorated on both sides in matching diaper piercing around the periphery, and with engraved masks at the base of the tines. The handle is also a match.

103. FISH SERVER PAIR, Martin Hall & Co., Sheffield, 1876. Knife, scimitar, length 32.5 cm; ivory handle. Fork, 26.5 cm; ivory handle. The flat unpierced blade has four negative cusps, and two positive ones at the rear of the cutting edge. The blade is decorated with a frieze of stamped radiating dots enclosed in lines of zigzag. It is engraved with a fish lying on a bed of reeds and ferns. The engraving is carried on both sides of the blade. The marks lie along the length of the blade on the top surface near the rear. There is no boss. The blade butts on a fluted, beaded ferrule, marked by Martin Hall, that holds a carved, crested ivory handle. The four-tine fork is also engraved on both sides in matching style to the knife. Ferrule and ivory handle match the knife. The marks lie under the stem. This pair is of lesser quality than the preceding one made by the same makers in the same year. Martin Hall were prolific manufacturers and their wares covered a range of customer interests.

104. FISH SERVER PAIR, Edw. Hutton, London, 1880. Knife, long-oval, length 30.7 cm; Celluloid or Ivorene handle. Fork, 25.5 cm; Ivorene handle. The blade is slightly double dished and has vestigial tail nubs. The top surface, only, is completely covered with a stamped leaf and flower design, with pierced birds on either side of a vase-shaped fruit stand on center. The flat-shaped stem is continuous with the blade and butts against a white handle. The marks lie along the underside of the stem. The four-tined fork is similarly decorated with matching handle and understem marks. This pair is an example of lower quality wares made attractively.

bladed server as an article of artistic expression, although production has continued throughout the present century. The most interesting exceptions are individual pieces made by the artist-designers of the various Arts and Crafts movements (8) of the early twentieth century and the legatees of the training programmes they helped to inspire. Several examples were presented in Figs. III 61-66. They display a high degree of originality.

American coin-silver (and later sterling) servers of the nineteenth century featured very little piercing. Notwithstanding, whereas it was seen that the highly pierced British slices of the 1830s and 1840s frequently became very coarse and uninteresting, American slices are characterized and enlivened by much hand-engraved, bright-cut, and engine-turned decoration. Quality articles feature hand-aided engraving of a wide variety of floral, naturalistic and geometric motifs — sometimes superimposed on an engine-turned background having a pounced finish [Figs. 111-114]. Fish slices are often unpierced but their function

201

105. FISH/CAKE SERVER pair; electroplate, Elkington and Co., Birmingham, 1865-1897. Knife, scimitar, length 34.7 cm; Old English handle. Fork, length 27 cm; Old English handle. The knife is stamped out. The blade has two negative cusps and a scrolled feature at the heel. The blades have been pierced, engraved, and chased by stamping in a pattern of C-scrolls and ovals. A pseudo-drop boss and side scrolls lift to the Old English monogrammed handle. The five-tine fork is unpierced, with matching stamped boss and decoration; unlike the knife, it is also decorated similarly on the underside of the heel. The Old English handle is upturned. The marks on both are on the upper stem. The whole aesthetic effect is still pleasing, although the pair cost only a small fraction of a sterling counterpart.

106. FISH SERVER pair; electroplate; unmarked; c. 1900. Knife, scimitar, length 32.5 cm; filled handle. Fork, length 25.5 cm; filled handle. The knife is unpierced and the right edge has three positive cusps and one negative cusp. It is decorated with machined scrolling foliage and a fish on water amid reeds — hence a fish slice in one convention. The underside has a small foliate scroll at the negative cusp. The right edge has three positive cusps and one negative cusp. The blade has a terminal heavy plate against which an ornate handle butts directly in line. It has stamped foliate scrolling and shell ornament. The heel of the five-tine fork is pierced; it is inconspicuously engraved and has a matching handle.

107. FISH SLICE, Thomas Rockwell, New London/Norwalk, Connecticut; c. 1795; length 30 cm; handle unmarked. The blade of this rare server has a positive cusp and a raised right edge. There is a frieze of engraved keyhole piercing around the whole blade. The inner reserve is bounded by a wavy line engraving and features an engraved, somewhat ill-tempered dolphin. A large shell boss intrudes on the piercing; it lifts on a round stem to a pseudo-ferrule that is soldered to a chamfered, hollow handle. The latter may well have been made by the smith, himself. Ensko (23) cites Rockwell's date of work as 1795, whereas Currier (24) gives this as the death date. The positive cusp certainly suggests the 1790s; the large size and breadth of this scimitar server blade suggest the latest possible date.
By cooperation and courtesy of Dr. Dale Bennett.

is denoted by engraved fish, fishermen and marine scenes; an unpierced blade may even have a fish or dolphin-like shape [Figs. 112,114]. In the latter half of the century, American slices tended to become smaller and lighter than their earlier counterparts. Manufacture of individual slices, in addition to pairs, also continued — unlike the British practice.

Continental slices of the early nineteenth century in Empire style also tend to be more decorative, on average, than British ones, both with respect to piercing and, especially, engraving [Figs. 128,132,134-137]. In this respect, American coin silver and Continental servers resemble one another. Some additional and interesting illustrations of the latter are found in Ref. (20). The pair by George Adams, 1845, mentioned above in the section on Blade Shape, is also unpierced, but is well engraved on a pounced background; on first sight it could be mistaken for a later American type. Like British servers, and at least for a time, later Continental servers in Biedermeier style also became less interesting after 1840.

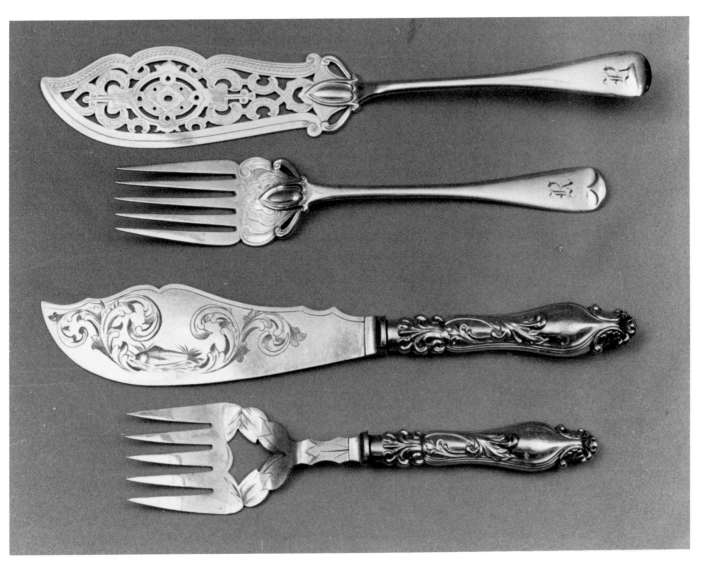

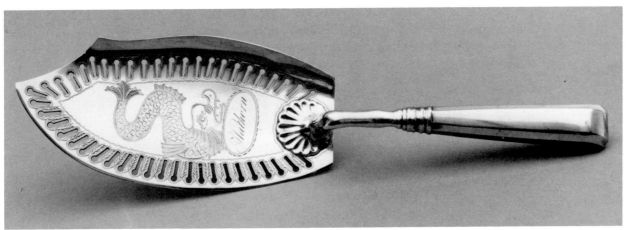

108.	FISH SLICE, Frederick Marquand, New York, c. 1825; length 30 cm; weight 5.7 oz; solid handle. The singly dished scimitar blade has a vertical hook in line with the raised waved right side that could be regarded as having four rounded positive cusps. The plain unreeded blade is pierced in a simple open pattern of stylized branch and leaves — not unlike provincial British slices of this time; cf. Figs. 35,72,73. The large rounded V-drop is decorated by a stamped shell, part of a handle that is double struck with Queen's pattern (5). However, there is no decoration at the heel of the blade. Like some other American slices, the boss is applied to the top surface of the blade with a discontinuity at the rear edge. The maker's mark and three silver standard marks of the period 1810-1850 (23) are on the back of the stem; the shoulders of the stem have been rounded into oblivion. American slices at this time were not yet as small, or lightweight, as many would become.

109.	FISH SLICE, no maker's mark, American, c. 1830; length 30 cm; mother-of-pearl handle. The plain unreeded blade is similar in shape to that of the preceding illustration. Both feature severely straight rear edges. The hook is reentrant and the blade tip lines up with the concave right side, which displays two negative cusps. The blade is plain and pierced with a large coarse oval arrangement of scrolled shapes and quatrefoils. A small V-boss, now smoothly joined to the rear edge (ct. the preceding example), rises by a sharply right-angled bend of a waisted stem. The rope-decorated, fluted ferrule of flattened shape holds a flattened, bevelled mother-of-pearl handle. There are three silver standard marks (23) laid perpendicular to the rear edge under the boss.

110.	FISH SLICE, Stevens and Lakeman, Salem, Massachusetts, c. 1830; coin silver; length 32 cm; solid handle. The unusual shape of the blade of this server makes uncertain whether it should be classified here as a scimitar, or in Chapter VI as a kidney shape [cf. Fig. 141b]. The blade 'tip' lies in line with the right edge and the server has a round front edge. The hook is vertical and the blade is concave between the two negative cusps. The perimeter carries a line of zigzag and the right edge a guilloche frieze. Pierced crescents outline an engraved fish. A semi-elliptical boss lifts on a shouldered bevelled stem to a monogrammed fiddle handle.
By cooperation and courtesy of Dr. Dale Bennett.

111.	FISH SLICE, Benjamin Gurnee, New York, N.Y., post-1835; coin silver; length 30 cm. The blade has a highly cusped and waved raised right edge. It is lightly pierced around the sides by large F-scrolls. The cutting arc is feather-edged. The whole blade is engraved with opposed, cross-hatched C-scrolls, other scroll work, two crossed fishes, and a lake and cottage scene. There is no boss; the reeded, upturned pointed Old English handle is continuous with the blade.
By cooperation and courtesy of Dr. Dale Bennett.


## Function

Having pronounced earlier that trowels were not meant for cutting, for reasons that included the lift of the stem so that handle and blade do not lie in the same plane, coupled with their delicate nature, we must now contend with the sharpened left-hand edge of the scimitar server, despite the lift of the handle stem. Scimitar servers are obviously broad-bladed knives that do have cutting functions. The solution to the apparent paradox lies, of course, in their sturdy and

204

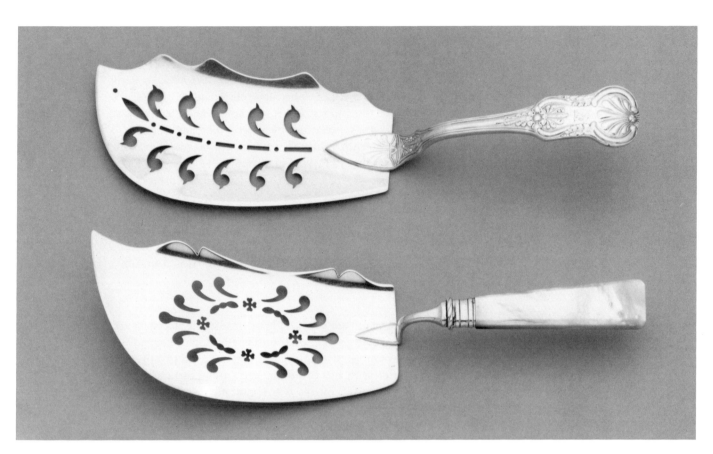

205

112.   FISH SLICE, Samuel Kirk, Baltimore, 1830-1846 (20,23-25); marked 10.15 (equal to 0.846 silver); length 29.5 cm; weight 5.7 oz; solid handle. The dished and rolled blade is in the shape of a comic rollicking dolphin with engraved features and scales, ruffed head and acanthus leaf. Superfluous, anatomically defective gills are represented by lunette piercing. The thread fiddle handle is single stamped in one piece with the turned-up (semi-apron) rear edge of the blade. The later date is favored by the Victorian style monogram.

113.   CAKE/PASTRY SLICE, Mulford and Wendell, Albany, N.Y., c. 1845; coin silver; length 27.3 cm. The unpierced scimitar blade is quite broad in its proportions. It has two positive cusps and one negative between. Although shaped as a scimitar, it is reminiscent of a trowel. It is unpierced and stamped over its whole surface with baroque-style foliate scrolls and large flower heads. The reeded handle stem is continuous with a rear apron and rises to an Albert finial.
By cooperation and courtesy of Dr. Dale Bennett.

114.   FISH SERVER PAIR, George B. Sharp for Bailey & Co., Philadelphia, c. 1851; coin silver. Knife, length 30.5 cm; solid handle. Fork, length 28 cm; solid handle. The blade is shaped and line engraved as a dolphin. The blade widens into a butt plate and is soldered to a pseudo-ferrule and flat, pointed handle. The latter, with zigzag outline, and crested cartouche (with date of 1860) and lozenge features, is completely covered with a cloth-textured background and a regular pattern of crosslets and bars superimposed. The fork is in matching style with four spreading tines, twist stem, and textured fork and matching handle. This blade shape and fork were featured by Mappin Brothers, Sheffield, in the Crystal Palace Exhibition, London, 1851.
By cooperation and courtesy of Dr. Dale Bennett.

compact construction. That they were used with force is manifested by occasional lateral deformation of the handle. The rectangular cross-section of the stem tends to resist such thrust, as is more readily revealed by servers having filled or ivory handles attached by less robust stems [Fig. 86]. The occasional example has been noted (9) in which the right-hand edge has been sharpened.

British scimitar servers are almost invariably called fish slices whether or not they display fish or marine themes. They may be used for parting, separating, skinning, cutting—both flesh and small bones—and serving fish. The sharpened left arc of the blade is the cutting edge. The hook has no explicit function, although in one replica of the Hester Bateman scimitar, the hook has been sharpened at some later time and its use as a cutter of the back bone of fish has been proposed (10); [cf. also Fig. 56]. They are also well adapted for the purpose of transferring a fish from a fish kettle to a mazarine (whether silver or ceramic) or to a platter; the fish could be served from the mazarine and sometimes was (Chapter II).

Both the asymmetric-shaped blade tip and especially the dishing of the blade seem to deny any optional identification of the early single (pre-pair) slices as cake or sweet pastry servers. Such early, unpaired broad-bladed British scimitars as are flat were usually flattened some time after making, with some detriment to

206

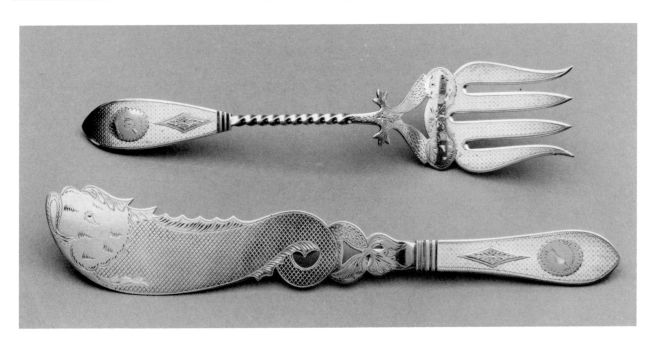

207

115. FISH SERVER PAIR, Albert Coles & Co., New York, c. 1850 (23-25). This is a very attractive set. Knife, length 30.5 cm; hollow handle. Fork, 25.5 cm; hollow handle. The flat scimitar blade has a multiply cusped — negative and positive — and waved right edge; the left edge is cusped at the rear. The blade is completely covered with machined engraving and bright cutting of leaves and bold scrolls and swags, in rococo style, and worked into the shaped edge. There is a central dolphin figure. The blade has a minimal row of pierced small scrolls parallel to the right edge. The underside of the blade has very minimal engraving of hit-and-miss peripheral lines. The marks lie along the underside rear of the right edge. A very short stem and butt plate are integral with the handle and soldered to a hollow handle stamped with intertwined dolphins holding a shell terminal in their mouths. Their progeny looks shyly at the scene. A beaded oval cartouche is empty. The fork has four spreading tines. The heel is pierced and the upper surface and tines are decorated with leaves and foliage in matching style. The underside is again lesser decorated. A stem of triangular cross-section leads to a matching handle.

116. FISH/CAKE SLICE, Peter L. Krider, Philadelphia, c. 1860; coin silver; length 28.5 cm; solid handle. The unpierced scimitar blade has an amorphously shaped right edge. It is beautifully decorated over the whole surface with bold baroque ornate scrolls and flowers on a woven background. The blade is continuous with a decorated rising handle and upturned Old English finial. A small cartouche holds a Victorian style monogram. Many servers were made smaller at this time.
By cooperation and courtesy of Dr. Dale Bennett.

117. FISH/CAKE SLICE, John Polhemus, New York, c. 1868, for Tiffany & Co., New York; sterling; length 28.3 cm; solid handle. The unpierced scimitar blade has an amorphous right edge, a formal, engraved flowered band around the circumference, and crisply engraved interlaced vine and realistically scribed leaves. The handle stem rises from the rear edge to a decorated reeded Old English handle with monogram.
By cooperation and courtesy of Dr. Dale Bennett.

118. FISH SLICE, Cortlan & Co., Baltimore; 1868-1870 (25); coin silver; length 30.3 cm; weight 3.4 oz; solid handle. Standard and maker's marks on bottom back of stem. The blade is of conventional dished scimitar shape with two negative cusps, but with concave right side and rolled up right edge; and with a rear apron and rising handle all in one piece. The pierced blade is completely covered with decoration. Double lines of zigzag, separated by a continuous series of boxed Xs, bound the edges of the blade. The center is covered with bold baroque scrolls and foliage; an inner reserve, defined by a conforming boundary of pierced F-scrolls, has a lake and castle scene. A double struck reeded handle leads to an upturned Old English finial showing a vaguely similar, single struck 'Queen's pattern.' Gorham has a similar pattern called "Josephine" (20), but many (most) names of American patterns are trivial and too numerous and variable to be diagnostic.

119. CAKE/TART SERVER, Tiffany & Co., New York, 1870-73; length 32 cm; weight 4.6 oz; solid handle, sterling. The blade of indefinite shape swells on the unsharpened, uninterrupted right edge and has a straighter, sharpened left edge. It is not a left-handed server. It is stamped in one piece with an upturned apron and rising handle. A machined design of rigid interlaced strapwork and other designs and minutiae cover the *rear* half of the blade — unusual. The handle is the "Italian" design patented in 1870 (27). Marks are on the bottom back of the stem.

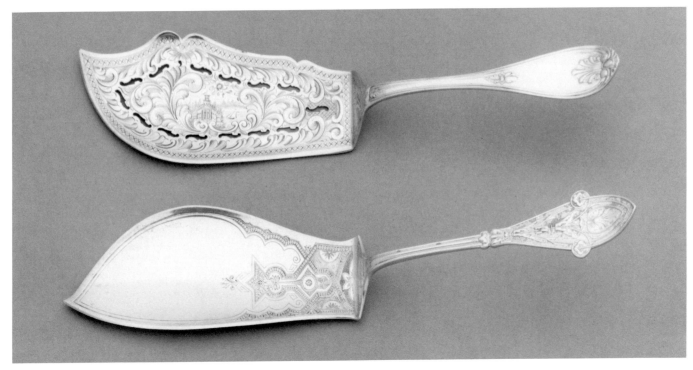

120.   CAKE/TART SERVER, Tiffany & Co., New York, c. 1873; length 29.5 cm; sterling; solid handle. The blade may be regarded as a highly stylized scimitar with a suspicion of a hook and curved arched right edge. The blade is stamped on the right side in a highly stylized pattern. The handle rises from the rear edge with complementary decoration on a modified up-turned Old English handle; compare the preceding figure.
By cooperation and courtesy of Dr. Dale Bennett.

121.   CAKE SERVER PAIR, James Watt, Philadelphia; c. 1875 (26). Knife, length 31.5 cm; weight 3.9 oz; solid handle. Fork, length 22.5 cm; weight 2.1 oz; solid handle. The lightweight knife has a flat scimitar blade with rolled up right side. The right edge is shaped in a broken pattern that must be seen to be believed. The perimeter of the unpierced blade is outlined by a broad double band of zigzag and dots. The surface is matte with an applied foliage pattern having a touch of Japonais and with bright cutting. The handle is integral and rises from the rear blade edge to a pointed finial, curved down around its long axis, and decorated in matching floral style to the blade with a sheaf of flowers. The marks are under the bottom of the stem. The unpierced fork has four spreading tines and a matte surface. All edges are outlined by a double band of dotted zigzag, and the surface with foliate engraving and bright cutting. The handle matches the knife.

122.   CAKE/PASTRY SLICE, Bailey, Kettell and Chapman, Boston (?), c. 1875; sterling; length 24.5 cm; weight 2.1 oz; solid handle. The small lightweight server has an unpierced flat scimitar blade with one rounded cusp and one lower positive cusp, and is stamped in one piece with a rising handle. The unpierced blade is outlined by a frieze of vine leaves and has a central engraved rococo pattern of scribed scrolls. The handle is double struck with reeding, including an underblade reeded drop, and with a double struck oak leaf and acorn pattern on the upturned pointed Old English finial. Marks are on back of the stem.

123.   PASTRY/ICE CREAM/PUDDING SERVER, no maker's mark, c. 1880; sterling; length 26.5 cm; weight 3 oz; solid handle. The atypical unpierced blade has an edge-fluted spoon-shape in the rear half, and scimitar shape with double positive cusp in the front, and with an uprolled right edge. The *left* edge is decorated with a frieze of zigzag lines with a matte and bright-cut band of leaves between. The stem is continuous and rises to a spatulate upturned finial that is decorated with a bright-cut floral bouquet having a Japanese feeling, and with a Georgian style, engraved initial C. A sterling mark is on the bottom back of the stem.

their condition (some exceptions, including American slices, have been noted in the section on Blade Shape). The dished asymmetric server can, however, function very well for the service of deep fish or meat pies or puddings of all sorts. The later, shortened, more spoon-like American sterling servers seem particularly well adapted for this use as well as for the service of other foods such as aspic and ice-cream; the ice cream server may be accompanied by a set of a dozen matching spoons. Indeed, a variety of American blade shapes, including long-ovals and *flat* knives, as well as scimitars, have been designated (20) as ice-cream servers [Fig. 123].

The most suggestively adaptable British server for cake or pastry is the (later) flat scimitar slice or the plain rectangular slice, especially a flat or unpierced one (Chapter VI). Whereas the fish slice or fish knife was included in standard

124.  FISH SERVER PAIR, Gorham Mfg. Co., Providence, c. 1885; sterling. Knife, length 26 cm; solid handle. Fork, length 22 cm; solid handle. This special order is lavishly decorated in Aesthetic/Japanese style with fish amid the lily pads. The unpierced knife blade is shaped as a butcher chopper and leads at the top rear edge to a shaped rectangular handle. The three-tine fork is in matching style. Obviously, this set will do very well for the service of cake, pie, etc; compare the following figure.
By cooperation and courtesy of Dr. Dale Bennett.

125.  CAKE/ICE CREAM SLICE, Bailey, Banks and Biddle, Philadelphia, 1878-1894; length 30.6 cm; weight 6.6 oz; solid handle; sterling. The server is in the shape of a meat chopper. The blade is decorated with bands of pseudo-bright cutting along both edges, and is engraved with a dragonfly and flower blossoms in Japonais style. The flat handle is integral with the blade and decorated with similar themes on a woven background. The underside is completely plain with marks along the back edge of the top side of the blade.

126.  FISH SLICE, Henri Polonceau, Montreal, c. 1810; length 37.5 cm. The blade is in the form of a rather stiff, realistic fish, complete with scales and fins, and is pierced in a regular complimentary pattern of holes (the dark circles in the photograph). Even more unusual is the boss and handle; the former, a hand holding the tail with a finger that curls underneath; the handle, a clothed, cuffed arm whose wrist (stem) lifts from the blade; and with a Georgian monogram in a bright-cut cartouche.
By courtesy of the Royal Ontario Museum, Toronto.

catalogue lists of British manufacturing silversmiths of the first half of the century (4), cake, tart or pudding servers were more often omitted. What alternative implement was intended is not clear; but Fig. 44 illustrates a rather rare English, unpierced, flat scimitar server of smaller size than the conventional fish slice and which is surely a cake or pastry server of this period; an occasional small long-oval of this period has also been seen. The conventional broad dished scimitar is presently titled as a cake or pastry server by some individuals and dealers. By contrast, both long-oval and asymmetric Continental servers of the nineteenth century are frequently designated as tart or pastry servers. Thus a Continental nineteenth-century scimitar slice having positive cusps by J. Gemza, Kasmark, is named as a "tortenschaufel" (11), whereas a similarly-shaped Swiss implement [Fig. 129] only 20 cm in total length, and thus smaller than conventional size, is likewise termed "pelle à tartelette" (III 40). In general, smaller servers of all countries, whatever their shape (see Chapters VI and VII), have been used as servers for baked goods.

Some (later) nineteenth century American scimitars are called cake servers, but the article that is frequently called a pastry server in Continental and American custom is the nineteenth-century flat trowel or long-oval server, whether pierced or not (Chapter III); contrarywise, Fig. III 94 illustrates a Norwegian trowel that is quite patently a fish server. To add to the confusion is the fact that a long-oval server, labelled as a pastry shovel in the last reference, is

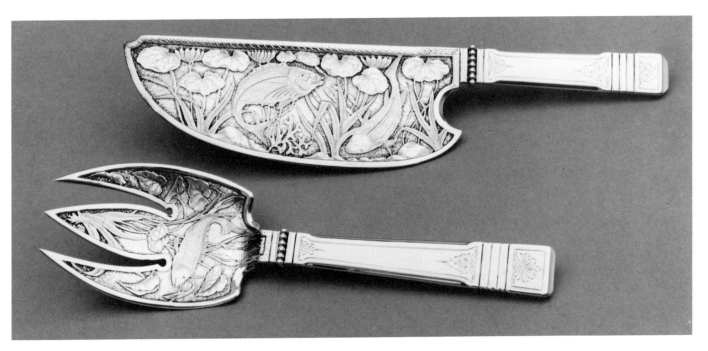

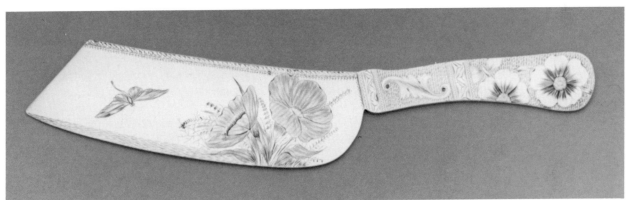

213

127. FISH SLICE, G.AA., Aurillac (France), 1798-1809 (28,29); length 36.5 cm; hollow handle. The very heavy cast blade is more or less in the 'English' shape, although larger than eighteenth-century scimitars. The piercing shows rounding and retraction in the corners, as well as remnants of flashing. It has an almost vertical hook, two negative cusps, and a concave right side. It is decorated along the right edge with a zigzag line and swags of bright cutting and pendant drops. A band of pierced diamond shapes, with wigglework and bright cutting along the side, parallels the right edge. An engraved snarling fish occupies the central panel; in Empire style. The blade evinces very light lavender fire stain. An integral faceted diamond-pointed boss and long flattened hexagonal handle is soldered to a reeded pseudo-ferrule and pointed reeded oval handle. The marks lie along the right side of the boss.

128. FISH SLICE, A.CC., Paris, 1798-1809 (28,29); length 36 cm; wooden handle. A beautiful pristine server in the second common style of Continental slices. The large doubly dished blade has a long moderate hook to a large positive cusp on the severely rolled up right side. It is highly decorated with zigzag and bright cutting on the periphery, with a frieze of zigzag engraved pierced scrolling foliage along the right edge, with a wide band of zigzag scribing that is bright cut with vine leaves and tendrils, and with a large sanguine completely scribed porpoise on the central panel; in Empire style. A faceted boss and stem rise to a conical holder of a turned balustered wooden handle. The four marks are rather carelessly disposed on either side of the boss on both top and bottom sides.

129. TART SHOVEL/SLICE, Mercier Antoine Pierre, 1800-1810, Lausanne; length 20 cm; wooden handle. The server has the prominent long hook and upper positive cusp that appears in the wares of Western European countries. The right side is raised and the unpierced blade is embellished with an engraved flowering branch. The oval boss leads by a long stem to the turned handle. The blade is quite small, and the whole is similar to the server of Fig. 134. The described function seems quite apt and, being unpierced, the server is somewhat sturdier than the comparison article. This article is the property of the Association of Vieux-Lausanne and the Community of Lausanne. It is in the Musée Historique de L'Ancien Évêché, Lausanne; see Ref. (III 40) for further details.
By courtesy of the Museum and of the publishers, Editions du Grand-Pont, Lausanne.

129a. FISH SLICE, C.L.S., Paris, 1819-1838; length 34.3 cm; ivory handle. The scimitar blade has a reentrant hook, an upturned right side on the lower two-thirds of the blade, and positive cusps. The blade is completely pierced with a frieze of triangles and a reticulated pattern. A split-penny boss, leads *via* a flattened shaped stem to the in-plane, natural coloured handle. Note: This example is slightly out of chronological order; cf. Figs. 135,136.

in fact of the abstract fish shape with tail-like projections. The corresponding British pastry server may be the oval and oblong servers that persist in the nineteenth century; but such usage comes under the optional proviso. Two designs of servers by G. Belli (c. 1800) (see also III 19) illustrate the slight differences involved; these are two flat *unpierced* ellipses, one having a fish engraving — hence a fish slice by fiat — and one without fish engraving — hence a cake slice [Fig. IV 46]. However, the pair of slices illustrated in Figs. 135,136 illustrate as well as any example both the arbitrariness of present nomenclature and the futility of rigid classification.

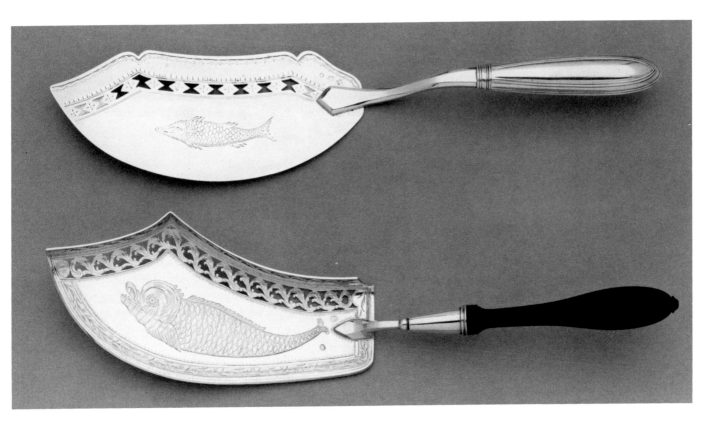

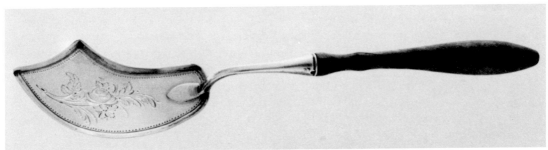

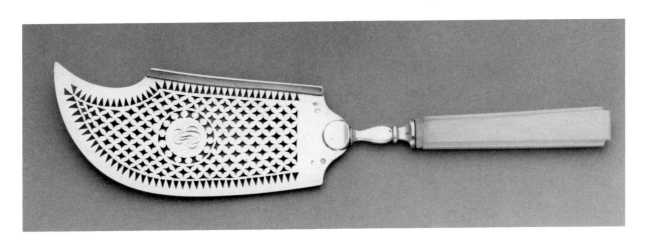

130.   FISH SLICE, IMS, Göteborg, c. 1810; length 29.5 cm; weight 3.4 oz; solid handle. The small blade of British shape has a reentrant hook, two negative cusps, a concave right side, and a kick to the right edge. It is engraved with lines of zigzag around the circumference that are also interlaced around pierced holes in a simple oval arrangement at the blade center [cf. Figs. 30 and 36]. The elliptical boss rises on a flared shoulder and bevelled stem to a late monogrammed fiddle handle. The use of this town mark ceased in 1812 (28,30). The marks are in a line under the center of the stem.

131.   FISH SLICE, V.A.D., Lisbon, 1814-1816 (28); length 33 cm; hollow handle. The large cast, robust blade is highly double dished, and is bevelled to an edge around the whole perimeter. The hook is highly reentrant, and the tip lines up with the single negative cusp and concave right side that turns convexly to the narrow rear edge. The blade is unreeded and unengraved but is completely pierced outside of a conforming narrow reserve in a pattern of notched pales and positive and negative interlaced heart shapes and arcs. The boss is a hollow cast anthemion with a complementary anthemion strengthening plate applied underneath. It joins a balustered waisted stem to whose butt plate is soldered the pseudo-ferrule of a flattened octagonal handle. Although stem and handle are in line with the blade, the dishing gives rise to an apparent lift. The marks are on top on either side of the boss which is highly encroached by the piercing.

132.   FISH/CAKE SLICE, maker K ? (rubbed); Utrecht (30), c. 1815; length 35.5. cm; wooden handle. The large blade is doubly dished in a characteristic Dutch style. It has a long highly reentrant hook that lines the tip up with the pronounced positive cusp at the center of the rolled up right side, which curves concavely into the straight rear edge of the blade. The decoration consists of a wide band of parallel pales and lunettes along the right side, which is embellished with a neoclassical (Louis XVI) frieze of small bright-cut lunettes, zigzag lines and flower heads along its left edge. The sharpened left arc of the blade is double reeded. By contrast with the naturalistic decoration of the following example, dated c. 1822, the estimated date of this one has been retarded as much as is allowed by the inauguration of the standard marks (1814). An oval boss is applied at the top of the rear edge. It lifts on a flattened, balustered, waisted stem to an oval conical holder of a pointed handle that is of flattened oval cross-section. Marks are on top on either side of the boss, at the blade tip, and with a later inland duty mark on the handle holder.

133.   FISH/CAKE SLICE, R.A. Verlegh (?), Breda, c. 1822 (31); length 37.5 cm; wooden handle. The large, slightly double-dished scimitar blade is again in one of the typical Dutch styles of this time. It has the remarkable reentrant hook and an equally pronounced positive cusp near the center of the rolled-up right edge. The heel of the blade has a flat edge. The server is highly pierced with zigzag scribed patterns of tulips and tendrils in a frieze along the right edge, and with more of the same, plus leaves and a flower head, in a circular central area with two complementary triangular pierced areas. The boss is a dolphin head that lifts to the conical holder of a turned balustered handle. The marks lie on top on either side of the boss.

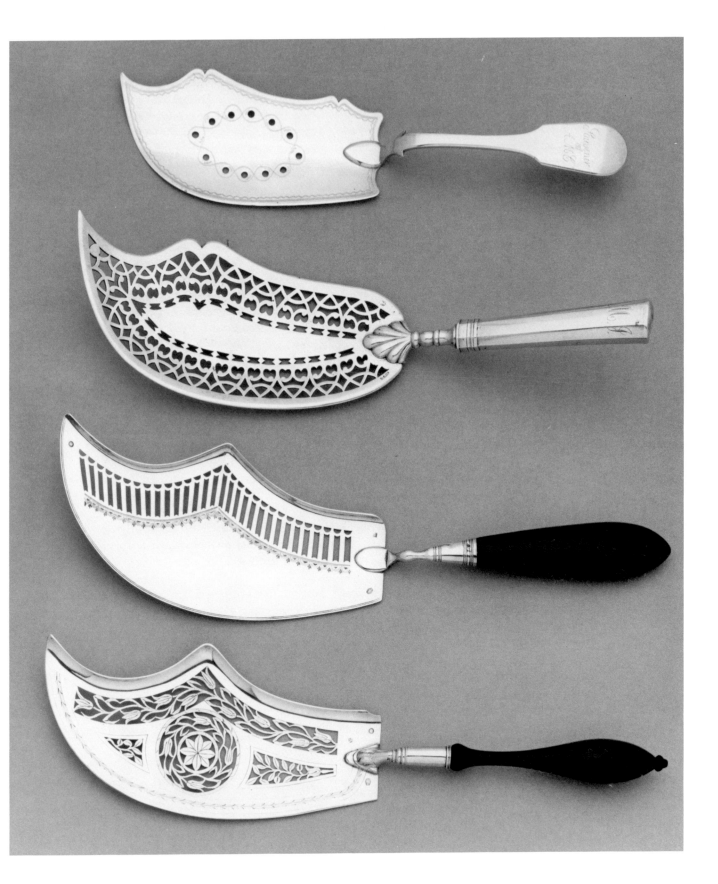

134.  MINIATURE SERVER, no maker's mark, France (Department rubbed); 1809-1819 (28-29); length 20 cm; wooden handle. The small flat blade has a positive cusp and uprolled side and resembles both Fig. 129 and the two following illustrations. It is engraved with various zigzag designs and foliate piercing on the right edge in Empire style. A faceted oval boss and stem rise to the conical holder of a pointed oval wooden handle. The blade is much smaller in proportion than is suggested by the total length. Suggestively a pastry server, the blade is too thin and light for anything more arduous than spooning light substances such as jelly or blancmange.
Gift of Henry W. Smart.

135.  FISH/CAKE SERVER, Louis Balthazard, Paris, 1823-1833 (29); length 34 cm, wooden handle. The blade is slightly double dished and has a rolled right edge. It is pierced, bright cut, and engraved in the same manner as the preceding miniature. The faceted V-boss and stem leads to a conical holder of a turned and highly shaped wooden handle. The marks are placed on either side of the boss. It would seem superfluous to take up space with two consecutive examples [Fig. 136] from the same town, same time, same size, same shape, same raised edge, and so on, and both decorated in Empire style, but this one is pierced and hence, presumably, adapted for the service of fish. The following illustration is unpierced, yet fish embellished and hence a "fish slice". So much for semantics!

136.  FISH SERVER, Francois-Pamphile Jozan, Paris, 1824-36 (29); length 32.5 cm; ivory handle. A slightly double raised blade with a long hook to a raised right side and positive cusp. The blade is *unpierced* but the article is called a fish slice by virtue of an engraved central fish. Multiple bands of dot lines, zigzag and bright-cut leaves parallel both edges of the blade. An anthemion boss lifts to a conical holder of a natural colored large baluster handle. The marks are on both sides of the boss.

137.  FISH/CAKE SERVER, I.A, Geneva, post-1815; length 35.7 cm; wooden handle. Another blade with long hook and marked positive cusp on an uprolled right side. The blade is decorated with a shaped U-frieze of inscribed leaves and flower heads and zigzag border, in style similar to the two preceding slices. The stamped shell boss lifts on a tubular stem to a plain turned handle. The marks are underside, on either side of the boss.

138.  FISH LIFTER/SLICE, Thos. Jensen Lange, Tondern, post-1820, wooden handle. This server displays the highly reentrant hook of several preceding Continental illustrations. However, the positive cusp(s) have degenerated into a flowing, waved right side. The hook is so pronounced that the leading edge is quite rounded and the tip is not serviceable. The server function is formally indicated by the central pierced reserve and engraved fish. A foliate pierced frieze follows the right side. A heavy wire stem leads to a holder for an oval wooden handle. This style is called Biedermeier; it could be called Regency, or Empire, elsewhere. See Fig. 3 of Ref. (III 18) for further description. The article may well serve also as a cake/pastry server.
By kind cooperation and courtesy of Dr. Wolfgang Scheffler.

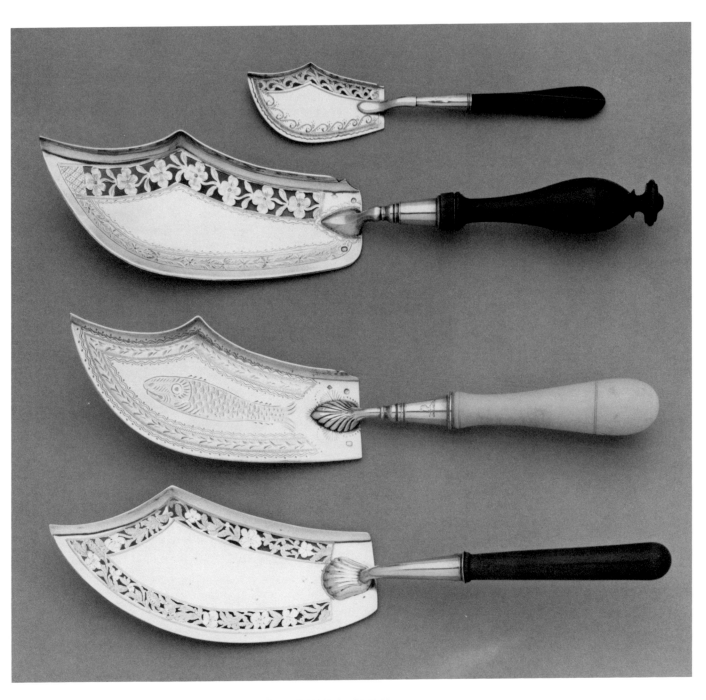

139. FISH/CAKE SLICE, Johan Heinrich Otto (?) (9); Copenhagen, 1852; P.R. Hinnerup, Assay Master (28); length 29.5 cm; handle, HO and PRH (conjoined), 1852. The doubly dished, lightweight blade has two (one and a half?) negative cusps and is outlined by a wide band of zigzag. It is pierced with a frieze of bold engraved scrolls and leaves along the right side. The conforming central reserve is set off by a line of hit-and-miss and is engraved with bold scrolls and floral motifs. The ornament is a mixed style. The stem is continuous with the blade; a narrow flat stem with slight shoulders leads to a soldered reeded pseudo-ferrule and hollow, reeded, waisted fiddle handle. Marks are on the back of the bottom of the stem, and matching marks lie in a line on the underside of the handle.

140. FISH/CAKE SLICE, ASN, Porto, 1853 (29); length 31.7 cm; weight 5.2 oz; solid handle. The plain undecorated blade has a slightly reentrant hook and two negative cusps on the right side, which is also positively cusped as it comes in to the narrow straight rear edge. The blade has a small lozenge-shaped area of pierced paling at the center of the blade. This might be called Biedermeier style, but compare the Exeter slice of forty years earlier (Fig. 35). A split boss — small drop on top and V-shape underneath — rises on a flat, worked stem to a shouldered, double-struck reeded fiddle handle that is crested and monogrammed in "Georgian" style. The marks are in line under the finial.

141a. FISH/CAKE SLICE, V.K., The Hague, 1861 (30); length 30.5 cm; weight 4.3 oz; solid handle. A very wide plain blade with two negative cusps on a wide rolled-up right edge. It is pierced over a large conforming central region in a coarse open scrolled pattern similar to contemporary English slices [Fig. 99]. The handle is continuous with the blade; it is a double stamped, upturned "Old English" Thread style, with a thread underblade drop. The marks are in a line at the top of the stem; the guarantee mark is located underblade at the rear edge.

141b. CAKE/PASTRY SERVER, J. Bryde, Drammen, 1861; length 25.7 cm, hollow handle. This stubby article is similar to the Brinck slice described in the text, but is unpierced. Unlike the conventional scimitar that narrows toward the tip, this slice broadens. The end is curved and the foremost point is not the tip; the latter lies beyond the midpoint of the right side. It has some of the characteristics both of an oblong and of a kidney slice (Chapter VI). The right edge has been raised by a stamped up-roll that has two negative cusps. It is decorated by a frieze of sinuous double dotted lines contained within double straight dotted lines. The flat stem is connected by an underblade circular boss; the anthemion at the rear of the blade is not part of the boss but is a rare top surface strengthening piece. The stem is soldered to a hollow double-waisted fiddle terminal; the marks are under the stem. Closely similar in shape is a "cake slice" by O. Sørum, Grimstad, in the Norsk Folkemuseum and illustrated in Ref. (III 38, p. 62); it is pierced and, also, uncusped on a gently waved right side. These smaller servers of the last half of the nineteenth century were intended for the service of baked goods rather than fish.

142. FISH/CAKE SLICE, P. Hertz, Assay Master S. Groth, Copenhagen, 1865; length 29 cm; weight 4.1 oz; solid handle. The blade is of unique spatulate shape, reminiscent of kidney servers in Chapter VI. It has a rounded front end, a single negative cusp, but with slightly concave sides both left and right. The front and left sides are bevelled to a cutting edge, although the shape makes only the front part of the blade suitable for cutting. The implement is a lifter. It has a conforming line of hit-and-miss around the blade with some piercing and bold rococo style engraved scrolling foliage and flowers. The double reeded, upturned incipient waisted fiddle handle is shouldered and continuous with the blade. There is no underdrop boss.

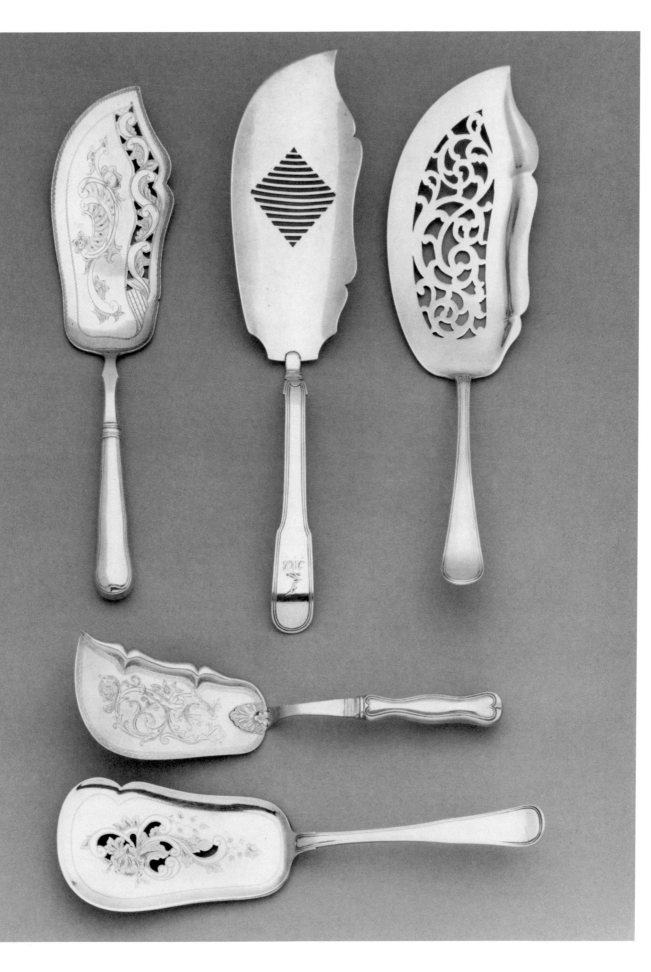

143.  FISH/CAKE SLICE, J.C.K, Austro-Hungarian Empire, post-1866; length 29.2 cm; handle unmarked. The flat blade is of heavy weight, with two negative cusps and a shaped rear edge. The blade is bevelled and sharpened on all edges, even the heel! It is pierced and engraved topside in an overall conforming reserve with baroque revival scrolls, flowers and a formal bouquet. A cast swan's head-and-neck-boss-and-stem lift to a long reeded and waisted pseudo-ferrule and soldered rectangular reeded hollow handle. The marks are on either side of the boss.

144.  FISH/CAKE SLICE, Emil Fischer, Austro-Hungarian Empire, post-1866; length 27.6 cm; weight 4.1 oz; solid handle. The flat blade is similar in weight and shape to the preceding example with one negative cusp on the right side and a shaped rear edge. It is sharpened on all edges. The blade is pierced and engraved topside over its whole surface with a baroque revival floral pattern. A small drop boss rises to a plain late-monogrammed Old English handle with underblade rib. The marks are on either side of the boss, and the standard is repeated under the stem.

145.  FISH SLICE, I.P. Khlebnikov; Assay Master I.K. (32), Moscow, 1878; length 31 cm; hollow handle. The blade has one negative cusp and a central circular reserve engraved with two crossed fish on a scribed background, and with a periphery of stylized pendant flower heads. The blade was completely pierced with angular interlaced tracery, above and below the reserve, by a slightly uncertain hand. A beehive boss rises on a faceted stem that is soldered to a waisted balustered pseudo-ferrule and a flattened hollow handle of decagonal cross-section. The piercing encroaches severely on the boss. Marks lie along the middle underside of the right edge.

146.  CAKE SERVER, BCAC (?, rubbed), France, post-1878; length 28.7 cm; weight 4.3 oz; solid handle. The gilted blade, which is worn to the silver down the center, is unpierced and in the form of a sleigh. It is stamped in one piece with the handle; with double thread line around the blade, and a scroll and flowering branch raised design. It has an underblade floral boss and a double-struck, reeded and scrolled waisted fiddle handle. The article is of lower quality and an example of mass machine production. It might well have been included in Chapter VI.

147.  FISH/CAKE SLICE, Trosdahl, Scandinavian, c. 1900. The blade has a rolled right side and two negative cusps. It is pierced in a large conforming reserve outlined by a dotted line and a rococo-style foliate scroll pattern. A long V-boss is attached under the blade and lifts on a bevelled stem to a soldered tapering reeded pseudo-ferrule and hollow, pointed, flattened handle that curves downward. The marks are on back of the stem.

Fish servers were not used in pairs, i.e., one in each hand. Left-handed servers were not made. Handedness was reinforced by the prescribed position of the fish to be served: set on a platter so that the head pointed to the left of the carver. In any case, only one fish slice was set out on the usual dinner table [Fig. II 3]. When a large group was entertained at dinner, two servers might be placed on the table, although not together but one at each end (12,13). If left-handed assistance was required, a large serving spoon was at hand on the table for such purpose. The later pair sets provided a fork to render such service (14,15). The narrowing and flattening of the blade of these pair sets made it even more knife-like and suitable for cutting soft meats, although fish server sets are not to be confused with conventional meat-carving sets; the latter are provided with steel-bladed knives.

222

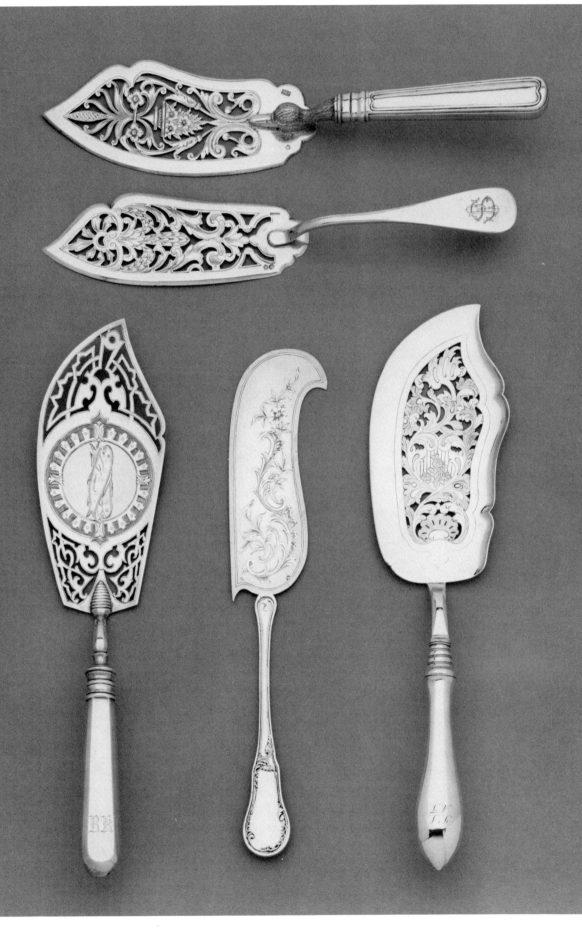

148. SERVER PAIR, A. Dragsted, Assay Master S. Groth, Copenhagen, 1894. Knife, length 31.5 cm; weight 8.5 oz; cast handle. Fork, length 29 cm; weight 9.6 oz; cast handle. An unusual set in a pattern used by a number of workers over a period of more than ten years. The knife blade has one leading negative cusp and two positive cusps, one on either edge at the rear of the blade. The right edge of the blade and large conforming pierced reserve have a single thread around. The reserve is hand pierced. It is engraved on both sides with foliate scrolling and flowers in rococo style. The back of the blade has a beaded engraved cap that carries into the cast handle. The latter is cast in florid baroque style with added chased, engraved and pounced details, and features rosettes and an animal figure. The marks lie along the rear underside of the right edge of the blade. The heavy cast handle of the fork is a related but differently arranged casting. It has a heavy cast stem and four scrolling tines. The marks are on back of the stem. Other pairs in this style resemble this one in general layout and arrangement, and in some details, but differ in proportions, nature of the piercing pattern (animal or floral), and many specific details of casting and engraving.

## Other Servers and Pair Sets

Some examples of British pair sets are shown in Figs. 96-106. As described above, although the wide, dished Georgian scimitar blades were intended primarily as fish servers, they were probably employed for other purposes, including the presentation of cake and pie, and antique shops presently sell them for that purpose. The later, narrow, flat Victorian fish carver knife (compare the example by Elizabeth Eaton [Fig. 96] was obviously more suited for the service of cake and tarts than its earlier predecessor. In the later nineteenth and twentieth centuries, specifically designated cake knives, in pair with forks (14), became common for the service of cake. With increase in the physical similarity of the two serving sets, the distinction between them became concomitantly attenuated. Although usually long-oval or scimitar in shape (or, more occasionally, of trowel shape as in one example by Francis Higgins, London, 1875), some advertised fish carver blades were simply pointed knife shapes, as was true of fish eater knives (18) as well (see Chapter VII). Similarly, although cake knives are frequently of the long pointed variety, sometimes with serrations along the back edge for severing tenacious textures, many are similar in shape to scimitar fish carver knives. The long cake (also pie) knife may have a rounded tip and (infrequently) be modestly pierced along the long axis; it frequently bears impressed decoration. The pair may be knife and spoon rather than knife and fork.

Some late nineteenth-century, both pierced and unpierced, elongated cake and pie trowel blades (16-18) even were advertised as fish carvers (18); but they were also made as individual servers. The trowel blade frequently has no boss junction; the rear of the blade may extend into an apron that is continuous with the stem of the handle. The handle may be solid or hollow, or made of other material, as for fish carvers, and usually has lift. Smaller versions of these shapes

224

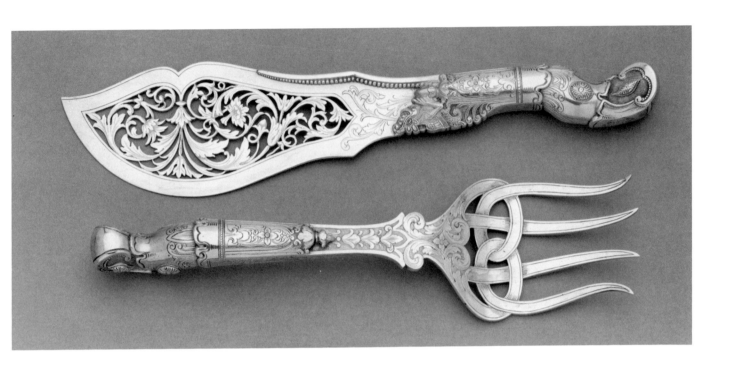

were also made as tart and pastry servers (see also Chapter III). In all of this discussion, it should be remembered that the word *pie* at this later time connotes a sweet fruit dessert rather than a savoury.

Still another carver pair that bears a close resemblance to the cake pair are melon servers (16,19) and salad servers (Chapter VII). Like the other pair sets, they were available in silver or in electroplate. The conventional price differential between the two materials was roughly a factor of two. The blade is usually of the customary knife shape or may have some scimitar influence. The offering of these implements in the advertising literature of the day was less frequent than that of cake and pie servers. Some catalogues (16) offered the two categories of servers as interchangeable.

American servers were so variable in shape and designation (20) that attempts at classifications become even more confusing.

Walker Hall, Sheffield, as well as other manufacturers (see, for example, Ref. 18) combined all of these closely related structures and functions in universal three-piece sets, called "Serve-Alls," that included knife, fork and spoon. The spoon shape of later nineteenth-century American servers also suggests other potential uses. One of these was as ice-cream server, and sets consisted of a server with, say, a dozen ice-cream spoons.

The style of knives, handle types, and attachment styles available from the various manufacturers run the gamut of variations described in this chapter and in Chapters III and IV. Stag antler handles also occurred more frequently at this time.

Although it would be logical to consider salad server pairs at this point, these servers have such long and co-mingled history that it has been elected to reserve their discussion to Chapter VII along with some other servers.

## *Marks and Makers*

Represented in the present collection of British scimitar servers extending over a period of more than a century, are some sixty-six makers. More, or different, examples could have lengthened the list. It is evident, however, that many spoon makers and small workers turned their hand to the making of these attractive objects or to their retailing. Silversmiths with two or more included examples are W. Eley and W. Fearn, S. Adams II, A. and G. Burrows, W. Welch, Wm. II and S. Knight, J. Gilbert, P. and W. Bateman I, J. Hayne, W. Traies, A. Walker, M. Chawner, B. Stephens, W. Eaton, G. Adams, Martin Hall Co. The selection of examples is somewhat adventitious and other prominent names include H. Chawner, J. Emes, T. Wallis, A. King, S. Hougham, T. Hayter, B. Smith, P. Storr, J. Taylor, T.C. Savory, W. Elliot, W. Chawner II, R. Gray & Son, C. Lias, S. Hayne and D. Cater, E. Eaton, W.R. Smily, Hilliard and Thomason, Elkington & Co. Obviously the list is not all inclusive. Provincial examples include Exeter, Birmingham, Sheffield, Newcastle, Edinburgh, Glasgow, Perth, Aberdeen, Dublin.

The marks on individual English servers with silver handles are placed in the same manner as spoons and ladles, i.e. under the finial or the top of the stem. Items with other than solid handles are usually marked in-line along the under edge of the blade, and usually on the right side. Exceptions occur more often later in the period. Provincial and, especially, Dublin examples are more frequently marked on the rear top surface of the blade and, in the latter case, on the handle as well. The marks on pair knives are more randomly placed, in general, even on London wares, and often on the top side of the blade. Continental servers tend to be marked on the top rear surface.

## *References*

1.  V. Brett, *The Sotheby's Directory of Silver,* Sotheby's Publications, London, 1986.
2.  G.B. Hughes, *Small Antique Silverware,* Batsford, London, 1957.
3.  I. Findlay, *Scottish Gold and Silver Work,* Chatto and Windus, Edinburgh, 1956.
4.  T. Cox Savory, *Manufacturer of Silverplate,* Cornhill, London, c. 1830.
5.  I. Pickford, *Silver Flatware,* Antique Collectors Club, Suffolk, 1983.
6.  a) J. Culme and J.G. Strang, *Antique Silver and Silver Collecting,* Hamlyn, London, 1973.

    b) D.S. Shure, *Hester Bateman,* Doubleday, New York, 1959, Plate LX.

7. M. Holland, *Silver*, Peerage Books, London, 1983.

8. a) F. Lucie-Smith, *Story of Craft*, Phaidon, Oxford, 1981.
   b) M. Haslam, *Marks and Monograms of the Modern Movement 1875-1930*, Lutterworth Press, Guildford, 1977.

9. Reference III 26, Lot No. 73b and others.

10. H.W. Smart, *Country Life*, December 26, 1974.

11. E. Toranova, *Goldschmiedekunst in der Slowakie*, Tatran, Bratislavia, 1975.

12. J. Williams, *The Footman's Guide*, Dean and Munday, London, c. 1836.

13. T. Cosnett, *The Footman's Directory*, Simpkin, Marshall and Colburn, London, 1825.

14. Mappin Brothers Illustration, Daily News, 1862.

15. Goldsmiths Alliance, *Catalogue*, London, 1868.

16. Mappin and Webb, *Catalogue*, London, 1900.

17. John Round, *Catalogue*, Sheffield, 1898.

18. Jas. Deakin, *Catalogue*, Sheffield, 1899.

19. N. Holdsworth, *Catalogue*, London and Sheffield, c. 1865.

20. N.D. Turner, *American Silver Flatware 1837-1910*, Barnes, Cranbury, N.J., 1972.

21. W. Scheffler, *Fischheber*, Kunst und Antiquitaten, Part 2, 1976.

22. Bonhams, London, Sale No. 23, 215a, 4 July 1984, Lot 74.

23. S.G.C. Ensko, *American Silversmiths*, Cracker Barrel Press, Southampton, N.Y., 1937.

24. E.M. Currier, *Marks of Early American Silversmiths*, Century House, Watkins Glen, N.Y., 1970.

25. D.T. Rainwater, *American Silver Manufacturers*, Crown, N.Y., 1975.

26. D. Bennett, personal communication; see V.S. Vaughan, *Silver*, May-June, p.8, Whittier, CA, 1988.

27. C.H. Jr. and M.G. Carpenter, *Tiffany Silver*, Dodd Mead, New York, 1978.

28. Tardy, *Poincons d'Argent*, 9th Edition, Paris.

29. E. Beuque, *Dictionnaire des Poincons*, Vol. I, De Nobele, Paris, 1924.

30. B.W.G. Wttewaall, *Nederlands Klein Zilver*, Allert de Lange, Amsterdam, 1987.

31. E. Voet, *Stichting, Alkmaarse Goud- en Zilversmeden 1753-1807*, Nijhoff, The Hague, 1974.

32. P.L. Paulson, *Guide to Russian Silver Hallmarks*, private publication, 1976.

Chapter **VI**

# TRANSIENT SHAPES: 1780-1840

## *History, Function and Decoration*

AFTER A PERIOD of roughly thirty-five years lasting until 1775, during which only trowels of rather standard shapes were made, the birth of the British long-oval server gave rise to a spate of inventive creation in server blade shapes that lasted for over fifty years, and longer in American practice. The term *transient* is applied to these, as opposed to the long-oval and scimitar shapes which continued in production without cease into the twentieth century. The appellation *experimental* has also been suggested (1), although it is highly problematical that the efforts of the industry were inspired by a search for new functional possibilities. The writer prefers to seek their source in artistic inspiration and expression. The dates given in the chapter title represent the period of maximum activity. In general, there is no Continental counterpart to this British excursion, but specific instances do occur.

As will be seen, some, but not all, of these servers are symmetric with respect to the long axis of the blade. Thus, like planar long-ovals, they have no handedness unless the blade acquires a raised edge or the handle acquires lift. The function served by these implements cannot be readily distinguished from those recounted for long-ovals and scimitar servers. As described below, those that more closely resemble the former in structure follow the discussion and arguments of Chapter IV; likewise, those kindred to the scimitar relate to Chapter V. Detailed repetition is unnecessary and present remarks will be restricted.

The transients were made by the same smiths who made the more common shapes. The handles and decoration of these articles and the placement of marks followed the custom and evolutionary trends described previously.

## *Oblong Servers*

The oblong or rectangular slice [Figs. 1-8] has already been introduced as a variant of the long-oval in Chapter IV [Figs. IV 12, IV 15]. They are the servers that are closest to the vulgar spatula shape. They are probably the most numerous and longest produced of all the transient types; they span the chapter title period. The form is related to the near-elliptical server. All blades are symmetric with respect to their long axis. Some examples do exhibit double symmetry about both major and minor blade axes [Figs. 1,6]. In both instances, of course, they lack an elliptical shape; the ends are sharply truncated and provide an oblong contour.

These servers occasionally display one or two negative cusps as a reversion to the scimitar custom. They may also exhibit remnant tail nubs at the rear end of the blade [Fig. 4], as well as other features related to deviant scimitars (cf. Chapter V, the Brinck slice) and long-oval slices [Fig. 1]. Some additional examples made by the Bateman firm may be seen in Ref. (2).

A relatively high proportion of very early rectangular blades have a raised right rim [Figs. IV 12,IV 15, and 1,2] — frequently scalloped along its edge and sometimes beautifully decorated with engraving and bright cutting. The early slices had nearly flat blades and qualify very well as tart and pastry servers. The edge may make them less well adapted for other purposes such as deep pudding servers. An occasional one has evident fish association [Fig. 6].

Later nineteenth-century examples have the less-ornate decoration characteristic of their time. Few of them are equipped with a sharply raised rim.

Irish makers [Fig. 6] seem to have produced a larger proportion of these shapes and to have continued with their production for a longer time than other provincial centres. Rectangular slices also appear in Continental wares [Fig. 7] and were presumably intended as cake servers.

## *Shaped Long-Oval Servers*

Only a few years after their inception, a variant of the long-oval shape appeared in the 1780s. These display a rim edge that is cut or clipped so as to produce a variety of polygonal 'oval' or 'elliptical' shapes. The number of edge segments is variable, and results in multisided blades varying usually from six to twelve sides. The side segments may be flat or concave; in some instances a series of mini-scallops create a highly multisided implement [Figs. 9-11, VII 20].

Where the resulting blade has a pointed tip, as in most cases, the piece is evidently merely a modification of the long-oval or elliptical server. In another instance, as in Fig. 1 which shows a flat leading end, the blade is doubly symmetric and this server by H. Chawner, London, 1791, may be regarded as a modified rectangular. Some of these slices have an applied vertical right edge; others display tail nubs (2).

These modified shapes, which are not rare, persisted for only a very short time and largely disappeared after 1800. The Bateman family was well represented in the manufacture of these items. Nothing new emerges with respect to their function and decoration.

1.     SHAPED OBLONG SERVER, Henry Chawner, London, 1790; length 29 cm; handle, Robert Twyford, London, 1791. The doubly symmetric, octagonal blade is slightly dished. It has a flat leading edge and an applied, cusped, raised right edge. The blade is decorated in neoclassical style. It is outlined by notched hit-and-miss lines; and a zigzag line runs around the blade and pierced horseshoe shaped reserve that also holds a bright cut starburst and a contemporary shield and crest. The pierced pattern has parallel bright-cut bows and swags separated by small ellipses. The underside is undecorated. A large faceted pointed oval boss and stem lift to a filled reeded handle. The marks lie under the lower right concave edge. A similar shape may be seen in the Victoria and Albert Museum, London.

2.     OBLONG SERVER, Michael Plummer, London, 1793; length 31 cm; handle, Moses Brent, 1793. The almost flat blade has rounded front corners, and has an applied, cusped, raised right side and cusped rear edge. There is double reeding around the free edges. It has a conforming central area that is pierced with outer bands of parallel pales, with a central engraved circle of flower heads around an ewer, and with a heart-shaped foliage burst and other scrolling themes. The blade is crested below the reserve; the underside is not engraved. A split-penny boss and waisted stem are in line with a reeded filled handle. The marks lie under the blade at the rear of the left edge. [cf. Figs. IV 12, IV 15].

3.     RECTANGULAR SERVER, John Shekleton, London, 1801; length 28 cm; handle, John Tatum, London, 1801. The rectangular blade has rounded corners. Lines of hit-and-miss and, in part, darts circumscribe the blade and a reserve in the forward half of the blade. The latter is pierced with a double tier of parallel pales with a surround of pierced swags interspersed with pendant bright-cut leaves, all decorated with lines of hit-and-miss. Below the reserve is a crested bright-cut laurel wreath cartouche. The pointed, faceted boss rises on a waisted stem to a reeded filled handle. The marks are under the rear of the left edge of the blade.

4.     OBLONG SERVER, Peter and Wm. Bateman, London, 1809; length 27 cm; Ivorene handle. The singly dished blade is sharpened on both edges. It has a rounded front contour, a waved rear edge, and negative cusps on both edges that give a likeness to a rudimentary fish tail. A line of hit-and-miss circumscribes the blade and boss. A horseshoe design of pierced and bright-cut circles envelop a scribed and bright-cut spine of scrolls. A pointed faceted oval boss rises to a reeded ferrule and a reeded and fluted replacement handle. The marks lie along under the left edge at the rear of the blade.

5.     OBLONG SERVER, Wm. Eley, Wm. Fearn and Wm. Chawner; London, 1811; length 28.3 cm; weight 4.8 oz; solid handle. The blade has rounded front corners but straight sharpened sides and sharp corners at the wide straight rear edge. The whole blade and a central rectangular reserve are double reeded on their perimeters. The reserve is pierced with a double set of parallel pales. The slightly rounded V-boss lifts on a robust stem to a monogrammed Old English handle. The marks lie in line under the finial.

6.     OBLONG FISH SERVER, Jas. Scott, 1818, Dublin; length 29.5 cm; weight 4.9 oz; solid handle. Apart from a slight taper to the blade, this one is almost doubly symmetric. The singly dished blade is sharpened on both sides. A line of waved hit-and-miss circumscribes the blade, and dotted lines follow a central pierced reserve of a crossed fish and dolphin, all suitably engraved. Pounced vine tendrils occupy the corners of the blade. A shaped rectangular boss leads to a shouldered fiddle handle. The marks are in line under the finial.

230

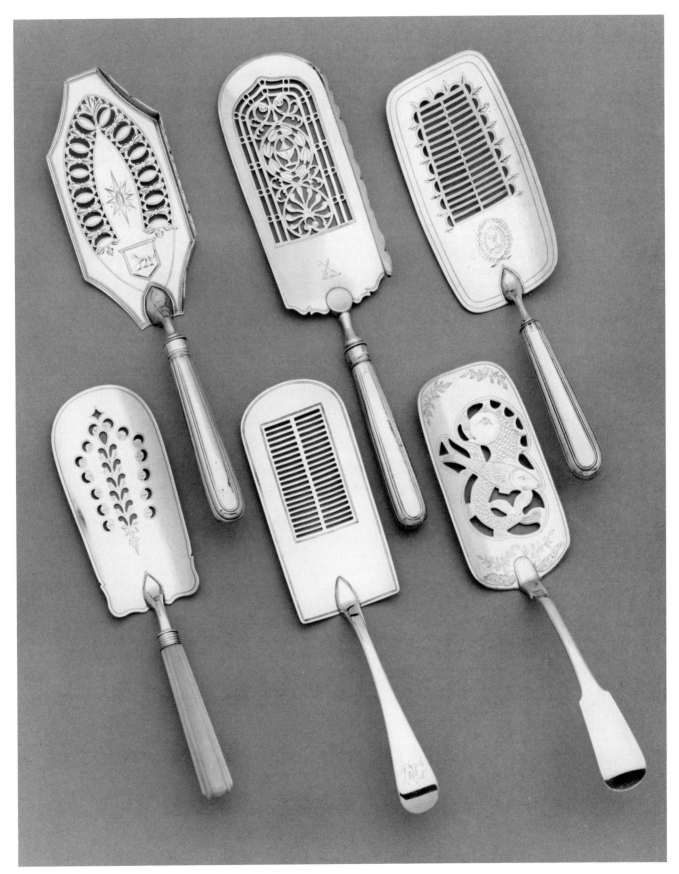

7.    CAKE/PASTRY SERVER, AN, Hamburg, c. 1812-1827; length 31 cm; ivory handle. The slightly tapering, flat rectangular blade has a sharply rolled narrow rim and a waved rear edge. It is outlined by a straight and waved dotted band. It has a central elliptical area hand-pierced with parallel pales and bounded by a waved dotted band. The blade has been heavily stamped with a symmetric frieze of imbricated acanthus leaves. The style is an Empire/Biedermeier mix and supports the later estimated date (date letter B). The cast anthemion boss and flat shaped stem lift to a long reeded ferrule that holds a flat tapering rectangular ivory handle that is parallel fluted over the rear half. The marks lie under the stem.

8.    OBLONG SERVER, Wm. Bateman II, London, 1836; length 30 cm; weight 4.3 oz; solid handle. The blade is sharply rectangular over most of its length but develops acorn-like protrusions of the edges in the bottom one-third. The blade is outlined by dotted waved lines that are interrupted by bright cut foliate sprays. The central reserve of conforming shape is pierced, bright-cut and engraved with an oak branch, leaves and acorn. It has a conventional V-boss and shouldered fiddle handle. The marks lie under the finial. This article might have been listed later with acorn slices.

9.    SHAPED LONG-OVAL SERVER, Wm. Plummer, London, 1790; length 28 cm; handle, John Tatum, London, undated. The nonagonal blade is symmetric about the long axis. It has a pointed tip and eight concave sides and a waved rear edge. The blade is reeded around the rim and a central conforming reserve that has an outer, shaped reticulated horseshoe frieze and an inner, bow-tied, scrolled foliate pierced bouquet. The blade is strongly double dished. The underside is plain. A split penny boss has a bright-cut surround and a monogram letter. The short waisted stem leads to a fluted oval filled handle. The marks lie along the underside of the middle right panel.

10.    SHAPED LONG-OVAL SERVER, Wm. Abdy, London, 1792; length 30 cm; handle, WA, London, undated. The eleven-sided pointed blade is symmetric about the long axis and slightly doubly-dished. There are multiple rows of dotted lines and bright-cut small circles and flower heads in a frieze around the blade; and a band of notched hit-and-miss lines and bright-cut lunettes around a pierced area having a dotted figure eight inset with two bright-cut floral bursts. A crested shield lies above the boss, which is a bright-cut, stepped semi-ellipse. The stem cranks sharply up to a stepped butt plate and octagonal reeded filled handle. Marks lie under the rear left edge of the blade.

11.    SHAPED LONG-OVAL SERVER, Henry Chawner, London, 1792; length 30 cm; ivory handle. The eleven-sided blade has a rounded tip and eight concave sides. There are multiple lines of dots engraved around the blade and horseshoe pierced design that is bright cut with chains of pendant flower heads, in neoclassic style. The faceted oval boss lifts to an egg-and-dart stamped ferrule, by R.M., Sheffield, 1883, and a rounded rectangular natural ivory handle.

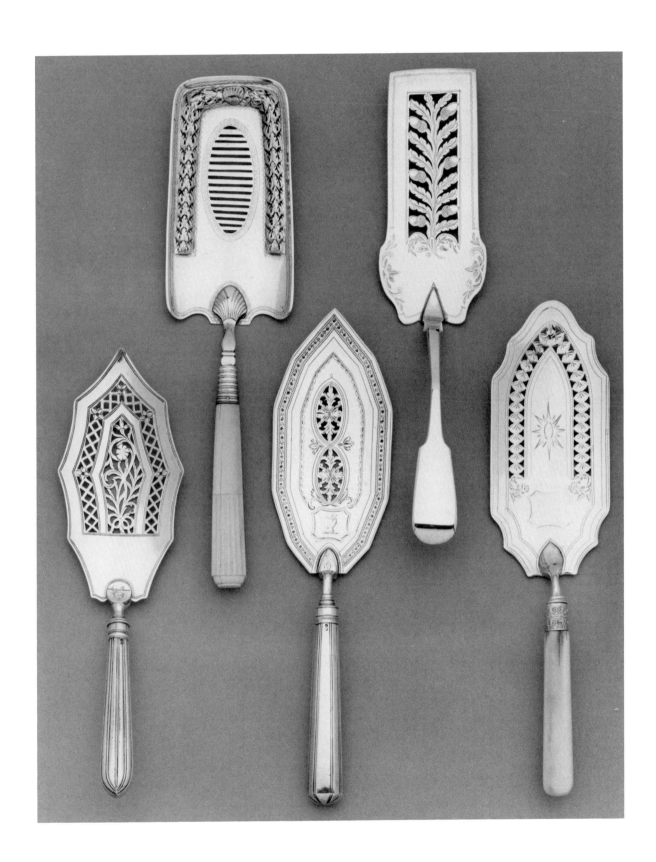

12.   MODIFIED SCIMITAR/LONG-OVAL SERVER, Henry Chawner, London, 1796; length 31 cm; handle, John Tatum, London. The blade of this unusual slice is truncated on the right side which is a straight line. The curved left edge is gently shaped in five segments. The blade is pierced on the right side by six long gill-like slits, embellished by floral engraving. A circular laurel cartouche and crest are placed above the faceted rounded V-boss. The latter is placed in the middle of the rear edge, which removes any question as to whether the right side of the blade has been sheared off. The waisted stem leads to a reeded filled handle.
By cooperation and courtesy of Dr. Dale Bennett.

13.   ACORN FISH SLICE, John Emes, London, 1802; length 29 cm; handle, John Tatum, London. The sharpened blade displays a fish allusion in the form of pairs of tiny fish nubs at the heel of the blade. The blade has a bright-cut leaf chain frieze around the top rim. The center is pierced with a reticulated lozenge; a monogram is in a laurel leaf cartouche. A split-oval boss and short waisted stem are in line with a filled reeded handle. See Ref. (4) for other description.
By kind cooperation and courtesy of Phillips, Blenstock House, London.

14.   FISH SERVER PAIR. Knife, L.B., Edinburgh, 1804; length 30 cm; weight 3.7 oz; solid handle. Fork, Wakely and Wheeler, London, 1896; length 24 cm; weight 3 oz; solid handle. The modified oval slice has an alate rear region that has some resemblance to the acorn servers, but is curved concavely rather than convexly, toward the back of the blade where there are a pair of fish tail nubs; it is doubly dished. The blade rim and interior decoration are outlined by lines of hit-and-miss. A pierced horseshoe frieze of bright-cut acanthus leaf tips, an engraved six-pointed pierced star, and other bright cut floral themes cover the interior region of the blade. A rounded V-bolster is laid on top of the blade in discontinuity with the underside. It rises on a shouldered stem to a fiddle finial; the handle is outlined by hit-and-miss design. The marks lie under the finial. The four-tine fork is pierced in matching leaf and star pattern with bright-cut floral scrolled engraving. The matching fiddle handle turns up. The marks are similarly placed.

15.   ACORN FISH SLICE, Robt. Gray and Son, Edinburgh (Glasgow), c. 1810 (date rubbed); length 28 cm; weight 3.9 oz; solid handle. The singly dished blade is embellished on each side by twin positive cusps or stylized fins at the rear; it is outlined by lines of hit-and-miss. The center of the blade is pierced by a vertical dolphin balanced on a wave, and with a foliate festoon suspended below. A V-boss and shouldered stem rise to a monogrammed fiddle handle. The marks are in line under the finial.


## Modified Scimitar or Long-Oval

An unusual and rare server is given in Fig. 12. It was made by Henry Chawner, London, 1796, who was a prolific maker of early scimitars in the 1790s. In effect, this slice is half of a conventional scimitar or long-oval server and represents an idea that was stillborn, although Chawner made a number of them. It is an attractive creation but is relatively fragile for use as a cutter and has a somewhat inadequate surface for use as a lifter.

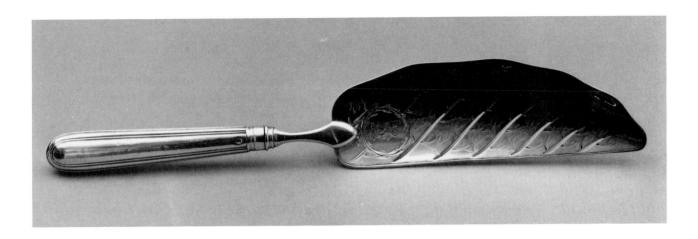

19.    KIDNEY SERVER, Gorham & Co., Providence, 1852-1865 (5); coin silver; length 31 cm; wooden handle. The unpierced flat blade has a modestly rolled right edge. It is engraved in bold rococo style with foliate scrolls enclosing a maiden. If one sought to find a correspondence in Continental style, it would be Biedermeier for this and other like ornamental articles. A long underblade rat-tail boss lifts on a waisted chamfered stem to a soldered fluted ferrule that holds a stained rectangular oak handle. This server is better adapted for the service of pastries than the dished examples. Maker's marks are on the rat-tail.

20.    SERVER, Wm. Theobalds, London, 1836; length 26.5 cm; handle, W.T., 1835. The blade is plain and unpierced; it has a sharpened front and left edge. It is double reeded on the right edge. As discussed in the text it is intermediate in shape between oblong and kidney, but much smaller than those. The blade is single dished, very robust, and lifts from a V-boss on an unusually stout short stem. The striking filled handle by Theobalds is an extremely weighty cast figure. What heavy duty this server was called on to perform is still a mystery — not quite flexible enough and too asymmetric for a royal shoehorn! The marks are underside on the rear of the right edge.

21.    SMALL SERVER; France, post-1738; length 20 cm; handle, EC (lozenge, long cross between initials). The worn dished blade is plain and unpierced and has a sharpened left edge. It is difficult to classify; it resembles the Theobald implement in shape, somewhat; save for a single lower negative cusp otherwise it is kidney shaped. It has an underblade drop, and balustered stem and replacement filled handle of earlier style. The guarantee mark is top side on the right rear corner.

22.    CIRCULAR SERVER, unmarked, Continental, c. 1880 (?); length 32.5 cm; wooden handle. This comparatively rare circular plain blade is pierced over its whole surface in a complex pattern of star shapes. The oblate oval boss is applied at the rear edge and is flush with the undersurface. It carries on a long straight rectangular stem to a soldered split boss attached to a tubular holder that is pinned to a long turned wooden handle. It is quite elegant in its simple clean lines. It could be a rice or small vegetable (peas?) server. Other possible uses include fruit strainer and egg poacher. The same object also appears with a round hoop of height ~2 cm, on a finger-operated spring mount, that sits on the perimeter of the blade and may be lifted up — another 'mystery.'

## *Kidney Shape*

Still another blade shape that appeared in the first quarter of the nineteenth century is the kidney shape. A strikingly beautiful, very early predecessor is the unique article displayed in Fig. 16. Made in London in 1781 by an unknown maker, it lacks the characteristic pointed tip of the long oval servers of this period. The standard type is illustrated by the rather plain example by T. Wallis, London, 1808 [Fig. 18]. A somewhat prettier Edinburgh example by F. Howden, 1814, is shown in Fig. 17. The decoration and piercing of both examples is representative of scimitar slices of the time. Their shape appeals to the writer as being a deviant

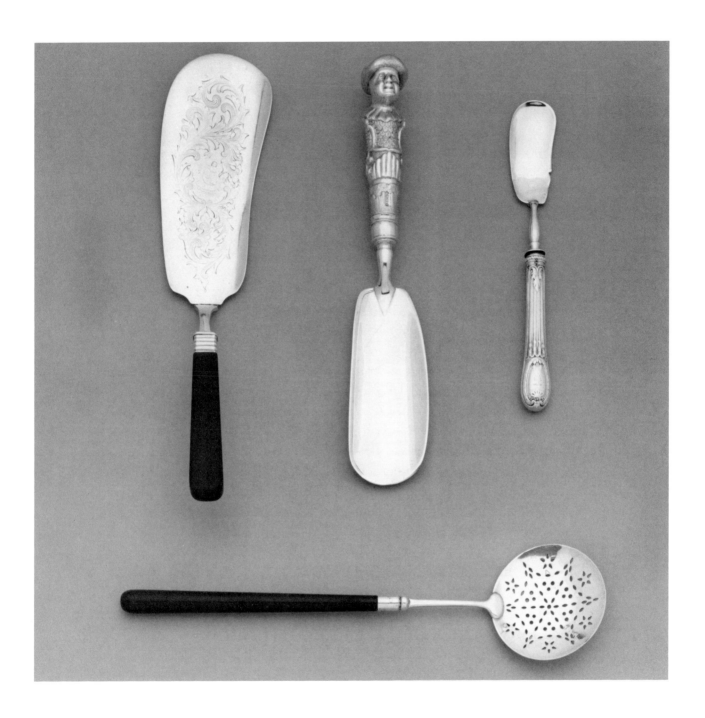

scimitar; it bears a resemblance to the scimitar of Fig. V 29, which has a similar strongly incurving right side but lacks the cusps of the latter. Inasmuch as the kidney server lacks a tip, its principal intended use may well have been as a lifter, say for a deep pie or pudding; the singly dished blade is not as well adapted for cake or pastry, but undoubtedly it saw service in various capacities. Indeed, one possible American example [Fig. V 110] does display a pierced fish. A later (c. 1858) unpierced coin silver example by Gorham is shown in Fig. 19. These servers are encountered only occasionally.

## Other Shapes

Occasional very rare shapes occur. Some are highly degenerate versions of more common shapes. One of these is a diamond-shaped blade. It may be regarded as an extreme version of a shaped or clipped long-oval.

Figure 20 displays an unusual example by Wm. Theobalds, London, 1836. It might appear to be an example of a rectangular server; however, it lacks the symmetry with respect to the vertical axis that those display; it swells on the left side somewhat like a kidney shape. It is further distinguished by the small size of the blade, only 13 cm long and 5 cm wide, and by the unusual shape of the hollow figure handle. The latter represents an ornate, richly clothed figure in dress of mixed, indeterminate and vaguely renaissance style. It is somewhat incongruous in association with the simple undecorated blade. This article might be a cake or pastry server but such purpose is belied by the dished shape of the blade. Its true identification remains as an unfinished project; possibly it is simply a multipurpose scoop.

A small post-1837 French server is shown in Fig. 21. Its shape is intermediate between kidney and the shape just discussed. Interestingly, it displays one *lower* negative cusp — a scimitar feature. It may be a butter server or possibly a cheese scoop discussed in Chapter VII.

Finally, although round silver servers "never" were made in the eighteenth century, an occasional one, having a dished blade, is found in the nineteenth century [Fig. 22]. They have persisted with considerable frequency of manufacture in the twentieth century up to the present time. They currently still appear as plated wares and have large (10 cm diameter) heavy blades that are pierced with an array of circular holes. The handles are of the same length as soup handles and are made in a variety of cutlery styles. They are sold as rice servers. Although evidently not transient in occurrence, they were nonetheless rare in the first half of the nineteenth century.

## References

1. H.W. Smart, *Country Life,* December 26, 1974.
2. D.S. Shure, *Hester Bateman,* Doubleday and Co., New York, 1959, Plate LX.
3. Jas. Deakin, *Catalogue,* Sheffield, 1899.
4. See (Ref. III 26, Lot 121).
5. D.T. Rainwater, *American Silver Manufacturers,* Crown, N.Y., 1975, p. 60.

# Chapter VII

## OTHER SERVERS

A VARIETY OF SERVERS were made, some of which have connections in function or shape with the various slices that have been discussed in the preceding chapters. But others are not definitely fish, pastry, or pudding servers. Some come under other categories, such as vegetable, salad, sandwich, melon, or chop servers. Their true nature is still not definitively known and some surmise and speculation enters the discussion.

In the case of those articles whose production continued into the twentieth century, the discussion is sometimes general and without specification as to whether the objects are made of silver or are plated. The principal distinction to be borne in mind is that the latter were less expensive and tended to be more utilitarian in nature, with less, or less elegant, decoration than the silver articles. This is only a rule of thumb to which exceptions exist.

Absent here is a discussion of the plethora of *ad hoc* servers, of specialized and overlapping function, toothed or otherwise, made especially in America in the latter part of the nineteenth century (43,53).

### *Fork-Slices*

The title of this section is a coined one that has no virtue other than to provide a succinct caption for two types of rather mysterious serving pieces. The first of these, illustrated in Figs. 1-5, have usually five or six broad fork-like tines at the forward side edge of what otherwise might appear to be an ordinary rectangular serving slice that has a curved sharpened edge. The second variant is a slice whose front end terminates in a set of five or six broad tines. It has a curved left side cutting edge that extends to the tip of the tines, so that the tine on the extreme left is part of the cutting edge and is wider than the others in order to withstand the cutting pressure. The pedestrian classification *side* fork-slice and *end* fork-slice, respectively, will be used to distinguish the two.

The side fork-slice was made in small numbers, mainly in the period 1800-1830. No doubt, some earlier examples may yet appear. The later end of the period is really not closed. No significant manufacture of this specific construction

241

1. SIDE FORK-SLICE, Thos. Wallis, London, 1806; length 26 cm; ivory handle. The plain blade is slightly single dished, and has six tines on the left front side that are concave upward. The right side is sharpened and has pierced parallel paling. A contemporary monogram is engraved in front of the shaped V-boss, which lifts on a chamfered waisted stem to a short fluted ferrule and twist-fluted, natural colored handle. The marks are underside along the rear of the right edge. The lift of the handle defines this to be a left-handed server because back-handed cutting involves an uncomfortable motion.

2. SIDE FORK-SLICE, Wm. Bateman I, London, 1818; length 27.3 cm; solid handle. The almost flat blade has a sharpened left edge; it has a slightly up-rolled, lower negative cusp and six *upturned* tines on the right side. A chain of engraved pendant leaves is parallel to the edge. The long graceful V-boss rises on a chamfered shouldered stem to a monogrammed fiddle terminal. This is a right-handed server.
By cooperation and courtesy of Dr. Dale Bennett.

seemed to have taken place in the years between 1830-1900 (excluding the multitude of forked servers that were made in the last half of the nineteenth century, as mentioned in the Introduction (I 2)). However, an identical type was made by W. Hutton, Sheffield, in the first quarter of the twentieth century and appears to have had some substantial circulation [Fig. 4].

These servers have very long pointed teeth, of length somewhat roughly equal to the width of the flat blade. Examination of the examples displayed in the figures shows that the decoration and handle styles correspond to prevalent custom described previously for scimitar slices of the Regency period. However, whereas a single band of piercing of an ordinary fish slice tends to follow the unsharpened rear right edge of the blade, the band of pales in the present examples is placed more randomly with respect to the two sides.

The twentieth-century implement illustrated in Fig. 4 displays the blade decor characteristic of the first decade of the nineteenth century, but also features a George II pistol handle. It represents an example of Victorian eclectism that sometimes was manifested so unfeelingly in the nineteenth century, and, as we shall argue below, so unthinkingly in this particular instance. A distant cousin of this server has been on display in the American wing of the Metropolitan Museum, New York. It was made by Tiffany & Co., 1870. It is a right-handed implement. It is furnished with a palmette style solid handle and differs from the present articles in having a row of short blunt dentillations along the length of its rear right edge. It is mentioned here because it was captioned as a *fish* server rather than for macaroni, tomato, cucumber, or whatever.

The side fork-slice has been described by dealers, other experts, and collec-tors as having any of several possible functions: a variety of fish slice, (1,2), which seems to be the majority view; a form of melon server, or, possibly, a cheese cutter and server, a minority view; a cake slice, one view; and, fifthly, as unknown and

242

possibly variable in purpose. The suggestion that the server is an altered fish slice may be immediately dismissed by consideration of the proportions of the blade and its decoration.

Some advocates of the description of this server as a form of fish slice suggest the use of the teeth as a help in skinning or descaling fish. This may be, but the tines of the examples examined by the writer are very sharp and might well tear the skin and flesh. Still another suggestion is its use for separating the flesh of a large fish, such as a salmon, from the bones, or for separating and presenting a portion of the fish flakes. A possible use for opening shell fish has also been invoked. In any case, objection to its characterization as a fish slice may be made. For one thing, the blades of these devices are usually flat, whereas almost every contemporaneous slice made was dished. For a second, these slices have lost the conventional pointed tip of the scimitar or long-oval slice that is so useful for getting under and lifting a serving; that is they are shortened to a very wide flattened leading edge, which limits this aspect of their usefulness as servers. For a third, asymmetric fish slices are exclusively right-handed, while the captions of Figs. 1-4 reveal that some

3.	SIDE FORK-SLICE, Wm. Knight II, London, 1828; length 26.3 cm; weight 3.4 oz; solid handle. The narrow flat blade has a sharpened left edge with five very long, very sharp tines that are markedly *downturned*. The left side of the plain blade is pierced with two conforming columns of paling. The V-boss lifts on a standard chamfered monogrammed fiddle handle; the marks are under the terminal. The lift defines this to be a right-handed server.

4.	SIDE FORK-SLICE, Holland, Aldwinckle and Slater, London, 1906; length 26.5 cm; handle, Wm. Hutton and Sons Ltd, Sheffield, 1906. The narrow flat blade is almost identical with that of Fig. 3; it only lacks one in the series of pales. The boss is a split penny. A George II-style filled pistol handle, decorated with stamped acanthus leaves, is attached by an in-line, short, waisted balustered stem. The slice is defined to be right-handed by the marks on the underside, along the rear of the right edge. The whole article is brightly gilded. Hutton and Sons made a number of these gilt servers in the first two decades of the century, some under their own mark and others with retailer's marks.

5.	SERVER, Richard Britton, London, 1817; length 28 cm; weight 3.4 oz; solid handle. This unusual article has a thin, almost flat blade that is reinforced by a channel wire that circumscribes the entire blade, except for a projecting toothed area on the left forward side of the blade; twelve bright-cut and engraved short triangular tines are capped by a flat sharpened wire and are functionally inoperative. The blade is outlined by wrigglework and by hit-and-miss around a central pierced and engraved area. A coach-and-four occupy the reserve; a cheerful bugler serenades the party. A conventional initialled fiddle handle rises from a drop bolster. The marks are under the terminal.

servers are intrinsically left-handed and others right-handed. A roughly equal division into these categories occurs amongst all those that the author has seen. A further example of a left-handed slice, by W. Eley and W. Fearn, London, 1800, with five, upward curving tines, and displayed at the Victoria and Albert Museum, London, is pictured in Ref. (1) (note that although the blade is furnished with a split-penny junction and filled handle having no lift, the top-side of the server is defined by a contemporary monogram; the underside carries the marks). Another server by these makers, but dated 1801, is very similar except that it features six tines (3). Still another left-handed side fork-slice, 1800, having a V-boss and lift to an ivory handle, and six up-curving tines, is illustrated in Ref. (2). It seems inconsistent that such different consideration would have been given to handedness for a server that ostensibly was a fish slice.

Finally, there is still another aspect that is troubling in understanding a well-defined function for these servers. Examination of Fig. 3 shows that the tines turn down for this right-handed slice. However, another right-handed server with lift to a fiddle handle, by W. Bateman, London, 1818 [Fig. 2], has a blade with *upturned* tines. This dilemma reaches its apex in the case of the twentieth-century servers in Fig. 4. These were presumably all made by William Hutton, Sheffield, and the other 'makers' are retailers. They feature a pistol grip handle that, in principle,

6.    END FORK-SLICE, Chas Eley, London, 1825; length 26.5 cm; weight 5.2 oz; solid handle. A relatively small, very heavy blade has a bevelled left edge and a straight blunt right edge; there are no cusps. The blade terminates in six short, sharp tines that are cut from the blade, although they are robust because of its thickness. The blade is reeded along the right edge and around a conforming rectangular reserve that is pierced in a contemporary pattern of parallel columns of flower heads and arcs that are separated by an anthemion spine [cf. Fig. V 53]. A faceted V-boss and shouldered stem lift to a monogrammed fiddle terminal under which are placed the marks.

7.    END FORK-SLICE, close plate, R. Silk, Birmingham, c. 1809; length 24.7 cm; hollow handle. The small blade is bounded by dotted and zigzag lines. It terminates in five pointed tines; the left one, on the cutting edge, is wider in order to take the pressure. The V-boss rises sharply on a bevelled stem to a *soldered*, flattened octagonal hollow handle. Up to the middle of the century, and frequently beyond, such handles were almost invariably filled in British manufacture.

8.    END FORK-SLICE, close plate, R. Silk, Sheffield, c. 1809; length 24.5 cm; ivory handle. The blade, boss and stem are similar to the preceding example. A reeded ferrule holds a bevelled rectangular ivory handle.

9.    PLACE MELON KNIFE, Jas. Dixon & Sons, Sheffield, 1870; length 21.8 cm; ivory handle. The name used in the original patent application (48) is "melon eater;" the designation used here is preferred (see text). The article is one of a boxed set of twelve. It has three tines but paradoxically, and presumably a simple defect in design, the widest one is on the blunt edge and is not for cutting. The butt plate and boss are combined. The length is similar to that of fruit/dessert knives.

By kind cooperation and courtesy of Brian Beet Antiques, London.

makes the hand grasp unique and permits no manual dexterity — such as reversing the hold — that otherwise might be judiciously attempted with an ordinary filled handle having no lift. This server in effect forbids the use of its tines by other than a contortionist; reversal of the pistol grip is both uncomfortable and contrary to its nature.

Although these articles possibly *are* fish slices, alternative five, above, is favoured for want of better insight. Thus, these implements might seem suited for the cutting and serving of melon such as watermelon, cantaloupe, or other soft melon that were popular in this period. However, this function conflicts with that of the end slice described below. Moreover, the existence and sale of flat, thinner, more knife-like melon carvers in the late nineteenth and twentieth centuries also countervails this possible function for the William Hutton implements of the Edwardian period.

But what about the third alternative — use of the slice as a cheese server? It must be admitted that this server could so function for the handling of softer and larger cheeses. Is it, perhaps, the big elder cousin of the still-contemporary,

familiar cheese knife whose blade is rather of dessert knife size, has a sharpened edge, and whose turned-back tip displays two or three short tines to assist in picking up the cheese slices? Actually, a Georgian analogue of such a cheese knife of similar shape exists in the collection of the Cutlers Guild (4). A variant of this cheese knife was made in the last half of the nineteenth century (5,6) in the form of an implement whose handle is in line with a blade that has a sharpened edge, and is usually made of steel to assist in cutting a hard cheese; but the striking feature of this implement is a set of four sharp tines approximately one centimeter in length that start at the tip of the blade and that run back on a diagonal line toward the rear edge of the blade. The tines are splayed backward in claw-like fashion and the tip of the fourth tine surpasses the rear edge of the blade. The knife may also be part of a set that includes a small broad fork and a small oval lifter. The handles of the knives were made in standard cutlery patterns. However, it is diminutive in size as compared to the fork slice whose tines are, in some implements, even longer than the width of the blade. It is concluded that the side fork slice is not a cheese server.

The ordinary cheese knives described above were also made for individual place service, with three or four tines and a blade length of 8 cm (6). Sadly, Britain did not entirely escape the American proliferation-of-function syndrome and this particular design was also marketed as a cucumber knife (7)! The turned-back tines were also consolidated into a single large tine, or point, and the implement thereby gained the name of oyster knife. Not all cheese knives were of the above design. Some have simple blades, reminiscent of dessert knives (7).

Other unknown uses probably exist. The writer has so far been unsuccessful in unearthing a source or an early catalogue that identifies these articles. In any case, whatever the intended usage, the whys and wherefores of the handedness of the implement and the optional curvature of the teeth presently remain a mystery.

A further element of obscurity is added by the right-handed server shown in Fig. 5. This is ostensibly an article related to the side fork-slice. It has twelve *short* teeth on the forward left side of the blade; but the teeth are capped by a band and have lost their dental function. This band is sharpened, whereas the rest of the perimeter of the blade is circled by a heavy wire rim that seems intended to preclude use of the rear or front edge. Thus, the teeth feature has become a decorated side-extension of a blade that has some different service function. We will return to this implement in the section on Asparagus Servers. The larger problem will be surrendered to further research.

The nature of the end fork-slice is perhaps less puzzling. Those so far encountered were made in the period 1800-1830 [Figs. 6-8]. They are right-handed and have the dished blade characteristic of the scimitar slice, but are of total size smaller than the side article and about three-quarters as large as an ordinary fish slice. The piercing and decoration is characteristic of scimitar slices. Fewer silver examples [Fig. 6] have been encountered than of the side variety; a rare pair (W. Chawner II, London, 1822) has recently surfaced. Several close plate specimens exist [Figs. 7,8], although those found so far have all been the product of R. Silk, c. 1809 (8); they are all unpierced. Why this company specialised in these implements, if indeed they did, is not clear. In any case, the very manufacture of close plate articles suggests some more general usage, as does the variety of handles — fiddle, ivory, and filled — that have been found even for the few examples seen so far. None of the side type has so far been seen in close plate.

The first matter to be disposed of with respect to end servers is the suggestion that these are later-altered fish slices. Several arguments refute this idea. First, the tines are more robust than would be the case if they arose by sawing an ordinary slice (compare a true salad server and one later-made from a spoon). Second, the server has no rear-edge cusps, positive or negative, as it would otherwise have. Third, they are smaller in size than a conventional fish slice. Finally, the central reserve is oblong and follows the overall shape of the present blade, rather than a headless fish shape that would be more typical for a scimitar fish slice from which it might have been derived.

Again, recourse to various sources of information has not yet revealed any direct clue to the identity of these servers. Like the side type, no mention has yet been found in the contemporary catalogues of manufacturers or of auction houses. Unlike the former, however, these serving pieces may have found a counterpart in later nineteenth-century individual place cutlery, just as fish eaters are the place setting counterparts of fish slices. Figure 9 pictures the item in question. It has a flat sharpened blade and, interestingly, displays one negative cusp. This example is one of a dozen cased replicas made by Jas. Dixon and Sons, Sheffield, 1870. It thus seems, unequivocally, to be an item of place cutlery. It has been suggested to be a melon knife (9); it has a sharpened left blade edge and broadened left tine and obviously it could be used to cut up a larger slab of melon. "I am like a melon-monger's knife, cutting here a slice, there a slice" (10). This suggestion has been confirmed (48) by the appearance of another registered set by Dixon & Sons that are termed "melon eaters" in the original Patent Office description. The tines could assist to convey pieces to the mouth — an all-in-one fork and knife (see later). Similar utensils of somewhat more amorphous shape were known in contemporary American manufacture as melon or orange knives (50). The end server is thus plausibly intended for the service of melon, as seems supported; this, of course, opens anew the question of how side type servers were employed.

## *Individual Place Service; Fish Pairs*

The increasing prosperity of the British Victorian era was accompanied by increasing elaboration and sophistication of large scale silver manufacturing. Attending this development came the proliferation both of serving implements and of place setting utensils that brought new articles to the dining room. One of these was the individual fish knife — not to be confused with the fish knife server or slice — known by the ungrammatical and inelegant name, "fish eater" knife. As a reflection of personal bias, in this book it will henceforth be called a *place fish*

10.   FISH PLACE PAIRS. a) Maker or retailer FAM (in a shield) Sheffield, 1885. Knife, length 22 cm; ivory handle. The flat blade is engraved and bright cut with baroque scrolling foliage and crossed fish in a pool. The handle has a fluted ferrule and a worn erased lion crest. Fork, length 19 cm; in matching style, with similar fish engraving and a de-pigmented crest. The heel of the fork is usually waisted in a characteristic fashion (see following examples).
By cooperation and courtesy of A. Pash and Son, London.

b) H.A. Sheffield, 1906. Knife, length 21 cm; weight 1.9 oz; solid handle. The plain long-oval blade is singly dished and is in one piece with the modified dognose handle. Fork, length 17 cm; weight 1.2 oz; in matching style. Victorian fish place sterling is much sought after and surprisingly elusive. Long-oval blade shape is less common than scimitar shape.
By cooperation and courtesy of S.J. Shrubsole, Ltd., London.

c) Electroplate, Harrison and Howson, Sheffield, c. 1907. Knife, length 22 cm; Ivorene oval handle. The scimitar blade has one positive cusp; the right edge is stamped with feather edging and a guilloche frieze with bright cutting; the marks are on the upper back surface of the blade. It has a sterling, gadrooned and scrolled ferrule by George Howson (52), Sheffield, 1907. The fork has four tines and matching features; length 19 cm.
By courtesy of Old World Shop, Seattle.

d) EPNS, no maker, c. 1890. Knife, length 20 cm; Ivorene handle. The scimitar blade has a single negative cusp and cursory stamped reeding and small C-scrolls; there is no stem. The oval handle butts against a split oval bolster that grasps the blade. This short knife might well be part of a 'fish and dessert' pair (see text). Fork, length 17.3 cm; it has four tines and is somewhat larger in size than the dessert forks in Fig. 11.

knife. It was the forerunner of the *place fish fork* and the pair, known as fish eaters, are here called *place fish pair*.

The advent of the place fish knife in large numbers occurred after 1850. It was first used in conjunction with a table fork. The place fish fork that made the pair did not follow for a number of years. Carrington and Hughes (11) in their survey of the plate of the Goldsmiths Company remark that place fish knives were only first purchased in 1875 and fish forks only in 1901 — although place fish forks had appeared by 1865 if not earlier. The time of earliest appearance of place fish knives seems uncertain. G.B. Hughes has cited 1815-1820 as the time of their introduction (2,12). But in a survey of the plate of the Mercers Company, Lane (13) notes that by c. 1817 there would have been no fish knives, "a piece of bread with a fork being used instead." They are not listed in a 1830s catalogue by a well-known maker (46).

The fish place setting articles resemble small serving pairs. The total length of the knife is approximately 17-25 cm — just slightly longer on average than a dessert knife — with a proportionately smaller fork, which has three or, usually, four tines and a waisted heel. The blade of the knife is most often a scimitar shape, sometimes long-oval, and may be similar to that of the conventional dessert knife

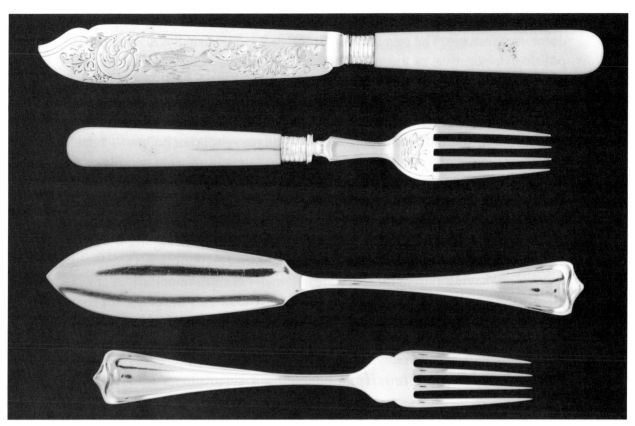

251

11.   DESSERT (FRUIT) PLACE PAIRS. a) Moses Brent, London, 1808. Knife, length 22.3 cm; ivory handle. It has a plain straight, slightly tapering blade with rounded end, a reeded ferrule, and an oval natural colored handle; the marks are on the rear underside of the blade. Fork, length 18.3 cm; ivory handle. It has four long tines and a shaped heel with balustered stem and matching handle; the marks are on the stem.

b)   Close plate, T. Harwood, Birmingham, c. 1814. Knife, length 20.5 cm; ivory handle. The plain, slightly tapering blade has a rounded end, a fluted ferrule, and a cusped-sided natural-colored handle with carved anthemion terminal. The marks are topside at the rear of blade. Fork, length 17 cm; ivory handle. There are four long tines; the stem is of diamond cross section. It has a ferrule and handle similar to the knife, but is straight sided. It is unmarked.

c)   Harrison and Howson, Sheffield, 1866. Knife, length 21.5 cm; mother-of-pearl handle. The straight blade has a rounded end and is stamped lightly on both sides with flower heads and a cusped line along the edge. A long ferrule is decorated with raised oval medallions; the handle is carved. The marks are on top at the rear of the blade. Fork; length 18 cm. It has a matching ferrule and mother-of-pearl handle; the marks are on the stem. The fork is in the same style as that in (b), and no change in pair style is apparent over the interval of fifty years.

d) Place fruit knife, Landers, Frary, and Clark, New Britain, Conn., 1865-97 (54); length 16.2 cm. The blade is of tapered, pointed cutlass type. It has a mother-of-pearl handle and a beaded sterling ferrule that is stamped with C-scrolls.

12.   FRUIT/BERRY SPOONS. a) I.S., Aberdeen, c. 1775; length 21.7 cm; weight 2.1 oz; Old English finial; two of a set of four. Eighteenth-century berry spoons are an extravagant variation of the companion tablespoon. They were differentiated by fluting of the bowl or other decoration — in this instance by a cusped edge and a zigzag tree in the bowl. The handle has a conventional underblade drop; it is feather edged and crested. The marks are seen on the lower back of the stem.

b)   IL, London, 1789; length 21.5 cm; weight 1.8 oz; Old English finial. The gilt bowl has been later decorated: it is heavily chased and embossed with fruits and leaves. The handle is stamped with dotted lozenges and flower heads. The marks are under the terminal.

shape, of the sinuous rounded-end Queen Anne type. They were also prone to less decoration (stamped or engraved) than fish service (5,7,24). The handles of these implements are also much the same as those for fish. Handles made of ivory (natural or synthetic) are usually in-line with the blade. Solid metal handles may be in-line or may display some lift.

Some enterprising manufacturers simply advertised their pairs as "fish and dessert pairs" (25); these might feature long-oval or scimitar blades and be provided with either continuous solid metal handles having lift, or with ivory or other hafts in-line with the blade. Needless to say, the fruit place pairs overlap the place fork-knife, described in an earlier section of this chapter, as implements for use with melon. Nonetheless, duplication of function by utensils of different

254

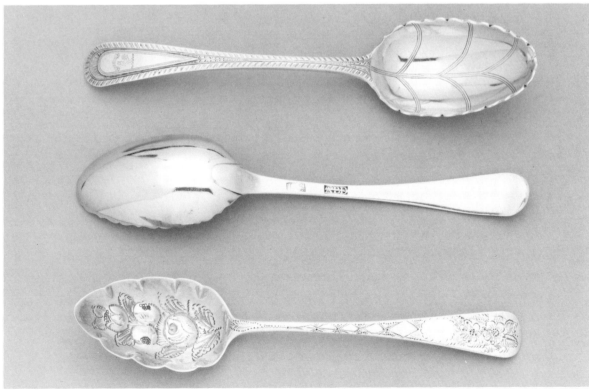

13.    DOUBLE-BLADED SERVER, Wm. Eley, London, 1796; length 31.5 cm; handle, John Tatum Sr. and Jr.; London, 1798. The slightly double-dished, small lower blade is of spade/heart shape [cf. Fig. III 57], and is doubly reeded around the perimeter and a conforming reserve that has reticulated piercing [cf. Fig. V 10]. An underblade drop boss connects by a long, flat, in-line stem to the filled reeded handle. The marks are under the rear of the left edge. The stem holds a stand-up sprung hinge, secured by a finger screw. The slightly smaller, matching top blade is barely double-dished upward and is decorated in matching pattern and is crested; it has a drop boss and a flat stem that is mounted on the hinge and has an upturned rolled flat end that is positioned conveniently to the user's thumb. The marks lie at the rear under the left edge of the blade.

14.    DOUBLE-BLADED SERVER, Abstainando King, London, 1798; length 32.8 cm; handle, Moses Brent, London, 1798. The server is similar in all major details of construction to Fig. 13. The lower blade is outlined by double lines of dots. An *oval* reserve is similarly outlined and is pierced with an engraved fish (shown). The upper blade is similarly outlined but a conforming *triangular* reserve is pierced in a floral design [cf. Fig. V 12]. There is a vacant laurel wreath cartouche. The marks are under both blades, this time along the rear of the right edges.

15.    DOUBLE-BLADED SERVER, John Shekleton, London, 1799; length 30.3 cm; handle, Moses Brent, London, 1799. The lower blade has now become long oval in shape, although the small upper blade remains heart-shaped. Both blades are very slightly dished in opposing fashion. They are double reeded as are the matching V-shaped reserves that are pierced with an oval zigzag pattern of oval elements. A split-penny boss passes by a round balustered stem to a pinned, reeded filled handle. It carries the conventional stand-up hinge mount for the upper blade, which has an applied hemi-circular boss. The marks lie under the rear of the right edge on both blades.

16.    DOUBLE-BLADED SERVER, George Cowles, London, 1802; length 30 cm; weight 6.5 oz; solid handle. Both blades are scimitar shaped, hence this is a less common article. The blades have conventional reeding and fish-bone pattern piercing. The lower blade has a standard shouldered crested fiddle handle, with a matching crest on the upper blade. See Ref. III 26, Lot 120 for further description.

By kind cooperation and courtesy of Phillips, Blenstock House, London.


shape and construction is well established; asparagus servers described later provide a notorious example.

## Double-Bladed Servers.

The period 1790-1830 saw the fabrication of still another kind of server. This is the two-bladed, scissor-like implement designed to pick up and grasp a portion of food. The dished lower blade of the server resembles contemporary fish and pudding slices. The examples shown in Figs. 13-20 illustrate the construction and stylistic evolution of these servers during the period of their production. Early examples featured small blades and an elongated shank leading to a filled handle [Figs. 13,14]; later servers had more conventional dimensions [Fig. 15]. The upper

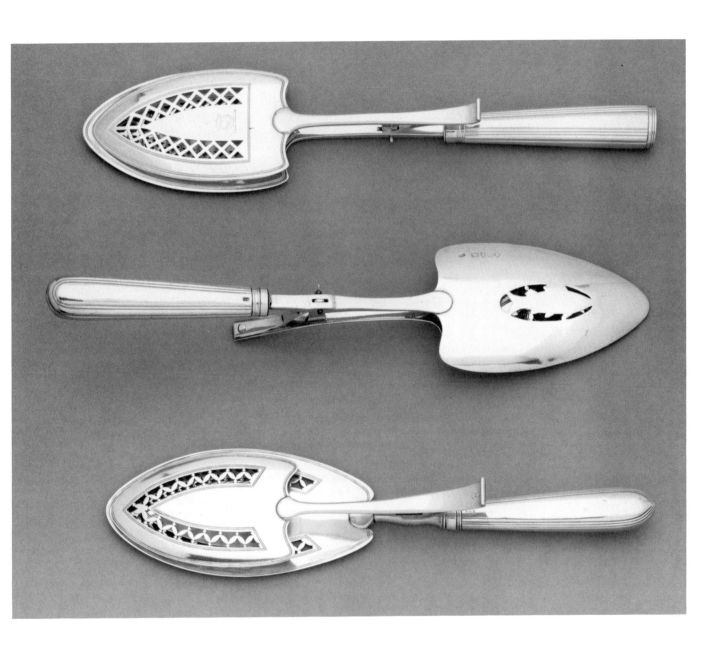

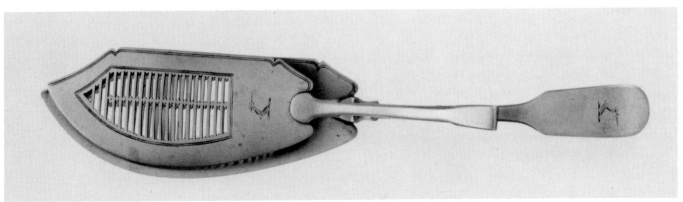

257

17.   DOUBLE-BLADE SERVER, Wm. Eley and Wm. Fearn, London, 1806; length 29.5 cm; weight 9.1 oz; solid handle. The lower and upper blades are the common long-oval and spade/heart shapes, respectively. They are double reeded and pierced in the sea-foam pattern; both have V-bosses. The handle is Hourglass pattern. The hinge action is a very rare one in silver [cf. Fig. 26] whereby the upper blade stem passes through the stout lower stem, which reverses the open and closed phases of the action. The upper blade and stem bear crests. The marks are under both stems.

18.   DOUBLE BLADED SERVER, Peter and Wm. I Bateman, London, 1809; length 29.5 cm; weight 6 oz. The singly dished, lower blade is rectangular with negative cusps toward the rear of both edges, in a vague allusion to a fish tail [cf. Fig. VI 4 by these makers]. The upper blade is much smaller and is of similar shape. Both are decorated with U-bands of highly engraved circles and diamonds and pendant foliage. There are a standard hinge, long tapering V-bosses, and a plain fiddle handle. The marks are under the finial and, unusually, under the center of the upper blade.

19.   DOUBLE-BLADED SERVER, Oporto, c. 1810; hollow handle. The blades are the more common oval and heart/spade shape. The rims of the blades are outlined by zigzag, waved, and leaf engraving. They are pierced with reticulation. A split penny lower boss and half-round upper boss lead to the conventional stems and hinge action. The crest on the octagonal handle is that of Major I. Atkins Davis who served in Portugal during the Peninsular War, and accounts for the close resemblance to British pieces. Note the engraved flat fishes.
By cooperation and courtesy of Dr. Dale Bennett.

20.   DOUBLE-BLADED SERVER, Wm. Gale & Son; New York, c. 1860; length 28.5 cm; hollow handle. This elegant article has two long oval blades, the smaller top one being larger than the analogs in Figs. 15, 17. Both blades are scalloped and pierced with lozenges in a conforming reserve in baroque revival style, and have additional fruit and leaf embellishment. The semi-elliptic boss of the lower blade leads to a shaped stem that carries a standard hinge mount applied to a short rectangular upper stem lever. The rectangular handle is scribed in a parquet pattern.
By cooperation and courtesy of Dr. Dale Bennett.

blade, flatter and smaller than the lower, and dished upward, is sprung on a mount that is hinged on the lower stem so that it is normally in the closed position. The hinge pin may be a finger screw, so that it is demountable, or it may be clinched. With the handle held in the hand, thumb pressure down on a truncated lever arm attached to the rear of the upper blade lifts the blade against the spring pressure and opens the server for the acquisition of the foodstuff. A slightly unnatural action of reverse thumb pressure may be applied in order to close the blade firmly on the food portion, inasmuch as spring pressure alone tends to be rather feeble.

   A very rare instance of an alternate, true-scissor, reverse hinge action is presented in Fig. 17. This server by W. Eley and W. Fearn, London, 1806, features a pass-through hinge arrangement. The spring maintains the server in the open

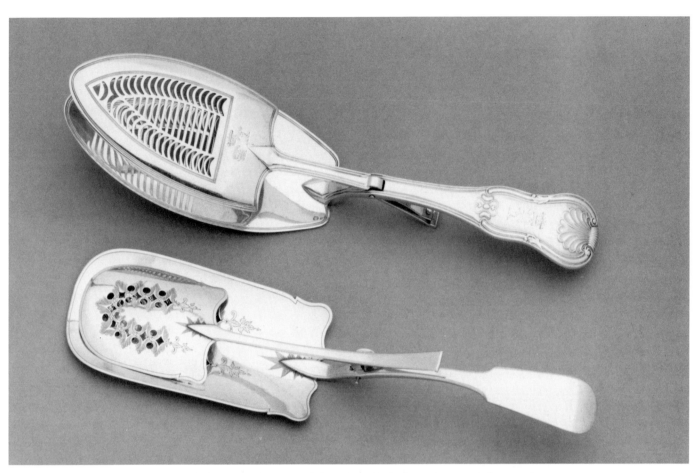

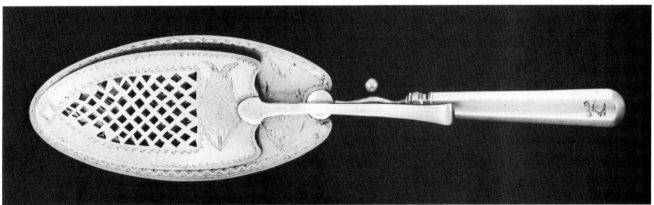

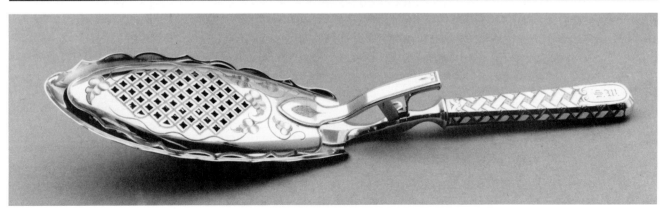

259

21.   DOUBLE-BLADED SERVER, George Nangle, Dublin, 1811; retailer West; length 27 cm; weight 8 oz; solid handle. A short broad doubly dished heavy blade (spoon shape) has seven sharp front tines, of length ~2 cm. The top blade is of conforming shape and is perfectly flat; its front edge has an applied down lip that conforms to the dishing of the tines. An underblade boss continues on a shouldered bevelled stem to the plain fiddle finial; the marks are under the terminal. A small rounded boss on the upper blade connects to the lever stem that is mounted on a conventional hinge; the marks are under the top end of the lever.

22.   DOUBLE-BLADED SERVER, Carden Terry and Jane Williams, Cork, 1809-1821; length 28 cm; ivory handle. The short broad lower blade is doubly dished and has ten short rounded front tines. The upper blade of conforming shape is oppositely dished and open at the leading edge. It is crisply decorated with festoons of flowers, pendant from a crested cartouche; it is bounded by an engraved twist frieze. A flat stem leads from the bottom blade to the oval natural ivory handle and carries a hinge mount. A half-round boss lifts on a flattened spreading stem-lever that displays a different crest.
By cooperation and courtesy of Dr. Dale Bennett.

position — a somewhat more awkward configuration of the blades when at rest — and a very firm grasp of the food portion is provided when pressure is applied to the lever arm simply by squeezing the hand to close the server.

The dished shape of the bottom blade of the 1796 slice by W. Eley I, London, [Fig. 13], is triangular or heart-shaped; the top blade is a little smaller, but is of the same shape and dished upward. A long-oval bottom blade is of later occurrence; the smaller top blade is still heart-shaped [Fig. 15] as in the server by J. Shekleton, London, 1798. Various other blade shapes occurred: Fig. 16 illustrates a scimitar shape by G. Cowles, London, 1802; Figure 18 by P. and W. Bateman, London, 1809, features rectangular blades. In at least one example of a later slice (London, 1815), both blades are heart-shaped, of the same general size and shape as those just cited; except that the top blade is modestly truncated at the front end and given a scalloped front edge. Although 1840 has been given as the inclusive date for these servers, occasional production continued for some time. An example by G. Adams, London, 1865, is in the author's collection; it is illustrated in Ref. (32) and is pierced with fish bone paling in a pattern that goes back sixty years [cf. Figs. 16 and V 23]; it is unusual in that the upper lever arm also has a fiddle finial rather than the common square truncated end. An American example by W. Gale, New York, c. 1862, is shown in Fig. 20.

The styles of the piercing and decoration of the earlier examples is geometric in nature, analogous to contemporary fish slices, and includes an instance of the popular sea foam pattern. The discussion of Chapter V applies here with regard to stylistic evolution in this period, examples of which need not be shown. As for handles, early filled types tend to give way to all-silver handles of plain fiddle shape. Other common cutlery styles were made [cf. Fig. 17]. The Victoria and Albert Museum, London, has displayed a long-oval example by P. Storr, 1816,

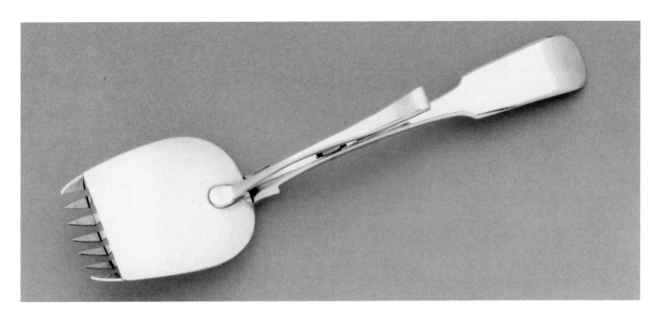

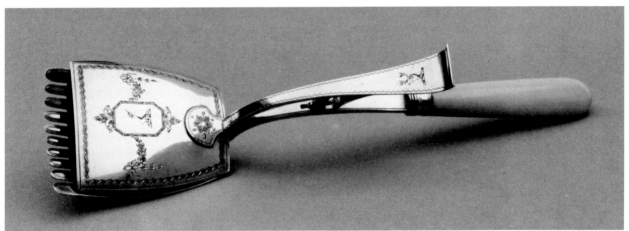

with Stag Hunt pattern handle, and scroll and star piercing. Ivory handled examples were also made.

A number of diverse opinions have been expressed with regard to the function of these double-bladed servers. One very common description (3) is as a fish slice — no doubt because of the marked similarity with the (lower) blade shape. Another designation is as an asparagus server (26). Clayton (27) has generalized their description to serving tongs, "perhaps for white bait"; another related fish application has been suggested (12). Confirmation of their use for fish service is found in the early example by A. King, London, 1798 [Fig. 14]. The server is of early type with elongated shank and two fully marked heart-shaped blades. The top blade is pierced with engraved flowers and leaves; the bottom is pierced with an engraved fish. Still another example of the fish association is provided by the engraved fish decoration on a Portugese implement, c. 1810, [Fig. 19], which was made for a British officer stationed in Portugal (3).

These servers obviously cannot function as cutters or slicers. Thus, their use for the service of a large fish would entail employment of still another slice for dividing the portions—seemingly unlikely. However, other applications as fish serving tongs cited above (12,27)—whether for a pile of white bait, or for individual small fish such as smelt or kipper that became breakfast fare in the nineteenth century, or even for fish cakes—seem quite apt.

What about other uses — say the suggested function as an asparagus server? This seems implausible. As described below, two types of asparagus tongs, bow and scissors, were already in contemporary usage for this purpose and were advertised as such (2). Moreover, the latter implements had flatter blades of much smaller area than the present dished servers. Were they also used as cutlet or chop (i.e. sliced meat such as mutton, pork or beef) tongs? This seems possible. Presumably they could also be used as pastry servers, or for tendering slices of cake; however, these servers are much larger than the double flat-bladed pastry and sandwich servers of the second half of the nineteenth century. Their use as vegetable or salad servers also seems possible, if less probable, given the existence of salad serving forks dating from the second half of the eighteenth century, and which even then could be used together with a large spoon for such purpose, as pairs, or even two spoons, still are now. In any case, the sole well-established use of the double-bladed implement is as a fish server. Their relative scarcity perhaps reflects a lack of popularity in the face of their higher cost.

A curious double-bladed article, intermediate in character between the double-bladed server and salad servers and quite mysterious in its own way, is shown in Fig. 21. It is an Irish piece by G. Nangle, Dublin, 1811. The mount and spring are the conventional ones described at the outset. The lower blade is a dished salad fork that has seven sharp pointed tines and connects to a fiddle handle *via* a short stem. The latter is more reminiscent of double bladed servers in length than of the longer shank of a salad fork [Fig. 25], or of ordinary Georgian basting spoons (that could double as salad servers). The top blade is flat and unpierced; it conforms to the shape of, and rests on, i.e., seals, the side and back edges of the lower spoon; but the truncated flat front end of the top blade terminates half-way along the lower tines. At first sight, the top blade seems merely to serve the function of grasping a serving of, say, salad more firmly. However, this blade has a perpendicular edge-plate attached under its forward end that is shaped to the dished contour of the spoon. Not only does this edge tend to obstruct the acquisition of a full serving when the server is open, but, when closed, it joins with the lower tines to form an ingenious strainer that allows liquid to flow out, leaving solid residue trapped. But for what food stuff? The true function and application of this device remains unresolved and the subject is

262

further vexed by other closely related examples. Two, by J. Shekleton, London, 1799 and 1801, have nine shorter (~1.5 cm) rounded-end tines and an oppositely dished top blade that lacks the perpendicular end plate. It cannot function as a strainer but allows freer acquisition of a serving. The type is illustrated in Fig. 22 by the article of Terry and Williams, Cork, c. 1813, which has ten short rounded tines. The subject of salad servers will be nibbled at in the following section.

## *Asparagus, Salad and Related Servers*

One of the most numerous survivors among British servers of the eighteenth and nineteenth centuries is the asparagus server, in all of its manifold forms. Examination of some dinner menus of the Worshipful Company of Goldsmiths, London, reveals some frequency attached to the serving of asparagus in the latter half of the eighteenth century. But so many servers survive today as to lead to some wonderment at the extent of the predilection throughout the British Isles (28) for the admittedly inexpensive 'sparagrass' or 'sparrow-grass' spears — especially in light of the large variety of vegetables and greens that were available (Chapter II). By the middle of the eighteenth century, salad (sallet) plates were a part of the table setting of the well-to-do (47).

Asparagus servers appeared in number in the second half of the eighteenth century. The earliest form had a scissor action designed for three-finger operation, with one smaller and one larger circular finger grip [Fig. 23]. The Victoria and Albert Museum displays one made by R.I., London, 1765. The blades were long and very narrow with a corrugated inner surface, for improved grasping. One blade had a perpendicular down lip or bar on the front edge — ostensibly better to secure the spears. These scissors are one of two variations that are known as tongs. The second type is the bow tongs, discussed below.

Considerable scepticism prevails among devotees of antique silver as to whether these scissors were actually intended for the service of asparagus, or whether they had other uses. The answer is probably *yes* in both cases. They were surely used for any purpose that suited their owners' needs. In addition to asparagus, this might include other stringy or green vegetables, cooked or raw, and salad of all kinds, as well as chops and even pastry. Figure 24 shows a pair of well decorated French "cake tongs" by J.F. Kirstein, Strasbourg, 1809-18, having blades apparently only a little wider than asparagus scissors and of very similar construction. Another cake tongs example by F.T. Burckhardt, Basel, 1781-1827 has corrugated unpierced blades; it may be seen in the Historisches Museum, Basel.

One should recall again the ubiquitous serving spoon, such as that commonly designated for stuffing or basting [also called a vegetable spoon (gemüse loffel) on the Continent] and much shrunken from the very large hash spoons or spoon ladles of the early half of the century [see Fig. II 3 and companion text]. It

23.    ASPARAGUS SERVER (SCISSORS), John Faux and Geo. Love, London, 1764-1772; length 25.5. cm; weight 4.7 oz. The plain narrow blades are corrugated and fit together when closed. The flat hinge is made of four interpenetrating circles. The handle is designed for three-finger action. The only ornaments are four carved scrolls between the branches. The marks are duplicated on the outside of the finger grips.

24.    CAKE TONGS (SCISSORS), Jacques Frédéric Kirstein, Strasbourg, 1809-1818; length 25.5. cm; gilted. The flat rounded end blades have no down bar [ct. Fig. 23]. They are scalloped and outlined with zigzag. Applied oval beaded medallions are stamped with rayed heads. The rear of the blades are decorated with acanthus leaves, and the hinge with a rose. The finger holes are beaded. The inner blade surfaces are corrugated for grasping. This article appears as Fig. 207 in H. Haug, L'Orfèvrerie de Strasbourg, Musées Nationaux, Paris, 1978.
Courtesy of Musée des Arts Décoratifs, Paris; photo Sully-Jaulmes.

25.    SALAD FORK, Wm. Turton, London, 1774; length 28.5 cm; weight 3.4 oz; Old English handle. The concave bowl has six oval tines, parallel sides, and an overall rectangular shape. The robust chamfered stem is integral with the bowl. The absence of a drop is another distinguishing feature from made-over English basting spoons. Marks are on the bottom back of the stem.

26.    SALAD SCISSOR TONGS, bone, French prisoner of war, English, c. 1800; length 30.8 cm. These articles are examples of scissor-type salad tongs. They were made by P.O.W.s held in Britain. The branches are decorated on both sides by carved bead work, flower heads, tendrils, and pseudo-acanthus leaves. The style is transitional for the period. The spoon and four-tined fork are joined by a pass-through hinge [cf. Fig. 17]. All combinations of spoons and forks were made.

could be employed either alone or in conjunction with another utensil, whether salad fork or table spoon or fork. The single spoon was also used by the diner to serve himself from a vegetable dish on the dining table.

In the last quarter of the eighteenth century, a serving article called an asparagus fork had appeared (16), although how differentiated from the salad fork is not clear. Figure 25 illustrates a salad fork by W. Turton, London, 1773. An earlier six-tine Old English example, dated 1764-66, may be found in the Victoria and Albert Museum. Such forks somewhat resemble a spoon-fork because they may be deeply dished. Indeed, their shape and relative rarity has frequently encouraged counterfeiting by the sawing of the bowls of contemporary basting spoons to produce tines; not only is the bowl shape of such fakes somewhat more curved than the genuine article, but the tines are flatter in contour, as derived from the original spoon.

A pair of bone, French 'prisoner-of-war', scissor salad tongs, of the kind made in camps in England into the nineteenth century (29), is shown in Fig. 26; such servers also featured two spoons, rather than fork and spoon, and, presumably, even two forks, at the whim of the maker. They seem to be as well, or better,

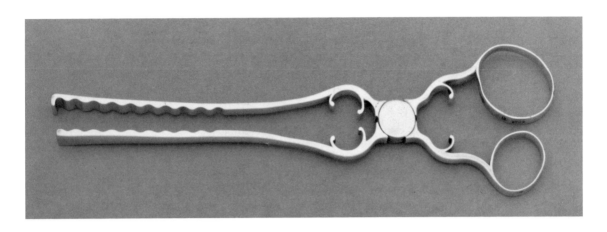

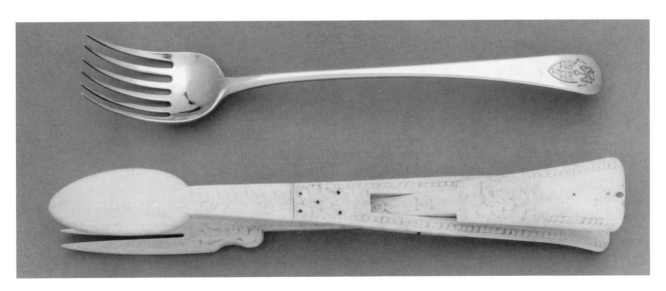

27.   ASPARAGUS SERVERS, bow tongs, George Smith III, London, c. 1780; length 25.3 cm; weight 5.1 oz. This is the early narrow-bladed type, with corrugated blades. The article is highly decorated with bright-cut zigzag around all edges and on the yoke, and with engraved birds, on oval matte backgrounds, on the blades; it is crested on the bow.

28.   ASPARAGUS SERVERS, hinged bow; Thos. Bowen (?), London, 1785; length 23 cm; weight 3.1 oz. This is the early narrow corrugated blade type, with tension supplied by a flat circular sprung hinge at the apex of the bow. There is no restraining yoke. This appearance has won the description, *wishbone* type. The straight stems of this type are turned transverse to the blades and transverse to the bow. The whole is plain and unadorned.

adapted for leafy salad than the narrow-bladed scissors or the scissor-like double-bladed servers of the preceding discussion. Scissor tongs furnished with various combinations of spoons and forks came into usage again after the mid-century — in parallel with the more popular bow tongs (see below). As was mentioned in Chapter V, later nineteenth-century silver and plated-silver manufacturers of serving pair sets also made pairs of salad servers. An early example of a matched pair of salad servers — a spoon and fork — is one by Wm. Eley and Wm. Fearn, London, 1821.

Following upon the earlier scissor-type asparagus servers was the bow tong type [Figs. 27-33], which appeared in Britain in the 1770s, if not before. They superseded the scissor tongs after the turn of the century, although the latter continued to be made on the Continent. They are said to have come into use in Ireland after 1780 (30). Their construction has three components: a broad U-bow handle that leads to narrower stems that join to the blades. The upper stem frequently acquired a down-step by the end of the century. The bow, which is work-hardened, supplies the spring tension; in some models of "wishbone" type, it is replaced by a flat, rotating, circular spring action to which the branch handles are attached [Fig. 28]. Some smaller late nineteenth-century articles had a spring hinge at the end of the handles. The handle sections were made in contemporary cutlery styles, such as Old English and fiddle, and including more ornate variations like King's pattern.

The very early bow tongs had rather narrow (1-1.5 cm), somewhat smaller, unpierced blades [Figs. 27,28]. By the turn of the century, most servers had acquired broader (2-2.5 cm), longer blades that were usually, but not always, pierced. They were made in the same styles as contemporary fish slices, both with respect to piercing and decoration, such as engraved, embossed, or stamped ornamentation, and which might extend to the bow [Figs. 27,30,33]. The hall-marks are found on the inside of the bow. Most blades are rectangular in shape and have parallel sides; their piercing may cover up to half or more of the surface area. Unpierced blades usually have a corrugated inner surface [Figs. 27,28,32]; pierced blades do more occasionally [Fig. 33]. Some implements, particularly

266

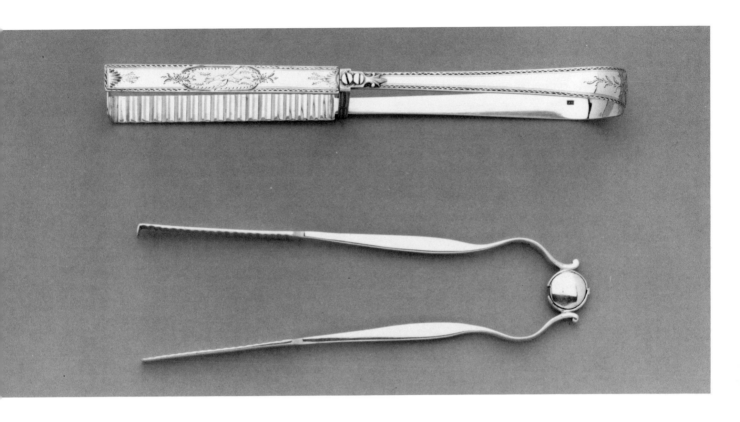

Continental ones, have tapered blades, which may either widen [Fig. 33] or narrow towards the ends; they sometimes feature an enlarged bow [Fig. 32]. Some servers have flaring blades or shaped blades [Fig. 30], which may also feature much open work [Fig. 31], such that they resemble later Victorian scissor-type sandwich servers. The blades are flat and the upper blade usually carries a retaining end bar or down lip for securing the charge. A small minority of implements have one narrower blade that is bowed, and whose tip fits into a horizontal slot near the end of the flat blade when the server is pressed shut. The blades are approximately 40-50% of the total length (~25 cm); early blades were proportionately longer (50%) than later articles (40%). Spread of the tong blades is usually restrained by a guide yoke, rigidly fixed to the lower stem, and close to the junction with the blades. In some later articles, the guide is a single capped rod that is attached to the lower stem and passes through the upper blade at the same relative location that the yoke would be found [Fig. 32]. The restriction of the permissible opening of the blades of a minority of these servers, especially by a rather useless down lip on the front edge of one blade, makes them less well adapted for the service of leafy or bulky vegetables or food stuffs. The bow servers have continued in production into the twentieth century.

Again, the question arises as to other possible functions for these devices. Vegetable and salad servers (30)? Sandwiches? Pastry? Chops? Presumably, all of

29.    ASPARAGUS BOW SERVERS, close plate, J. Gilbert, Birmingham, c. 1812; length 26 cm. The broad blades are double reeded and stamped with a pierced pattern of whole and part quatrefoils. V-bosses and stems lead to a fiddle style bow; one V-boss on the stepped stem is stamped, the other is screwed to the blade and carries the restraining yoke.

30.    ASPARAGUS BOW SERVERS, Elizabeth and John Eaton (52), London, 1858; length 27.8 cm; weight 7 oz. The wide Victorian double reeded blades have waved sides and canted corners. They are pierced with an open, coarse, scrolled pattern similar to contemporary fish slices (Chapter V). The stems are reeded; the bow is single struck with King's pattern handles and carries a repeated shamrock crest.

31.    ASPARAGUS BOW TONGS, Thos. Smily (52), London, 1862; length 27.8 cm; weight 5.8 oz. The blades are completely pierced (stamped) and lack the conventional wide silver edge. The latter is scalloped and part of the pattern of hearts, tear drops and lozenges. Plain stems lead to a fiddle bow.

32.    ASPARAGUS BOW TONGS, A. Bonebakker and Son, Amsterdam, 1867; length 23 cm; weight 5.4 oz. The article is single reeded around the edges. The simple rectangular corrugated blades pass by a waisted stem to a swelling bow; the stem has no step. The conventional yoke is here replaced by a restraining rod. The marks are on the insides of the stems. A swelling bow of enlarged radius of curvature appears occasionally in British work, even as early as 1794 as in an example by A. and P. Bateman, London.

33.    ASPARAGUS BOW TONGS, LC, Paris, post-1838; length 25 cm; weight 6.8 oz. The corrugated blades are straight sided and diverge towards the ends; they have inner side corrugations. They are doubly reeded and have stamped, applied, rococo style floral bosses and are (crudely) hand pierced in an intricate engraved foliate pattern. The stems and bow are stamped, reeded, and embellished with rococo foliate scrolling and cartouche. The apex of the bow is enlarged to make a Continental-type "cap." There is no step to the stem. The marks are on the outside of each stem (cf. British placement; see text). Notwithstanding the somewhat dull impression conveyed by the machine *and* hand work, the article is first standard alloy (0.950).

these were uses. They were advertised as asparagus servers, but are so numerous in their survivorship as to invite the belief that they were found to be very useful, multi-purpose tongs. Thus, the record of a Christie's (St. James's, London) auction of 1817 lists a pair of *vegetable* tongs (9 oz). In a discussion of Regency dining table appointments, Williams (31) shows the placement of a fish slice beside the fish plate, but does not provide any special serving utensil other than a large spoon proximate to the asparagus dish [Fig. II 3].

Not all Georgian 'asparagus' tongs had narrow blades. An occasional variant is found that has broader, shorter, and pierced rectangular blades. Such an implement was well adapted also as a pastry or sandwich server, or as tea tongs. A bow tong server of exceptional shape is the Old Sheffield article (c. 1800) shown in Fig. 34. Rather than the long rectangular blades of asparagus servers, it

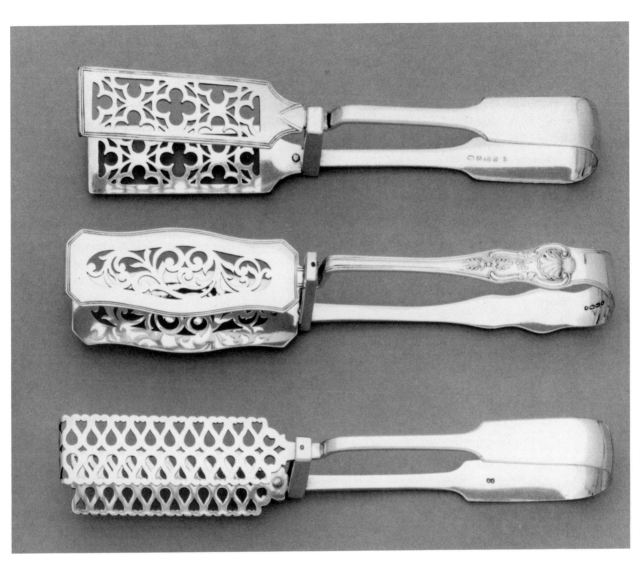

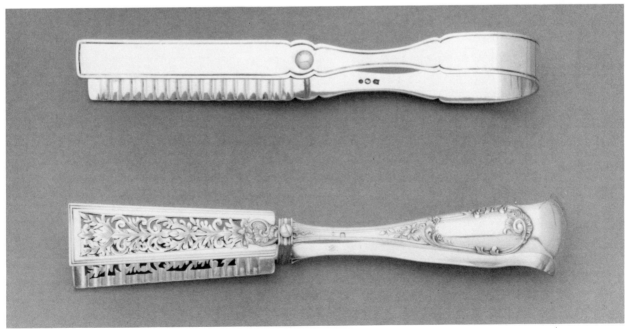

has heart-shaped blades similar to the upper blade of double-bladed servers [Figs. 13-15]; it has a conventional restraining yoke. It is possibly an asparagus or vegetable server, or could be used for small fish or white bait, or one of the other uses mentioned earlier. Some bow-tong implements, of which one by Wm. and Samuel Knight, London, 1813, may be noted, have two pierced spoons (of dessert spoon bowl size) that replace the blades; this suggests their use as vegetable or salad servers.

The bow servers were made in their Georgian form right through the nineteenth century. A smaller, but structurally similar bow tongs of length 18 cm by G. Adams, 1856 [Fig. 36], has almost square, toothed grid ends. The teeth mesh for a bull-dog grip. This might be a chop tongs, but it could function just as well as ice tongs; it is larger than superficially similar Russian sugar tongs and was made into the twentieth century. An amusing variant called a "chicken server," as in an 1865 American example by Gorham, substitutes a splayed chicken foot for the upper blade (32).

A smaller, less ornate form of bow tongs also appeared in the later part of the nineteenth century and early twentieth century. Their blades are frequently much shorter and wider and two forms were made: those having the longer blade axis parallel to the bow handle and those having it transverse (23). Not all of these exhibit a retaining yoke or clip (33). The piercing is frequently rudimentary and may consist of three or four large longitudinal pales; some blades were unpierced and had corrugations. These tongs are larger than the sandwich server tongs that were advertised by the same maker (22) at a lower price. However, still other manufacturers (6,7) evidently found it more practical to consolidate their inventory and listed "asparagus or sandwich" tongs in various styles, of length 17-23 cm, as well as "asparagus, sandwich *and* salad" serving tongs. Examples in silver of the bow tong type of salad server are well known in Dutch and Continental manufacture of the middle nineteenth century. Like the bone tongs cited earlier, these may combine a spoon and fork, and are of generous proportions and somewhat bulkier than asparagus tongs.

Further evidence supporting the multiple use postulate for such servers was provided later in the nineteenth century with the appearance of still another server labelled frankly in supplier catalogues as "asparagus *or* sandwich servers" (6). These embrace some physical constructional features of both of the two principal types: namely, a sprung hinge mount action, or a scissors action similar to the Georgian/Regency double bladed servers described in an earlier section. They employ an even broader lower blade than that of either the earlier scissors or bow tongs, together with a (frequently) smaller top blade. Both blades may or may not be pierced and feature more or less open-work piercing. Total length of these implements is 18-25 cm and the length of the lower blade is 7-9 cm. The lower blades are frequently akin to those asparagus bow tongs described above as having flaring or shaped blades. Blades may be rectangular, pointed, or shaped; the top blade varies greatly in shape and relative size — roughly one-quarter to one-half of the bottom blade. It is possible that a familial constructional similarity has encouraged the present-day characterization by some silver experts of the very early double-bladed articles as asparagus servers.

It should be noted for all of these later Victorian tongs, whether bow, spring or scissors type, that examples occur of blade shapes of almost every permutation of form, size and piercing [Fig. 35]. Stems and handles resemble double-bladed servers and may be solid or hollow, or made of ivory, agate, and the like. These servers tend to be much smaller than the Georgian double-bladed implements discussed earlier.

Still another innovation in the second quarter of the nineteenth century was the widespread appearance of an implement that may be termed an asparagus slice or scoop. It features a very wide, rectangular pierced blade, rolled up at the rear end and having an under-blade boss that leads *via* the shank to a filled handle, or to material such as ivory. A French example in Fig. 37 has a mother-of-pearl handle. Some of these articles assist their identification by displaying asparagus in their decorative pattern (34) and are evidently well-suited as lifters of asparagus from a flat serving dish. The earliest onset of this server or related type is not well known. Jackson (35) mentions the assay in 1787 of an "asparagus shovel" made by Christopher Haines, Dublin. If this was indeed a related type, then these servers were contemporaneous with the two earlier types already described. The writer has not encountered early articles or their descriptions. The reader may be reminded, however, of the side fork-slice having capped teeth that was described earlier [Fig. 5], and which was conceivably used as a lifter for asparagus, vegetables, or other foods. Servers of this basic type continued to occur in the later nineteenth and twentieth centuries, becoming simpler, smaller in blade, and more utilitarian in nature, as made by the mass-production industry. The blade may be quite undecorated, and have rounded shoulders, parallel or tapering sides, and crude longitudinal pale piercing that resembles capped tines. They have evolved in the present day into the omnipresent, quasi-rectangular, plastic or steel kitchen spatulas that have two to four large pales and somewhat longer handles than the nineteenth-century forebears. The 'caps' sometimes disappeared and a very wide fork with broad flat tines, as in the example of Fig. 38, resulted. Small prototypes of the capped server are sometimes called sardine servers.

Although there is no intention to discuss dishes here, it may be mentioned that Victorian asparagus servers were sometimes part of a complete asparagus service. It might, as in one Elkington plated example, comprise a footed stand, a long pierced concave or flat bed dish for holding the spears, and a long-handled shovel or scoop of matching curvature and shape for slipping under the spears and lifting them. Ceramic asparagus dishes were also made; the bed might be made up of parallel spears. A complete set includes special place plates, each with a butter well. Finally, asparagus was frequently eaten by hand as it is today. In the

34.    BOW TONGS SERVERS, Old Sheffield, c. 1795; length 27.5 cm. The plain spade/heart shaped blades are pierced in a conforming U-pattern by triangles and lozenges that enclose pales and have just a hint of a flower head. The blades have silver edges. Pinned oval bosses lead by plain stems to a reeded bow that is decorated with anthemion. A yoke restrains the action. This article may well be a bow variant of the double-bladed server, rather than of asparagus servers.

35.    SPRING TONG SERVER, Francis Higgins, London, 1864; length 19.5 cm; weight 4.8 oz. The small heart-shaped blades are oppositely dished. The decoration of tendrils, leaves and flowers was cast and applied to the surface; the sandwich was then pierced through. The handles are also similarly decorated and pierced. A small interlocking cylindrical hinge is activated and sprung in the same manner as the double-bladed servers. The marks are on the rims of the blades. These serve very well for sandwiches or any small foodstuff.

36.    BOW TONGS SERVER, George Adams, London, 1856; length 18 cm. The small rectangular blades have an inner grid of prongs that mesh. Small V-bosses attach to straight stems and a fiddle bow. These smaller tongs are unsuited for many of the possible uses of double-bladed and asparagus servers, but would do very well for sandwiches, smaller pastries, chops, ice, and so forth.

By cooperation and courtesy of Schredds, Portobello Road, London.

late eighteenth century, long creamware boats or shells with one open end might be used to hold the spears; at that time, and in the nineteenth century, the more familiar flat, tapering ceramic asparagus dishes, having vertical converging sides and open at both ends, were frequently employed. These holders were filled and brought to the table arranged on a serving plate that might include a liquid butter or sauce bowl.

Individual silver bow tongs for holding asparagus spears appeared in the latter half of the nineteenth century. In such manner did dining become more fastidious. These holders, sometimes listed as "asparagus eaters" (7,23) [Fig. 39], bear a close resemblance to sardine tongs [Fig. 40a] and are of the approximate length (8-12 cm) of small sugar tongs. The spoon or claw ends of the latter are replaced by a pair of either semicircular channels or dished spread ends, around 3-4 cm long, with their major axis placed at, or near, right angles to the stems. A less familiar type is one that has a hinge at one end and a split, flattened channel shape that may be decorated with an asparagus motif [Fig. 40b]. They are still made today.

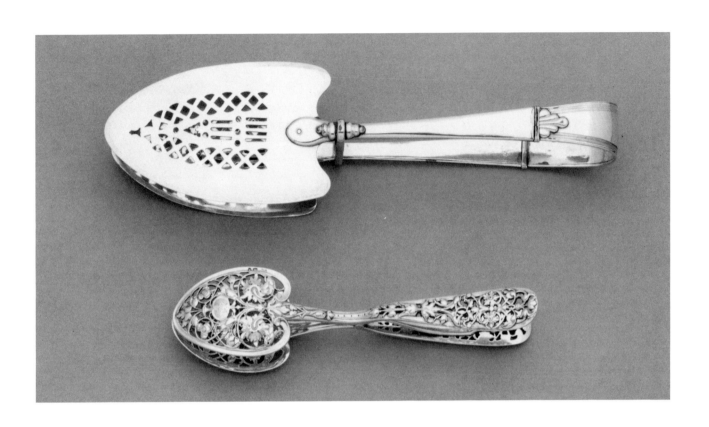

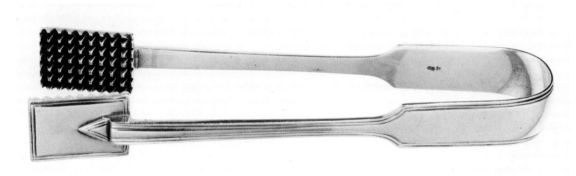

37.    ASPARAGUS/VEGETABLE SERVER, P.D.R., France, post-1838; length 27 cm; mother-of-pearl handle. The oblong blade has rounded front corners and a waved rear edge. It is much broader than those of Figs. VI 2-7. It also differs from those in that it is very strongly dished around the short axis. Apart from the plain peripheral rim, the whole blade is completely hand pierced with scrolls, flowers, and a central bouquet. A drop boss attaches under the rear of the blade and leads in-line by a flattened balustered stem to an elaborate beaded ferrule in the shape of festooned acanthus leaves. It holds the oval mother-of-pearl handle. Although it is suitable for the service of asparagus and other vegetables, the imagination extends its use even to omelets or pancakes.

38.    ASPARAGUS SERVING FORK, length 25.7 cm; weight 5.7 oz. The article is a marriage of blade and handle. Handle, Tiffany & Co., New York, 1890-1891, in the Broom Corn pattern (53). The large broad blade has four 'tines;' it was cut from a sheet and is hand pierced and chased to make a rudimentary scrolled pattern. The double-stamped handle has a small, underblade, hemicircular boss. Turner (50) shows a similar article called an oyster or entree server; it differs negligibly from an asparagus server also pictured there.

39.    ASPARAGUS PLACE TONGS, electroplate, John Round and Son, Sheffield, c. 1890; length 13.2 cm. Channel blades, 4.3 cm long, are connected continuously by bevelled shouldered stems to a fiddle bow. The channel is set at an angle of approximately ten degrees from the normal. Why this displacement is the commonly preferred 'magic angle,' designed ostensibly for greater ease and facility of use, is not clear [see Fig. 40].

40a.   SARDINE PLACE TONGS, electroplate on brass, unmarked, c. 1900; length 12 cm. Channel blades, 5.5 cm long, shaped as fish and cursorily stamped with anatomic details, are connected continuously with stamped pseudo-drop bosses to beaded stems and Old English bow. In this case the 'magic angle' is zero [cf. Fig. 39], i.e. the blades are set at right angles to the stems.

## Butter and Tart Servers and Related Implements

These small objects appear, at first sight, to be quite removed from the type of servers that have been considered so far. However, at one time or another they have demonstrated all of the principal blade shapes that have been encountered to this point so that their consideration has some associated interest; moreover, butter trowels may resemble small pastry servers.

Butter servers and spreaders appeared only during the second half of the eighteenth century (since butter had been served earlier in semi-liquid form) and took a triangular spade or trowel form. An order for a "butter trowel" is recorded in the Garrard Ledgers of 1774 (51). Servers ranged between 15-22 cm in total length, including the ivory or wooden handle. Some early ones had solid cutlery handles, but these are rarer [Fig. 42]. One cutlery piece by John Stoyte, Dublin, 1792, is a trowel pierced with a frieze of lunettes and fitted with a pointed Old English handle (judged to be approximately 12-15 cm in length), and labelled as

274

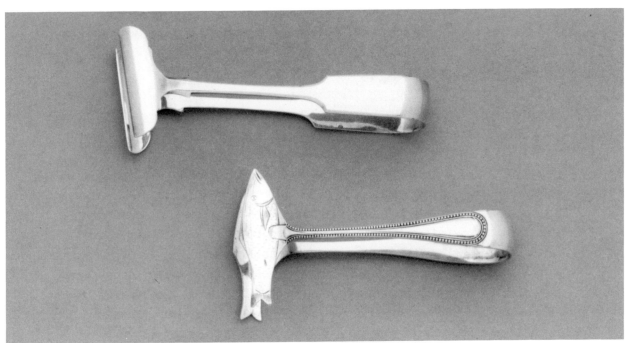

40b.   ASPARAGUS TONGS, unmarked, late nineteenth century probably; length 12.5 cm; plated silver. The heavy blades are shaped as asparagus stalks and channeled along the long axis. They are hinged at the rear end. Thumb and two-finger loops provide a facile way of holding, and opening and closing, the tongs. Despite their short length, the sturdy construction and width of the blades (2 cm) indicate that these devices could be servers or individual place cutlery. A French example by Christofle is in the writer's collection.
By cooperation and courtesy of Mrs. Mildred Corcoran.

41.   BUTTER SHOVEL, maker unknown, Germany; length 19 cm; solid Old English style handle. The date is given as c. 1750 in the reference below. The oval spoon-like blade is flattened; the function of, and necessity for, the corrugations is not clear, since the implement is obviously intended for handling solid material. This server is described as Fig. 369 in M. Meinz, *Schönes Silber*, Klinkhardt und Biermann, München, 1964.
Courtesy of Dr. Manfred Meinz; photography by the Worshipful Company of Goldsmiths, London. Private collection, Hamburg.

41a.   BUTTER SERVER/PASTRY TROWEL, Thomas Chawner, London, c. 1780; length 19cm; weight 1.3 oz; solid handle; bottom marked. The whole perimeter is bright cut. The neoclassical blade is pierced and machine engraved with circumferential decoration. The Old English handle is attached by an underblade small drop that has suffered slightly in the piercing.

42.   BUTTER SERVER/PASTRY TROWEL, George Smith III, London, 1784; length 18.5 cm; weight 1.7 oz; solid handle. The small trowel blade is of robust construction, undecorated and unpierced. There is no boss, and a solder joint of the blade to the stem, if any, has been skilfully hidden. The handle is Old English; the marks are under the terminal.

43.   BUTTER SERVER/PASTRY/TART TROWEL, George Adams, London, 1864; length 17.7 cm; weight 1.5 oz; solid handle. The small trowel is highly pierced in an open scrolling pattern. A V-boss and sturdy rounded stem lift to an Old English finial; the marks are on its reverse. The blade is thick enough so that it is quite robust despite the piercing.

English handle (judged to be approximately 12-15 cm in length), and labelled as a "cheese" trowel (36). The larger of these may be confused with tart or pastry servers. Figure III 33b illustrates a small "pelle à tarte", Strasbourg, 1773, i.e., a "tart shovel" trowel, that is 18 cm in length. It might just as well function as a butter server, or vice versa, and, indeed, a similar, contemporary Strasbourg object is characterized as a "butter spade" by Brunner (18). Two such are illustrated in Ref. (16). They are not pierced and are thus suited to the somewhat arduous task of a spreader. A Hester Bateman, 1788, small unpierced spade, illustrated and called a spreader by Shure (37), is similar to the Strasbourg article. Some other British spades or trowels of the late eighteenth century were also unpierced and of very rugged construction; these *could* have served as spreaders or servers, whether for butter, pastry or *any* small foodstuff. An example in cutlery style was cited in Fig. 42. Reference (49) illustrates a prettier bright-cut Old English style spade, 19 cm in length, by George Smith III and Wm. Fearn, London,

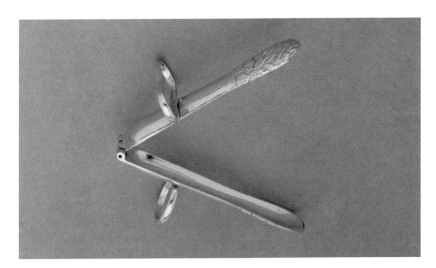

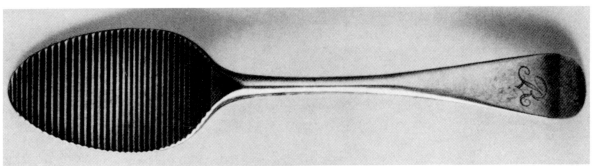

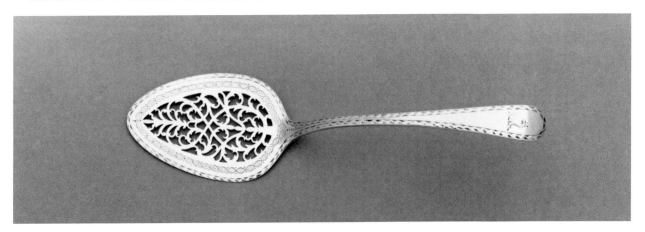

44a.   BUTTER SERVER, Wm. Bateman I, London, 1816; length 19.5 cm. Made in one piece, without boss. The blade is sabre or kidney shaped, with an unreeded, uncusped, waved right side. The handle is a shouldered fiddle.

44b.   BUTTER SERVER, Wm. Knight II, London, 1819; length 19.8 cm. The scimitar blade is dished around the long axis. It is double reeded with two negative cusps on the right side. There is no boss. The handle is a stamped King's pattern in one piece with the blade and with a shell under the heel.

44c.   BUTTER SERVER, Wm. Chawner II, London, 1829; length 19.5 cm. The scimitar blade is flat. It has double reeding and two negative cusps on the right side. The V-boss and reeded fiddle handle are integral with the blade.

44d.   BUTTER SERVER, Robt. Wallis, London, 1847; length 20.5 cm; stamped in one piece; the scimitar blade is double reeded with double negative cusps; the handle is reeded fiddle with an underblade stamped drop.

44e.   BUTTER KNIFE, A.C. Wortley, retailer H & S, American, c. 1870; length 18.5 cm; weight 1.5 oz. The plain scimitar blade has triple negative cusps and is turned at right angles to the flat handle, which carries a stamped pattern. The article is a late coin silver example.

44f.   BUTTER KNIFE, A. Edward Jones, Birmingham, 1908; length 14.2 cm. The article is Art Nouveau style. The blade is sabre shaped. It is held in a flattened hollow oval handle that is decorated with rope bands at both ends and with a terminal inset green cabachon. As judged by size, this article might well be a place item or have other function.


spade blade, a V-boss and stem that accepts an ivory handle and is approximately 16 cm in length. These contrast with the smaller, more fragile pierced trowel described earlier in Chapter III [Fig. III 56], which simply could not function in such capacity and survive whole. However, even the sturdier articles would seem to be better adapted to the function of server rather than that of spreader; a side knife could serve that purpose. Moreover, the former use is a better adaptation for single articles that are not individual place items. In any case, the Bateman shop made a heart-shaped article similar to Fig. III 56, having an ivory handle and pierced with foliage and paterae, that was called a *cake slice* in a 1976 sale at Christie's, London. References (17) and (18) illustrate a similar, slightly longer (23 cm) unpierced trowel (Strasbourg c. 1780) also called a cake slice (see Chapter III). Related to these is a silver eighteenth-century German implement called a "butter shovel" (38), having an Old-English style handle and a trowel, or spoon-shaped, flat corrugated blade [Fig. 41].

None of the above objects are to be confused with the cheese scoop or its elongated kin, the so-called butter scoop, an illustration of which by Samuel Pemberton, Birmingham, 1802, is given in Ref. (39); it has a total length of 15 cm, a long narrow concave blade 5.5 cm in length, and a baluster ivory handle. On the

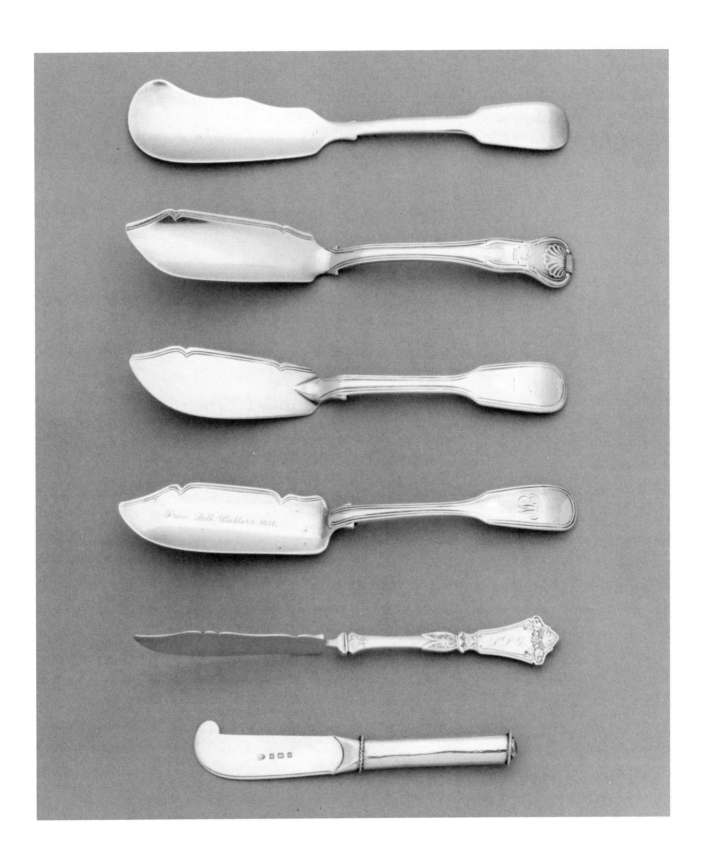

other hand, small French trowels are described, called "pelles à glace," that are very similar to the so-called "pelle à tarte" cited earlier. Reference (40) provides illustrations of several such trowels: one (Paris, 1785) that is 24 cm in length and has a conventional boss and shank leading to a baluster handle, and a gilded pair (Strasbourg, 1750-1789), of length 18.8 cm, that have rear aprons and shanks leading to baluster wood handles. Very small silver versions of conventional work shovels, of lengths similar to the above ice trowels and called ice shovels, were made in the late eighteenth and through the nineteenth century. Smaller spoon size versions were made as individual ice cream spoons. An even smaller miniature is the familiar salt shovel.

The distinction between butter spades and triangular jam or jelly spoons is also not always clear. The latter are usually smaller and may be flat but are usually dished; their appearance may vary from trowel-like to spoon-like. They have bigger (usually raised) shoulders than do butter spades. Jam or preserve trowels (and long-oval servers) advertised in the late nineteenth and twentieth centuries (22,41) could serve in both capacities.

The small butter spades and pastry or tart trowels of the last half of the nineteenth century were more robust than many of their more decorative eighteenth-century prototype. They feature heavier unpierced blades that are up to the work of serving. By this time the more versatile butter knife greatly preponderated for the service of butter. A pierced article by G. Adams, 1864 [Fig. 43], *is* a sturdy item, but is obviously not as well adapted for butter. Small pastry/tart servers took many shapes, of course, including oblong as well as unpierced scimitars, as in American and Continental manufacture (Chapter V).

At the turn of the eighteenth century, in parallel with the evolution of the scimitar fish slice, the well-known butter knives appeared (4) that resembled miniature scimitar slices except that their blades are unpierced. Figure 44 illustrates the type. They are typically 16-24 cm in length. They usually display (6,25) single or double positive and/or negative cusps, or other imaginative combinations and edge shapes, and may not have a double band of reeding along the right edge. The early blades are frequently not otherwise decorated. More of the later nineteenth-century blades carry stamped 'chasing.' The handles represent all the conventional cutlery pattern, but fiddle and pressed patterns, such as King's, do predominate.

Although the scimitar blade shape is the most characteristic, other shapes frequently appeared particularly later in the century (5,43). They included long-ovals, the sabre-like, curved rounded-end style and the parallel-edge dessert knife type (6). Scimitar blades may be dished or flat. The handles may be of silver or of other materials such as natural or synthetic ivory, and pearl. They may be in-line or, particularly when solid, display lift. Some articles feature a flat blade that is twisted at right angles to the handle [Fig. 44e]. All conventional cutlery patterns are represented. One manufacturer's catalogue (44) features as many as 13 variations of butter knives — ten scimitar, two long-oval, and one with short end tines as a combination butter fork and knife (see below) that is somewhat reminiscent of a sardine fork, on the one hand, and of a place melon knife, on the other. All but one display stamped decoration.

What function was served by butter knives? Ostensibly they were servers, and, especially adaptable for flat-bladed cutlery, they could also be used as spreaders — but by whom? Not by most diners at a large table throughout most of the nineteenth century because these articles were not used as place cutlery in Britain. The well-known firm of Walker and Hall advertised (23) a complete canteen that included 12 table knives, 12 cheese knives, but only one pair of fish carvers and one butter knife. In a larger service that included 18 table knives, the number of butter knives increased to two. Deakin and Sons (7) offered a 108-piece canteen that included one butter knife. Thus, cheese (dessert) knives might be place cutlery as befitted the importance of that dessert item, but not the butter knife, which is revealed as a 'master' server and, other than on informal small occasions, not a spreader. The discussion by Cosnett (28) earlier in the century, though not entirely clear, seems to support this conjecture. Advertisements of another manufacturer in the 1860s (45) conform also. No doubt some side knife, the fish, cheese, or dessert knife served as butter spreader. Matching butter forks in common cutlery styles were available (23); these were also servers to be used with a butter dish containing diced butter pats. The advent of butter knives as place cutlery seems to be a twentieth-century development, although very early on in America. These articles are smaller (12-17 cm long) than a master butter server; they usually have flat blades and appear in all styles [cf. Fig. 47f].

As presented in the manufacturers' catalogues, butter, fruit, dessert, "tea," and hors d'oeuvres knives were all very similar (23).

# References

1.  G.B. Hughes, *Small Antique Silverware,* Batsford, London, 1957.
2.  M. Holland, *Silver,* Octopus Books, London, 1973.
3.  Dale Bennett, personal communication.
4.  C. Blair, personal communication.
5.  Elkington & Co., *Travellers' Sample Pattern Sheets,* Victoria and Albert Museum, London.
6.  John Round, *Catalogue,* Sheffield, 1898.
7.  Jas. Deakin, *Catalogue,* Sheffield, 1899.
8.  F. Bradbury, *History of Old Sheffield Plate,* Northend, Sheffield, 1968.
9.  Brian Beet, London, personal communication.
10. *New English Oxford Dictionary,* J.A. Murray, ed., Oxford Clarendon Press, 1901, Vol. VI, p. 323.
11. J.B. Carrington and G.R. Hughes, *The Plate of The Worshipful Company of Goldsmiths,* Oxford University Press, 1926.
12. G.B. Hughes, *Sheffield Silver Plate,* Praeger Publishers, New York, 1970.
13. R. Lane, *The Mercers Company Plate,* A.H. Jolly, London, 1985.
14. C.J. Jackson, *An Illustrated History of English Plate,* Batsford, London, 1911.
15. G.E.P. and J.P. How, *English and Scottish Silver Spoons,* 1952.
16. I. Pickford, *Silver Flatware,* Antique Collectors Club, Suffolk, 1982.
17. E. Lassen, *Knives, Forks and Spoons,* Høst, Copenhagen, 1960.
18. H. Brunner, *Old Table Silver,* translated by J. Seligman, Faber & Faber, London, 1967.
19. A.J. Collins, *Inventory of the Jewels and Plate of Queen Elizabeth I,* Cambridge University Press, 1955.
20. B. and T. Hughes, *Three Centuries of English Domestic Silver,* Lutterworth Press, London, 1952.
21. M. Snodin, *English Silver Spoons,* C. Letts, London, 1974.
22. M. Willis, *Catalogue,* Sheffield, 1907.
23. Walker and Hall, *Catalogue of Gold and Silver Plate Cutlery,* Sheffield, c. 1915.
24. Goldsmiths Alliance, *Catalogue,* London, 1868.
25. Mappin and Webb, *Catalogue,* London, 1900.
26. H. Wykes, Antiques Magazine, Vol. 10, No. 2, 1926.
27. M. Clayton, *Christie's Pictorial History of English and American Silver,* Phaidon, Oxford, 1985.
28. T. Cosnett, *The Footman's Directory,* Simpkins, Marshall and Colburn, London, 1825.
29. C.I.A. Ritchie, *Bone and Horn Carving,* Barnes, New York, 1975.
30. I. Delamer, *Irish Silver, An Exhibition,* Irish Printer, Dublin, 1971.
31. J. Williams, *The Footman's Guide,* Dean and Munday, London c. 1836.
32. Argentum & The Leopard's Head, *Catalogue,* San Francisco, 1988.

33. J.B. Chatterley, *Catalogue*, Birmingham.

34. Henry W. Smart, personal communication.

35. C.J. Jackson, *English Goldsmiths and Their Marks*, Macmillan, London, 1921.

36. K. Ticher, Collector's Guide, November, 1973.

37. D.S. Shure, *Hester Bateman*, Doubleday, New York, 1959. Plate XXXV.

38. M. Meinz, *Schönes Silber*, Keysersche Verlagsbuchhandlung, Munich, 1964.

39. R.R. Wark, *British Silver in the Huntingdon Collection*, Castle Press, 1978.

40. *Orfèvrerie Francaise des XVI^e, XVII^e, XVIII^e Siecles*, Musées des Arts Decoratifs, Flammanon, Paris, 1984.

41. Jas. Rodgers, *Catalogue*, Sheffield, 1900.

42. Orfèvrerie Christofle, *Catalogue*, Paris, 1898.

43. R.F. Osterberg and B. Smith, *Silver Flatware Dictionary*, Barnes, New York, 1981.

44. Taylor's, *Eyewitness Catalogue*, Sheffield, undated.

45. Mappin Bros., Advertisement, Daily News, 1862.

46. T.C. Savory, *Catalogue*, London, c. 1830.

47. E. Barr, George Wickes, *Royal Goldsmith 1698-1761*, Rizzoli, New York, 1980.

48. Molly Pearce, City of Sheffield Museum, personal communication.

49. Mary Cooke, *Catalogue No. 6*, London, July 1988.

50. N.D. Turner, *American Silver Flatware 1837-1910*, Barnes, Cranbury, N.J. 1972.

51. Helen Clifford, Ph.D. Thesis, Royal College of Art, London, 1988, and personal communication.

52. J. Culme, *The Directory of Gold and Silversmiths*, Vol. II, Antique Collectors Club, Woodbridge, Suffolk, 1987.

53. C.H. Jr. and M.G. Carpenter, *Tiffany Silver*, Dodd Mead, New York, 1978.

54. D.T. Rainwater, *American Silver Manufacturers*, Crown, New York, 1975.

# INDEX*

*Makers*

Aase, M. **III 61**

Abdy, W. IV 148,**VI 10**

A.CC. **V 128**

AN **VI 8**

ASN **V 140**

Adam, E. 54

Adams, G. 150,155,171,199,202,
    226,260,270,280, **V 3a,91-95,99,VII 35,43**

Adams, II, S. 226, **V 14,24,29**

Aldridge, C. 112,139,140,148, **III 37,45,48,
    IV 4,9,17,23**

Aldridge, E. 112, **III 20**

Angenend, W. 52

Appleby, M. **III 66**

Arthur, P. **V 72**

Atsma, H. 50, **III 13**

Bailey, Banks and Biddle **V 125**

Bailey, H. **III 38**

Bailey, Kettell and Chapman, **V 122**

Balthazard L. **V 136**

Barnard, W. and J. **IV 21**

Bateman, A. 148, **IV 37**

Bateman, H. 72,113,120,128,148,150,
    154,206,229,276,278, **IV 14,20,28,V 2**

Bateman, P. 128,148,226,260, **IV 37,
    V 36,37 VI 4, VII 18**

Bateman I, W. 226,244,260, **V 36,37,41,
    VI 4, VII 2,18,44a**

Bateman II, W. 236, **VI 7, VII 10**

BCAC **V 146**

Belli, G. 144,224, **IV 46**

Berg, H.J. 86, **III 81**

Beyer, P.C. 86, **III 85**

Billon, A.C. **III 96**

Birks, H. **III 63b**

Blake, J. **IV 32**

Bobbink, L.H. 50, **III 12**

Bond, W. 58,60, **III 42**

Bonebakker,A. and Son **VII 32**

Bot, J. **III 10**

Boulton, M. 30,32,57,74,106,117, **IV 1,2**

Bowen, T. **VII 28**

Brandt, S.S. 86, **III 84**

Brenner, G.C. 84

Brent, M. 136, **IV 22,27-29,37, V 1,9,
    VI 2,16, VII 11a,14,15**

Brinck, F.J. 167,170

Britton, R. **VII 5**

Bruff, C.O. 60

Bryde, J. 167,170, **V 141b**

Burckhardt, J.F. 263

Burrows, A.&G. 64,90,117,226, **III 58,
    V 18,20**

Buttner, J.F. **II,** 111,III 83

Buysem, J. 128

Cater, D. 226, **V 86**

Chatterton, W. G 94

Chawner, H. 58,138,148,151,226,229,234,
    **III 57, IV 30, V 6, VI 1,11,12**

Chawner, M. 226, **V 74,80**

Chawner, T. **VII 41a**

Chawner II, W. 196,226,248, **V 33,67, VI 5,
    VII 44c**

A. Clark Mfg. Co. **V3b**

Clérin, A.C. 87, **III 89**

C.L.S. **V 129a**

Coles A. & Co. **V 115**

Collings, W. **III 51**

Cortlan & Co. **V 118**

Courtauld, S. 94

Cowles, G. 260, **VII 16**

Cox, W. **III 51**

Cripps, W. 112

Daniel, T. 148, **IV 11**

Davenport, B. 112,148, **IV 10,22**

Dawson, N. 66

D.D. **V 84**

Deakin and Sons 281

De Lamerie, P. 37,42,44,48,56,57,64,68,
    70,95,102,104,117,118, **III 1,27a**

Denn, B. 112, **III 49,50**

Denziloe, J. **V 7**

Dixon, J. & Sons 249, **VII 9**

D.G. **V 47**

*Note. Roman citations are to page numbers; bold face citations refer to figures.*

284

*Note. Page and figure references for subjects that may be readily found in the Table of Contents are not
included here, but references for such subjects located elsewhere in the book are included.*